Law, Governance and Technology Series

Volume 69

The *Law, Governance and Technology Series* is intended to attract manuscripts arising from an interdisciplinary approach in law, artificial intelligence and information technologies. The idea is to bridge the gap between research in IT law and IT-applications for lawyers developing a unifying techno-legal perspective. The series will welcome proposals that have a fairly specific focus on problems or projects that will lead to innovative research charting the course for new interdisciplinary developments in law, legal theory, and law and society research as well as in computer technologies, artificial intelligence and cognitive sciences. In broad strokes, manuscripts for this series may be mainly located in the fields of the Internet law (data protection, intellectual property, Internet rights, etc.), Computational models of the legal contents and legal reasoning, Legal Information Retrieval, Electronic Data Discovery, Collaborative Tools (e.g. Online Dispute Resolution platforms), Metadata and XML Technologies (for Semantic Web Services), Technologies in Courtrooms and Judicial Offices (E-Court), Technologies for Governments and Administrations (E-Government), Legal Multimedia, and Legal Electronic Institutions (Multi-Agent Systems and Artificial Societies).

Rosa Ballardini • Rob van den Hoven van Genderen • Sari Järvinen
Editors

Emotional Data Applications and Regulation of Artificial Intelligence in Society

Springer

Editors
Rosa Ballardini
Faculty of Law
University of Lapland
Rovaniemi, Finland

Rob van den Hoven van Genderen
Faculty of Law
University of Lapland
Rovaniemi, Finland

Sari Järvinen
VTT Technical Research Centre of Finland
Espoo, Finland

ISSN 2352-1902 ISSN 2352-1910 (electronic)
Law, Governance and Technology Series
ISBN 978-3-031-80110-5 ISBN 978-3-031-80111-2 (eBook)
https://doi.org/10.1007/978-3-031-80111-2

This work was supported by Business Finland

This Springer imprint is published by the registered company Springer Nature Switzerland AG
The registered company address is: Gewerbestrasse 11, 6330 Cham, Switzerland

Contents

Introduction

Rosa Ballardini, Rob van den Hoven van Genderen, and Sari Järvinen

1 Objectives and Novelty

This revolutionary new book on processing human data to infer information on emotions by artificial intelligence (AI) seeks to raise awareness, thoroughly discuss through a multidisciplinary perspective, and, in this way, disseminate research findings that elaborate on the topic of current and future regulatory needs for responsible and ethical developments and uses of emotional AI.

Emotional AI refers to solutions where AI is used for processing emotions and developing emotion-aware services.[1] Amongst the most sensitive human information are biometric and psychological data, and the objective of the book Emotional Data Applications and Regulation of Artificial Intelligence in Society is to provide a holistic understanding of key challenges and propose novel, workable, substantive and methodological solutions for navigating the existing and future legal and ethical needs and tensions within the processes of developing and using emotional AI.

Although scholarship literature and policy actions have intensively discussed issues of ethical regulation of AI, there is a limited understanding of the opportunities and risks related to emotional AI and its potential technology developments. Yet, emotional AI is one of the most promising areas for the adoption of AI-based solutions and applications since it will affect the daily lives of citizens and impact large user groups. Though, on the one hand, several of these innovations could be

[1] Bryson Joanna (2019) [The future of AI's impact on society | MIT Technology Review].

R. Ballardini (✉) · R. van den Hoven van Genderen
Faculty of Law, University of Lapland, Rovaniemi, Finland
e-mail: rosa.ballardini@ulapland.fi; rob.vandenhovenvangenderen@switchlegal.nl

S. Järvinen
VTT Technical Research Centre of Finland, Oulu, Finland
e-mail: sari.jarvinen@vtt.fi

R. Ballardini et al. (eds.), *Emotional Data Applications and Regulation of Artificial Intelligence in Society*, Law, Governance and Technology Series 69,
https://doi.org/10.1007/978-3-031-80111-2_1

perceived as welcome in our society as they can improve our well-being and experiences in many ways, on the other hand, these innovations might also have a negative effect on the privacy, interdependence and autonomy of natural persons, producing a problem in both a legal and an ethical sense. Thus, their societal acceptance might be challenged by several legal provisions in the European Union, such as the General Data Protection Regulation (GDPR),[2] the Artificial Intelligence Act (AI Act),[3] as well as regulations on communications, social platforms, and marketing. In addition, the implementation of these innovations require considerable investments. Thus, legal incentives such as intellectual property rights (IPRs) are crucial to supporting investments in these fields. Moreover, several other legal issues arise in the context of emotional AI including data regulation and liability challenges, to name but a few. Yet, the current legal landscape for emotional AI in Europe appears quite unclear. Such uncertainty becomes even more palpable when we look at the global picture of the regulatory framework for emotional AI.

In this book, a wide range of world top experts address these issues engaging in a multidisciplinary study related to the techno-economic-legal developments of emotional AI, its impacts and needs for action. The book will contribute with deep scientific and societally relevant insights on the past, present and future of emotional AI in general, especially its many implications for law and policies by:

- Providing a holistic overview of the role of law in supporting the development and uses of emotional AI;
- Engaging in in-depth multidisciplinary discussions encompassing legal, ethical, business and technological aspects in the context of emo-AI and emo-data; and
- Giving unique legal and ethical overviews on topics illustrating the already wide applications of emotional AI in society.

Thus, this book contributes to the thinking about AI processing emotional data as well as the creation of emotions by AI applications and whole AI systems from a positive legal and business enhancing perspective. Not only the existing regulatory framework but also the required guidance for future developments in society by AI will be presented by a unique set of authors. Although the scholarly literature is quite abundant when it comes to addressing issues related to law and ethics of AI, in general and in fields such as privacy and data protection especially, to date there is no book available on the market that discusses the specific needs and challenges but

---

[2]Regulation (EU) 2016/679 OF THE EUROPEAN PARLIAMENT AND OF THE COUNCIL of 27 April 2016 on the protection of natural persons with regard to the processing of personal data and on the free movement of such data, and repealing Directive 95/46/EC (General Data Protection Regulation).

[3]Regulation (EU) 2024/1689 of the European Parliament and of the Council of 13 June 2024 laying down harmonised rules on artificial intelligence and amending Regulations (EC) No 300/2008, (EU) No 167/2013, (EU) No 168/2013, (EU) 2018/858, (EU) 2018/1139 and (EU) 2019/2144 and Directives 2014/90/EU, (EU) 2016/797 and (EU) 2020/1828 (Artificial Intelligence Act) (Text with EEA relevance). [https://eur-lex.europa.eu/eli/reg/2024/1689/oj].

also highlights the opportunities and ways to boost them via appropriate regulation that promotes ethical and responsible developments and uses.

2 Common Definitions

The various chapters of this book rely first on the definitions existing in European laws and regulations. In particular, for all definitions concerning the regulatory application of AI systems, we refer to article 3 of the AI Act.[4] When European legislation lacks definitions, the chapters rely on widely accepted scholarly concepts and descriptions used in research and practice, as per below.

Emotion

While "emotion" is not directly defined in any legislation in Europe, the definition provided by the American Psychological Association (APA) is widely accepted. Accordingly, emotion is defined as "conscious mental reactions (such as anger or fear) subjectively experienced as strong feelings usually directed toward a specific object and typically accompanied by physiological and behavioural changes in the body".[5]

In the APA dictionary, emotion represents a complex reaction pattern, involving experiential, behavioural, and physiological elements, by which an individual attempts to deal with a personally significant matter or event. The specific type of emotion (e.g. fear, shame) is determined by the specific significance of the event. For example, if the significance involves threat, fear is likely to be generated; if the significance involves disapproval from another, shame is likely to be generated. Though emotion typically involves feeling, it differs from feeling in having an overt or implicit engagement with the world.[6] Emotions are how individuals deal with matters or situations they find personally significant. Emotional experiences have three components: a subjective experience, a physiological response and a behavioural or expressive response.[7]

Feelings

Feelings arise from an emotional experience. Because a person is conscious of the experience, this is classified in the same category as hunger or pain. A feeling is the result of an emotion and may be influenced by memories, beliefs, and other factors.

According to the APA dictionary, a feeling is a self-contained phenomenal experience. Feelings are subjective, evaluative, and independent of the sensations, thoughts, or images evoking them. They are inevitably evaluated as pleasant or unpleasant, but they can have more specific intrapsychic qualities, so that, for

---

[4] Ibid.

[5] See: <https://www.apa.org/topics/emotions> (accessed 8.8.2024).

[6] See APA Dictionary of Psychology at: https://dictionary.apa.org/emotion (accessed 8.8.2024).

[7] Rainer et al. (2020), pp. 81–100. https://doi.org/10.1017/9781108264822.009.

example, the affective tone of fear is experienced as different from that of anger. The core characteristic that differentiates feelings from cognitive, sensory, or perceptual intrapsychic experiences is the link of affect to appraisal. Feelings differ from emotions in being purely mental, whereas emotions are designed to engage with the world.[8]

Biometric Data

According to the AI Act (AIA) Article 4(14) biometric data means "personal data resulting from specific technical processing relating to the physical, physiological or behavioural characteristics of a natural person, such as facial images or dactyloscopic data". In the preamble of the AIA, the explanation is even more encompassing: "(15) The notion of 'biometric identification' referred to in this Regulation should be defined as the automated recognition of physical, physiological and behavioural human features such as the face, eye movement, body shape, voice, prosody, gait, posture, heart rate, blood pressure, odour, keystrokes characteristics, for the purpose of establishing an individual' identity (. . .)".

Emotion Recognition System

In the preamble of the AIA, an emotion recognition system is defined as follows: "(18) The notion of 'emotion recognition system' referred to in this Regulation should be defined as an AI system for the purpose of identifying or inferring emotions or intentions of natural persons on the basis of their biometric data. The notion refers to emotions or intentions such as happiness, sadness, anger, surprise, disgust, embarrassment, excitement, shame, contempt, satisfaction and amusement. It does not include physical states, such as pain or fatigue, including, for example, systems used in detecting the state of fatigue of professional pilots or drivers for the purpose of preventing accidents. This does also not include the mere detection of readily apparent expressions, gestures or movements, unless they are used for identifying or inferring emotions. Those expressions can be basic facial expressions, such as a frown or a smile, or gestures such as the movement of hands, arms or head, or characteristics of a person's voice, such as a raised voice or whispering".

Emotional Data

Although there is no separate definition of "emotion data" or "emotional data" in the AI Act, in the literature emotional data is often defined as information related to human emotions that can be extracted from various sources, such as text, images, or audio.[9] It is information about a person's emotional state, such as his/her subjective response to a certain stimulus. Emotional data can be both quantitative and qualitative, including, for example, physiological measurements, facial expressions, speech, and self-reports of feelings captured through technical means.[10] In affective computing, different taxonomies have been developed to categorize emotions in

[8] See APA Dictionary of Psychology at: https://dictionary.apa.org/feeling (accessed 8.8.2024).

[9] Häuselmann et al. (2023), pp. 1–8.

[10] Pal et al. (2021), p. 5554.

everyday experiences, the most popular being 'basic emotions', which comprises the following six basic emotion categories: anger, disgust, fear, happiness, sadness, and surprise.[11] Additional categories such as anxiety, guilt, shame, pride, compassion, relief, hope, and love have been included to elaborate the taxonomy. Emotional data, even when derived from identifiable biometric data (such as facial images and speech), as such, does not contain personal characteristics necessary for identification of an individual.

Artificial Intelligence
According to the AIA Art. 3.1., an "AI system" means a "machine-based system that is designed to operate with varying levels of autonomy and that may exhibit adaptiveness after deployment, and that, for explicit or implicit objectives, infers, from the input it receives, how to generate outputs such as predictions, content, recommendations, or decisions that can influence physical or virtual environments".

Emotional AI
Emotional AI is built on the scientific basis of affective computing, which focuses on systems that recognize, interpret, and respond to human emotions.[12] These systems use sensory inputs (like facial expressions, voice tone, and physiological data) to understand emotional states, with the goal being to create technology that interacts with humans in an emotionally intelligent and empathetic manner, bridging the gap between emotions and technology.[13] Basically, an emotional AI system is an AI system able to access and process emotional data.

Emotion-Aware Service
An "emotion-aware service" is able to detect, interpret, and respond to human emotions in both physical and online spaces. In emotion-aware services, technology is harnessed to understand and respond to human emotions.[14]

Personal Data
In the GDPR, "personal data" means "any information relating to an identified or identifiable natural person ('data subject'); an identifiable natural person is one who can be identified, directly or indirectly, in particular by reference to an identifier such as a name, an identification number, location data, an online identifier or to one or more factors specific to the physical, physiological, genetic, mental, economic, cultural or social identity of that natural person".

---

[11] Cabanac (2002), pp. 69–83.

[12] Picard (2000).

[13] Kumar and Martin (2023), p. 118651, ISSN 0957-4174, https://doi.org/10.1016/j.eswa.2022.118651.

[14] Anderson and Ostrom (2015), pp. 243–249.

3 Organisation of the Book

In addition to this introduction, this book features 15 chapters, which are divided into two main parts. The first part of the book discusses the recent advances in sensor technologies, computing platforms and connectivity enable development and deployment of AI-driven solutions for use cases, which were previously unsolvable either from the perspective of technical feasibility or economic viability. The second part sheds light on several legal issues and open questions related to emotional AI regulation, largely focusing on the European Union context but also including perspectives from other jurisdictions (e.g. US, Asia).

More specifically, in the first part, the book discusses technological and business aspects related to the development of emotion-aware services and usage of emotional AI. **Järvinen & Kallio** start by presenting some exemplary use cases of emotion-aware services for physical spaces and their technical requirements. The chapter includes insights on the business viability of the emotion-aware services in different industry domains (lighting systems, intelligent furniture and safety applications). Following this, different viewpoints on the usage of personal data from a technology development perspective are discussed by **Vildjiounaite et al**. Finally, to improve the user acceptability of AI-driven solutions, explainable AI methods are proposed (**Zhukov et al.**).

The second part of the book then begins with several chapters exploring different issues related to privacy, data protection and fundamental rights applications of some of the most sensitive aspects of human nature: emotional behaviour. **Van den Hoven van Genderen** tackles questions concerning the influence of AI on emotions and wellbeing of natural persons, as well as whether the ex-ante risk-based regulation in the so-called AI Act and parallel development of new regulations is a risk concerning the influence on the wellbeing of society. As emotional AI can fall entirely outside the remit of the GDPR, **Leijten & Lodder** further question how to deal with emotional data in the existing data protection legal framework of the GDPR. Thus, the authors ask: what regulatory frameworks may apply to the deployment of emotional AI and the data processed by emotional AI? Thereby, several unresolved questions are highlighted. In this context, a use case considering the applicability and impact of data protection law on emotional data points is also considered by using facial coding and the (facial) expressions collected and from which the necessity of regulating emotional data points within the scope of data protection law is examined (**Salami**). Furthermore, **Vesala et al.** continue on the issue of privacy by highlighting interesting nuances that emotional AI triggers in relation to our understanding of consent under the GDPR. To tackle some of the challenges implied with the processing of emo data, **Hartzog & Richards** address the proposal of creating a duty of loyalty in a later chapter.

Subsequently, the book addresses the important issue of the use of specific personal and emotional data where AI is given a pivotal role to combat the online solicitation of children, as a speaker, eavesdropper and collector of suspect language is addressed (**de Hingh**; **Alen-Mäihäniemi**).

Thereafter, the chapters delve into some of the core—yet quite under investigated—issues on the role of law to promote and foster innovations and diffusion of emotional AI. Here, a plethora of central legal disciplines namely IPR, liability, corporate social responsibility as well as contractual frameworks is investigated in relation to their effects on emotional AI developments and uses. **Ballardini & Pitkänen** shed light on the issue of fair data governance regulation and models in the EU, highlighting the interaction but often unaddressed clashes between IPR and privacy regulations in the context of emo-data regulation and governance. In their comparison between the EU and the Southeast Asian Nations regulatory frameworks, **Dermawan & Mezei** delve into novel issues related to generative emotional AI and copyright law. While **Schutte** digs into the EU liability framework in the context of damages caused by emotional AI in the EU context, **Drake** highlights the important issue of responsible and ethical use of emotional AI by companies in light of corporate social responsibilities regulations. **Hurmerint-ä-Haanpää et al.** continue on the topic of responsibility in the specific context of proactive contracting as a methodology for enhancing ethical practices with emotional AI.

4 Overall Contribution and Future Research

Until now, most publications about AI regulation have been rather general on the risk-based approach. This book opens the discussion about a rather sensitive and not strictly defined concept as emotional data and their use as processed by AI and the related ethical and regulatory aspects. It takes an in-depth observation of a specific area of using AI as a processing instrument for emotional data and the ethical and legal aspect of the effects on natural persons and groups. Additionally, the effects on the regulation of liability and intellectual property are taken into account concerning the specific use and influence of emotional data. Special attention is given to the pejorative effects on the investment of emotional AI applications by restrictive regulatory measures and the possibility of legal uncertainty for investors and users by ex-ante legal requirements for still developing technology. This aspect of the book requires continuous scholarly attention and promises more research opportunities, specifically concerning the beneficial use of AI in the stimulation of efficiency in sustainability and interaction between people on all levels of society.

The book Emotional Data Applications and Regulation of Artificial Intelligence in Society provides a solid guide for academics working in the field of law and policy as well as technology and business in the context of emotional AI, as well as for legislators, policymakers and organizations dealing with this matter. Considering the scarcity of literature on emotional AI regulation, on the one hand, and the speed of development and innovation in this area, on the other, the book holds great potential for both academic and societal impact.

References

Anderson L, Ostrom AL (2015) Transformative service research: advancing our knowledge about service and well-being. J Serv Res 18(3):243–249. https://doi.org/10.1177/1094670515591316

Bryson Joanna J (2019) The future of AI's impact on society, As artificial intelligence continues its rapid evolution, what influence do humans have? MIT TR. December 18, 2019

Cabanac M (2002) What is emotion? Behav Processes 60(2):69–83

Häuselmann A, Sears AM, Zard L, Fosch Villaronga E (2023) EU law and emotion data. 1–8. https://doi.org/10.1109/ACII59096.2023.10388181

Kumar H, Martin A (2023) Artificial emotional intelligence: conventional and deep learning approach. Exp Syst Appl 212:118651, ISSN 0957-4174, https://doi.org/10.1016/j.eswa.2022.118651

Pal S, Mukhopadhyay S, Suryadevara N (2021) Development and progress in sensors and technologies for human emotion recognition. Sensors 21(16):5554. https://doi.org/10.3390/s21165554

Picard RW (2000) Affective computing. MIT Press. https://doi.org/10.7551/mitpress/1140.001.0001

Rainer R, Andrea H, Weber H (2020) Personality and emotions. In: Corr PJ, Matthews G (eds) The Cambridge handbook of personality psychology. Cambridge University Press, pp 81–100. https://doi.org/10.1017/9781108264822.009

Regulation (EU) 2016/679 OF THE EUROPEAN PARLIAMENT AND OF THE COUNCIL of 27 April 2016 on the protection of natural persons with regard to the processing of personal data and on the free movement of such data, and repealing Directive 95/46/EC (General Data Protection Regulation)

Regulation (EU) 2024/1689 of the European Parliament and of the Council of 13 June 2024 laying down harmonised rules on artificial intelligence and amending Regulations (EC) No 300/2008, (EU) No 167/2013, (EU) No 168/2013, (EU) 2018/858, (EU) 2018/1139 and (EU) 2019/2144 and Directives 2014/90/EU, (EU) 2016/797 and (EU) 2020/1828 (Artificial Intelligence Act) (Text with EEA relevance)

Part I
Technology and Business

Adding Emotional Intelligence to Physical Spaces: Data-Driven Solutions for Measuring, Analysing, and Responding to User Needs and Expectations

Sari Järvinen and Johanna Kallio

Abstract Although emotions can influence our living, experiences, and performance in different contexts, current immersive services in physical environments are failing to read, interpret and respond to our emotions. This study aims to provide understanding of how to enhance physical spaces with emotionally aware, intelligent, and integrated services meeting the expectations of the users. It focuses on three different environments (office, public space and transport) and defines the high-level requirements for the technologies needed for the implementation of emotionally intelligent services, as well as identifies the stakeholders involved in service creation and data processing. Service concepts were generated in collaboration with experts from academia and industry using co-creation methods. The industrial partners of this study see that the novel sensing capabilities and artificial emotional intelligence-based solutions for behaviour analysis and situational awareness have the potential to enable new services, for both the space operators and the users. For such services, the pipeline from data to information and actions must be streamlined and modular, which requires research on technologies, analytics methods, service, and business model design. Ultimately, such services will enable businesses to provide experiences that understand and respond to human behaviour and emotional responses in everyday life, while interacting with technology.

1 Introduction

Remarkably, emotions influence human experiences, performance, and everyday living. However, the current technologies struggle to read and interpret human emotions accurately in real-life settings,[1] and consequently there are no widely used emotion-aware digital services. The purpose of this study is to discuss how to

[1] Tzirakis et al. (2021).

S. Järvinen (✉) · J. Kallio
VTT Technical Research Centre of Finland, Oulu, Finland
e-mail: sari.jarvinen@vtt.fi; johanna.kallio@vtt.fi

R. Ballardini et al. (eds.), *Emotional Data Applications and Regulation of Artificial Intelligence in Society*, Law, Governance and Technology Series 69,
https://doi.org/10.1007/978-3-031-80111-2_2

enhance the physical spaces with emotionally aware, intelligent, and integrated services able to respond to the demands and expectations of the users who are accustomed to personalized intelligent online services. Such services will understand and respond to human behaviour and emotional experience in everyday life: at work or home, at school or in a car, in public or private spaces, while interacting with technology. This will be achieved, for example, by improving the experience of using a space or a service, detecting increased risk events, and supporting vigilance, productivity, and well-being.

Currently, the user expectations and the commercial state-of-the-art of digital services in physical spaces do not meet. The commercial services able to react to human behaviour or changes in the environment are based on the usage of simple sensor data of physical nature (e.g. presence, temperature, CO2) to estimate the usage of the space and adapt by adjusting, e.g. lighting or air-conditioning. Although there are approaches where human behaviour and even emotions, as interpreted from facial expressions, are monitored using video cameras, the applicability of these is limited as the solutions are sensitive to changes in lighting and require a high-quality facial view from close range. In many cases, the privacy sensitivity of video data is a challenge for wider adoption of such technologies.[2]

However, recent advances in research and technology related to artificial intelligence (AI) methods, computing platforms, networking technologies and sensor solutions have enabled the creation of novel technology components required for real-time remote measurement of human behaviour and emotional experience as well as the surrounding environment.[3] The main challenge is to close the large gap between the fragmented, service-specific experimental laboratory prototypes and commercially feasible services in the adoption of the measurement technologies to real-world services able to derive emotional insight from the measured biosignal data and to combine it with the situational-awareness information.[4] This chapter aims to narrow this gap by co-creating emotion-aware service concepts in collaboration with industry experts and by providing industry insight on the research and development of enabling technologies and implementation of the services. The results are expected to contribute to the design of future research, development, and innovation activities.

2 Methodology

This study adopts different methods for research, development, and innovation with industry experts, the companies of whom provide lighting solutions, furniture and space services, public safety and mobility solutions, and data-driven service

[2] Hernandez et al. (2021).

[3] Booth et al. (2019); Fernandes et al. (2022).

[4] Fernandes et al. (2022).

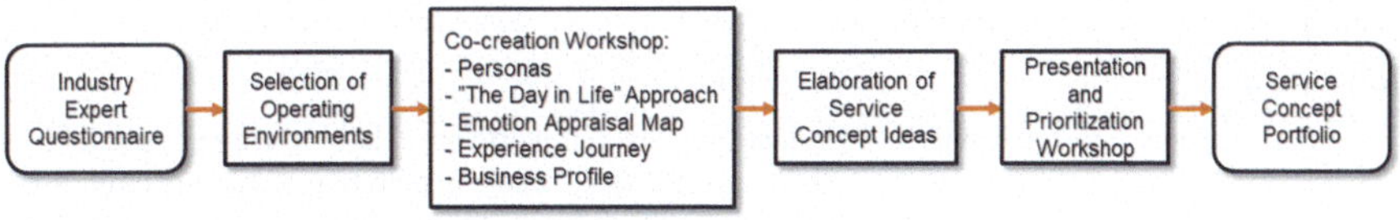

Fig. 1 First phase of the study—service concept co-creation

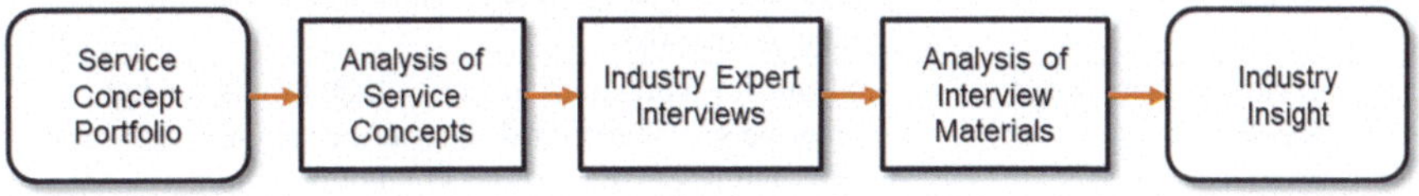

Fig. 2 Second phase of the study—Interviews for industry insight

innovation support to B2B customers. First, co-creation methods were applied, aiming to identify potential service concepts and second, semi-structured interviews for collecting business insights. Both these activities aim to ensure the inclusion of business perspective into the design and development of emotion-aware services. The concepts resulting from the co-creation activities define functional requirements and characteristics of the services without considering technical implementation details.

In the first phase of the study (Fig. 1), the industry experts completed a questionnaire aiming at engaging them in the topic and providing insights into the intended application contexts and end-users. Based on the conducted expert survey and the business interests of the companies', business areas and environments for co-creation were selected. Following this, consortium members (industry experts, technology, and law researchers) participated in a two-day workshop to explore potential solutions for the selected environments. The participants were instructed to innovate omitting the limitations of current technologies or regulation. Through co-creation methods, such as personas, the "day in the life" approach, an emotion appraisal map, an events-driven experience journey, and a business profile, concept ideas were identified. After the two-day workshop, the consortium members developed their ideas further according to instructions and met again on a third day to pitch and prioritize the best concepts in an online meeting.

A year after the service concept ideation and analysis of the service concept portfolio (Fig. 2), the second phase of the study started with a thorough analysis of the service concept portfolio and continued with semi-structured interviews where the company representatives shared their business insights on development and commercialization of emotion-aware products and services. A total of five company partners and ten persons (two female and eight male) participated to the 45–60-minute interviews.

First, the participants were asked for their professional background and a short description of their company. The company representatives have typically been working in the same company for 5+ years and hold expert or management positions related to research and development of new products, product management and

Table 1 Thematic categorization of the developed emotion-aware service concept ideas

No	Theme	Description
1	Performance booster services	Protect the personal workspace, help to trigger, and take advantage of a flow state and help to regulate the cognitive load when a focused, uninterrupted work time is needed or desired.
2	Empathic environment services	Data-driven environment control and space adjustment services, providing an environment that is sensitive to human emotions.
3	Services for emotional self-reflection	Means for individuals to learn which factors, including other people's emotional states or behaviours, cause positive and negative reactions or emotions.
4	Services for managing public comfort and safety	Support the staff, management, and security operators of a public area by providing alerts upon detecting anomalies in the normal behavioural and emotional patterns or flow of events.
5	Emotion-aware service delivery guidance systems	Improve the public or commercial services offering and delivery, and customer satisfaction by using the information on behaviour and emotional state of the customer or end-user as a cue for service needs.
6	Automatic customer feedback services	Capture customer emotion and behaviour to provide objective measurement and verification of customer satisfaction with services and offerings provided.

innovation. Then, the service themes (Table 1), which were already familiar to the interviewees from previous project activities, were reviewed briefly and reasoning inquired for the selection of company focus on service themes. As an "emotion-aware" service or product can be understood in many ways, a specific question was posed for the interviewees to define an emotion-aware service or product from their company perspective. Following this, the interviewees answered questions regarding the development status of emotion-aware products or services, expected added value of these to their customers, business potential, target markets and customers as well as time scale for a market entry. The final questions asked for the biggest challenges identified and need for collaboration partners in development and adoption of emotion-aware technologies.

3 Emotion-Aware Services and the Enabling Technologies

In both physical and online spaces, the concept of "emotion-aware service" integrates advanced technologies to detect, interpret, and respond to human emotions. The integration of emotion-aware services represents a transformative approach to service design, where technology is harnessed to understand and respond to human

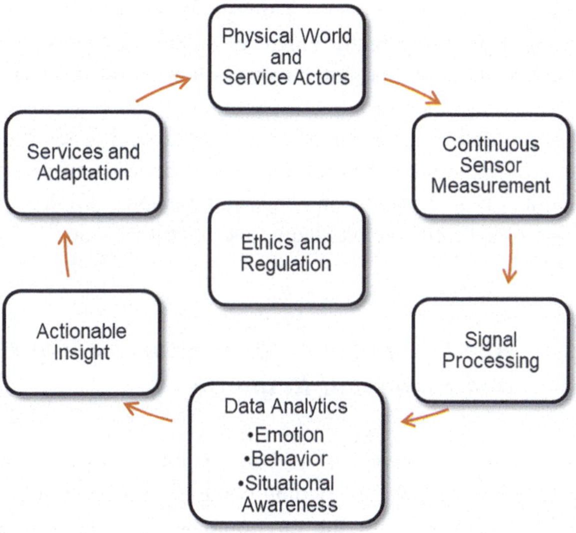

Fig. 3 The overall concept of continuous human behaviour and emotion analysis providing actionable insight as input for the immersive, adaptive services in a physical space with the objective to improve the human experience and space performance

emotions.[5] The overall concept of an emotion-aware service in a physical space (the target context in this study) is based on continuous analysis of human behaviour, emotional state, and the surrounding environment, where the connected immersive services can adapt in real-time using the actionable insight on human needs and expectations. Figure 3 depicts the continuous process of measuring and analysing human behaviour and adjusting the environment and services accordingly. By leveraging different technologies for human behaviour measurement and emotion recognition, these services aim to create personalized, empathetic, and responsive experiences.

3.1 *Emotion-Aware Services*

Emotion-aware services can be applied in various domains, including retail, healthcare, transportation, education, and customer support. The potential benefits of these include enhanced user engagement, improved customer satisfaction or employee experience, and increased performance. In retail environments, for instance, facial recognition technology and different sensor technologies can be employed to assess customers' behaviour and emotional states. Adaptive in-store experiences, such as dynamic lighting and personalized recommendations, can then be tailored based on these cues.[6] Furthermore, healthcare settings benefit from the ability to gauge patients' emotional well-being, enabling a more personalized and

[5] Anderson and Ostrom (2015).

[6] Luomala et al. (2023).

empathetic care approach.[7] Through the implementation of emotion-aware services, the transportation sector enhances safety by adapting to drivers' emotional states, thereby mitigating potential risks, or increases the wider adoption of public transport services by measuring and optimizing the passenger experience. For example, services built on measured data such as occupancy measurement and solutions to avoid the overcrowding of vehicles became significant during the COVID-19 pandemic.[8] In office environments, remote sensors integrated into the workspace can assess the employee wellbeing and cognitive load.[9]

3.2 Key Technologies for Measurement of Human Behaviour and Emotional Response

Emotion-aware services need to be able to measure the emotional state, human behaviour and the surrounding context. This section presents examples of technologies integrated into the environment enabling remote measurement of human behaviour (trajectories, movement, and activities) and features related to emotional state.

Human behaviour measurements can be done using a variety of technology solutions from radio-based positioning and Global Positioning System (GPS) to optical sensors such as RGB cameras and depth sensors. In this study, we mainly focus on indoor solutions, where GPS is not applicable, and the optical sensors typically outperform the radio-based positioning systems in accuracy. Although early depth-based people tracking systems initially used stereo or time-of-flight (ToF) cameras to generate disparity or depth maps, these faced challenges due to changing conditions, were expensive and less accurate for people tracking. However, a turning point was made with the introduction of the Microsoft Kinect, an accurate depth camera. Subsequent studies explored depth-based and RGB-D (RGB and depth) people detection and tracking.[10] Recent advancements in machine vision solutions have rendered RGB camera-based people tracking an attractive choice for certain applications. Indeed, RGB camera tracking often offers broader coverage compared to depth sensors, the video data enables object and activity recognition, and the cost of the sensor can be lower. An overview of these advancements is presented by Iguernaissi et al.[11] Additionally, recent experiments indicate the viability of using mm-wave radar for measuring people trajectories and activities in indoor environments. Moreover, the remote sensors enable analysis of more detailed activities such as human pose, sports activities, activities of daily living and specific

---

[7] Vildjiounaite et al. (2017); Lin et al. (2016).

[8] Tirachini and Cats (2020).

[9] Vildjiounaite et al. (2019); Kallio et al. (2020).

[10] Camplani et al. (2016).

[11] Iguernaissi et al. (2019).

gestures.[12] Such information contributes to the creation of a situational awareness view enhancing the understanding of the relation between the environment, humans and their recognized emotions.

Human emotions are traditionally categorized into six prototypes: anger, disgust, fear, joy, sadness, and surprise.[13] Though many studies aim to recognize the macro-expressions of humans from facial images[14] or analyse the micro-expressions indicating more subtle emotions,[15] the facial expressions do not always reveal the actual emotions. Another approach is to focus on the physiological responses associated with emotions, which are not highly specific to individual emotions, but reflect broader emotional characteristics.[16] These emotional dimensions include valence (positive—negative emotion), arousal (relaxed—aroused), and dominance (submissive—dominating). Notably, the arousal dimension plays a significant role in measuring autonomic nervous system (ANS) responsivity. While valence typically induces heightened arousal in both very positive and very negative emotions, low dominance tends to influence the arousal effect and subsequent ANS response, creating a more nuanced understanding.[17] The state of the ANS is reflected in various physiological signals, e.g. heart rate (HR), heart rate variability (HRV) and skin conductivity (electrodermal activity, EDA). In addition to wearable sensors, recent advances in measurement technologies suggest that the remote measurement of these physiological signals could be done with various technologies such as video and thermal cameras,[18] as well as novel radar-based approaches. Indeed, the mm-range radar signal is extremely sensitive to microscopic movements that convey information down to the level of the users' heartbeat and breathing rates.[19] The radar technology is invariant to many environmental variables, such as lighting and weather conditions that typically hinder visual based sensing methods.[20]

Considering the technology readiness level of the different technologies, solutions for detecting emotions from facial expressions using normal RGB cameras are the most used in different applications. Based on a recent review, their accuracy varies from 76% to 99%.[21] The accuracy of RGB technologies (both for facial expression analysis and for measurement of physiological signals) is affected by the lighting conditions, movement of the target person and angle of view as well as the resolution of the image. Current implementations of radar-based measurement of

[12] Fu et al. (2020).

[13] Cabanac (2002).

[14] Canal et al. (2022).

[15] Ben et al. (2022).

[16] Russell and Mehrabian (1974).

[17] Kreibig (2010).

[18] Wang et al. (2017); Casado et al. (2024).

[19] Kiuru et al. (2016).

[20] Jardak et al. (2019).

[21] David and Samraj (2020).

physiological features require an optimal view on the target person and limit the movement.

4 Emotion-Aware Service Ideas and the Operating Environments

The consortium co-created service concept ideas following the first phase of the study methodology (Sect. 2) starting with six environments: 1. movie theatres and cultural centres, 2. transportation terminals and public transport areas, 3. shopping malls and department stores, 4. libraries and learning environments, 5. workplaces and offices, and 6. restaurants and food courts. This selection was based on the questionnaire answers provided by the industry experts. The two-day co-creation workshop resulted in 37 service concept ideas of which 11 were elaborated further for presentation to the consortium members and prioritization.

Since the aim was to innovate freely without considering the limits of current technologies, the service concept ideas contained a myriad of both realistic and imaginative features. In the initial analysis, we clustered the concept ideas according to identifiable themes or intended purpose. As a result, there were six themes defined based on the intended purpose (Table 1) for further processing. Although the goal of most concept ideas was to trigger or guide some specific actions, some ideas aimed to provide information for self-reflection, and some to verify the performed action. While the temporal focus of most concept ideas was present, some aimed to analyse longer-term trends, and some even to predict the future state.

In the second phase of the study, in collaboration with the consortium members, selected environments related to the service concept themes were analysed in more detail. The selection of environments was done with respect to the business aspects of the company partners. Three areas were the focus of the analysis: the office environment, where the interest is in knowledge workers' performance and experience; public spaces (such as stores, restaurants, and movie theatres), where the customer experience is highly important; and public transport, specifically focusing on on-board passenger behaviour and safety. The variety of the selected environments ensures that different aspects related to the design and development of emotion-aware services are considered. In the following, we describe each environment, its characteristics and provide some examples of potential services.

4.1 Office: Measuring Knowledge Workers' Performance and Experience

A smart office is a technologically advanced workspace that leverages artificial intelligence and Internet of Things (IoT) devices and sensors to optimize and automate various aspects of the work environment, such as energy efficiency, productivity, security, and employee comfort.[22] The goal of a smart office is to create a more efficient, comfortable, and productive workspace for employees, in which AI and IoT devices make it possible to gather data and automate various tasks, including controlling lighting, heating, and air conditioning systems.[23]

The emotion-aware office is designed to optimize the work environment, improve productivity and collaboration, and provide a safe and comfortable workplace for employees. In addition, the office environment is a dynamic space with various factors that can affect the accuracy and reliability of sensor-based measurements, e.g. the movement of people and objects can interfere with occupancy sensors. Therefore, it is essential to consider these factors when designing and implementing smart office technologies. Typically, the office environment has a known user or group of users whose activities and experiences can be monitored over the long term, which makes it possible to develop personalized models and tailored interventions to improve the office environment based on individual needs and preferences. An emotion-aware office can assess individuals' emotions, comfort levels and employee experience, monitor individuals' presence, movement, and activity within meeting rooms, observe behaviours at desks, identify anomalies in behaviour and environmental conditions, track people flow throughout the office to identify trends and patterns as well as assess the overall atmosphere and feeling of the office space e.g. energy levels, boredom, drowsiness and enthusiasm. In most cases, it is possible to obtain consent from individuals to monitor their activities in the office environment. Informed consent provides information about the nature and purpose of the monitoring system, data collection and usage. In addition to remote measurements, when obtaining consent and working with known users, wearable sensors can be utilized to capture physiological data, movement patterns, and environmental factors directly from the individuals wearing them. Indeed, wearable sensors can enhance the accuracy and granularity of the system, enabling a deeper understanding of individual behaviour and emotional state. Moreover, long-term measurements can provide insights into work patterns, productivity, well-being, and the effectiveness of emotion-aware services. However, using sensors to monitor employees in the workplace could raise privacy concerns. To address these concerns, it is important to ensure that emotion-aware services are designed and implemented in accordance with ethical and legal guidelines and that appropriate measures are taken to protect the privacy and autonomy of individuals. Data ownership and control should be transparently defined, allowing individuals to decide how their personal data is used and shared. In the office environment, the principles of MyData[24] can guide the responsible handling of personal data.

[22] Zhang et al. (2022).

[23] Ibid.

[24] MyData (2024).

SERVICE EXAMPLE: The **Flow Catcher** is an advanced productivity tool designed to help individuals maintain focus and composure under high-stress conditions, particularly when faced with stringent deadlines or critical tasks. Consider an individual who must complete a sales pitch within an hour but is plagued by constant interruptions from phone calls, messages, and colleagues. As time pressure mounts, anxiety increases, and distractions make it difficult to start the task. Flow Catcher intervenes by blocking these interruptions. It curtails incoming phone calls, messages, and other digital notifications that could disrupt the workflow. Additionally, a traffic light system signals the user's "do not disturb" status to colleagues, preventing unnecessary intrusions during critical work periods. Flow Catcher also optimizes the physical environment by adjusting lighting and temperature to create an ideal working atmosphere. It dispenses a calming scent to reduce stress and enhance mental clarity. When stress levels rise, Flow Catcher prompts brief mindfulness sessions to help the user regain composure, refocus, and approach tasks with a clear mindset.

By minimizing distractions and optimizing the working environment, Flow Catcher makes complex tasks more approachable and manageable. Users can complete their work quickly and effectively, with time to review and practice, ensuring high-quality outcomes.

4.2 Public Spaces: Remote Measurement of Customer Experience

People tracking in public spaces, such as stores, restaurants, and movie theatres, refers to automatically monitoring customers' trajectories, movements, and emotions within the space. The main goal in this environment is to provide real-time insights into customer satisfaction and experience by capturing data such as dwell times, points-of-interest, and emotional responses to different stimuli, which can help businesses identify improvement areas, optimize their operations, and ultimately enhance the overall customer experience.

Public spaces, such as restaurants and malls, are known for their dynamic and open environments, characterized by constant movement and unrestricted access. Consequently, this can affect the installation and maintenance of measurement devices, resulting in potential inaccuracies in data and modelling. Factors such as crowd density, noise, and the continuous entry and exit of people can influence sensor measurements. In this context, the target users and groups of users are unknown. Indeed, the diverse range of people entering the space makes it challenging to understand in depth the individual behaviour or emotional responses, which often manifest themselves differently based on personal background and characteristics unknown for the emotion-aware service in public spaces. The real-time measurement of human behaviour, emotions and the physical space focuses on creating a snapshot view on the atmosphere and the situation in the environment enabling trend analysis and anomaly detection, for example. Due to the high volume of people and the dynamic nature of the space, obtaining consent from individuals in crowded public places can be challenging. While active consent methods, such as verbal or written consent, may not be practical or feasible in such settings, passive consent methods, such as prominently displaying signs or notices indicating the presence of monitoring or measurement systems, could be used to inform individuals that their activities may be monitored. However, the latter methods can be problematic from ethical and legal perspectives. Therefore, to facilitate an informed decision, clear and concise information about the purpose and scope of the monitoring should be provided. Regarding privacy, it is crucial to handle data collection, storage, and analysis in accordance with ethical and legal guidelines. Public spaces typically have multiple service providers operating within them, such as shops, restaurants, or entertainment venues. Moreover, each service provider may have different policies and technologies, which can impact adoption of emotion-aware services. Consequently, coordination and collaboration among these providers are necessary to ensure a holistic understanding of the environment.

SERVICE EXAMPLE: The **Save the Day** service is designed to enhance customer experiences in entertainment venues by promptly addressing unforeseen disruptions. By detecting anomalies and assessing their severity, this service ensures that minor incidents do not escalate into significant disturbances, thereby maintaining a pleasant environment for all patrons. Consider the scenario where five-year-old Sara has eagerly awaited the release of a new movie. Upon finally entering the cinema with her mother, Sara accidentally drops her popcorn, resulting in potential chaos and crying, which could disrupt the experience for her, her mother, and other customers. Save the Day intervenes by swiftly identifying such events. The system detects the anomaly and evaluates its severity. It then immediately alerts the cinema staff, who respond by quickly cleaning the affected area and providing Sara with a new portion of popcorn. This timely intervention prevents the incident from escalating. It also minimizes the disruption for other patrons, maintaining a calm and enjoyable cinema experience for everyone. By efficiently managing unexpected events, Save the Day enhances operational efficiency and customer satisfaction, creating a smoother and more enjoyable environment in entertainment venues.

4.3 Public Transportation: On-Board Passenger Experience

The global climate crisis necessitates a shift from using private motor vehicles to using public transportation services such as trains, trams, buses, and undergrounds. To comprehend the barriers to the wider adoption of public transportation services, understanding perceived passenger experience is important. Concurrently autonomous mobility services are being developed, and, when aiming for optimized safety and comfort, solutions for automatic measurement and analysis of passenger behaviour are of the utmost importance.

Public transportation, including trams, trains, and buses, operates in a dynamic and open environment characterized by constant movement, crowded spaces, and unrestricted, public access. Therefore, when designing monitoring technologies to ensure data quality in this environment, passenger flow, noise, vehicle vibrations, and other external factors should be carefully considered. In addition, the moving vehicles challenge the connectivity between the local sensor system and the remote backend, thus different edge analytics solutions might be considered to minimize the need for data transfer. Public transportation involves a diverse range of passengers, including unknown target users and dynamic groups with different characteristics and behaviours. Monitoring systems need to account for this diversity and capture data representing the broader passenger population, enabling the tracking, and understanding of actions and interactions within these dynamic user groups. Furthermore, advanced monitoring systems and data modelling methods are required to extract valuable insights from the complex and ever-changing public transportation environment. Due to the high volume of people and the dynamic nature of the space, obtaining consent in public transportation presents unique challenges. As traditional consent methods such as verbal or written consent are not feasible or practical, alternative approaches can be explored, for example, providing clear signs indicating the presence of monitoring systems and their purposes, combined with an opt-out mechanism for passengers who do not wish to be monitored. Also, in public transportation, there are privacy concerns about collecting personal information through sensors or other monitoring systems. Similarly to the previously presented environments, in public transportation, it is also crucial to carefully evaluate the need for the collection of personal data and naturally handle data collection, storage, and analysis in compliance with the regulatory requirements as legal and ethical guidelines. Thus, anonymization techniques should be employed to protect individual identities, and only aggregated data should be used for analysis. Moreover, transparent communication about the privacy measures in place, including data security protocols, should be provided to reassure passengers and address their concerns.

SERVICE EXAMPLE: The **Disturbance Detector** activates on measuring emotions and physiological data of individuals or groups in public places, as in the case of stations, stadiums, or specific areas. It warns authorities such as

(continued)

police, fire alarm, or health authorities of any expected disturbance and helps to prevent and/or mitigate hostile, criminal, and disruptive actions or health risks in public places. It monitors the emotions that indicate a safety risk through abnormal behaviour of both the crowd (activity indicating emotions of fear/anxiety) and individuals (activity indicating emotions of aggression/ hostility), alerts the security staff/operator to increase presence, pinpointing the area and possible threats (individuals) to be monitored more closely. As a result, operational efficiency increases, while people feel safe and comfortable in the area because disturbances are contained promptly.

4.4 Analysis of Environments for Emotion-Aware Services and Technology Context

During service development and implementation, each environment presents unique considerations. The office environment is characterized by known target users with identifiable identities, enabling long-term monitoring and modelling. In contrast, public spaces and transportation include diverse unknown users and ever-changing groups of users, making it challenging to understand the behaviour and emotions which often manifest themselves in different ways in different people. While these environments present special measurement, analysis, and adaptation challenges, the enabling technologies should be applicable across various domains and environments. Table 2 provides an overview based on the analysis of characteristics of 11 service concept ideas, which were elaborated further, in relation to the selected environments (office, public space and public transport).

5 Industry Perspective

Based on the interviews, the company partners prioritized themes 1. *Performance booster services*, 2. *Empathic environment services*, 4. *Services for managing public comfort and safety*, and 5. *Emotion-aware service delivery guidance systems*. Theme 3., *Services for emotional self-reflection*, did not fit into the company partners' area of business; and though theme 6., *Automatic customer feedback*, was considered interesting, it was not a priority. Since the selected themes were a priority for 1–2 companies, the company interest became scattered as expected due to the different business domains the partners are working on. The basis for the selection of the themes and focus is two-fold. First, the choices were based on the identified customer need, which is derived from discussions and workshops with current and potential customers as well as other stakeholders. Secondly, the company partners

Table 2 Analysis of the service concept ideas and the environments

	OFFICE (5 service concepts)	PUBLIC SPACE (5 service concepts)	PUBLIC TRANSPORT (1 service concept)
SERVICES & ADAPTATION	Recommendations for personal activities Office space allocation Office environment (lighting, HVAC, audio landscape) adjustment Guidance to the optimal workspace location Data-driven space management	Human intervention by the staff Automatic people flow guidance Manual space and process adjustment Predictive resourcing Automatic HVAC adjustment	Security personnel intervention
ACTIONABLE INSIGHT	Cognitive load Stress Anxiety Emotion heatmap over time Personal state of mind Employee experience	Anomaly detection (both behavioural and environmental) Severity of the anomaly Customer experience Customer flow Customer bounce rate	Disturbing behaviour detection Discomfort recognition
DATA ANALYTICS: EMOTION	Emotion	Valence Arousal	Valence Arousal
DATA ANALYTICS: BEHAVIOUR	Location Activity	Activity Trajectory	Activity Trajectory
SENSOR MEASUREMENT & SIGNAL PROCESSING	Continuous time-series data on the target user Continuous time-series data from the environment	Continuous time-series data from the environment	Continuous time-series data from the environment
ACTORS	End-user/employee Empathic service provider Service provider/Employer Personal wearable technology provider Solution provider Data provider Platform/technology developer Platform provider (e.g. AWS) Facility manager Facility owner Architect	Customer Employee Empathic service provider Security service provider Service provider Data provider Technology developer Facility owner Facility manager Policy maker and legislator Designer Investor	Passenger Empathic service provider Security service provider Public transport operator Public security authorities Platform/technology provider Governmental and municipal authorities Research organizations

have visions on how to build on their existing technologies and products to widen their offering with novel emotion-aware solutions and new business models (e.g. transformation from a technology provider to a data provider).

Even though the "emotion-aware service or product" term had many different interpretations and providing a clear definition was difficult, the interviewees' opinions also bore similarities. Based on the participants' answers, the basis for an emotion-aware service or product is in understanding of human behaviour and needs without explicit human-technology interaction. Not only does emotion-awareness require measurement or monitoring of human or group behaviour, but it also needs inference to information, which can be used to control the functionality of the services and products. The adaptation of the services and products can be either fully automatic or supervised by human experts. In addition, the information on emotional atmosphere in a space can be communicated to the users currently present. In this case, the aim is not to adapt the product or service but to influence on human behaviour in space.

In their responses, most of the company partners identified initial emotion-aware product and service ideas. First potential use cases are targeted at providing actionable insight on user behaviour and mental state to the organization. Thus, the organization could adapt their processes and ways of working to better meet the user needs, which would be implemented as a service business. Also, the space could react to user needs with subtle changes or detect anomalies and provide mitigation actions. According to the responses, the companies are mainly in a research phase with their emotion-aware offering development. For example, they are investigating how AI can be used in human behaviour analysis or how to integrate measurement and analysis technologies into their products. The aim is to evaluate the feasibility of different technologies and create a related value proposition to be used for a product development plan. Additionally, the companies are developing further their existing technology platforms to support the integration of new services providing human behaviour and emotion insight data.

The motivation to invest in the development of emotion-aware solutions is in the added value it would provide to B2B customers and the users of the spaces. Indeed, the products and services must fulfil a user and customer need. Moreover, the emotion-awareness would be a competitive advantage for the companies and the same concepts could be adopted in different environments. In their responses, the companies are also looking for support for their brand image as a company investing in future technologies. Thus, the value proposition of emotion-aware products and services is in their expected ability to enhance the performance of organizations, spaces, and humans in addition to the well-being of all. Compared to the current implicit surveys, the actionable insight provided would be more comprehensive as it would be based on continuous measurement. Furthermore, it could improve the decision-making processes (regarding, e.g. investments, space controls, space usage) and enable new inspiration. In the future, the behaviour and emotion data could have value as well. As the business environment is evolving, customers have new critical requirements, e.g. related to safety and security.

As target users, the companies in this study are focusing on groups with special needs. The range in the target groups is broad, from older adults to global high-tech companies prioritizing the employee well-being and experience. In selecting the target group, an essential consideration is the company's ability to distinguish itself from competitors through a unique offering. All the companies interviewed have international customers, most of whom are working globally with the ambition to widen the international customer base further. The expected business impact is manifold, and the competitive advantage provided by the emotion-aware solutions would lead to new customers, increased sales, and growth in revenue. Furthermore, the margins would be improved and new offering, novel business models and sales channels adopted.

In the development and commercialization of emotion-aware products and services, the main challenge identified is in customer interaction; how to proof the added value of these solutions and how to create the customer need for a totally new type of offering. Introducing a new type of product to conservative customers poses a particular challenge, as some organizations or business domains may be resistant to change and more inclined to stick to traditional choices. The second important challenge identified are regulations present both in Europe and globally, as the usage of specific sensor technologies or AI methods might be unfeasible due to current and upcoming regulations. A further factor is the changing regulatory landscape causing uncertainty and hindering investments. In addition to the two main challenges mentioned, technology maturity, privacy, trust and accuracy of technologies, user acceptance and cost of the systems were identified as challenges for development and commercialization.

In this study, the companies under focus expect to be able to introduce the first simple emotion-aware products or services relatively soon with a timeframe of one to two years. The commercialization of more complex emotion-aware solutions able to respond automatically to human behaviour and emotions is estimated to take more than five years. Thus, for these solutions to become mainstream, a change in customer company culture or in their value network may be required, which might take years. All the interviewed companies have identified a need for collaboration to be able to build the emotion-aware products and services. Thus, expertise is required on sensor technologies, data acquisition, analysis, and interpretation.

6 Discussion and Conclusions

By adopting co-creation methods with a multidisciplinary team including experts from industry, technology, and law research, this study approaches the challenge of narrowing the gap between laboratory research and the commercialization of emotion-aware services. Via a long-term collaboration, the team has created an emotion-aware service concept portfolio to be used to guide future technology development activities and to offer a basis for discussion on ethics and regulation related to the emotion-aware technologies and services.

The literature studies and the industry expert interviews demonstrate that the definition of an emotion-aware service is as complex and varied as the expression of human emotions. However, based on the interviews there is a general consensus that emotion-awareness necessitates not only measurement and analysis of human behaviour and emotional state but also the ability to interpret and derive actionable insight to adapt either automatically or manually the services in the physical space to respond to human needs and expectations.

Based on the company views, customer and user needs are the key drivers for the development and deployment of emotion-aware services. It has been natural for the consortium members to place themselves in the shoes of a user of emotion-aware services during the co-creation work. In this study, the consortium came up with many service ideas with real-life applications. While some concept ideas are more complex and require a strong technological development push, others will require more work on building trust and growing acceptance from users. As user acceptance is a crucial factor considering the privacy challenges related to usage of personal data, a clear benefit for the user must be identified and communicated. Therefore, methods for data minimization, anonymization and aggregation should be considered, keeping in mind the need for transparent and trustworthy solutions. Moreover, user studies on comparing different emotion and behaviour assessment techniques, such as type of sensors, privacy, trust, and personal aspects, influencing social acceptance, are necessary. Indeed, legal aspects in relation to measurement and analysis technology choices should be studied further and potential harm caused by emotion-aware service in physical spaces reflected on. While emotion-aware services hold promises in enhancing user experiences, ethical considerations and privacy implications must be carefully navigated. Striking a balance between technological innovation and user protection is essential to ensure responsible deployment.

In conclusion, emotion-aware services represent a promising frontier in service design and development, offering a pathway to more empathetic, responsive, and user-centric interactions. By understanding and adapting to human behaviour and emotions, these services have the potential to revolutionize various domains. The authors knowledge that this study is a starting point for a more thorough investigation on potential of data-driven solutions to be used for adding emotional intelligence to physical spaces. Thus, the applicability of the emotion-aware solutions should be researched separately for the target environments and more precise scenarios involving the potential user groups to the co-creation process. In addition, it is imperative to approach their implementation with ethical considerations at the forefront to foster responsible and sustainable technological advancements.

References

Anderson L, Ostrom AL (2015) Transformative service research: advancing our knowledge about service and well-being. J Serv Res 18(3):243–249. https://doi.org/10.1177/1094670515591316

Ben X, Ren Y, Zhang J, Wang S-J, Kpalma K, Meng W, Liu Y-J (2022) Video-based facial micro-expression analysis: a survey of datasets, features, and algorithms. IEEE Transact Pattern Anal Mach Intell 44(9):5826–5846. https://doi.org/10.1109/TPAMI.2021.3067464

Booth BM, Mundnich K, Feng T, Nadarajan A, Falk TH, Villatte JL, Ferrara E, Narayanan S (2019) Multimodal human and environmental sensing for longitudinal behavioral studies in naturalistic settings: framework for sensor selection, deployment, and management. J Med Inter Res 21(8): e12832. https://doi.org/10.2196/12832

Cabanac M (2002) What is emotion? Behav Process 60(2):69–83

Camplani M, Paiement A, Mirmehdi M, Damen D, Hannuna S, Burghardt T, Tao L (2016) Multiple human tracking in RGB-depth data: a survey. IET Computer Vision. https://doi.org/10.1049/iet-cvi.2016.0178

Canal FZ, Rossi Müller T, Matias JC, Scotton GG, de Sa R, Junior A, Pozzebon E, Sobieranski AC (2022) A survey on facial emotion recognition techniques: a state-of-the-art literature review. Inf Sci 582:593–617. https://doi.org/10.1016/j.ins.2021.10.005

Casado CÁ, Räsänen P, Nguyen L, Lämsä A, Peltola J, Bordallo López M (2024) A distributed framework for remote multimodal biosignal acquisition and analysis. In: Särestoniemi, M et al (eds) Digital Health and Wireless Solutions. NCDHWS 2024. Communications in Computer and Information Science, vol 2084. Springer, Cham. https://doi.org/10.1007/978-3-031-59091-7_9

David DS, Samraj M (2020) A comprehensive survey of emotion recognition system in facial expression. Artech J Effect Res Eng Technol 1:76–81

Fernandes JM, Silva JS, Rodrigues A, Boavida F (2022) A survey of approaches to unobtrusive sensing of humans. ACM Comput Surv (CSUR) 55(2):1–28. https://doi.org/10.1145/3491208

Fu B, Damer N, Kirchbuchner F, Kuijper A (2020) Sensing technology for human activity recognition: a comprehensive survey. IEEE Access 8:83791–83820. https://doi.org/10.1109/ACCESS.2020.2991891

Hernandez J, Lovejoy J, McDuff D et al (2021) Guidelines for assessing and minimizing risks of emotion recognition applications. In: 2021 9th International conference on affective computing and intelligent interaction (ACII). IEEE, pp 1–8. https://doi.org/10.1109/ACII52823.2021.9597452

Iguernaissi R, Merad D, Aziz K et al (2019) People tracking in multi-camera systems: a review. Multimedia Tools Appl 78:10773–10793. https://doi.org/10.1007/s11042-018-6638-5

Jardak S, Alouini M, Kiuru T, Metso M, Ahmed S (2019) Compact mmWave FMCW radar: implementation and performance analysis. IEEE Aerosp Electr Syst Magaz 34(2):36–44. https://doi.org/10.1109/MAES.2019.180130

Kallio J, Vildjiounaite E, Koivusaari J, Räsänen P, Similä, H, Kyllönen V, Muuraiskangas S, Ronkainen J, Rehu J, Vehmas K (2020) Assessment of perceived indoor environmental quality, stress and productivity based on environmental sensor data and personality categorization. Build Environ 175:Article 106787. https://doi.org/10.1016/j.buildenv.2020.106787

Kiuru T, Metso M, Jardak S, Pursula P, Hakli J, Hirvonen M, Sepponen R (2016) Movement and respiration detection using statistical properties of the FMCW radar signal. In: Proceedings of 2016 Global Symposium on Millimeter Waves (GSMM) & ESA Workshop on Millimetre-Wave Technology and Applications, Espoo, Finland, pp 1–4. https://doi.org/10.1109/GSMM.2016.7500331

Kreibig SD (2010) Autonomic nervous system activity in emotion: a review. Biol Psychol 84(3): 394–421

Lin K, Xia F, Wang W, Tian D, Song J (2016) System design for big data application in emotion-aware healthcare. IEEE Access 4:6901–6909

Luomala HT, Järvinen S, Peltola J, Pennanen K, Sihvonen J (2023) Priming shoppers' well-being goal in grocery stores: moving toward healthier food choices? Food Q Pref 108:104882. https://doi.org/10.1016/j.foodqual.2023.104882

MyData (2024). https://github.com/mydataglobal/declaration/raw/master/1.0/EN/MyData_Declaration_v1.0_EN.pdf. Accessed 16 Feb 2024

Russell JA, Mehrabian A (1974) Distinguishing anger and anxiety in terms of emotional response factors. J Consult Clin Psychol 42(1):79–83. https://doi.org/10.1037/h0035915

Tirachini A, Cats O (2020) COVID-19 and public transportation: current assessment, prospects, and research needs. J Public Transp 22(1). https://doi.org/10.5038/2375-0901.22.1.1

Tzirakis P, Chen J, Zafeiriou S, Schuller B (2021) End-to-end multimodal affect recognition in real-world environments. Inform Fusion 68:46–53. https://doi.org/10.1016/j.inffus.2020.10.011

Vildjiounaite E, Mäkelä S-M, Keränen T, Kyllönen V, Huotari V, Järvinen S, Gimelfarb G (2017) Unsupervised illness recognition via in-home monitoring by depth cameras. Pervasive Mobile Comput 38(Part 1):166–187. https://doi.org/10.1016/j.pmcj.2016.07.004

Vildjiounaite E, Huotari V, Kallio J, Kyllönen V, Mäkelä SM, Gimel'farb G (2019) Unobtrusive assessment of stress of office workers via analysis of their motion trajectories. Pervasive Mobile Comput 58:Article 101028. doi:https://doi.org/10.1016/j.pmcj.2019.05.009

Wang W, den Brinker AC, Stuijk S, de Haan G (2017) Algorithmic principles of remote PPG. IEEE Transact Biomed Eng 64(7):1479–1491

Zhang X, Zheng P, Peng T, He Q, Lee C, Tang R (2022) Promoting employee health in smart office: a survey. Adv Eng Inform 51:101518. https://doi.org/10.1016/j.aei.2021.101518

Research Challenges Along the Data Analysis Chain for Emotional AI

Elena Vildjiounaite, Julia Kantorovitch, Johanna Kallio, Vesa Kyllönen, and Jenny Benois-Pineau

Abstract Emotional AI represents a relatively new research area, and to date, its focus has been on the development of AI methods to recognise instantaneous human states, for example, whether a person is currently happy or experiencing acute stress. However, because the majority of emotion detection studies to date have been conducted in laboratory settings, many technologies are not yet sufficiently mature for real-world applications. For example, though truly emotionally intelligent AI should be convenient for the users, adaptive to their personalities (given that the expression of the same emotion can vary across individuals), and capable of also assessing long-lasting human conditions, such as chronic stress, research into these problems is only starting. This chapter offers an overview of the most popular data sources and AI methods and discusses the main challenges that must be addressed to develop emotional AI methods for long-term real-world use.

E. Vildjiounaite (✉) · J. Kantorovitch · J. Kallio · V. Kyllönen
VTT Technical Research Centre of Finland, Espoo, Finland
e-mail: elena.vildjiounaite@vtt.fi; julia.kantorovitch@vtt.fi; johanna.kallio@vtt.fi; vesa.kyllonen@vtt.fi

J. Benois-Pineau
LaBRI, UMR CNRS 5800, University Bordeaux, Talence, France
e-mail: jenny.benois-pineau@u-bordeaux.fr

R. Ballardini et al. (eds.), *Emotional Data Applications and Regulation of Artificial Intelligence in Society*, Law, Governance and Technology Series 69,
https://doi.org/10.1007/978-3-031-80111-2_3

1 Introduction

Emotion recognition is an active research area, with numerous reviews summarising research on specific data sources, such as physiological data,[1] text and speech,[2] faces,[3] eyes,[4] body,[5] and device usage,[6] while other reviews focus on particular settings, such as office[7] and mobility,[8] or particular AI methods, such as fusion of multiple data sources.[9]

However, these reviews primarily target researchers with AI and emotion recognition expertise and focus on recognising ***instantaneous emotions***, whereas important ***long-lasting conditions*** such as chronic stress or seasonal mood variations are seldom addressed.[10] A reason for this is that most emotion recognition studies are conducted in laboratory settings, where it is only possible to induce instant stress. Even recent surveys on mobile devices have observed that research is typically conducted in controlled lab environments, primarily with university students.[11] Furthermore, in our research, we did not find many ***practical*** recommendations regarding which information source and which AI methods could be ***realistically*** used in which settings.

The main difference between laboratory settings and real life is that in labs, human subjects behave as requested by researchers to provide the best possible data for sensors, even if it is inconvenient for them. Conversely, in real life, individuals prioritise their own convenience and privacy. Therefore, methods, developed in labs, may not perform well in real-life scenarios.[12]

The main contributions of this paper are twofold: (1) providing a high-level overview of various data sources and AI methods, along with their suitability for different real-life settings; and (2) outlining the major research challenges for developing suitable for real life emotion recognition methods.

---

[1] Can et al. (2023); Egger et al. (2019).

[2] Schuller and Schuller (2021); Poria et al. (2023).

[3] Dalvi et al. (2021); Ekundayo and Viriri (2021); Zhao et al. (2023).

[4] Lim et al. (2020).

[5] Noroozi et al. (2021).

[6] Yang and Qin (2021).

[7] Alberdi et al. (2016).

[8] Sarsenbayeva et al. (2023); Yang et al. (2023).

[9] Naveed et al. (2023).

[10] Vildjiounaite et al. (2023); Dávila-Montero et al. (2021).

[11] Yang et al. (2023), annex B.

[12] Dávila-Montero et al., ibid.

2 Overview of Developing AI Models

Emotional intelligence in computer applications refers to their capability to understand human mental conditions (emotions, moods, chronic stress etc.) and to utilise this comprehension wisely. Though the use of human mental states by computer applications is beyond the scope of this chapter, we recommend that the choice of AI methods for assessing human conditions should align with the application goals. Figure 1 presents an overview of a typical data flow for assessing human mental conditions, along with an inexhaustive list of popular data sources, described in the next section in more detail.

A data flow for assessing human mental conditions is usually organised as follows:

Monitoring data on human physiological parameters and/or behaviour is acquired from physical or virtual sensors. For example, computer users may have their faces monitored by computer cameras (physical sensors), while a specialized computer application ("virtual sensor") logs keystrokes. When mobile, users may wear wrist devices recording heart rate and wrist motion, while a dedicated phone application gathers their phone screen usage data and locations.

Feature Extraction certain characteristics are extracted from the collected data, for example, how many times the "delete" key was pressed. Feature extraction can be organised in two ways. The first approach involves storing raw data, such as video footage of a user's face and all typed symbols along with their timestamps, and then calculating data features. The second approach is to extract data features and to store only these features. For instance, facial expressions and heart rate can be extracted from face data and stored instead of a video, while typing speed can be stored instead of typed letters. Storing raw data poses more privacy risks but allows for system updates (e.g., counting the usage of more keys than the initially selected).

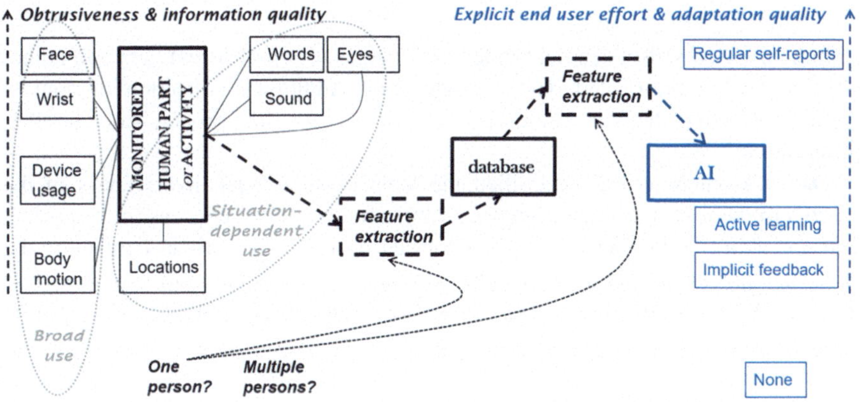

Fig. 1 Overview of a typical data flow for assessing human mental conditions

Additionally, storing raw data enables the use of modern deep learning methods, which automatically extract features.

AI Training and Using the Trained AI Models to output their opinions about current users, AI models need to be trained to map input data into stress or emotions. Training typically requires two types of input: examples of data and their corresponding labels (e.g. "this is stress," "this is happiness," etc.). Given the complexity of assessing human conditions, the most common approach to training AI models is fully supervised, where each data sample is accompanied by a label. Alternative training options include semi-supervised (where only some data samples have labels) and unsupervised (where no data samples have labels), but these are less common due to their lower accuracy.

AI methods for assessing human emotions fall into two main categories: "traditional" and "deep learning" methods. Traditional methods typically process data features. For instance, the traditional method to detect stress from a user facial video would involve detecting the user's heartbeat, calculating heart rate variability (HRV) before using HRV as an input feature. In contrast, deep learning methods can take raw data as input instead of pre-extracted features, as they perform feature extraction internally. Therefore, the primary advantage of the deep learning methods lies in their capability to learn complex data patterns directly from the data. However, these methods require large training datasets and significant quantities of labels.

Although traditional methods can learn from notably smaller datasets, they require carefully designed features because improper features reduce recognition accuracy. For example, if a system designer forgets to use mouth shape features, traditional methods would fail to recognise smiles. Since obtaining labels always require human effort and is thus costly, the choice of AI method should depend on the availability of labels and the trade-off between labelling efforts and benefits.

3 Popular Data Sources

Commonly used sensors capture video and images (often of faces), text and audio, physiological, motion, and device usage data. Additional collection of context factors, affecting human emotions, is rare, except for privacy-safe weather information.[13]

Dávila-Montero et al.[14] classified the level of superficial invasiveness of the sensors to the user into three categories: skin contact (sensor requires direct contact with the skin); body contact (sensor is placed on the body without contacting the skin); and no contact. Of these categories, skin contact was the most invasive while no contact was completely non-invasive. For example, physiological data can be

[13] Bogomolov et al. (2014).

[14] Dávila-Montero et al. (2021).

obtained by wrist-worn devices, requiring skin contact, or via non-contact video cameras in the environment; body motion can be obtained via accelerometers in wrist-worn devices and mobile phones, or via infrared cameras in the environment. In contrast to numerous other studies, Dávila-Montero et al. employ the term "invasiveness" to assess user convenience rather than privacy threats, while threats are evaluated based on the nature of the data. For instance, physiological data poses the same level of privacy risk regardless of the sensors used to collect it.

The deployment of emotion assessment methods in real life requires user acceptance, which is influenced by both sensor invasiveness and privacy threats. ***Perceived sensor potential*** to threaten privacy often affects personal attitudes more than the actual sensor functionality. For instance, Dávila-Montero et al.[15] included audio in their review, but excluded video and image, arguing that images and video are more privacy threatening. On the other hand, in another study,[16] the audio was rejected as highly privacy threatening, whereas video from a wearable camera was accepted on the condition of eliminating all image elements from the data which would lead to the identification of persons, such as photos, mirror reflexions, caregivers or family members. In our view, privacy threats of both audio and video data can be very high or moderate, depending on how data are transmitted and stored.

Sensor invasiveness also affects their suitability for different situations. When the user is actively moving, sensors requiring skin contact often lose contact, leading to dramatic deterioration in data quality. Although sensors, when placed in the environment, are usually convenient for the users, they cannot collect data if the users move out of their field of view. An ideal data source would continuously provide highly informative data without being intrusive or posing privacy threats, but such sensors do not yet exist. Consequently, the choice of the data source typically involves a compromise between data quality and privacy/intrusiveness. Below, we outline such compromises for the most popular data sources:

Text (Spoken or Written) This is a non-invasive and highly informative data source capable of providing user feelings and reasons behind them. Due to its high informativeness, text presents significant privacy threats. Hence, its applicability is limited to public situations, such as analysing written public reviews, and safety issues, e.g. detecting threats in social networks. Research into written text-based emotion recognition usually utilises internet data, e.g. news headlines, TV show transcripts, tweets etc., annotated by human observers.[17]

User Face This is a non-invasive and highly informative data source that can provide: (1) facial expressions corresponding to basic emotions (joy, fear, surprise, etc.); (2) heart rate; (3) eye gaze, blinking, and pupil dilation; and (4) micro-expressions—subtle facial movements that can reveal users' feelings even when

[15] ibid.

[16] Mallick et al. (2022).

[17] Deng and Ren (2023).

they attempt to conceal them. Facial expression data are also usually obtained from lab studies and from the internet, but less privacy-threating (than raw videos) heart rate data have also been collected in real life during the everyday work of computer users.[18] Although privacy threats depend on the type of data stored (e.g. video stream vs. heart rate), individuals may perceive face monitoring as "Big Brother watching" regardless. User face is best applicable for computer users since computer web cameras can continuously monitor the users. Mobile phone cameras can also be used, but only intermittently.

User Wrist This is an invasive (requiring skin contact) and relatively informative data source. Commercially available wrist-worn devices can continuously provide heart rate and accelerometer data; some also provide skin conductivity data. Moreover, heart rate and skin conductivity data can be used for stress and emotion recognition, although device shifts during physical activity negatively affect data quality.[19] Unlike text and face, wrist data cannot be obtained from the internet in large quantities. It is usually collected from volunteers in labs or in real life, and far too often from young and healthy subjects. Privacy threats are moderate with user wrist data: although in theory, heart rate in connection with motion data can reveal certain health problems, in reality, data quality is usually too low for that. An important factor to consider is user willingness to tolerate the weight and charging requirements of wrist devices.

Sound A non-invasive and relatively informative data source, as features such as voice loudness, speech dynamics, and pitch have been used for emotion and stress detection.[20] Speech data can be obtained from the actors, from lab studies and from the internet (videos). Although privacy threats depend on the stored data type (e.g. audio stream or features only), users may generally perceive microphones as "Big Brother listening". Sound analysis is best applicable for users who speak a lot, such as salespersons and service support personnel, while others may utilise mobile phones, but only intermittently.

Eyes (When Tracked Separately from Faces) This is a relatively invasive data source as accurate eye trackers are either using infrared projectors or are embedded in virtual/augmented reality headsets; less invasive web camera-based eye tracking is also less accurate.[21] However, the eye behaviour is a rather informative data source because pupil dilation and eye blinking can be used to detect stress and certain emotions, while eye gaze direction can provide insights into the reasons for emotions. With this data source, privacy threats are relatively low and mainly depend on detecting reasons for emotions. Applicability is limited to situations

[18] Rodrigues and Correia (2024).

[19] Can et al. (2023); Egger et al. (2019).

[20] Latif et al. (2023).

[21] Lim et al. (2020).

where people face infrared-based eye-trackers or wear headsets, such as games or training. Data are usually collected in the labs.

Device Usage This is a data source obtained through the use of computer peripherals (mouse, keyboard), mobile phone screen touches, used applications, phone calls/SMS, etc. Though this is a non-invasive data source, it can drain batteries on phones. Privacy threats depend on stored details; for example, if only mouse coordinates are logged, privacy threats are low, but privacy threats increase if typed texts or URLs of visited web pages are logged. With this source, applicability is limited to applications not requiring real-time emotion detection, as device monitoring cannot detect instant emotions or stress. Being non-invasive, this data type suits well for real-life data collections; nonetheless, to date, the majority of studies have been conducted in labs,[22] although phone usage data have been used to detect stress on a daily basis in real-life studies[23] and computer usage data have been used to detect stress during student exams.[24]

Body Motion This is a non-invasive data source when motion is obtained from depth cameras, infrared sensors, and pressure mats. This source requires body contact when motion is obtained from wrist devices and phones and may drain phone batteries. Privacy threats are low because such sensors do not identify users. With body motion, data are usually obtained from volunteers, and usually in the labs. Although applicability is limited to applications not requiring real-time emotion detection, motion data have allowed for the assessment of daily stress in real-life scenarios.[25]

Locations This is a source where outdoor locations are obtained from mobile phones, while indoor locations are obtained from dedicated positioning systems, requiring users to wear badges or cameras, which makes location data somewhat invasive. Data are usually obtained from volunteers. Privacy threats depend on the level of detail of location data, such as GPS versus mobile network cell ID, but any location information can cause problems if it reveals that a person was not at home or at work when expected. Location data are usually used as an auxiliary data source. To date, locations have only been used as the sole data source to address health disorders, such as Alzheimer's and depression.[26]

[22] Yang et al. (2023), annex B.

[23] Ferdous et al. (2015).

[24] Carneiro et al. (2015).

[25] Garcia-Ceja et al. (2016); Vildjiounaite et al. (2019).

[26] Shin and Bae (2023); Dovgalecs et al. (2013).

4 Major Challenges

Reviews on emotion detection using various data sources highlight several common challenges in this research area.

4.1 Lack of Real-Life Sensor Data

To recognise human conditions in real-life settings, AI models need to be trained on examples of these conditions. If the training samples are not sufficiently similar to real-life data, the accuracy of AI models decreases. Nevertheless, currently, most studies develop and test AI methods using data collected in laboratory settings, while their suitability to real-life data remains unknown. For instance, emotions in labs are often induced by tasks such as public speaking, mental arithmetic or watching movie clips[27] and are therefore short-lived. However, it remains unexplored whether errors in mental arithmetic are manifested in the sensor data in a similar way as real-life stressors, such as missed trains, conflicts with colleagues, project deadlines or family issues, the effects of which may last for a long time.

The dominance of laboratory studies is observed for all data sources, with phone location data being the only exception. For instance, a recent overview of approaches to physiological data analysis[28] listed 12 sets of collected data, of which only two were gathered in the real world. Similarly, a list of facial expression recognition datasets[29] primarily contains lab data or data obtained from the internet, where annotations are provided by external observers rather than the individuals experiencing the emotions. Such annotations can be oversimplified or erroneous since external observers may miss subtle emotions or misinterpret them. While it may be reasonable to assume that sad faces appear similar across different contexts (e.g. after watching a video clip in a lab and after receiving a phone call in real life), real-life emotions are often more complex. For example, while a carefully chosen video clip may indeed induce only sadness, a phone call could evoke a range of emotions, e.g. self-satisfaction of the kind "I knew it was coming!".

When collecting real-life data, it is crucial to consider several key aspects:

Diversity of Subjects Research on the analysis of human faces and physiological data is already rather mature, but surveys[30] have nevertheless emphasised the need for facial datasets to include a more diverse range of cultures, races, ages, and levels of emotion intensity. Similarly, many studies on physiological data analysis primarily involve young, healthy adults. For example, the only large real-life dataset

[27] Can et al. (2023).

[28] Ibid.

[29] Ekundayo and Viriri (2021).

[30] Dalvi et al. (2021); Ekundayo and Viriri (2021).

listed[31] contains data from 88 individuals with an average age of 21.5 years. Another real-life physiological dataset (not publicly available) predominantly includes educated employees with sedentary jobs.[32] Studies collecting device usage data often exclude participants with hypertension and musculoskeletal disorders, as well as those who are left-handed.[33] It is also important to include individuals with varying reactions to emotional stimuli: for instance, some people are more prone to stress than others. Indeed, a study by Smets[34] reported that detecting stress in physiological data is more challenging in individuals who experience stress frequently compared to those who rarely experience it. Studying whether the analysis of behavioural data presents similar or different challenges requires appropriate data.

Variety of Human Conditions and Activities As explained above, lab studies typically induce short-lived and relatively mild emotions, with subjects primarily engaging in given tasks and relaxation in between. Unfortunately, this approach fails to capture mixed emotions and natural behavioural responses to real life events. For instance, lab studies often use time pressure as stressor.[35] Consequently, commonly used features for detecting stress from computer data, collected in the lab, include typing tempo and usage of the "delete" key.[36] However, in real life, stressors include social interactions, lack of inspiration, and boredom.[37] Moreover, the behaviours of individuals under stress vary considerably; some may seek social support, while others may abandon a work task to start searching for a new job, but data, containing real human behaviours, are not publicly available. However, a study by Vanttola et al.[38] analysed real-life computer data and did not observe significant correlations between stress and usage of the "delete" key.

Variety of Durations of Human Conditions The majority of studies are relatively short: lab experiments typically span only a few hours, while real-life studies may last only a few days or weeks.[39] In their work, Vildjiounaite et al.[40] found only 11 real-life stress detection studies lasting at least four weeks, conducted during the last decade, none of which explored such an important human condition as chronic stress. Similarly, studies focusing on emotion and mood assessment tend to capture the immediate "now" or "today" state, rather than longer-term trends. However, many aspects of human life are influenced by prolonged trends rather than immediate conditions; for instance, persistent low-intensity stress may pose greater health

[31] Can et al. (2023).

[32] Smets et al. (2018).

[33] Yang and Qin (2021); Yang et al. (2023).

[34] Smets et al. (2018).

[35] Vildjiounaite et al. (2023).

[36] Yang and Qin (2021).

[37] Vildjiounaite et al. (2023).

[38] Vanttola et al. (2024).

[39] Can et al. (2023); Smets et al. (2018).

[40] Vildjiounaite et al. (2023).

risks than short-lived high-intensity stress.[41] Decisions such as changing jobs or ending relationships also often depend on the duration of dissatisfaction with the current situation. Currently, however, there are no data, suitable for detecting trends and persistent issues in real-life scenarios.

Variety of Settings Although lab studies are usually designed to collect detailed data, achieving a similar level of detail in the real world may be impossible. For instance, in a lab study by Koldijk et al.,[42] subjects were positioned so that depth cameras could capture their entire body, whereas in a real-life study by Vildjiounaite et al.,[43] office furniture obstructed camera views so that only head trajectories were recorded. Privacy and security concerns can also limit level of details. For example, a review by Yang et al.[44] lists keyboard data features used in lab studies, and these features include counts of lowercase and uppercase letters, numbers, punctuation, and special keys. In real life, such detailed data collection could compromise user privacy and security, particularly concerning passwords.

4.2 *Quality of Real-Life Labels*

In real-life studies, labels are usually self-reports from users. As observed,[45] the compliance of test subjects in providing these labels depends on the frequency of label requests and the required level of detail. The higher the requested user effort, the less likely it is that test subjects will provide all the required labels, and test subjects may even abandon data collection altogether.

Typically, subjects provide labels upon system prompts. Hence, the reported condition may have started just before or long before the label was recorded. Then, the subjects may experience multiple emotions during the reporting period. For instance, if a subject felt both stress and joy during the reporting period, how should one label it? While subjects can be given an option to provide labels whenever they want, this does not guarantee well-labelled data, as in real life reporting is usually a low priority activity.

Additionally, subjects' assessment of their own conditions highly depends on culture and personality, e.g. some individuals can be stressed by a lack of inspiration,[46] while others may perceive stress very differently. For example, the authors of this paper were sometimes asked "How can you study stress? It is such a rare occasion, like when your close relatives die".

[41] Lamb and Kwok (2016).
[42] Koldijk et al. (2018).
[43] Vildjiounaite et al. (2019).
[44] Yang and Qin (2021).
[45] Sarsenbayeva et al. (2023).
[46] Vildjiounaite et al. (2019).

Consequently, labels are highly person-dependent and often imbalanced. For example, some persons may never experience anger during data collection, while others may be too absorbed in their feelings to report anger, so anger will be under-represented in the data. This contrasts with lab studies, where the study protocol aims to induce the same emotion in everybody and defines when this emotion should be observed in the data. Transitions between emotions are also clearer in lab studies because test subjects usually relax before being placed in the next situation.

Currently, there is no established approach to handling real-life labels, and researchers may even refuse to use available real-life data due to its difficulty. For example, Vos et al.[47] did not utilize real-life stress data published[48] because they found it challenging to distinguish stress periods from normal ones.

4.3 AI Adaptivity

4.3.1 User Diversity

AI models typically require labelled data for training, and obtaining these labels involves significant human effort. An ideal solution would be "***general models***", trained on data from multiple individuals to work universally for all users without needing their labels. However, general models demand substantial training data and can be only trained for common expressions of emotions, such as raised eyebrows when surprised. Currently, general models can be trained for texts, images, and videos, where data are sourced from the internet and labelled via crowdsourcing.

General models, however, fail to recognise individualized expressions of emotions if such expressions vary significantly between individuals. For instance, while some individuals may become more communicative when stressed, others may withdraw; similarly, while some may "freeze" under stress, others may fidget. Moreover, general models fail in unusual cases, such as individuals who are unable to raise their eyebrows due to muscle problems, or when eyebrows are obscured by hair. Additionally, general models cannot reliably estimate emotion intensity because behaviours that seem normal for one person may signal extraordinary emotions in another (e.g. a young girl screaming and jumping when only mildly excited, compared to a middle-aged man).

Since general models lack adaptability, a basic usability requirement is to describe their applicability—for whom the model is expected to perform well and for whom it is likely to fail. However, currently, there are no established practices to do this.

One further approach is to develop ***person-specific models*** by using only the data of a person in training. These models can accommodate any data source and learn

[47] Vos et al. (2022).

[48] Hosseini et al. (2022).

individual nuances, such as freezing when stressed or fidgeting when tired. This approach (also called the "one-person" scenario[49]) is best suited to those cases when emotional manifestation highly depends on the individuals and may evolve with time. For example, during normal work (i.e. in a calm state), some persons may have a lot of meetings with minimal computer usage, some others may type a lot, while others may use a mouse a lot. Under stress, some of these persons may start using computer more actively, while others take a break to think. However, a change in work tasks/ hobbies and ageing may affect both "calm" and "stressed" computer patterns.

Another example is where an elderly person may show signs of depression or lower motor capacities with time, and this evolution is highly person specific. Hence, the monitoring tool should adapt to each user instead of generalising for the whole population. Such adaptation can be done incrementally: first, some data quantity is collected and used to train the initial model, then the model is updated when more data become available. However, the drawback here is that each user must provide labels for training, which can be burdensome. Hence, the individuals should value the provided services highly enough to invest efforts in training underlying AI models. Yet, in any case, training data in such cases are never abundant. Therefore, it would be highly desirable to reduce the number of labels required for training person-specific AI models. However, this research is still in its early stages, particularly for behavioural data.[50]

Hybrid models offer a compromise, using data from multiple individuals but requiring fewer labels per user compared to personalized models. For example, one hybrid approach is to model groups of similar users; but defining similarity between human beings is a tricky problem. For facial images, similarity by age, race and gender might work, but how should one measure the similarity of computer users?

Another hybrid approach involves training AI on data from numerous individuals, with certain model parameters shared among all users while others personalized.[51] However, more commonly, models are tailored not to individuals but rather to databases, e.g. the specifics of data collection conditions.[52]

4.3.2 Data Availability

Currently, most studies utilize a single data source. When multiple sources are used, it is often assumed that data from all sources are always available, such as students

---

49 Mallick et al. (2022); Mallick et al. (2022).

50 Vildjiounaite et al. (2023).

51 Taylor et al. (2020).

52 Dalvi et al. (2021); Zhao et al. (2023).

wearing wrist devices and using mobile phones daily.[53] However, in reality, all desired data sources may not always be available: users may not always be near cameras or they may forget to charge wearables. Additionally, some users may perceive video cameras as privacy threats, while others may dislike wearing wristwatches.

Hence real-life scenarios necessitate the development of methods to utilize data from various sources based on their availability: for instance, using face data when a video is accessible and phone data when it is not. Research in this area is still in its early stages; for example, a recent survey on multimodal emotion recognition[54] did not include methods for processing asynchronous data or real-life datasets containing data from multiple sensors.

4.3.3 Addressing Time

Although there are emotion detection methods capable of identifying the onset, development, and cessation of emotions, these methods have mainly been developed for physiological and facial data in laboratory settings. In real-life studies, researchers typically select specific periods (e.g. five minutes or a whole day) for classification and treat these periods independently of each other, even though human emotions rarely change instantly. For instance, participants have reported that although the current day seemed ordinary, they still felt stressed due to lingering issues from the previous day.[55] However, only a few studies have attempted to model the effects of past experiences,[56] necessitating the need for further research.

Another time-related challenge is that individuals evolve over time. This evolution can be assessed by either asking the user if the model's accuracy is still satisfactory or by evaluating discrepancies between AI models trained on past data and those trained on recent data. However, to date, human evolution has not been studied due to a lack of long-term data.

4.3.4 Use of Context

Context influences emotions (e.g. weather impacts mood), data quality (e.g. physical activity and food intake affecting heart rate) and ways how people express emotions (e.g. they are usually more reserved in public spaces). Moreover, context is important for assistive applications: for instance, knowing the reasons for stress can help reduce it, and understanding what scares an elderly person can prevent risky

[53] Vildjiounaite et al. (2023).
[54] Naveed et al. (2023).
[55] Vildjiounaite et al. (2019).
[56] Vildjiounaite et al. (2023).

situations in the future.[57] Nevertheless, the collection of contextual data alongside emotional data is infrequent, except for physical activities. As a result, there is limited research on incorporating context into emotional intelligence.

4.3.5 User Preferences and Needs

Emotions are intense and fleeting, while moods are diffuse and longer-lasting conditions.[58] Both emotions and moods are influenced by context, personal traits (such as the Big Five), and attitudes (such as beliefs).

Personal attitudes also influence user preferences regarding which data sources they would be willing to use. For instance, some users may find facial analysis intrusive, feeling that, e.g. "Big Brother is watching", while others may not be bothered. Similarly, some users may enthusiastically wear wrist devices daily and keep them charged, while others may feel the effort outweighs the benefits; mobile phones can be perceived as more "personal" devices than workstations and so on. The number of labels users are willing to provide for training emotion detectors also depends on their personal traits and attitudes: for example, curiosity may prompt some users to interact with emotion detectors more frequently. However, ultimately, users' willingness to invest effort in AI training depends on the benefits they perceive from the service.

Currently, most developers of emotion detectors prioritise achieving high accuracy in recognizing instant emotions, despite it requiring significant human labelling efforts. While some studies have assessed daily stress levels or predicted mood for a day, longer time periods and trends are rarely evaluated. However, using less accurate, but less obtrusive data sources and AI methods would be beneficial for users who dislike obtrusive data sources (top sources in Fig. 1) or are unwilling to provide many labels.

For instance, individuals with seasonal affective disorder (SAD) often experience worsening mood during specific seasons, typically winter. As winter approaches, their mood tends to decline, and detecting this trend using unobtrusive data sources would be sufficient to suspect SAD, whereas employing highly accurate but intrusive data sources would be excessive and potentially unpleasant. Similarly, for preventing burnout or the resignation of an unhappy employee, simply recognizing frequent stress could suffice.

Figure 2 presents the timescale of various conditions and trends, along with recommended types of technologies. For some purposes, such as stress mitigation or reducing risks for the elderly, it is necessary to recognise instant human reactions and their reasons. These can only be identified through the most informative (albeit intrusive) methods, such as facial analysis and contextual analysis through cameras.

[57] Mallick et al. (2022); Mallick et al. (2024a); Mallick et al. (2024b).

[58] Dávila-Montero et al. (2021).

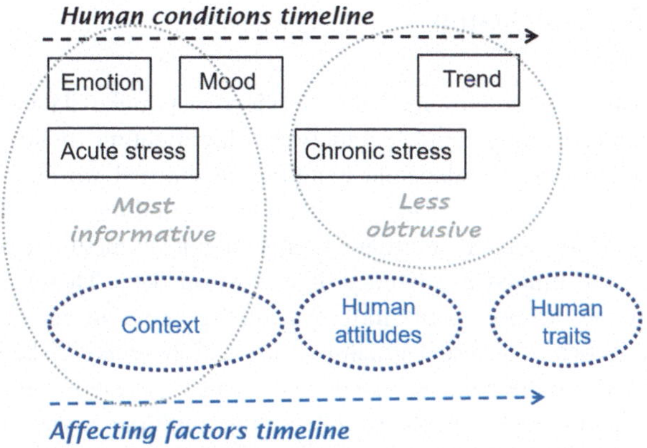

Fig. 2 Emotional conditions and factors affecting them

To assess trends and chronic conditions, less intrusive but less accurate methods can suffice. For example, the unobtrusive collection of motion and device usage data, while relatively privacy-safe, can help to assess the day as stressful or normal. However, this method requires many labels from each user. Therefore, to assess trends conveniently for the user, it is necessary to develop semi-supervised training methods and methods to evaluate long time periods "as a whole". Currently, long time periods are typically evaluated by summing up daily scores, which ignores the influence of past days. Hence, key research challenges for trend assessment are (1) addressing user diversity, which is much more notable in motion data and device usage data than in physiological and face data; (2) developing methods to learn from small datasets (because this kind of data cannot be collected in large quantities); and (3) addressing the temporal aspect.

Workplace applications, aiming at replacing manual surveys,[59] would also require privacy-safe and easy-for-users emotion detectors, capable of assessing average team conditions and trends. This can be achieved using the bottom sources in Fig. 1. On the other hand, personal assistants, especially of vulnerable groups,[60] should be able to accurately assess personal emotions and context, which can be only achieved by using top data sources. Personal assistants should also benefit from understanding user traits and attitudes. Being long-lasting characteristics, traits might be learnable in a manner similar to evaluating long time periods, although this issue remains largely unexplored. While a few studies have attempted to assess personality traits using voice and words as data sources, there has been no attempt to evaluate attitudes.[61] This is likely due to the need for systematic long-term monitoring of context, which has not been undertaken to date.

[59] Vildjiounaite et al. (2020).

[60] Mallick et al. (2022); Mallick et al. (2024a); Mallick et al. (2024b).

[61] Dávila-Montero et al. (2021).

5 Conclusion

This chapter presented an overview of popular data sources and AI methods for understanding human emotions, highlighting major challenges that must be addressed to understand emotions in the real world. These challenges stem from the wide variety of real-world situations and the diversity among individuals.

Unfortunately, current systems are not yet mature to address these challenges due to the limited availability of real-world data. Therefore, the first crucial step for future developers of emotional intelligence is to gather large databases of real-life data across different situations via multiple sensors. The subsequent critical step is to leverage these datasets to develop realistic emotion detection methods that are user-friendly and capable of integrating multiple asynchronous data sources. These methods should be able to assess both momentary emotions and long-lasting conditions, such as chronic stress, trends, personality traits, and attitudes.

While these challenges to understand emotions in the real world are not easy to overcome, it will be achieved in the future because emotional intelligence is currently a very active research area.

References

Alberdi A, Aztiria A, Basarab A (2016) Towards an automatic early stress recognition system for office environments based on multimodal measurements: a review. J Biomed Inform 59:49–75

Bogomolov A, Lepri B, Ferron M, Pianesi F, Pentland AS (2014) Daily stress recognition from mobile phone data, weather conditions and individual traits. MM 2014:477–486

Can YS, Mahesh B, André E (2023) Approaches, applications, and challenges in physiological emotion recognition—a tutorial overview. Proc IEEE 111(10):1287–1313

Carneiro D, Novais P, Pêgo JM, Sousa N, Neves J (2015) Using mouse dynamics to assess stress during online exams. In: International Conference on Hybrid Artificial Intelligence Systems, pp 345–356

Dalvi C, Rathod M, Patil S, Gite S, Kotecha K (2021) A survey of AI-based facial emotion recognition: features, ML & DL techniques, age-wise datasets and future directions. IEEE Access 9:165806–165840

Dávila-Montero S, Dana-Lê JA, Bente G, Hall AT, Mason AJ (2021) Review and challenges of technologies for real-time human behavior monitoring. IEEE Transact Biomed Circuits Syst 15(1):2–28

Deng J, Ren F (2023) A survey of textual emotion recognition and its challenges. IEEE Computer Society Press 14(1)

Dovgalecs V, Megret R, Berthoumieu Y (2013) Multiple feature fusion based on co-training approach and time regularization for place classification in wearable video. Adv Multim 2013:175064:1–175064:22

Egger M, Ley M, Hanke S (2019) Emotion recognition from physiological signal analysis: a review. Electron Notes Theor Comput Sci 343:35–55

Ekundayo OS, Viriri S (2021) Facial expression recognition: a review of trends and techniques. IEEE Access 9:136944–136973

Ferdous R, Osmani V, Mayora O (2015) Smartphone app usage as a predictor of perceived stress levels at workplace. In: 9th International Conference on Pervasive Computing Technologies for Healthcare

Garcia-Ceja E, Osmani V, Mayora O (2016) Automatic stress detection in working environments from smartphones' accelerometer data: a first step. IEEE Journal of Biomedical and Health Informatics

Hosseini S, Gottumukkala R, Katragadda S, Bhupatiraju RT, Ashkar Z, Borst CW, Cochran K (2022) A multimodal sensor dataset for continuous stress detection of nurses in a hospital. Sci Data 9:255

Koldijk S, Neerincx MA, Kraaij W (2018) Detecting work stress in offices by combining unobtrusive sensors. IEEE Transact Affect Comput 9(2):227–239

Lamb S, Kwok KCS (2016) A longitudinal investigation of work environment stressors on the performance and wellbeing of office workers. Appl Ergon 52:104–111

Latif S, Rana R, Khalifa S, Jurdak R, Qadir J, Schuller B (2023) Survey of deep representation learning for speech emotion recognition. IEEE Transact Affect Comput 14(2):1634–1654

Lim JZ, Mountstephens J, Teo J (2020) Emotion recognition using eyetracking: taxonomy, review and current challenges. Sensors 20(8)

Mallick R, Yebda T, Benois-Pineau J, Zemmari A, Pech M, Amieva H (2022) Detection of risky situations for frail adults with hybrid neural networks on multimodal health data. IEEE MultiMedia 29(1):7–17

Mallick R, Benois-Pineau J, Zemmari A (2024a) A hybrid transformer with domain adaptation using interpretability techniques for the application to the detection of risk situations. Multimed Tools Appl

Mallick R, Benois-Pineau J, Zemmari A (2024b) IFI: Interpreting for improving: a multimodal transformer with an interpretability technique for recognition of risk events. MMM 4:117–131

Naveed A, Al Aghbari Z, Girija S (2023) A systematic survey on multimodal emotion recognition using learning algorithms. Intelligent Systems with Applications, p 200171

Noroozi F, Corneanu CA, Kaminska D, Sapinski T, Escalera S, Anbarjafari G (2021) Survey on emotional body gesture recognition. IEEE Trans Affect Comput 12(2):505–523

Poria S, Hazarika D, Majumder N, Mihalcea R (2023) Beneath the tip of the iceberg: current challenges and new directions in sentiment analysis research. IEEE Transact Affect Comput 14(1)

Rodrigues F, Correia H (2024) Semi-supervised and ensemble learning to predict work-related stress. J Intell Inform Syst 62(1)

Sarsenbayeva Z, Fleming C, Tag B, Withana A, van Berkel N, McEwan A (2023) A review on mood assessment using smartphones. INTERACT 2023

Schuller DM, Schuller BW (2021) A review on the recent and near-future developments in computational processing of emotion in the human voice. Emot Rev 13(1):44–50

Shin J, Bae SM (2023) A systematic review of location data for depression prediction. Int J Environ Res Public Health

Smets E et al (2018) Large-scale wearable data reveal digital phenotypes for daily-life stress detection. npj Digital Medicine

Taylor S et al (2020) Personalized multitask learning for predicting tomorrow's mood, stress, and health. IEEE Transact Affect Comput 11(2)

Vanttola P, Vildjiounaite E, Sallinen M, Kallio J, Paajanen TI, Lukander K, Kyllönen V, Puttonen S (2024) Different methods to detect stress in knowledge workers: a pilot study for long-term monitoring. J UOEH 46(1):103–112

Vildjiounaite E, Huotari V, Kallio J, Kyllönen V, Mäkelä S-M, Gimel'farb G (2019) Unobtrusive assessment of stress of office workers via analysis of their motion trajectories. Pervasive Mob Comput 58

Vildjiounaite E, Kallio J, Kantorovitch J, Kyllönen V, Räsänen P, Ronkainen J (2020) Towards social enterprise with internet of office desks. HCC 2020

Vildjiounaite E, Kallio J, Kantorovitch J, Kinnula A, Ferreira S, Rodrigues MA, Rocha N (2023) Challenges of learning human digital twin: case study of mental wellbeing. PETRA 2023:574–583

Vos G, Trinh K, Sarnyai Z, Azghadi MR (2022) Ensemble machine learning model trained on a new synthesized dataset generalizes well for stress prediction using wearable devices

Yang K et al (2023) Survey on emotion sensing using mobile devices. IEEE Transact Affect Comput 14

Yang L, Qin S-F (2021) A review of emotion recognition methods from keystroke, mouse, and touchscreen dynamics. IEEE Access 9:162197–162213

Zhao G, Li X, Li Y, Pietikäinen M (2023) Facial micro-expressions: an overview. Proc IEEE 111(10):1215–1235

Explainable AI in Image Classification Tasks: How to Choose the Best?

Alexey Zhukov, Jenny Benois-Pineau, Romain Giot, and Romain Bourqui

Abstract The most popular methods in AI-machine learning paradigm are mainly black boxes. For user acceptance of these methods in various tasks, explanations are necessary for why an AI tool takes such a decision, as it is a matter of user trust in AI. Although dedicated explanation tools are being massively developed, the users and decision makers do not know which are the most appropriate for them. In this chapter, we will propose a taxonomy of the AI-explanation methods. This contribution is aimed at helping users in their choice of explanation methods for AI (XAI).

1 Introduction

Nowadays, artificial intelligence (AI) is increasingly being used to perform various human functions. Indeed, application domains such as medical image analysis[1] or industry of 5G,[2] human behaviour[3] are critical. For AI to be adopted in such areas, user trust in its decisions is crucial, requiring explanations of why AI makes certain decisions. This is especially relevant in the context of new EU directives regarding privacy[4] but also the intensive European activity on the standardization of explanations of AI.[5]

These authors contributed equally to this work.

[1] Litjens et al. (2017).

[2] Cayamcela and Lim (2018).

[3] Belmonte et al. (2023).

[4] European Commission (2019).

[5] European Parliament and Council of the European Union (2024).

A. Zhukov (✉) · J. Benois-Pineau · R. Giot · R. Bourqui
University of Bordeaux, CNRS, LaBRI, UMR 5800, Talence, France
e-mail: alexey.zhukov@u-bordeaux.fr; jenny.benois-pineau@u-bordeaux.fr; romain.giot@u-bordeaux.fr; romain.bourqui@u-bordeaux.fr

R. Ballardini et al. (eds.), *Emotional Data Applications and Regulation of Artificial Intelligence in Society*, Law, Governance and Technology Series 69,
https://doi.org/10.1007/978-3-031-80111-2_4

Due to the shift of the paradigm in AI, the most used tools nowadays represent Neural Networks (NN), and more precisely, Deep Neural Networks (DNNs). These constitute part of purely machine-learning—based decision makers[6] or of hybrid systems with symbolic AI[7] or with a human in the loop.[8] In recent years, numerous methods for explaining neural networks have been proposed.[9] These methods, have received the name of Explainable Artificial Intelligence (XAI). Some of these represent *local* approaches, which explain individual predictions, while others are *global*, which explain a model on a dataset as a whole. When a user of an AI framework would like to understand why it has taken such a decision on the input data, he/she will have to choose an explanation method for this AI tool. There is no consensus on how to choose an explanation method, how to evaluate its quality. Each user still has to choose the explainer accordingly to their intuition and some partial information they have about its functioning.

In this chapter, our goal is to give a potential user an overview of explanation methods, focusing on a specific family of these methods. The latter makes it possible to explain the decision for one given data sample. The best kind of data on which one could illustrate XAI methods are images: "one picture is worth a thousand words". In the follow-up, this is why we focus on the overview of XAI methods in image classification tasks. Our study provides a comprehensive taxonomy of XAI methods, offering clear guidance for users in selecting appropriate explanation techniques based on their specific needs.

However, future research should address limitations that still remain in the dynamic nature of XAI research and the need for extensive empirical validation of different methods in real-world applications.

2 Interpretation and Explanation

Although deep Neural Networks (DNNs) are popular for decision-making, they are often seen as black boxes due to their lack of transparency.[10] To clarify DNN models, two terms are used: *interpretability* and *explainability*.[11]

Interpretability enables developers to delve into the model's decision-making process, boosting their confidence in understanding the model's results. Interpretation techniques provide interfaces that explain the AI system's underlying

[6]LeCun et al. (2015).

[7]Besold et al. (2017).

[8]Amershi et al. (2019).

[9]J.Benois-Pineau et al. (2023); Ayyar et al. (2023).

[10]Hassija et al. (2024).

[11]Ali et al. (2023).

functioning, aiding developers in understanding the DNN model. For instance, the visualization of features[12] helps one comprehend the learning process of a DNN.

In contrast, *explainability* provides insight into the DNN's decisions for the common end-user, building trust in the AI's correctness and lack of bias. In healthcare, AI-based visual analysis, such as medical image analysis and emotional status monitoring,[13] relies on explanation methods such as "feature attribution". These methods highlight those image areas contributing most to decisions, making the information clear through the human visual system.

Explainers provide insights into DNN decisions. La Rosa et al.[14] categorize explainers into *Feature attribution*, *Learned features*, *Explanations by examples*, *Counterfactuals*, and *Model Behaviour*. This chapter aims to help users choose suitable AI explanation methods, focusing on the most understandable: Feature Attribution.

3 Feature Attribution Methods

Feature attribution methods assign scores to input features based on their impact on model predictions.[15] They reveal where the model focuses to make predictions and provide insights into why a specific output is produced. These methods can be applied *globally* to the entire dataset or *locally* to individual samples. Feature attribution can be implemented through post hoc techniques or self-explainable networks, leading to a variety of techniques.

Examples of feature attribution methods include gradient-based methods (Gradient-weighted Class Activation Mapping [Grad-CAM],[16] Integrated Gradients[17]), propagation methods (Layer-wise Relevance Propagation [LRP][18]), perturbation-based methods (Local Interpretable Model-agnostic Explanations [LIME],[19] SHapley Additive exPlanations [SHAP][20]), and intrinsic methods using model properties and attention weights. Two examples of feature-attribution explainers are shown in Fig. 1, with the original image from the Salicon[21] dataset.

For users seeking explanations as to why an image has been classified into a specific class, the AI framework is effective if it bases its decision on meaningful

[12] Halnaut et al. (2020).
[13] Belmonte et al. (2023).
[14] La Rosa et al. (2023).
[15] Sundararajan et al. (2017).
[16] Chattopadhyay et al. (2017).
[17] Sundararajan et al. (2017).
[18] Binder et al. (2016).
[19] Ribeiro et al. (2016b).
[20] Lundberg and Lee (2017).
[21] Jiang et al. (2015).

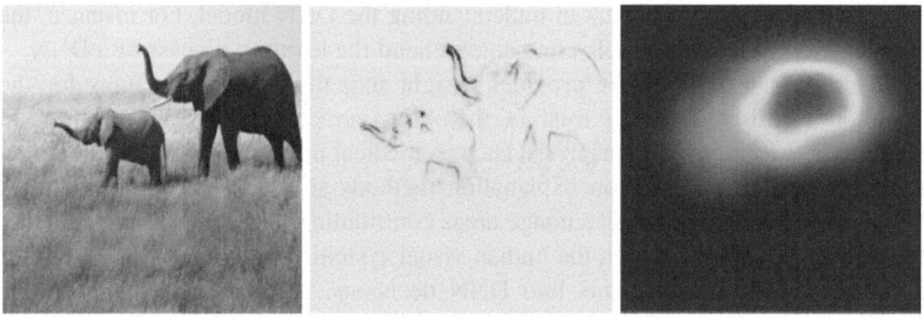

(a) Elephant (b) VGG16 - LRP (Elephant) (c) ResNet - FEM (Elephant)

Fig. 1 Original image (**a**). LRP (**b**) can be used with a colour-coded heatmap for feature attribution on images. In this method, thin black lines and thick black lines indicate input pixels that have positively or negatively contributed to the prediction, respectively. By hypothesis of Feature Explanation Method (FEM) [Ahmed Asif Fuad et al. (2020)] (**c**), in the last layer of convolution, the strongest features are the representations of the most relevant regions in the input image. These are displayed in the explanation map from important (red) to unimportant (dark blue), (or from a central grey colour to the peripheral lighter grey in the print version). (**a**) Elephant; (**b**) VGG16—LRP (Elephant); (**c**) ResNet—FEM (Elephant)

regions in the image that, in the user's opinion, support that class. For example, in recognizing architectural styles in historical buildings,[22] humans focus on central architectural details. If the explainer of the DNN classifier highlights the same relevant regions when the image is correctly classified, it is considered an adequate explainer for the AI tool. Feature attribution methods fulfil this task by highlighting the regions the DNN classifier used for its decision.

To grade features based on their contribution to a classifier's decision, explainers use methods such as importance maps superimposed on images[23] or selected regions.[24] Notable methods include Grad-CAM,[25] LIME,[26] Integrated Gradients,[27] LRP[28] and SHAP.[29] These methods assist both deep learning specialists and general users in selecting tools for explaining AI decisions.[30]

To assist decision-makers in AI explanation tasks, we propose a hierarchical two-level taxonomy of feature attribution methods. This taxonomy, shown in Fig. 2,

[22] Obeso et al. (2022).

[23] Selvaraju et al. (2016).

[24] Ribeiro et al. (2016b).

[25] Chattopadhyay et al. (2017).

[26] Ribeiro et al. (2016b).

[27] Sundararajan et al. (2017).

[28] Ivanovs et al. (2021).

[29] Lundberg and Lee (2017).

[30] Ayyar et al. (2021)

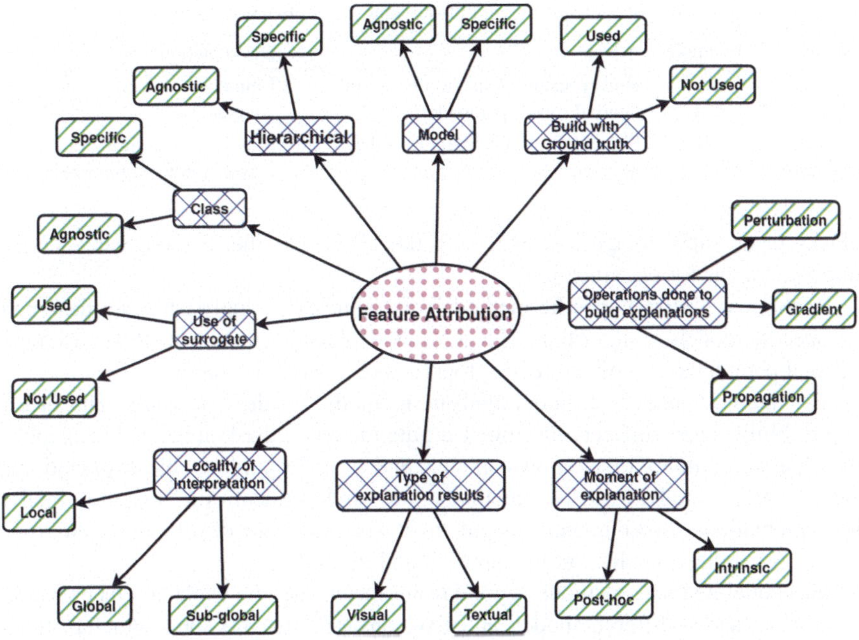

Fig. 2 A two-level taxonomy of feature attribution explanation methods

includes ten families of methods at the first level, categorized by their design attributes, while the second level involves specific attributes of each family.

As depicted in Fig. 2 according to the colour (and the markings inside the boxes), methods can be divided into the following hierarchy:—*families,—detailed attributes*.

Thus, we introduce the families: *Model, Class, Hierarchical, Build with ground truth, Operations done to build explanations, Moment of explanation, Representation of results, Locality of interpretation, Use of surrogate models*, which we describe in detail.

3.1 Model

3.1.1 Model: Specific, Agnostic

"Model agnostic methods" or "black-box" approaches explain model decisions without depending on the model architecture or learning algorithm. They analyse how input features interact with output predictions. For example, masking square

Table 1 Comparison of model-specific and model-agnostic explanation methods

Method	Example	Advantages	Disadvantages
Model-Specific	Grad-CAM	Higher accuracy due to the use of internal model parameters.	Limited to specific model architectures.
Model-Agnostic	LIME	Flexibility, applicability to different models.	May be less accurate due to abstraction from the model.

blocks in an input image and analysing the DNN classifier's score can identify important areas for classification.[31]

In contrast, "Model specific methods" or "white-box" approaches are designed for specific models or algorithms. To generate explanations, these methods leverage internal parameters, architecture, or properties of a particular model.

The main advantage of model-agnostic methods[32] is their flexibility and broad applicability across different machine learning models. Based on general principles, they handle complex or unknown models and provide interpretable explanations. Additionally, model-agnostic methods are independent of specific model implementations, making them useful in diverse software development environments. A synthesis of this family can be found in Table 1.

For model-agnostic methods, a good result means that the explanations provided make sense across different models and give consistent insights about which features are important. If the results seem inconsistent or irrelevant, this may indicate a poor application of the method or that the model's behaviour is too complex to be captured. For model-specific methods, a good result will provide detailed and accurate insights specific to the model's internal workings, showing how particular features influence the model's decisions. If the explanations are unclear or do not match expectations, it may suggest that the method is not well-suited to the model or there is an issue with how the model is being interpreted.

3.2 *Class*

3.2.1 Class: Specific, Agnostic

In this family, we separate methods as explaining a score of a specific class or explaining the decision for all classes. *Class agnostic* methods do not assume knowledge about specific classes of data. This approach makes it possible to show which features in the input have contributed the most in the decision of the NN classifier w.r.t. in the whole set of classes. Examples of such methods are FEM[33] and

[31] O.Gorokhovatskyi et al. (2023).

[32] Ribeiro et al. (2016a).

[33] Ahmed Asif Fuad et al. (2020).

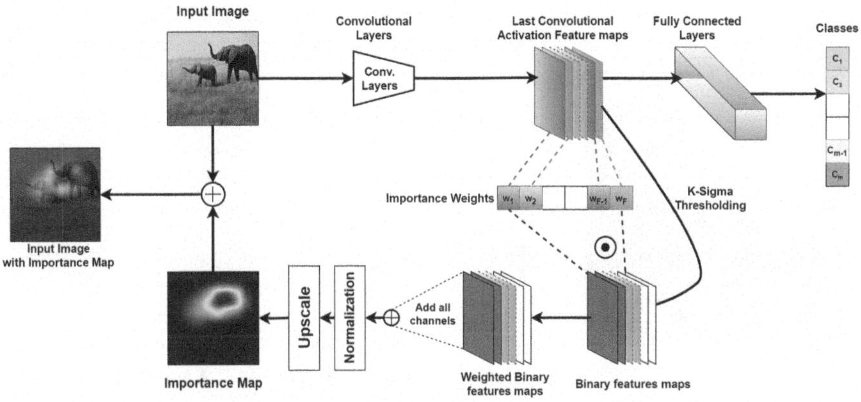

Fig. 3 Block-diagram of FEM accordingly to Zhukov et al. (2023)

Multi-Layered FEM,[34] which perform statistical analysis of features at the layers of a DNN, more precisely of a Convolutional Neural Network (CNN) classifier, before propagating them on the input. For the overall decision of the network, they show the grading of importance of all input data elements. A block-diagram of FEM is displayed in Fig. 3. Initially, the features are extracted from the final convolutional layer after the activation process (upper segment). Subsequently, binary feature maps are created, and importance weights are computed. The importance map is then generated by normalizing a linear combination with channel weights before finally presenting this map as a heat-map overlay on the original image for visualization purposes.[35]

Class specific methods can discover and explain dependencies that are unique to a particular class of data. An example of such methods is the LRP,[36] which focuses on a specific neuron, responsible for the decision for a given class and back propagates the relevance (score) throughout the network classifier, via receptive fields of neurons in the layers before going to the pixels of the input image. A flowchart of an example of the LRP method for CNNs can be found in Fig. 4. The original image is taken from Salicon[37] dataset.

The advantage of class agnostic methods is their versatility and applicability across different types of data. They are able to discover common patterns that can be useful not only for explaining patterns, but also for understanding the data and drawing more generalized conclusions. However, class specific methods can be useful when it is necessary to find and explain dependencies that are specific only to particular classes of data. The synthesis of this family can be found in Table 2.

[34] Bourroux et al. (2022).

[35] Ahmed Asif Fuad et al. (2020).

[36] Binder et al. (2016); Zang et al. (2021).

[37] Jiang et al. (2015).

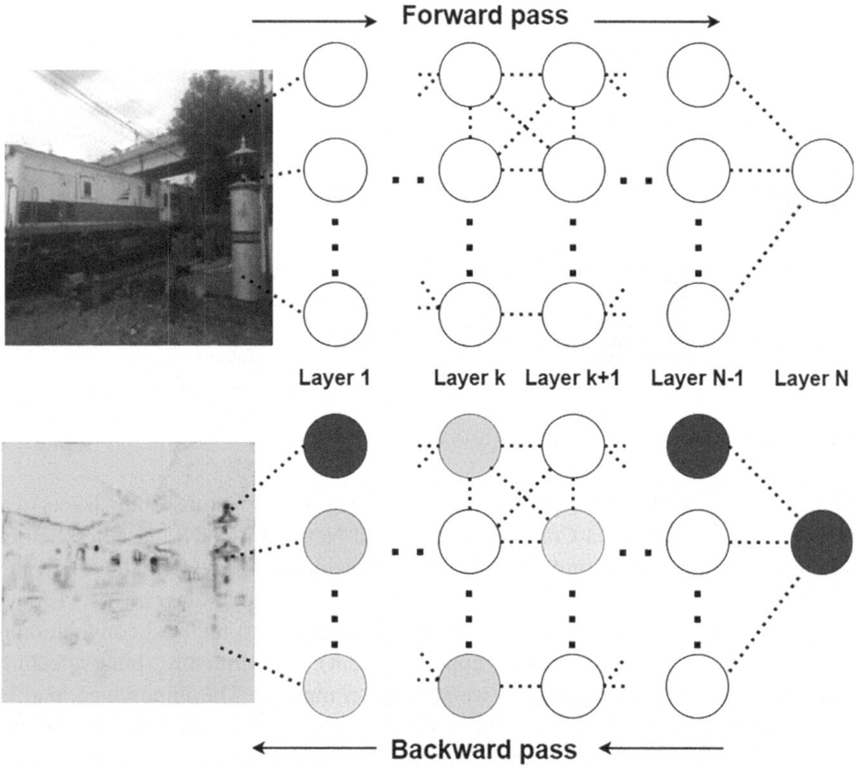

Fig. 4 Flowchart of LRP method for CNN accordingly to Cruciani et al. (2023)

Table 2 Comparison of Class-Specific and Class-Agnostic Explanation Methods

Type	Example	Advantages	Disadvantages
Class-Specific	LRP	Identifies class-specific patterns.	May not generalize well to other classes.
Class-Agnostic	FEM	Discovers common patterns across all classes.	May overlook specific class details.

3.3 Hierarchical

3.3.1 Hierarchical: Specific, Agnostic

The *hierarchical*—this element of the taxonomy indicates that the explanation model can use hierarchical representation of input data, namely images. Hierarchical segmentation is an image segmentation method that uses a hierarchical structure to partition images into regions of monotone granularity. We can cite here, for instance,

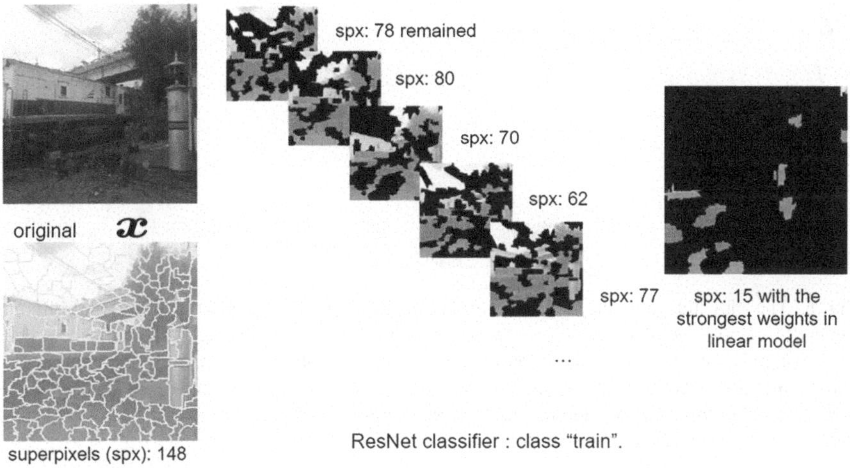

Fig. 5 Explaining a prediction with LIME

a fundamental work on binary partition trees.[38] These methods allow the creation of a more detailed segmentations while retaining contextual information about the image structure. The most regular kind of such a segmentation is the partition with quad trees, which has been recently proposed for input masking.[39]

Image segmentation can be used in various XAI methods to explain the behaviour of models and identify important regions in images. Some of the methods that can use hierarchical segmentation include:

- Feature importance analysis: Using segmentation to calculate the importance of image regions and determine which features contribute most to model predictions, as is the case of Local Interpretable Model-agnostic Explanations (LIME).[40] A visualization of the explanation process with LIME is shown in Fig. 5.
- Explanation visualization: Using segmentation to create visual explanations that show which areas of the image affect specific model predictions, as in Shapley Additive explanations (SHAP).[41] The Fig. 6[42][43] demonstrates the working principle of SHAP.

[38] Salembier and Garrido (2000).

[39] O.Gorokhovatskyi et al. (2023).

[40] Ribeiro et al. (2016b).

[41] Lundberg and Lee (2017).

[42] https://github.com/shap/shap#deep-learning-example-with-deepexplainer-tensorflowkeras-models.

[43] License - https://github.com/shap/shap?tab=MIT-1-ov-file.

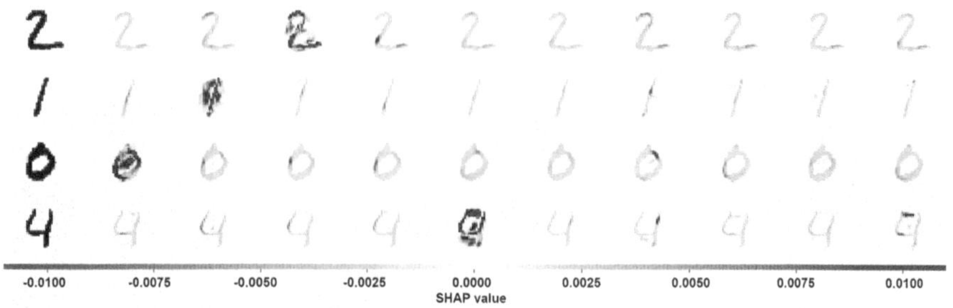

Fig. 6 The plot illustrates the impact of different pixels on the model's output for ten different digits (0-9) across four distinct images. In the given black and white image, Dark noise (the higher the value, the more intense the black colour) corresponds to an increase in the model's output score, while Grey noise (the lower the value, the more intense the grey colour) leads to a decrease in the output score. In this example, the largest number of black pixels are on the third two, the second one, the first zero, and the fifth four

Table 3 Comparison of Hierarchical and Non-Hierarchical Explanation Methods

Explanation Type	Example	Advantages	Disadvantages
Feature Importance Analysis	LIME	Uses segmentation to determine the importance of image regions.	Requires computational resources for segmentation.
Explanation Visualization	SHAP	Creates visual explanations showing important image areas.	May require many model evaluations.
Not Using Segmentation	LRP, Grad-CAM	Directly uses pixel information for explanations.	May miss higher-level contextual information.

However, not all XAI methods can use image segmentation, e.g. methods that rely on pixel information such as LRP,[44] GradCam[45] and its variations.[46]

To use hierarchical methods in explainable AI, which involve hierarchical representation and segmentation of input data such as images, a user needs to understand image segmentation and its application in model explanations. Although this approach makes more detailed and contextual segmentation of images possible, aiding in feature importance analysis and explanation visualization, it does not require deep expertise in the underlying model mechanics. The synthesis of this family can be found in Table 3.

[44] Binder et al. (2016).

[45] Selvaraju et al. (2016).

[46] Sundararajan et al. (2017).

Table 4 Comparison of Methods Using and Not Using Ground Truth

Ground Truth	Example	Advantages	Disadvantages
Used	ML-FEM	Provides more accurate explanations.	Requires access to ground truth data.
Not Used	LIME	Can work without ground truth data.	May be less accurate.

3.4 *Build with Ground Truth*

3.4.1 Build with Ground Truth: Used, Not Used

To build an efficient explainer some methods, such as ML-FEM[47] need a ground truth (of explanation). Thus, we introduce a classification of explainers accordingly to this feature.

Ground truth methods require access to the true labels or values of the target variable in the training data. These methods use information about the correct answers to create explanations or assess the importance of features. Moreover, they use ground truth to compare model predictions or partial explanations as in[48] with true values and identify the influence of certain features on predictions. The basic idea is that access to the correct answers can help explain the reasons why the model makes certain decisions.

In contrast, the *Methods without Ground truth* do not require access to ground truth, as their name indicates. For example, methods such as LIME[49] or SHAP[50] can create local models and analyse their behaviour without full information about ground truth.

The choice between methods requiring ground truth and agnostic methods depends on the task, the availability of ground truth and the required level of interpretability. If access to the ground truth is limited or impossible, agnostic methods can be used to explain the model. However, methods that require ground truth can provide more accurate explanations, especially if one needs to understand which features or aspects of the data have the greatest impact on the predictions of the model. The synthesis of this family can be found in Table 4.

[47] Bourroux et al. (2022).

[48] Bourroux et al. (2022).

[49] Ribeiro et al. (2016b).

[50] Lundberg and Lee (2017).

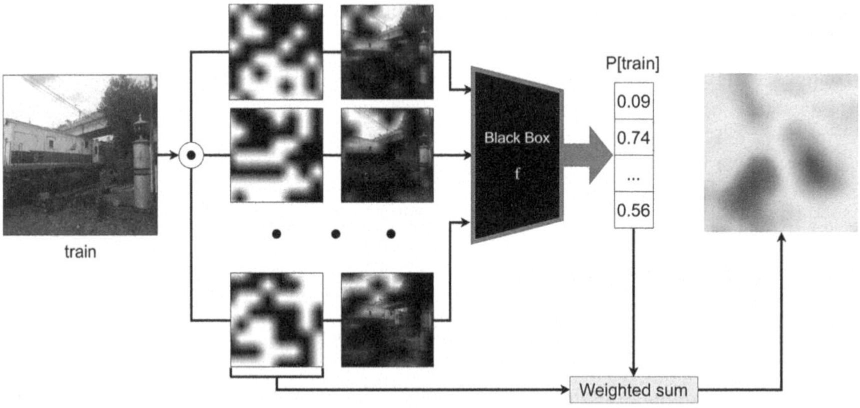

Fig. 7 RISE Overview, accordingly to Petsiuk et al. (2018)

3.5 Operations Done to Build Explanations

3.5.1 Operations Done to Build Explanations: [Gradient Computation, Perturbation, Propagation of Relevance or Gradients]

Despite the fact that this classification covers a number of heterogeneous approaches—both white-box and black-box, it seems interesting to us to identify this family. Furthermore, the inputs to these methods are also different. Operations[51] are performed both on the input of the network and its partial outputs, there of which are:

1. *Gradient computation*: Gradients are vector derivatives of the loss function with respect to input features, showing the direction of the greatest change in the loss function. They estimate each feature's contribution to model predictions, with higher values indicating a stronger influence. These methods use features from the last layers of the network.[52]
2. *Perturbation-based methods*: These methods analyse how model predictions change when one or more input features (pixels) are altered. By adding perturbations to original images, they assess model sensitivity without needing access to model parameters. These black-box methods require only forward propagation passes and include techniques such as LIME,[53] SHAP,[54] and RISE.[55] Figure 7 illustrates the RISE method, where the input image is multiplied by random

[51] Abhishek and Kamath (2022).

[52] Selvaraju et al. (2016).

[53] Ribeiro et al. (2016b).

[54] Lundberg and Lee (2017).

[55] Petsiuk et al. (2018).

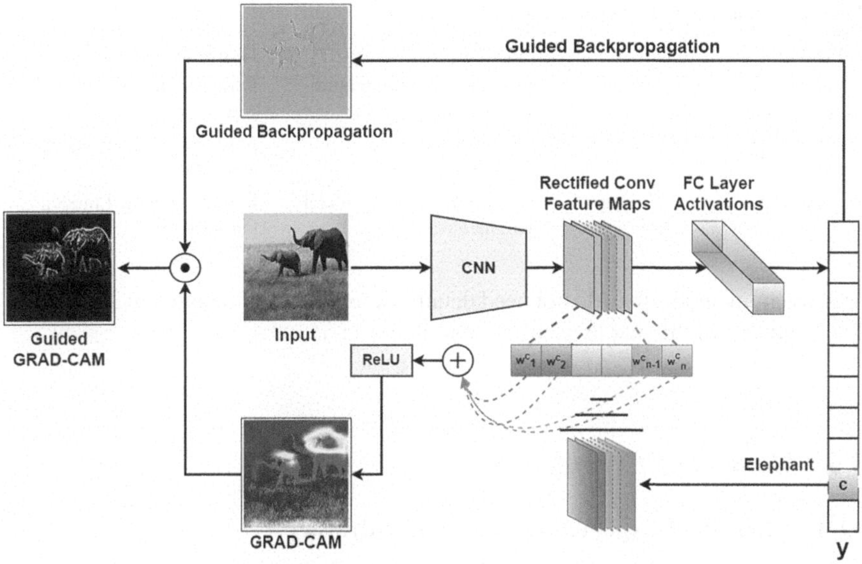

Fig. 8 Grad-CAM Overview: Given an image and a class of interest as input, we need to pass the image through a part of the CNN model, and then through calculations depending on the task we choose to obtain an initial estimate for the category. Accordingly to Zhukov et al. (2023)

masks. The resulting saliency map is a linear combination of the masks, weighted by the target class score of each masked image.

3. *Propagation of relevance or gradients*: This involves back-propagating information from the output to the input, as in LRP,[56] or from the last convolutional layer, as in CAM.[57] Some methods use forward propagation to integrate features from different layers.[58] These "white box" methods often limit understanding to the last convolutional layer, computing gradients as in GradCam[59] (Fig. 8). Other methods, such as LRP or Multi-Layered FEM, use internal propagation algorithms or model details, incorporating gradients, neuron activations, or other characteristics to create explanations.

To use gradient computation methods, users need a basic understanding of calculus and neural network architecture. However, for perturbation-based methods, which involve changing input features to see how predictions change, users only need a basic grasp of machine learning and forward propagation. Although users should understand back-propagation and neural network layers to use relevance propagation

[56] Binder et al. (2016).
[57] Selvaraju et al. (2016).
[58] Bourroux et al. (2022).
[59] Selvaraju et al. (2016).

Table 5 Comparison of Operations Done to Build Explanations

Operation	Example	Advantages	Disadvantages
Gradient Computation	Integrated Gradients	Provides accurate feature importance.	Requires access to model gradients.
Perturbation	LIME, SHAP	Does not require model gradients.	May require many model evaluations.
Propagation	LRP, Grad-CAM	Can utilize internal model parameters.	Requires detailed model knowledge.

or gradient methods, they do not need detailed knowledge of the internal algorithms. The synthesis of this family can be found in Table 5.

3.6 *Moment of Explanation*

3.6.1 Moment of Explanation: [Post-hoc, Intrinsic]

This classification refers to the timing of the explanation. For instance, in a decision tree classifier, the explanation through the choice of a meaningful data partition attribute is already achieved during the training process. In contrast, methods such as CAM, GradCam, FEM, and SHAP provide post-hoc explanations, which occur after the model is trained. More formally, they can be divided into two subgroups:

Intrinsic refers to methods that create machine learning models with built-in explanation mechanisms. These methods, also known as "explanations-by-design", make the model self-explanatory during the learning process. Such models can be more interpretable and understandable.[60] Examples include linear regression, logistic regression, decision trees,[61] RuleFit,[62] naive Bayes, and k-nearest neighbours.

Post-hoc refers to methods that create explanations for models after they have been trained and used. The explanation is generated independently of the model itself and can be applied to any model without altering it. Post-hoc explanations can be created using various methods, whether they are white-box or black-box. The choice between *Post-hoc* and *Intrinsic* approaches depends on the requirements and context of the explanation task.

While *Post-hoc* methods are preferable for obtaining explanations for already trained models without altering their structure, *intrinsic* methods are preferable if it is important to have built-in explanation mechanisms and interpretability during model training. Post-hoc explanation methods can provide insights into a black-box model in two ways: globally, offering an overview of the model's behaviour on the entire

[60] Chen et al. (2019).

[61] Hastie et al. (2001).

[62] Friedman and Popescu (2008).

Table 6 Comparison of Intrinsic and Post-hoc Explanation Methods

Moment	Example	Advantages	Disadvantages
Intrinsic	Decision Trees, Linear Regression	Higher interpretability from the beginning.	Often less flexible and may not perform as well in complex tasks.
Post-hoc	SHAP, LIME, Grad-CAM	Can be applied to any pre-trained model.	May not fully capture the model's internal mechanics.

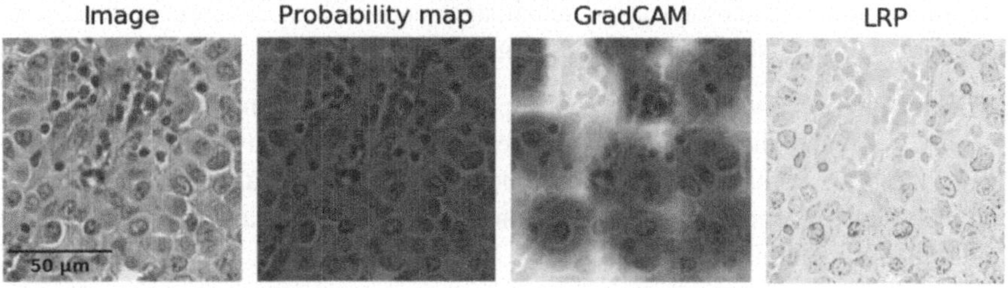

Fig. 9 Different [Hägele et al. (2020)] granularity levels of visual explanations—from patch level (middle left) to pixel-wise heatmaps (right)

dataset, or locally, focusing on explaining a specific example. A synthesis of this family can be found in Table 6.

3.7 *Representation of Results*

3.7.1 Representation of Results: [Visual, Textual]

Visual and *Textual* are two types of explanations that can be used to represent interpretations of a machine learning model.

1. *Visual Explanations* are explanations presented using visual elements such as images and heatmaps, which show how different features influence the model's predictions. For example, a heat map can highlight which parts of an image affect the model's decision the most. Visual explanations are usually easier to understand than abstract numerical data. They can also help identify patterns and relationships between features and predictions. Different levels of visual explanations are shown in Fig. 9 below.
2. *Textual Explanations* are explanations given as text descriptions or rules. They use natural language to explain the importance of features, the model's logic, or the reasons for a decision. Depending on what is needed, text explanations can be brief or detailed. They can appear as comments or reports that explain which factors the model considered important for its prediction. This type of explanation

Table 7 Comparison of Visual and Textual Explanation Methods

Representation	Example	Advantages	Disadvantages
Visual	Grad-CAM	Intuitive and easy to understand.	May require expertise to interpret correctly.
Textual	Rule-based explanations, textual summaries in SHAP	Accessible to a wider audience.	May not capture all the nuances of visual data.

is often used in fields such as medical image analysis,[63] where users prefer textual reports and may not be experts in Image Processing.

The choice between visual and textual explanations depends on the requirements of the XAI task and the preferences of the people who will use and interpret the explanations. A combination of both types can also be useful to provide a more complete and understandable explanation of the machine learning model.[64] The synthesis of this family can be found in Table 7.

3.8 *Locality of Interpretation*

3.8.1 Locality of Interpretation: [Local, Global, Sub-global]

Local, *Global* and *Sub-global* are three levels of explanations that can be used to understand how machine learning models work.

1. *Local Explanations* explain individual model predictions for specific data instances. They show which features or feature areas influence specific predictions and why. Local explanations are often displayed as heatmaps, graphs, or lists of features that indicate their contribution to a particular classification. Moreover, they provide detailed information about the model's behaviour at an individual level. Methods such as LIME, SHAP, FEM, GradCam are typically local explainers.
2. *Global Explanations* are designed to understand the overall behaviour of the model across the entire dataset or within a broad context.[65] These explanations provide generalized information about the model, showing the overall contribution and importance of features in the decision-making process. A global explanation can be created by aggregating local explanations of features across the dataset. In the text domain, Ribero et al.[66] propose aggregation of the importance of each word in the text through the dataset, for instance.

[63] van der Velden et al. (2022).

[64] Koitka et al. (2020).

[65] Mishra (2022).

[66] Ribeiro et al. (2016b).

Table 8 Comparison of Local, Global, and Sub-global Explanation Methods

Locality	Example	Advantages	Disadvantages
Local	LIME, SHAP	Detailed, instance-specific insights.	Not easily generalizable.
Global	Aggregated local explanations	Holistic view of the model.	Less detailed on individual instances.
Sub-global	Grouping explanations by feature importance	Balances detail and generalizability.	Complexity in identifying meaningful subsets.

3. *Sub-global Explanations*. In van der Linden et al.,[67] the authors describe another method to generalize local explanations as proposed by Ribera et al.[68]: showing a group of data samples where the attribute has a high global importance score. As a result of this, sub-global explanations can be discussed. These explanations focus on a narrower context, highlighting features and their relationships within small groups or subsets of data. Sub-global explanations help understand which features and combinations of features are important for the model in specific situations or for certain data subgroups. They can be presented as groupings of features that show their importance for various subcategories or subgroups of data.

Each of these levels of explanation provides a different level of detail and makes it possible to understand the model at different levels of abstraction. The synthesis of this family can be found in Table 8.

3.9 Use of Surrogate Models

3.9.1 Use of Surrogate Models: [Used, Not Used]

Surrogate-based models involve training a surrogate model that approximates the original complex machine learning model. This surrogate model should be simple and interpretable enough for easy analysis (e.g. a linear model[69]). Then, the attributions of feature importance are computed directly for this surrogate model. The advantage of this approach is that the surrogate model is often more straightforward and understandable, making the explanations derived from it easier for humans to interpret. One example of a method that uses a surrogate model to create an explanation is LIME.[70]

[67] van der Linden et al. (2019).

[68] Ribeiro et al. (2016b).

[69] J.Benois-Pineau et al. (2023).

[70] Ribeiro et al. (2016b).

Table 9 Comparison of Surrogate-Based and Non-Surrogate-Based Explanation Methods

Surrogate Model	Example	Advantages	Disadvantages
Used	LIME	Simpler, easier to understand.	May not fully capture the complexities of the original model.
Not Used	Integrated Gradients, SHAP	Maintain accuracy and complexity of the original model.	More complex to interpret.

In contrast, *non-surrogate-based models*, directly analyse the original machine learning model to compute feature attributions and explain its predictions. Since training an additional model is not required, they can be more computationally efficient and accurate. The advantage of *non-surrogate-based* approaches is that they preserve the accuracy and complexity of the original model, though they may be more challenging for humans to comprehend due to this complexity. Integrated Gradients[71] and SHAP[72] are examples of these methods.

To use surrogate-based models, which approximate complex machine learning models with simpler, interpretable ones for easier analysis, a user should understand basic model training and interpretation concepts. However, one does not need expertise in the original model's complexity. In contrast, non-surrogate-based models, which directly analyse the original model for feature attributions, require a deeper understanding of the model's internal workings. The choice between using a surrogate model or not depends on the trade-off between interpretability and accuracy, as well as the requirements for computational efficiency and the availability of training data for the surrogate model. A synthesis of this family can be found in Table 9.

4 Conclusion

In this chapter, we presented an extensive overview of Explainable AI (XAI) methods, which are crucial for ensuring user trust in AI decisions. The need for explainability arises from the increasing deployment of AI systems in areas where their decisions directly impact human lives, well-being, industrial development, and security.

Given the importance of image classification in many data analytic frameworks, and to enhance reader comprehension, we focused on XAI approaches in image classification tasks. Among the various approaches, we concentrated on those most relevant to non-IT users, such as medical doctors or industrial engineers. These methods, called *feature attribution methods*, identify the pixels in input images that

[71] Sundararajan et al. (2017).

[72] Lundberg and Lee (2017).

contribute to the AI framework's decisions. We provided a taxonomy of these methods and analysed their strengths and weaknesses.

Our study has introduced a comprehensive taxonomy of feature attribution methods, a fundamental aspect of XAI. This taxonomy categorizes the methods based on several criteria, including model specificity, class focus, hierarchical segmentation, use of ground truth, operations involved in explanation generation, moment of explanation, representation of results, locality of interpretation, and the use of surrogate models. By structuring these methods into distinct families, we aimed to provide clarity and guidance for users and developers in selecting the most appropriate XAI techniques for their specific needs. To our knowledge, this is the first attempt to build a taxonomy on multiple features of the methods, which might be understandable to application domain experts.

Our study has revealed that:

- Model-agnostic methods are flexible and applicable to various models, while model-specific methods offer higher accuracy.
- Class-specific methods identify unique patterns for particular classes, whereas class-agnostic methods find common patterns across all classes.
- Hierarchical segmentation of images used for masking of regions enhances the interpretability of complex models by providing detailed and context-aware explanations.
- Methods requiring ground truth data generally offer more accurate explanations but are limited by data availability.
- Intrinsic methods provide AI models, interpretable by their design, while post-hoc methods offer flexibility after model training.
- Visual explanations are more intuitive, and textual explanations are more accessible to non-experts.
- Local explanations give detailed insights for specific instances, and global explanations offer a comprehensive view of model behaviour on the whole dataset and not only on a single image.

Taking to the account a large variety of XAI methods which have been already developed, future research has to focus on their evaluation. We have to give objective, numerical criteria in terms of quality metrics, to the user in order to facilitate his choice of a XAI method in his task.

More user-centric studies are needed to understand how different stakeholders perceive and use these explanations. Practical challenges like computational efficiency, scalability, and user interface design should be addressed for integrating XAI methods into real-world systems. Additionally, we do not consider our proposed taxonomy as a fixed one. The research in XAI is highly dynamic. Therefore, it is necessary to keep an eye on new technologies to expand it.

References

Abhishek K, Kamath D (2022) Attribution-based xai methods in computer vision: a review. arXiv preprint arXiv:221114736 https://doi.org/10.48550/arXiv.2211.14736

Ahmed Asif Fuad K, Martin PE, Giot R et al (2020) Features understanding in 3D CNNs for actions recognition in video. In: Tenth International Conference on Image Processing Theory, Tools and Applications, IPTA 2020, Paris, France, https://hal.archives-ouvertes.fr/hal-02963298

Ali S, Abuhmed T, El-Sappagh S et al (2023) Explainable artificial intelligence (xai): what we know and what is left to attain trustworthy artificial intelligence. Inform Fusion 99:101805. https://doi.org/10.1016/j.inffus.2023.101805

Amershi S, Weld D, Vorvoreanu M, et al (2019) Guidelines for human-ai interaction. In: Proceedings of the 2019 CHI Conference on Human Factors in Computing Systems. Association for Computing Machinery, New York, NY, USA, CHI '19, pp 1–13, https://doi.org/10.1145/3290605.3300233

Ayyar MP, Benois-Pineau J, Zemmari A (2021) Review of white box methods for explanations of convolutional neural networks in image classification tasks. J Electr Imaging 30(5). https://doi.org/10.1117/1.JEI.30.5.050901

Ayyar MP, Benois-Pineau J, Zemmari A (2023) Chapter 5 - a feature understanding method for explanation of image classification by convolutional neural networks. In: Benois-Pineau J, Bourqui R, Petkovic D et al (eds) Explainable deep learning AI. Academic Press, pp 79–96. https://doi.org/10.1016/B978-0-32-396098-4.00011-9

Belmonte R, Allaert B, Tirilly P et al (2023) Impact of facial landmark localization on facial expression recognition. IEEE Trans Affect Comput 14(2):1267–1279. https://doi.org/10.1109/TAFFC.2021.3124142

Benois-Pineau J, Bourqui R, Petkovic D et al (eds) (2023) Explainable deep learning AI. Elsevier Academy Press. https://doi.org/10.1016/B978-0-32-396098-4.00004-1

Besold TR, d'Avila Garcez AS, Bader S et al (2017) Neural-symbolic learning and reasoning: a survey and interpretation. In: Frontiers in artificial intelligence and applications, vol 309. IOS Press, pp 1–18. https://doi.org/10.3233/FAIA210348

Binder A, Montavon G, Bach S, et al (2016) Layer-wise relevance propagation for neural networks with local renormalization layers. CoRR abs/1604.00825. http://arxiv.org/abs/1604.00825

Bourroux L, Benois-Pineau J, Bourqui R, et al (2022) Multi layered feature explanation method for convolutional neural networks. In: International conference on pattern recognition and artificial intelligence (ICPRAI), Paris, France, https://doi.org/10.1007/978-3-031-09037-049

Cayamcela MEM, Lim W (2018) Artificial intelligence in 5g technology: a survey. In: 2018 International Conference on Information and Communication Technology Convergence (ICTC), IEEE, pp 860–865

Chattopadhyay A, Sarkar A, Howlader P, et al (2017) Grad-cam++: Generalized gradient-based visual explanations for deep convolutional networks. CoRR abs/1710.11063. http://arxiv.org/abs/1710.11063,1710.11063

Chen C, Li O, Tao D, et al (2019) This looks like that: deep learning for interpretable image recognition. In: Wallach HM, Larochelle H, Beygelzimer A et al (eds) Advances in neural information processing Systems 32: annual conference on neural information processing systems 2019, NeurIPS 2019, December 8-14, 2019, Vancouver, BC, Canada, pp 8928–8939, https://proceedings.neurips.cc/paper/2019/hash/adf7ee2dcf142b0e11888e72b43fcb75-Abstract.html

Cruciani F, Brusini L, Zucchelli M et al (2023) Chapter 6 - explainable deep learning for decrypting disease signatures in multiple sclerosis. In: Benois-Pineau J, Bourqui R, Petkovic D et al (eds) Explainable deep learning AI. Academic Press, pp 97–123. https://doi.org/10.1016/B978-0-32-396098-4.00012-0

European Commission (2019) Ethics guidelines for trustworthy ai. https://digital-strategy.ec.europa.eu/en/library/ethics-guidelines-trustworthy-ai

European Parliament and Council of the European Union (2024) Regulation (eu) 2024/1689 of the european parliament and of the council of 13 june 2024 laying down harmonised rules on artificial intelligence and amending regulations (ec) no 300/2008, (eu) no 167/2013, (eu) no 168/2013, (eu) 2018/858, (eu) 2018/1139 and (eu) 2019/2144 and directives 2014/90/eu, (eu) 2016/797 and (eu) 2020/1828 (artificial intelligence act) (text with eea relevance). http://data.europa.eu/eli/reg/2024/1689/oj

Friedman JH, Popescu BE (2008) Predictive learning via rule ensembles. Ann Appl Statistics 2(3): 916–954. http://www.jstor.org/stable/30245114

Hägele M, Seegerer P, Lapuschkin S, et al (2020) Resolving challenges in deep learningbased analyses of histopathological images using explanation methods. Sci Rep 10(1):6423. https://doi.org/10.1038/s41598-020-62724-2

Halnaut A, Giot R, Bourqui R, et al (2020) Deep dive into deep neural networks with flows. In: VISIGRAPP (3: IVAPP). SCITEPRESS, pp 231–239, https://hal.science/hal-02492393

Hassija V, Chamola V, Mahapatra A et al (2024) Interpreting black-box models: a review on explainable artificial intelligence. Cogn Comput 16(1):45–74. https://doi.org/10.1007/s12559-023-10179-8

Hastie T, Tibshirani R, Friedman J (2001) The elements of statistical learning: data mining, inference, and prediction. Springer series in statistics. Springer, https://books.google.fr/books?id=VRzITwgNV2UC

Ivanovs M, Kadikis R, Ozols K (2021) Perturbation-based methods for explaining deep neural networks: a survey. Pattern Recogn Lett 150:228–234. https://doi.org/10.1016/j.patrec.2021.06.030

Jiang M, Huang S, Duan J, et al (2015) Salicon: saliency in context. In: The IEEE Conference on Computer Vision and Pattern Recognition (CVPR)

Koitka S, Kim MS, Qu M et al (2020) Mimicking the radiologists' workflow: estimating pediatric hand bone age with stacked deep neural networks. Med Image Anal 64:101743. https://doi.org/10.1016/j.media.2020.101743

La Rosa B, Blasilli G, Bourqui R et al (2023) State of the art of visual analytics for explainable deep learning. Comput Graph Forum 42(1):319–355. https://doi.org/10.1111/cgf.14733

LeCun Y, Bengio Y, Hinton G (2015) Deep learning. Nature 521:436–440. https://doi.org/10.1038/nature14539

Litjens G, Kooi T, Bejnordi BE et al (2017) A survey on deep learning in medical image analysis. Med Image Anal 42:60–88. https://doi.org/10.1016/j.media.2017.07.005

Lundberg SM, Lee SI (2017) A unified approach to interpreting model predictions. In: Proceedings of the 31st International Conference on Neural Information Processing Systems. Curran Associates Inc., Red Hook, NY, USA, NIPS'17, pp 4768–4777, https://doi.org/10.48550/arXiv.1705.07874

Mishra P (2022) Practical explainable AI using python: artificial intelligence model explanations using python-based libraries, extensions, and frameworks. Apress, https://doi.org/10.1007/978-1-4842-7158-2

O.Gorokhovatskyi O, Peredrii N, Vlasenko V (2023) Explainable deep learning AI, chap explanation of CNN image classifiers with hiding parts. In: BenoisPineau J et al (2023) https://doi.org/10.1016/B978-0-32-396098-4. 00004-1

Obeso AM, Benois-Pineau J, García-Vázquez MS et al (2022) Visual vs internal attention mechanisms in deep neural networks for image classification and object detection. Pattern Recognit 123:108411

Petsiuk V, Das A, Saenko K (2018) RISE: randomized input sampling for explanation of black-box models. BMVC. BMVA Press, p 151, https://api.semanticscholar.org/CorpusID:49324724

Ribeiro M, Singh S, Guestrin C (2016a) Model-agnostic interpretability of machine learning. arXiv e-prints

Ribeiro MT, Singh S, Guestrin C (2016b) "why should i trust you?": explaining the predictions of any classifier. In: Proceedings of the 22nd ACM SIGKDD International Conference on Knowledge Discovery and Data Mining. Association for Computing Machinery, New York, NY, USA, KDD '16, pp 1135–1144

Salembier P, Garrido L (2000) Binary partition tree as an efficient representation for image processing, segmentation, and information retrieval. IEEE Trans Image Process 9(4):561–576. https://doi.org/10.1109/83.841934

Selvaraju RR, Das A, Vedantam R, et al (2016) Grad-cam: why did you say that? visual explanations from deep networks via gradient-based localization. CoRR abs/1610.02391. http://arxiv.org/abs/1610.02391,1610.02391

Sundararajan M, Taly A, Yan Q (2017) Axiomatic attribution for deep networks. In: Proceedings of the 34th International Conference on Machine Learning - Volume 70. JMLR.org, ICML'17, pp 3319–3328, http://arxiv.org/abs/1703.01365

van der Linden I, Haned H, Kanoulas E (2019) Global aggregations of local explanations for black box models. ArXiv abs/1907.03039. https://api.semanticscholar.org/CorpusID:195833815

van der Velden BH, Kuijf HJ, Gilhuijs KG et al (2022) Explainable artificial intelligence (xai) in deep learning-based medical image analysis. Med Image Anal 79:102470. https://doi.org/10.1016/j.media.2022.102470

Zang B, Ding L, Feng Z et al (2021) Cnn-lrp: Understanding convolutional neural networks performance for target recognition in sar images. Sensors 21(13). https://doi.org/10.3390/s21134536

Zhukov A, Benois-Pineau J, Giot R (2023) Evaluation of explanation methods of ai – cnns in image classification tasks with reference-based and no-reference metrics. Adv Artif Intell Mach Learn 3(1):620–646. https://www.oajaiml.com/uploads/archivepdf/20401143.pdf

Part II
Law and Ethics for and with Emotional AI

Artificial Intelligence, Threat or Enhancement of the Quality of Our Wellbeing and Personal Life?

Rob van den Hoven van Genderen

Abstract Although the AI processing of personal and, specifically, emotional data can enhance the wellbeing of people, it can also intrude on fundamental rights, such as physical and mental integrity, autonomy and privacy. In this respect, the main attention of European legislators as well as many scholars is directed at the risks and dangers of AI processing (See a.o.: https://www.pewresearch.org/internet/2023/06/21/themes-the-most-harmful-or-menacing-changes-in-digital-life-that-are-likely-by-2035/.). Instruments such as the European Artificial Intelligence Act (AIA; Official version of the Act: https://eur-lex.europa.eu/eli/reg/2024/1689/oj) concentrate on risk assessment and avoiding the risks and perceived dangers of the use of AI systems, thereby negating the positive aspect in increasing wellbeing by AI.

1 Introduction

Society will not escape the increasing use of AI technology. Industrial production, healthcare but also personal life will be dependent on AI in many aspects. Indeed, artificial intelligence is the motor that depends on the fuel consisting of data and often personal data. The focus of this chapter will be on so-called emotion data, derived bio signals and the psycho data of natural persons on the basis of their physical emotional or psychological behaviour perceived and processed by the use of wearables, sensors, cameras, and radar technology used in emotion recognition systems.[1] In addition, here, AI systems that influence or create emotional effects on human actors are considered emotion processing systems. Those data can be

[1]Compare this with recital 15 of the AIA: The notion of 'biometric identification' referred to in this Regulation should be defined as the automated recognition of physical, physiological and behavioural human features such as the face, eye movement, body shape, voice, prosody, gait, posture, heart rate, blood pressure, odour, keystroke characteristics.

R. van den Hoven van Genderen (✉)
Faculty of Law, University of Lapland, Rovaniemi, Finland
e-mail: rob.vandenhovenvangenderen@switchlegal.nl

R. Ballardini et al. (eds.), *Emotional Data Applications and Regulation of Artificial Intelligence in Society*, Law, Governance and Technology Series 69,
https://doi.org/10.1007/978-3-031-80111-2_5

processed to increase the welfare and wellbeing of natural persons. By processing emotion data, though AI could increase medical improvements, agriculture, security and comfort, it could also be used to influence, manipulate and control people by governments, industry and other organizations. Moreover, people with criminal intents could manipulate the autonomy of people and even the psychic situation of people.

It is an ironic fact that the application of legal instruments aimed to protect personal life and to avoid the risks of AI can be counterproductive to the positive applications and can even be a danger to legal certainty and the peace of mind of people. For instance, the requirement of transparency in the AI processing of data could endanger the wellbeing of persons by exposing and therefore limiting fundamental values such as privacy, integrity, inviolability, anonymity in the freedom of thought, personal life and more non personal rights such as trade secrets and intellectual property rights.

A clear example of the complexity is found in the evolution of the texts of the European General Data Protection Regulation (GDPR) and the AI Act. The definitions of AI are in constant adaption in line with perceiving changes in technology and knowledge about application and effects. Coming from the first description by John McCarthy in 1955, "the science and engineering of making intelligent machines", AI came to the more specific definition proposal of AI, to be equal to the latest definition of the OECD of 23 November 2023 as it is integrated in Article 3 of the EU AI Act, according to which: "*An AI system is a machine-based system that, for explicit or implicit objectives, infers, from the input it receives, how to generate outputs such as predictions, content, recommendations, or decisions influence physical real or virtual environments*". Therefore, the final version of the AI Act is almost comparable, but with the addition of the following: "*to operate with varying levels of autonomy and that may exhibit adaptiveness after deployment*".[2] This notion of varying levels of autonomy is an important difference to the OECD definition as AI is under constant adaption not to miss a future development that could escape regulation. Mentioning this varying level of autonomy can be considered a portent to legal uncertainty.[3] In other words, there will hardly be a system that is not considered AI. This uncertainty is made clear by the descriptions in the recitals of December and February in the draft Act:

[2]Article 3.1 of the AIA, see Introduction for full text.

[3]This also accounts for the AI convention of the Council of Europe: Article 2—Definition of artificial intelligence systems.

For the purposes of this Convention, "artificial intelligence system" means a machine-based system that for explicit or implicit objectives, infers, from the input it receives, how to generate outputs such as predictions, content, recommendations or decisions that may influence physical or virtual environments. Different artificial intelligence systems vary in their levels of autonomy and adaptiveness after deployment.

Council of Europe Framework Convention on Artificial Intelligence and Human Rights, Democracy and the Rule of Law. https://rm.coe.int/1680afae3c.

> The notion of AI system in this Regulation should be clearly defined and closely aligned with the work of international organisations working on artificial intelligence to ensure legal certainty, harmonization and wide acceptance; while providing the flexibility to accommodate the rapid technological developments in this field.
>
> Moreover, it should be based on key characteristics of artificial intelligence, such as its learning, reasoning or modelling capabilities, so as to distinguish it from simpler software systems or programming approaches. AI systems are designed to operate with varying levels of autonomy, meaning that they have at least some degree of independence of actions from human controls and of capabilities to operate without human intervention.

Instead, this last part was replaced by the following text in the February 2024 version:

> Moreover, it should be based on key characteristics of artificial intelligence systems that distinguish it from simpler traditional software systems or programming approaches and should not cover systems that are based on the rules defined solely by natural persons to automatically execute operations. A key characteristic of AI systems is their capability to infer. This inference refers to the process of obtaining the outputs, such as predictions, content, recommendations, or decisions, which can influence physical and virtual environments and to a capability of AI systems to derive models and/or algorithms from inputs/ data.[4]

Again, in the final version of the recital in the AIA, this has been changed:

> The notion of 'AI system' in this Regulation should be clearly defined and should be closely aligned with the work of international organisations working on AI to ensure legal certainty, facilitate international convergence and wide acceptance, while providing the flexibility to accommodate the rapid technological developments in this field.
>
> Moreover, the definition should be based on key characteristics of AI systems that distinguish it from simpler traditional software systems or programming approaches and should not cover systems that are based on the rules defined solely by natural persons to automatically execute operations. A key characteristic of AI systems is their capability to infer. This capability to infer refers to the process of obtaining the outputs, such as predictions, content, recommendations, or decisions, which can influence physical and virtual environments, and to a capability of AI systems to derive models or algorithms, or both, from inputs or data.[5]

It is interesting to see that in the recital in the final version "*harmonization*" is replaced by *facilitate international convergence*, which, in my view, is a more technical term and not an all-encompassing policy of harmonization.

By reference to physical environments, the changes to the recital imply that outcomes can have an effect on human behaviour and wellbeing as the most important aspect of a physical environment and as a specific capability of AI. However, is this not just a part of all use of technology and all human actions? This description seems to be inspired by the fear of non-controllable effects or the misuse of AI. In the clarification of the prohibition of AI systems that infers emotion in Article 5 of the AI Act, it is stated that the uncertainty and unpredictability leads to this recital:

---

[4] Recital 6 AIA. (February 2024).

[5] Recital 12 AIA.

> (44) There are serious concerns about the scientific basis of AI systems aiming to identify or infer emotions, particularly as expression of emotions vary considerably across cultures and situations, and even within a single individual. Among the key shortcomings of such systems are the limited reliability, the lack of specificity and the limited generalisability. Therefore, AI systems identifying or inferring emotions or intentions of natural persons on the basis of their biometric data may lead to discriminatory outcomes and can be intrusive to the rights and freedoms of the concerned persons. Considering the imbalance of power in the context of work or education, combined with the intrusive nature of these systems, such systems could lead to detrimental or unfavourable treatment of certain natural persons or whole groups thereof. Therefore, the placing on the market, the putting into service, or the use of AI systems intended to be used to detect the emotional state of individuals in situations related to the workplace and education should be prohibited. That prohibition should not cover AI systems placed on the market strictly for medical or safety reasons, such as systems intended for therapeutical use.

By describing the concerns and uncertainties as key characteristic of AI as a pejorative element one could create a negative view on AI systems inferring emotions. However, this influencing of physical and virtual environments can have a positive effect as well.[6]

In the European General Data Protection Regulation (GDPR), the definition personal data '*means any information relating to an identified or identifiable natural person ('data subject')*'.[7] Moreover, the identification of natural persons is clearly dependent on the state of technology. All data, which increasingly can be made identifiable by technology such as AI, will thus fall under the definition of personal data and therefore be subject to the GDPR.[8] With the increasing capability of AI technology considering personal activity and behaviour, there will be hardly any data left considering the activities of natural persons that could not be considered personal data. Consequently, the use of AI to process personal, sensitive data, such as medical data or any data that is considered to have biometric or mental characteristics, will be under scrutiny of the AI Act and the GDPR and will require severe assessment based on the critical risks that such processing will provide.

The question in this and the following sections will be whether it will be even possible in a practical sense to control and protect personal data and protect the personal sphere as well as wellbeing by adaptive regulations as GDPR and the AIA in the era of AI. Furthermore, could this lead to an increasing risk of legal uncertainty?

---

[6](34) 'emotion recognition system' means an AI system for the purpose of identifying or inferring emotions or intentions of natural persons on the basis of their biometric data.

[7]For complete definition see introduction.

[8]Any information relating to an identified or identifiable natural person ('data subject'); an identifiable natural person is one who can be identified, directly or indirectly, in particular by reference to an identifier such as a name, an identification number, location data, an online identifier or to one or more factors specific to the physical, physiological, genetic, mental, economic, cultural or social identity of that natural person.

2 Scope, Wellbeing AI and Emotional Data

Wellbeing can be considered a subjective feeling of a complex system of the qualities of physical and mental life and differing circumstances. This complexity makes it difficult to pinpoint the elements that add to a certain feeling of wellbeing. There are several international organisations that mention different aspects that form a combination to a general feeling of wellbeing. For example, Article 25 of the Universal Declaration on Human Rights states: "*Everyone has the right to a standard of living adequate for the health and well-being of himself and of his family, including food, clothing, housing and medical care and necessary social services, and the right to security in the event of unemployment, sickness, disability, widowhood, old age or other lack of livelihood in circumstances beyond his control"*. The wellbeing of people consists of a mixture of all these mentioned elements. Moreover, general instruments such as the International Covenant on Economic, Social and Cultural Rights give an enumeration of rights that add up to the wellbeing of the population.[9] Another example, Article 17 of the United Nations Convention on the Rights of the Child (20 November 1989), requires the signatory states to protect the "social, spiritual and moral wellbeing and physical and mental health" of all children on their territories. Moreover, the Children's Rights Convention (CRC) reflects the general provisions of the Universal Declaration of Human Rights (UDHR), 10 December 1948, including the right to life (UDHR, Article 3; ECHR, Article 2) and to health and wellbeing as referred to in UDHR, Article 25.[10] Quality of life or wellbeing is dependent on primary material aspects such as housing, enough food, energy to create warmth and light, and all requirements for a satisfactory life, personal mobility, etc. However, quality of life is also dependent on personal wellbeing in environmental acceptable circumstances, e.g. clean air and water, and psychological stability, i.e. not to be disturbed by the manipulation of information and conspiracy theories. There is a requirement of living in a well-regulated state of being under the rule of Law, which could mean a political and socially acceptable state, based on the acceptance of fundamental and social rights; with freedom to express oneself; credible media and democracy, based on the rule of law; and respect for fundamental rights. In a more psycho-physical way: healthy circumstances in a wide sense. As John Locke stated: "people should have the right to comfortable enjoyment of their lives, liberty, and property."[11] Certainly, research on the effects of AI certainly has to be centred on the influence on human life and fundamental

[9] https://www.ohchr.org/en/instruments-mechanisms/instruments/international-covenant-economic-social-and-cultural-rights.

[10] https://www.living-democracy.com/principals/activity/awareness/physical-activity-human-right/. See also: Article 25 of the UDHR.. https://www.un.org/en/universal-declaration-human-rights/index.html.

[11] John Locke,Two treatises of Government Chapter II, para 6., https://oll.libertyfund.org/title/hollis-the-two-treatises-of-civil-government-hollis-ed#lf0057_label_207.

requirements and rights, but it also must be directed on stimulating investments and legal protection of AI-related innovations...

However, both investments in and the legal protection of AI systems processing emotional data might be challenged by several legal provisions in the EU such as the GDPR and the AI Act. In addition, the new European Data strategy, including the Data Act and Data Governance Act, could endanger the further development and investment in AI systems that process or create emotion data for new AI applications because of the transparency and data sharing requirements in those regulations. In a data driven society, though transparency is a good principle, it could also endanger wellbeing by impairing autonomy, integrity, personal life and security. The wellbeing connected to AI is openly stimulated in soft- and harder law instruments.

Already in 2019, the Ethics guidelines for trustworthy AI were developed by the independent High Level Ethics Group (AI HLEG) appointed by the Commission.[12] In those guidelines, the AI HLEG developed seven non-binding ethical principles for AI which are intended to help ensure that AI is trustworthy and ethically sound. These seven principles include human agency and oversight; technical robustness and safety; privacy and data governance; transparency; diversity, non-discrimination and fairness; societal and environmental wellbeing; and accountability.

The legal process of protecting and stimulating new applications in the field of processing emotional data by AI systems in processing and creating emotions has to be scrutinized and developed to good use for an AI driven society. For the ethical and legal acceptance of AI and emotional data, it is also of the utmost importance that there will be a balance between the further development of AI and the protection of personal data and personal life as well as fundamental rights as the autonomy and integrity of the human mind for the wellbeing of society. Human rights Organizations such as the Council of Europe see this as a relevant perspective as they do not perceive to prevent research in AI if there is no relevant risk for fundamental rights, as stated in article 3.3 of the Framework Convention on Artificial Intelligence, Human Rights, Democracy And The Rule Of Law of the Committee on Artificial Intelligence.[13]

2.1 Quality of Life, Wellbeing in What Sense?

Naturally, quality of life is not just dependent on the way of using technology and the protection of a personal life environment. According to Maslow's theories of an

[12] https://www.europarl.europa.eu/cmsdata/196377/AI%20HLEG_Ethics%20Guidelines%20for%20Trustworthy%20AI.pdf.

[13] 3 Without prejudice to Article 13 and Article 25, paragraph 2, this Convention shall not apply to research and development activities regarding artificial intelligence systems not yet made available for use, unless testing or similar activities are undertaken in such a way that they have the potential to interfere with human rights, democracy and the rule of law. https://rm.coe.int/1680afae3c accepted on 5th May 2024.

ideal life and a good life, known as "Maslow's Hierarchy of Needs", to have "the ideal life" or a "good life" (in other words, to have a quality of life), it is necessary to satisfy the eight needs that make up his "Hierarchy of Needs". These needs are: (1) physiological needs, (2) the needs for safety and peace of mind, (3) belonging needs, (4) self-esteem needs, (5) cognitive needs, (6) aesthetic needs, (7) self-actualization needs, and (8) self-transcendence needs.[14]

Much earlier than the ideas of Maslow, the school of philosophy called Epicureanism, founded by the ancient Greek philosopher Epicurus (341–270 BCE), taught that pleasure is the highest good. Epicurus's concept of pleasure, however, is not simply physical and is far from being extravagant, materialistic, or indulgent. Epicurus taught that a life of moderation, virtue, and philosophy would be the most pleasurable. Moreover, he believed it was important to tame wild desires that are impossible to satisfy and that cause unhappiness and dissatisfaction with life by focusing on methods for achieving freedom from mental, emotional, and physical pain through tranquillity (*ataraxia*).

In addition to Maslow and Epicurus, others have contributed ideas to achieving greater wellbeing. Indeed, the concept of utilitarianism of Jeremy Bentham (1748–1832) and John Stuart Mill (1806–1873) can be described as a method for maximizing wellbeing. For Aristotle, the concept of wellbeing in his *Nicomachean Ethics* starts from an observation about "some good" as the object of all human striving that soon turns to "the good," that is, "the best good",[15] which is then equated to *eudaimonia* (commonly translated as "happiness").[16] Aristotle notes at this point that it is generally agreed that "living well and doing well are the same as being happy".[17] Even Aristotle extends his concept of wellbeing to a broader level when it concerns countries or governments that pursue wellbeing as a common advantage. : "The political community seems to have come together from the beginning and to abide for the sake of advantage (*sumpherontos*). For it is at this that the lawgivers aim, and justice, they say, is the common advantage (*sumpheron*). So the other communities aim at some portion (*kata mere*) of what is advantageous (*sumpherontos*) . . . but the political community does not aim at the present advantage (*sumpherontos*), but at the whole of life."[18]

Yet, naturally there are other ways to measure the quality of life. For instance, Numbeo measures the quality of life country wise and publishes a list of all different countries in grading the quality of life based on: (1) cost of living index, (2) crime index, (3) healthcare index, (4) pollution index, (5) property prices, and (6) traffic

[14]In: Maslow, 1962; Ventegodt et al. (Maslow, 1943; 1954; 1962; 1970a; 1970b; 1987, 2003a; 2003b; 2003c). Maslow (1962), also: Maslow AH American Journal of Psychoanalysis; New York Vol. 23, Iss. 2, (Jan 1, 1963): 117.

[15]Aristotle, *Nicomachean Ethics* (I.2 1094a21–22).

[16]Idem, (I.4 1095a18).

[17]Kraut (2015) https://www.routledgehandbooks.com/doi/10.4324/9781315682266.ch2.

[18]Idem, (1160a11–23) Kraut p. 24.

index.[19] However, quality of life can be measured in many ways whereby it must be determined on which scale this is measured and on basis of which parameters. On a country scale, since 2012, there has been the well-known "happiness report", which is based on certain questions that are variable due to the perceived importance in the view of the researchers. The 2023 report was based on the following questions:

1. What is the consensus view about measuring national happiness, and what kinds of behaviour does it require of individuals and institutions? (Chapter 1)
2. What is the consensus view about measuring national happiness, and what kinds of behaviour does it require of individuals and institutions? (Chapter 1)
3. How have trust and benevolence saved lives and supported happiness over the past three years of COVID-19 and other crises? (Chapter 2)
4. What is state effectiveness and how does it affect human happiness? (Chapter 3)
5. How does altruistic behaviour by individuals affect their own happiness, that of the recipient, and the overall happiness of society? (Chapter 4)
6. How well does social media data enable us to measure the prevailing levels of happiness and distress? (Chapter 5)[20]

Evidently, this report only refers to the broad picture of a certain country (and a certain time frame, ref.to COVID). On the basis of a developed standard, other organizations are also trying to measure wellbeing worldwide. For example, the newly organized World Wellbeing Movement (WWM) has set up a measurement of wellbeing on the basis of research by Academic, industrial and political participants.[21] If we look at a personal subjective scale, one sees that the feeling and emotions determine the rating quality of life too and that it is a very subjective state of mind within a more general perception of general wellbeing in different certain political or cultural circumstances. Referring to the Greek concept as used by Aristotle of wellbeing Kraut describes the more personal state of mind as that when one asks whether someone is "eudaemon", one is asking whether he/she is living well. Naturally, this depends on what kind of life one has, as unless one knows what good things or bad things are in someone's life, one cannot assess how well it is being lived.[22] To conclude this shallow search for the concept of happiness and wellbeing, the observation of the Greek philosophers and myself is that it depends on the personal feelings and emotion perception of every different individual. On a more general level, one could connect to the utilitarian observation that happiness

---

[19] Numbeo is the world's largest cost of living database. Numbeo is also a crowd-sourced global database of quality of life data: housing indicators, perceived crime rates, healthcare quality, transport quality, and other statistics. https://www.numbeo.com/quality-of-life/rankings_by_country.jsp.

[20] https://happiness-report.s3.amazonaws.com/2023/WHR+23.pdf(This is clearly influenced by the.

[21] The World Wellbeing Movement (WWM), a not-for-profit social impact organisation working at the intersection between academic experts, and decision-makers in both business and policy to translate evidence-informed wellbeing insights into real-world impact. https://worldwellbeingmovement.org/.

[22] Idem Kraut p. 24.

and wellbeing is the sum of the most positive effects on the population in a society by the policy decisions made by the accepted authorities (the acceptance of the "best" authority is also part of wellbeing). Concerning the emotions and feelings that will determine the state of happiness and wellbeing, it must be taken in account that the value as well as the manifestation of those emotions will differ depending on geographical position, culture and of course the individual.

Since feelings and emotions are most intimate aspects of human behaviour, the combination of emotion data derived from natural persons and processing by AI systems is considered a frightening perspective by many scholars, politicians and international organisations.

Emotions can be positive or negative. They can be physically felt or/and have a psychological impact, and they vary in their personal impact. According to Psychology Today, both emotional experiences and physical sensations—such as hunger or pain—bring about 'feelings'. Feelings are a conscious experience; although not every conscious experience, such as seeing or believing, is a feeling, as explained Reisenzein c.s..[23] According to the same article, an emotion "can only ever be felt [...] through the emotional experiences it gives rise to, even though it might be discovered through its associated thoughts, beliefs, desires, and actions".[24] Emotions are not conscious but instead manifest in the unconscious mind. These emotions can be brought to the surface of the conscious state through extended psychotherapy.[25] This range of emotions is impacted by such factors as their behaviour, the culture they come from, and their possible previous traumatic experiences.

If emotions are perceived differently, it will be difficult to use Artificial Intelligence to process emotional data to adapt to every individual person in all circumstances in order to enhance the feelings of comfort and wellbeing. Yet, those emotions that cause a positive experience are shown to differ between cultures. For example, "European Americans (as well as 'real' Europeans) typically preferred excitement and elation" as positive emotions, while Chinese populations "preferred calm and relaxation more".[26] This difference is seen in, e.g. advertising, which utilizes the positive experience emotions to craft messages for maximum impact. Therefore, what kind of emotions will be triggered and how they are valued is also culturally dependent.

One may conclude that creating a positive emotional response and/or processing emotion data by AI applications to enhance wellbeing is not an absolute concept but depends on culture, circumstances and certainly the individual perception of the different values that create it. Although taking into account background and circumstances, knowledge of emotional behaviour can certainly have a positive effect. As a result of a study already in 2011, authors concluded that organizations and individuals may benefit from the development and utilization of behaviours attributed to

[23] Rainer et al. (2020), pp. 81-100.

[24] Idem note 5. See also Damasio and Carvalho (2013), pp. 143–152.

[25] Brackett et al. (2004), pp. 1387–1402.

[26] Dawson (2018). https://www.psychologicalscience.org/observer/the-fluidity-of-time.

emotional intelligence. The practical application of emotional intelligence skills can enhance individual and group decisions and outcomes.[27]

3 Psychological Influences of the Use of Emotion Generative AI on the Wellbeing of People

The use of emotional data and AI not only has applications in the job market, in the admission process to studies, finding emotionally disturbed people and possible criminal activities but it also helps the elderly by the use of on body sensors or face recognition. This can have a positive but also a negative impact on their psychological status. There is also always a chance that the used data derived from people can be biased in the analysis by AI. Furthermore, data used in training the AI can be biased. By using subliminal techniques or the use of image and voice manipulation by AI, even the use of corrected data can have negative influences on the state of one's mind. Moreover, predictive AI can lead to certain policies having an influence on individuals as well as groups. One well-known (albeit negative) example from forensic and criminal psychology is the use of predictive models to allocate policing resources to some neighbourhoods. Another example from clinical psychology in the domain of health interventions is the mining of text or voice data to identify people who are at risk of or experience mental health issues and subsequent automatic referrals to human counsellors.[28] The use of AI to make high-stakes decisions such as these is quite broad, touching most if not all domains of psychology across a wide spectrum of human activity.[29] Indeed, the use of emotions in influencing people can have positive effects to stimulate people or relieve depressive feelings as well. Considering the use of Large Language Models (LLM) as ChatGPT in recognizing and processing emotional data, recent studies indicate that although ChatGPT has successfully generated theoretical information in multiple fields, its ability to identify and describe emotions is still unknown. Emotional awareness (EA), the ability to conceptualize one's own and others' emotions, is considered a transdiagnostic mechanism for psychopathology.[30]

The use of AI technology can have a positive influence when concerns a specific group and a specific culture (Japan). In an experiment conducted in Japan on the effects of using AI in educational activities, students supported by a mobile

[27] Hess and Bacigalupo (2011), ISSN: 0025-1747, Article publication date: 31 May 2011.

[28] Graham et al. (2019), p. 116.

[29] Landers Richard and Behrend Tara (2023).

[30] This study utilized the Levels of Emotional Awareness Scale (LEAS) as an objective, performance-based test to analyse ChatGPT's responses to twenty scenarios and compared its EA performance with that of the general population norms, as reported by a previous study. A second examination was performed one month later to measure EA improvement over time. Elyoseph (2023).

(intelligent) agent, performed better in terms of mental health, interpersonal sensitivity, anxiety, learning pressure, emotional and psychological balance of autonomy, responsiveness, initiative, and mobility than the group that did not use the agent.[31]

4 European Regulations That Influence Processing Emotional Data and Wellbeing by AI

The European Charter is mainly developed to create a fundamental rights framework for the European Union.[32] As stated in the preamble to the European Charter, the pursuit of happiness and wellbeing will certainly encompass the statement: *"Conscious of its spiritual and moral heritage, the Union is founded on the indivisible, universal values of human dignity, freedom, equality and solidarity; it is based on the principles of democracy and the rule of law. It places the individual at the heart of its activities, by establishing the citizenship of the Union and by creating an area of freedom, security and justice"*.[33] Article 7 and 8 of the Charter stand for the protection of a private and personal life, communication and the protection of personal data. Moreover, in other regulations, a reference to the idea of general wellbeing is often mentioned as the basis for regulating in a very general sense, before restricting activities in the rest of the document that could work counterproductive to this preamble.[34]

4.1 The GDPR

As stated above, existing and draft European regulations have their effect on the development on the use of AI to create wellbeing by using emotion data. The big question is whether wellbeing is a leading principle of these regulations and thus has to be taken into account in any regulation considering AI. One answer could be derived from recital (4) of the GDPR: "The processing of personal data should be designed to serve mankind. The right to the protection of personal data is not an absolute right; it must be considered in relation to its function in society and be balanced against other fundamental rights, in accordance with the principle of proportionality". This recital is in line with the ongoing debate that modern technology should improve the lives, wellbeing, privacy and security of individuals and not undermine fundamental rights.

[31] Yanqi (2023). (PsycInfo Database Record (c) 2023 APA, all rights reserved).

[32] CHARTER OF FUNDAMENTAL RIGHTS OF THE EUROPEAN UNION (2000/C 364/01).

[33] https://www.europarl.europa.eu/charter/pdf/text_en.pdf.

[34] Universal Declaration of Human Rights, Article 25; European Convention of Human Rights, Article 2.

One of the defining features of applying AI in relation to personal data is the emergence of new products and services such as smart wearables and even in-body devices and apps that leverage algorithm-based AI systems. These new developments create challenges for regulators and other policy makers, in particular in the context of privacy.[35] However, these challenges, can also bring new opportunities. For instance, will it be possible in an increasingly complex system of using these personal data by other parties to ensure the data subjects of their information sovereignty over their own data and their physical and psychological integrity? Crucially, personal data should be treated as an extension of the individual's own personality right, granting protection to their personal development.[36] The European Data Protection Supervisor (EDPS) Ethics Advisory Group has warned against increasingly remote algorithmic profiling".[37] The transcription of behaviours and propensities is neither neutral nor exhaustive. The question is whether the digital representation of persons may expose them to new forms of vulnerability and harm. Data protection is not a technical or legalistic matter; it is a profoundly human one. The protection of fundamental rights is also considered an essential aspect of the creation of an enhanced level of wellbeing. Certainly, the possibility to control your own informational autonomy and sovereignty creates self-consciousness and peace of mind as an element of well-being.

One of the more difficult requirements to be met under the GDPR is the requirement that personal data must be processed "transparently" and with the explicit consent of the data subject. Article 6 of the GDPR describes the options available to process personal data without the express consent of the data subject. Under sections E and F, this article offers several possibilities by mentioning the grounds for processing without the consent of the data subject, namely in the vital interests of the data subject or the public interest. Paragraph 3 provides that processing data without consent is governed by (a) Union law; or (b) the national law to which the controller is subject. One could extend this to the acceptance that wellbeing too is of vital interest, essential for the life of the data subject.

Emotional data will fall under the GDPR if those data are considered personal data, as defined in Article 4, as long as they are identifiable. Importantly, emotional data (for instance, collected or used in Artificial Intelligence systems") can be considered sensitive data, defined in Article 4.[38] Emotional data can be considered a sub-category of "biometric data". Biometric data are personal data resulting from

---

[35] In the context of healthcare, see, e.g. Corrales Compagnucci (2021), Cambridge Bioethics and Law (2022).

[36] Van der Sloot (2015), pp. 25–50.

[37] Peter Burgess et al. (2018), p. 11, available at: https://edps.europa.eu/sites/default/files/publication/18-01-25_eag_report_en.pdf (accessed on 4 August 2023).

[38] (1) "personal data" means any information relating to an identified or identifiable natural person ("data subject"); an identifiable natural person is one who can be identified, directly or indirectly, in particular by reference to an identifier such as a name, an identification number, location data, an online identifier or to one or more factors specific to the physical, physiological, genetic, mental, economic, cultural or social identity of that natural person.

specific technical processing relating to the physical, physiological or behavioural characteristics of a natural person, which allow or confirm the unique identification of that natural person, such as facial images or dactyloscopic data(14) And (15) "data concerning health", meaning personal data related to the physical or mental health of a natural person, including the provision of health care services, which reveal information about his or her health status. Emotional data can easily reveal the physical or mental status of a person, which is an area where (physical) feelings and emotional expressions merge.

Therefore, emotional data can be considered sensitive data under the special regime of Article 9 of the GDPR, according to which:

> [. . .] the processing of genetic data, biometric data for the purpose of uniquely identifying a natural person is forbidden except with the consent of subjects, or other legitimate reasons listed in the article as securing the data subject's vital interest or reasons of national (security) interest.

If it could be considered that wellbeing is of vital interest, this would be a reason to further develop the AI system that processes the sensitive emotion data.

A complicating issue is the requirement of transparency in Article 12 of the GDPR as well as for emotional AI Systems, where the data subject has to be informed about the data processing, its purpose and possible extensions, in a concise, transparent, intelligible and easily accessible form, using clear and plain language.[39] Using an AI system will not be easy to present this. In addition, there are the information rights of the data subject, which are specified in other articles of the GDPR—access, change, control, storage information, retraction of consent, complaints procedure, etc.—to enhance the understanding of what happens with the subject's data. By their complexity, these positively inclined rights could also result in negative effects on the feelings of the wellbeing of (elderly) people by creating too much, often complex information and intruding on their autonomy.

Lastly, Article 22 of the GDPR states that:

> The data subject shall have the right not to be subject to a decision based solely on automated processing, including profiling, which produces legal effects concerning him or her or similarly significantly affects him or her.

Although there will be ample AI applications processing emotions that can be considered automated processing in this sense, still it is not always notable to the subject that this is the case. Indeed, it will be difficult to object to actions one does not have knowledge about.

[39] Concerning high risk systems in article 13 AIA, the deployers have to be informed about purpose and outputs not the data subjects.

4.2 *Draft ePrivacy Regulation and the e-Privacy Directive*

4.2.1 The Draft ePrivacy Regulation[40]

Although still in draft form since 2017, it is worth mentioning the draft ePrivacy Regulation because it considers the use of sensors and the connections to other sources and recipients of personal and emotional data as on- and in body devices. Such devices can be used in personal and public use for medical, psychological or simply for commercial purposes. This regulation is meant to be more extensively applied to consider also internet-based social platform services and other content related services to replace the "old fashion "directive that does not apply to those so called "Over the Top services".[41] Until now, the ePrivacy directive is still the applicable legal document. The draft ePrivacy Regulation also refers to the emotional sensitive aspect of data in its recital 2:

> (2) The content of electronic communications may reveal highly sensitive information about the natural persons involved in the communication, from personal experiences and emotions to medical conditions, sexual preferences and political views, the disclosure of which could result in personal and social harm, economic loss or embarrassment. Similarly, metadata derived from electronic communications may also reveal very sensitive and personal information.

In sum, all data that is considered to be identifiable to a natural person will fall under the reign of the GDPR. The more advanced the technology is, the greater the chance that seemingly neutral data can be considered identifiable. It is questionable whether the draft ePrivacy Regulation, which has been debated for a long time, will take AI technology developments into account, striving for technological neutrality.[42] Consequently, European privacy rules might pose several challenges for the use of emotional data and its processing.

[40] Proposal for a Regulation of the European Parliament and of the Council concerning the respect for private life and the protection of personal data in electronic communications and repealing Directive 2002/58/EC (Regulation on Privacy and Electronic Communications), COM(2017) 10 final.

[41] These Over-the-Top communications services ("OTTs") are in general not subject to the current Union electronic communications framework, including the ePrivacy Directive. Accordingly, the Directive has not kept pace with technological developments, resulting in a void of protection of communications conveyed through new services. https://eur-lex.europa.eu/legal-content/EN/TXT/PDF/?uri=CELEX:52017PC0010.

[42] COM(2017) 10 final2017/0003 (COD)Proposal for a Regulation of the European Parliament and of the Council concerning the respect for private life and the protection of personal data in electronic communications and repealing Directive 2002/58/EC (Regulation on Privacy and Electronic Communications).

4.3 The AI Act: Possible Repercussions on Emotional AI, Threat to Wellbeing?

Based on the concept of risk assessment, the Artificial Intelligence Act[43] (AIA) is being enacted to regulate AI. The AIA can be classified as a form of preventive or proactive (as opposed to reactive) law, meaning that the approach to law is based on an ex-ante, rather than an ex-post view.[44] In April 2021, the Proposal for the Act was published by the Commission aiming to address different risks of AI applications, divided into four different risk categories: unacceptable risk, high risk, limited risk, and minimal risk. In the Act, although the text is presented as being "technology neutral", this seems rather strange as the act regulates the technological character of AI and the claim to technological neutrality is also disproved by mention of different technological AI applications in the different annexes. The question is whether the risk-based approach is not hampering the use of AI and emotional data in circumstances that could enhance the wellbeing of people, for instance, help of the elderly, by making it more complicated to use sensoring devices for biometric and emotional signals.

The scope of the AIA is directed to all AI providers and users, also outside the EU if the output or result is in the EU.[45] The orientation is a human-centric approach, in the sense that all development and use of AI-related applications should be guided by certain essential (human) value-oriented principles. This is believed to enhance and promote the protection of rights covered by the European Charter of Fundamental Rights (CFR), especially human dignity, democracy, respect for human rights, and the rule of law. Depending on the level of risk the AI can generate, the AIA follows a risk-based approach and establishes obligations for providers and users. With an unacceptable level of risk to people's safety and integrity, under the act, AI systems would be strictly prohibited, including systems that deploy subliminal or purposefully manipulative techniques (as explained in the next section), exploit people's vulnerabilities or are used for social scoring (for instance, classifying people based on their social behaviour, socio-economic status, or personal characteristics). Although there might be some "lighter" AI applications, emotion-related AI systems are mainly categorized under the category forbidden or are at least high-risk level. This means that wellbeing enhancing AI systems will be hindered by complex assessment procedures or will even be prohibited to use under workplace or education related circumstances.

---

[43] REGULATION (EU) 2024/1689 OF THE EUROPEAN PARLIAMENT AND OF THE COUNCIL of 13 June 2024 laying down harmonised rules on artificial intelligence and amending Regulations (EC) No 300/2008, (EU) No 167/2013, (EU) No 168/2013, (EU) 2018/858, (EU) 2018/1139 and (EU) 2019/2144 and Directives 2014/90/EU, (EU) 2016/797 and (EU) 2020/1828 (Artificial Intelligence Act) [https://eur-lex.europa.eu/legal-content/EN/TXT/HTML/?uri=OJ:L_202401689]

[44] Brown Louis (1950).

[45] Scope, article 2 AIA.

Looking at the AI Act, several of the current articles could play a role in terms of the acceptability or non-acceptance of emotional AI systems. Indeed, Article 5 in the final text bans certain applications because of: "the potential threat to citizens' rights and democracy posed by certain applications of AI". Article 5 provides examples of such applications: "the co-legislators agreed to prohibit: biometric categorisation systems that use sensitive characteristics (e.g. political, religious, philosophical beliefs, sexual orientation, race); untargeted scraping of facial images from the internet or CCTV footage to create facial recognition databases; emotion recognition in the workplace and educational institutions; social scoring based on social behaviour or personal characteristics; AI systems that manipulate human behaviour to circumvent their free will; AI used to exploit the vulnerabilities of people (due to their age, disability, social or economic situation)". Specifically a ban on the use of an important element of human well-being in the form of processing and interpreting emotions could have counter-productive effects as now ordained in the area of education and workplace in Article 5.1. (f) "the placing on the market, the putting into service for this specific purpose, or the use of AI systems to infer emotions of a natural person in the areas of workplace and education institutions, except where the use of the AI system is intended to be put in place or into the market for medical or safety reasons".

Logically, the (mis)use of AI systems in these examples could deprive people of a feeling of wellbeing. However, the positive use of AI systems should also be possible in the case of using emotion data for avoiding stress or detecting anomalies in the workplace and educational institutions as relevant human-centric applications. Even though the ban would not be that absolute concerning emotion recognition systems if it concerns safety and medical applications,[46] it is still a quite restrictive approach, based on the fears as describe in recital 44 of the AIA:" There are serious concerns about the scientific basis of AI systems aiming to identify or infer emotions, particularly as expression of emotions vary considerably across cultures and situations, and even within a single individual. Among the key shortcomings of such systems are the limited reliability, the lack of specificity and the limited generalisability. Therefore, AI systems identifying or inferring emotions or intentions of natural persons on the basis of their biometric data may lead to discriminatory outcomes and can be intrusive to the rights and freedoms of the concerned persons. Considering the imbalance of power in the context of work or education, combined with the intrusive nature of these systems, such systems could lead to detrimental or unfavourable treatment of certain natural persons or whole groups thereof. Therefore, the placing on the market, the putting into service, or the use of AI systems intended to be used to detect the emotional state of individuals in situations related to the workplace and education should be prohibited. That prohibition should not cover AI systems placed on the market strictly for medical or safety

[46] https://www.europarl.europa.eu/news/en/press-room/20231206IPR15699/artificial-intelligence-act-deal-on-comprehensive-rules-for-trustworthy-ai. See all documents concerning the AIA: https://artificialintelligenceact.eu/documents/.

reasons, such as systems intended for therapeutical use. It should be considered that physical expressions-data that would be allowed also are representations of emotions, and the extended processing would be acceptable. Also, the inference of emotions by AI systems resulting in changing the atmosphere and physical environment by sound, lightning, vibrations or other physically enhancing systems should not be excluded from being further developed and introduced into the market if they clearly enhance the comfort and wellbeing of people in the workplace environment and educational institutions Indeed, one could easily be positively influenced by AI initiated music or lighting during work or an exam. In this respect, what is the difference with non-AI initiated emotions? Recognizing and inferring emotions for the good of people on an individual- or group basis should be allowed when they are sufficiently informed according to the legal requirements.[47] Moreover, the use of wellbeing enhancing AI, specifically oriented to disabled and elderly people can be considered positive, but the question is if it will be allowed under the specifications in Article 5.

4.3.1 Psychological Influence of Subliminal Techniques

In addition to the aforementioned, 'the placing on the market, putting into service or use of an AI system that deploys subliminal techniques beyond a person's consciousness in order to materially distort a person's behaviour in a manner that causes or is likely to cause that person or another person physical or psychological harm' can certainly influence one's well-being.[48] Although not specifically directed at the prohibition of emotional data, but rather directed at biometric and other characteristics-related data that seem to include emotional data, there is the exception that this prohibition will not apply to AI systems intended to be used for approved therapeutic purposes based on the specific informed consent of the individuals that are exposed to them or, where applicable, of their legal guardian. This exception could very well be extended to more specific AI applications that process emotional data, certainly if it can be used to improve the physical and/or mental wellbeing of people. Therefore, necessary human-centric applications in the workplace could be allowed to increase safety and wellbeing.

[47] Article 52 (2) AI Act sets out that people exposed to emotion recognition systems must be informed about it. Any data must be processed in accordance with the GDPR.

[48] Also, the digital service Act (DSA Article 25(1)) specifically targets these practices, prohibiting platforms from using interface designs that mislead, manipulate, or impair users' abilities to make informed decisions. However, this article is limited to 'online platforms', not including any other applications. The DSA is directed to the users autonomy, choices, and decision-making processes.

5 Conclusion: Increasing Wellbeing with a Little Help of My Friend AI?

If we want to stimulate the use of AI to create a higher level of well- a more positive oriented regulation of AI technology would help to create a sustainable future. Considering AI as well as the use of personal data to increase wellbeing in the emotional AI domain, we have to take into account the latest principles of the UN advisory group of December 2023.[49] The first and foremost principle is stated:

> AI should be governed inclusively, by and for the benefit of all", meaning that: "Despite its potential, many of the world's peoples are not yet able to access and use AI in a manner that meaningfully improves their lives. Fully harnessing the potential of AI and enabling widespread participation in its development, deployment, and use is critical to driving sustainable solutions to global challenges. All citizens, including those in the Global South, should be able to create their own opportunities, harness them, and achieve prosperity through AI. All countries, big or small, must be able to participate in AI governance.

Stressing the wellbeing of all people by using the potential of AI and actively participate in the further development of its use, beneficial to all should be more stressed in the AI Act as well.

Principle 5 of the UN group has a keen eye on the wellbeing of people regarding human rights and sustainability by stating that: "AI governance should be anchored in the UN Charter, International Human Rights Law, and other agreed international commitments such as the Sustainable Development Goals". There are more AI applications that can use data as well to create emotional effects for the good of deprived or disabled people. Within the actual text of Article 5 of the AIA, AI systems that analyse and create positive emotions and change of behaviour in education and in workplaces would also be forbidden. A more specified description is needed here. Therefore, it would help to define emotion data and stimulate the beneficial use of emotional AI systems that improve wellbeing. Moreover, it should be clear that only the harmful use of such systems would be forbidden. Currently, there is no clear line between emotion data, emotional AI systems and biometric data processing systems and the application of Article 5. Consequently, the regulators of the EU must take the principle of stimulating wellbeing in its widest sense into account. This kind of more openness to flexibility, recognizing the positive effects of processing emotional data would thus create wellbeing in society and benefit the developers of AI systems.

Legal Instruments

Council of Europe Framework Convention on Artificial Intelligence and Human Rights, Democracy and the Rule of Law. https://rm.coe.int/1680afae3c

[49] Interim Report: Governing AI for Humanity http://www.un.org/en/ai-advisory-body.

Charter Of Fundamental Rights Of The European Union (2000/C 364/01)
Regulation Of The European Parliament And Of The Council Laying Down Harmonised Rules On Artificial Intelligence, May 2024, 2021/0106(COD)
Regulation (EU) 2022/2065 of the European Parliament and of the Council of 19 October 2022 on a Single Market For Digital Services and amending Directive 2000/31/EC (Digital Services Act)
Proposal for a Regulation of the European Parliament and of the Council concerning the respect for private life and the protection of personal data in electronic communications and repealing Directive 2002/58/EC (Regulation on Privacy and Electronic Communications). COM(2017) 10 final2017/0003 (COD)
International covenant economic social and cultural rights (1969)
Universal Declaration on Human Rights (1948)
The United Nations Convention on the Rights of the Child (20 November 1989),

Reports a.o.

Interim Report: Governing AI for Humanity http://www.un.org/en/ai-advisory-body
Numbeo, quality of life https://www.numbeo.com/quality-of-life/rankings_by_country.jsp.
World Happiness Report https://happiness-report.s3.amazonaws.com/2023/WHR+23.pdf(This

References

Aristotle, Nicomachean Ethics (I.2 1094a21–22)
Brackett MA, Mayer JD, Warner RM (2004) Emotional intelligence and its relation to everyday behaviour. Pers Individ Dif 36:1387–1402. https://doi.org/10.1016/S0191-8869(03)00236-8
Brown Louis M (1950) Preventive law. Prentice-Hall, New York
Corrales Compagnucci M, Fenwick M, Haapio H, Minssen T & Vermeulen EPM (2021) Technology-driven disruption of healthcare & “UI Layer” privacy-by-design. In: Corrales Compagnucci M, Wilson ML, Fenwick M, Forgó N, Bärnighausen T (eds) AI in eHealth: human autonomy, data governance & privacy in healthcare. Cambridge University Press, Cambridge
Damasio A, Carvalho GB (2013) The nature of feelings: evolutionary and neurobiological origins. Nat ReNeurosci 14:143–152. https://doi.org/10.1038/nrn3403
Dawson J (2018) The fluidity of time: scientists uncover how emotions alter time perception (Oct. 2018) https://www.psychologicalscience.org/observer/the-fluidity-of-time
Elyoseph Z (2023) ChatGPT outperforms humans in emotional awareness evaluations. Front Psychol Emotion Science 14:1199058l. https://doi.org/10.3389/fpsyg.2023.1199058
Graham S, Depp C, Lee EE, Nebeker C, Tu X, Kim HC, Jeste DV (2019) Artificial intelligence for mental health and mental illnesses: an overview. Curr Psychiatry Rep 21(11):116. https://doi.org/10.1007/s11920-019-1094-0. PMID: 31701320; PMCID: PMC7274446

Hess JD, Bacigalupo AC (2011) Enhancing decisions and decision-making processes through the application of emotional intelligence skills. Manage Decision 49(5):ISSN: 0025-1747, Article publication date: 31 May 2011

Kraut R (2015) Citing: Aristotle on well-being (1095a1from: The Routledge handbook of philosophy of well-being. Routledge

Landers Richard N, Behrend Tara S (2023) Auditing the AI auditors: a framework for evaluating fairness and bias in high stakes AI predictive models. Am Psychol 0003066X, 20230101, 78(1)

Locke J, Two treatises of Government https://oll.libertyfund.org/title/hollis-the-two-treatises-of-civil-government-hollis-ed#lf0057_label_207

Maslow 1962; Ventegodt et al. (Maslow, 1943; 1954; 1962; 1970a; 1970b; 1987, 2003a; 2003b; 2003c). Maslow (1962), also: Maslow, Abraham H. Am J Psychoanal New York 23(2)

Peter Burgess J, Floridi J, Pols A, van den Hoven J (2018) Towards a digital ethics EDPS Ethics Advisory Group, Report 2018, p 11, Available at: https://edps.europa.eu/sites/default/files/publication/18-01-25_eag_report_en.pdf

Rainer R, Andrea H, Weber H (2020) Personality and emotions. In: Philip JC, Matthews G (eds) The Cambridge handbook of personality psychology. Cambridge University Press, pp 81–100. https://doi.org/10.1017/9781108264822.009

Van der Sloot B (2015) Privacy as personality right: why the ECtHR's focus on ulterior interests might prove indispensable in the age of "Big Data". Utrecht J Int Eur Law 31(80):25–50

Yanqi G (2023) Examining the impact of assistive technology on psychological health, family education, and curriculum research in Japan: insights from artificial intelligence. J Autism Dev Disord. (PsycInfo Database Record (c) 2023

On AI That Knows How We Feel, Without Knowing Who We Are: EU Law and the Processing of Soft Biometric Data by Emotional AI

Eline L. Leijten and Arno R. Lodder

Abstract Increasingly, peoples' emotions are datafied through emotional AI. In recent years, the development and deployment of emotional AI has evolved rapidly. One category of data processed by emotional AI is biometric data: hard biometric data, relating to identified or identifiable individuals, and soft biometric data, that cannot identify or single out individuals. Both the processing of hard biometric data and soft biometric data allow to manipulate individuals, and as such may constitute a violation of fundamental rights: in particular, the right to human dignity; the right to a private and family life; and the right to the protection of personal data. Besides those human rights, at an EU level, hard biometric data fall within the scope of the General Data Protection Regulation (GDPR). By definition, as soft biometric data do not enable the identification of an individual, they remain outside the remit of the GDPR. In this chapter we argue that the European Union (EU) regulatory regime governing the usage of emotional AI technologies that process soft biometric data insufficiently safeguards the full exercise of the aforementioned fundamental rights. We analyse the AI Act, and the various inconsistencies it exhibits, prompting questions on its expected effectiveness in regulating the processing of soft biometric data by emotional AI.

1 Introduction

Arguably, few functions of the human brain are more intriguing and intimate than emotions. Emotions are paramount aspects in the context of self-construction and self-perception, play an essential role in social interactions, and define human relationships, influencing how people relate to one another as well as to the external

E. L. Leijten (✉) · A. R. Lodder
Amsterdam Law and Technology Institute, Vrije Universiteit, Amsterdam, The Netherlands
e-mail: e.l.leijten@vu.nl; a.r.lodder@vu.nl

R. Ballardini et al. (eds.), *Emotional Data Applications and Regulation of Artificial Intelligence in Society*, Law, Governance and Technology Series 69,
https://doi.org/10.1007/978-3-031-80111-2_6

world.[1] Until recently, human emotions were merely captured through non-automated processes, e.g. displayed in works of art, described in reports, photographed, or filmed. However, since the emergence and widespread adoption of technologies that allow for the datafication of practically all facets of human life,[2] and specifically the rise of affective computing, emotions can be converted into machine-readable data and processed at scale. In 1995, the term 'affective computing' was coined by Picard, as 'computing that relates to, arises from, or influences emotion'.[3] While commonly used interchangeably with affective computing, emotional AI specifically refers to the application of AI in the field of affective computing: 'technologies that use affective computing and artificial intelligence techniques to sense, learn about and interact with human emotional life'.[4]

Next to a widening range of emotional AI applications used in public services, such as healthcare, education and border controls, emotional AI is rapidly gaining traction in the private sector, ranging from, e.g., the retail sector and the workplace to the automotive industry.[5] The rollout of a myriad of emotional AI technologies naturally results in extensive data processing. From a data protection perspective, it is critical to note that the deployment of emotional AI does not necessarily lead to the ability to either directly or indirectly identify the people whose emotions are processed. A well-known example is sentiment analysis on social media. This form of analysis is not focused on who says what, but aims to derive sentiments at an aggregate level. In this chapter, we focus on another category of emotional data, i.e., biometric data. Two types of biometric data processed by emotional AI can be distinguished.[6] Firstly, biometric data processed by emotional AI that allow for the identification of data subjects are referred to as hard biometric data.[7] If, however, biometric data processed by emotional AI fail to identify individuals, those data fall within the second type of biometric data, the realm of soft biometrics, a term introduced by Jain et al.:

---

[1] Albano (2008), pp. 494–497.

[2] Newell and Marabelli (2015), pp. 3–14.

[3] Picard (1995).

[4] McStay (2020), pp. 1–12.

[5] In the workplace, emotional AI is a.o. used to foster employee happiness and productivity by optimising the timing of breaks, to improve interaction with audiences during virtual presentations and to deploy after-meeting feedback loops. Examples in the other industries will be elaborated in the next section. See Roemich et al. (2023).

[6] Besides biometric data, AI systems can process other data on the basis of which information about peoples' emotions can be inferred, commonly referred to as 'emotional data'. For example, this holds for AI technologies monitoring (comment sections on) social media platforms, since messages shared on social media platforms can reveal information about a person's emotional state. A message on social media does not constitute biometric data, yet could amount to emotional data. This chapter solely focuses on (soft) biometric data processing by emotional AI.

[7] Biometric data that allow for the singling out of individuals are thereby classified as hard biometric data, see McStay (2020), pp. 1–12.

> We define soft biometric traits as characteristics that provide some information about the individual, but lack the distinctiveness and permanence to sufficiently differentiate any two individuals.[8]

For long, biometric data was not explicitly regulated within the EU. Although Directive 95/46 was applicable to biometric data, it did not mention biometric data.[9] However, this changed when the GDPR introduced a definition of biometric data. Obviously, within the context of the GDPR this only concerns hard biometric data.[10] Unlike hard biometric data, the processing of soft biometric data by emotional AI is hardly regulated, while the application of emotional AI processing soft biometric data may seriously hinder the exercise of fundamental rights.

This chapter assesses whether the EU regulatory regime governing the processing of soft biometric data by emotional AI is adequate to safeguard the fundamental rights that may be affected by it, and if not, whether additional regulation is required for EU member states to fulfil their positive obligations to safeguard their citizens' effective exercise of fundamental rights, also in horizontal relations. The chapter is structured as follows. To set the scene, Sect. 2 discusses a non-exhaustive range of examples of applications that use emotional AI to process soft biometric data. Then Sect. 3 assesses to what extent fundamental rights may be impacted by the processing of soft biometric data by emotional AI, covering the right to human dignity, as enshrined in Article 1 of the EU Charter of Fundamental Rights (Charter); the right to private and family life further to Article 7 of the Charter and Article 8 of the European Convention on Human Rights (ECHR); and the right to the protection of personal data, as established in Article 8 of the Charter. This is followed by Sect. 4 which discusses the EU regulatory regime governing the processing of soft biometric data by emotional AI. This section starts with an analysis of the definition of personal data as laid down in the GDPR, to substantiate why soft biometrics fall outside of the GDPR's scope. It proceeds with an exploration of the relevant provisions in the Artificial Intelligence Act (AI Act), demonstrating that the AI Act fails to adequately safeguard the fundamental rights that may be violated by non-identifying emotional AI. Section 5 concludes with an analysis on whether the current EU regulatory regime governing the processing of soft biometric data by emotional AI is sufficiently equipped to uphold the fundamental rights that may be compromised by these data processing practices, and if not, how this could be remedied.

---

[8] Jain et al. (2004).

[9] Directive 95/46/EC of the European Parliament and of the Council of 24 October 1995 on the protection of individuals with regard to the processing of personal data and on the free movement of such data, *OJ L 281, 23.11.1995*; Sprokkereef and Cehajic (2009).

[10] Regulation (EU) 2016/679 of the European Parliament and of the Council of 27 April 2016 on the protection of natural persons with regard to the processing of personal data and on the free movement of such data, and repealing Directive 95/46/EC (General Data Protection Regulation), *OJ L 119, 4.5.2016.*

2 Non-Identifying Emotional AI: A (Non-Exhaustive) Overview of Applications

Technological advances have catalysed the adoption of (emotional) AI across industries. An example of 'non identifying emotional AI' can be found in stationary (food) retail. Shops seek recourse to emotional AI to track visitors' moods (often claimingly without the ability to identify them) with the purpose of improving the in-store experience based on these data, e.g. through personalised advertising. For instance, Pizza Hut has recently rolled out "an AI-powered mood detector technology" in a range of its restaurants. Based on their detected moods, allegedly without identifying them, this detector delivers tailor-made recommendations to visitors on what pizza to order.[11] As the aim of linking the mood to a particular pizza can be realised without knowing which person's emotions are being processed, there is no need to identify the individual. Naturally, it is conceivable that identification of the visitor whose mood is detected *is* possible when combining multiple datasets, in this example, e.g. after payment of a pizza, in combination with personal data linked to a loyalty card programme. However, without additional data, 'non-identifying emotional AI' is not able to identify individuals. Obviously, the person may be identified if some crime took place in the Pizza Hut, but in that case the detected mood is irrelevant.

A second example concerns the experimentation with AI-powered 'communicative prostheses' for people who encounter difficulties in communicating with others, for instance because of autism spectrum disorders,[12] helping them to 'read' emotions of those they interact with.[13]

Third, with the aim of enhancing road safety, ongoing innovation in the automotive industry under the umbrella of 'in-vehicle connectivity' has yielded a range of emotional AI systems implemented in vehicles to monitor emotions in order to detect drivers' attention or distraction.[14] In the context of autonomous cars, the enhancement of *perceived* car safety is a key purpose to which emotional AI is considered to contribute, further fostering the advent of emotional AI within the

[11] Hindustan Times Tech (2023).

[12] Xiao et al. (2020); Somers (2019).

[13] One technology named the 'Brain Power Autism System' combines augmented reality and emotional AI in smart glasses that help children with autism recognise other peoples' emotions. It entails a game that lets children find faces of people around them, detects the emotional state of these faces, and asks the children to pick the right emotion. See Keshav et al. (2017); Forbes (2018).

[14] The development of this category of emotional AI in the automotive industry is exacerbated by the European Commission's determination to involve technology in pursuit of its goal to reduce road fatalities, as illustrated by the EU's General Safety Regulation, Regulation 2019/2144 (GSR), mandating in Article 6(1)(d) GSR the installment of advanced driver distraction warning (ADDW) systems in all new vehicles per 7 July 2024. Although arguably ADDW systems under the GSR do not necessarily amount to emotional AI, under the same umbrella of the advancement of road safety, the systems car manufacturers install in practice often do involve emotional AI. See McStay and Urquhart (2022).

automotive industry. This is illustrated by the EU-funded project 'SUpporting acceptance of automated VEhicle' (SUaaVE), launched to develop in-vehicle software that detects the emotions of passengers of autonomous vehicles. As the purpose of the detection of emotions enables vehicles to react to their passengers' detected emotional states, e.g. through adjustment of driving style,[15] the vehicles are referred to as 'empathic vehicles'.[16]

Although the accuracy of emotional AI technology in detecting human emotions remains subject to scrutiny,[17] it is expected that its emergence will not come to a halt anytime soon.

3 Soft Biometrics and Emotional AI from a Fundamental Rights Perspective

As soft biometric data are non-identifying, one could argue they therefore do not impact the person to whom the data are related. In this section, we refute such a claim and contend that the processing of soft biometrics by emotional AI can be at odds with several fundamental rights.

3.1 The Right to Human Dignity (Article 1 of the Charter)

As the basis of all fundamental rights,[18] and a founding value of the EU further to Article 2 of the Treaty on the European Union (TEU), the right to human dignity is inviolable and inalienable.[19] Despite its significance, as also witnessed by being Article 1 of the Charter, the Charter lacks clarity on the exact meaning of human dignity. This remarkable ambiguity, in combination with a scarcity of CJEU case

[15] These systems will likely process a combination of hard biometric data, or personal data under the GDPR, and soft biometric data. Note, however, that De Montjoye et al. demonstrated that 95% of all individuals are uniquely identifiable based on only four spatio-temporal points (pieces of information, regarding space and time), e.g. collected from smartphones. It thus seems unlikely that persons who frequently travel in a particular vehicle and connect their mobile devices to the car's audio system are not identifiable on the basis of their data processed by in-vehicle emotional AI. These data hence presumably constitute hard biometric data. Conversely, depending on the emotional AI system, occasional passengers whose emotions are detected by emotional AI may be unidentifiable. See De Montjoye et al. (2013); Article 29 Working Party (2013); European Network and Information Security Agency (2018); De Conca (2021) Accessed 25 January 2024.

[16] European Commission (2023).

[17] See, e.g., Whittaker et al. (2018).

[18] See also Universal Declaration of Human Rights (UDHR), Article 1 'All human beings are born free and equal in dignity and rights'.

[19] Dupré (2013), p. 319.

law on Article 1 of the Charter, has led scholars to argue that human dignity ought to be left undefined, i.e. held *conceptually open*, for the concept to remain an 'anthropological reservoir of meaning' (*anthropologisches Sinnreservoir)* that can serve as the basis for the formulation of new approaches to safeguarding humanity.[20]

The conceptualisation of human dignity as it has evolved in existing scholarship is most notably rooted in the work of Immanuel Kant, in which the concept revolves around the unequivocal prohibition to instrumentalise people, that is, to use people simply as means.[21] Moreover, human dignity is closely tied to autonomy and agency. The human rights discourse on human dignity has focused on protecting bodily integrity rather than mental autonomy.[22] However, the emergence of AI has given rise to the question whether human dignity provides an appropriate basis to restrict or prohibit certain artificial intelligence applications, hence to prevent humans from being instrumentalised or objectified. Specifically, UNESCO names ethics as 'a dynamic basis for the normative evaluation and guidance of AI technologies', and mentions human dignity as one of the cornerstones to serve as a compass.[23]

Assessing the relevance of human dignity firstly requires acknowledging that despite the inability to identify, soft biometric data can be deployed to manipulate people.[24] To address the sophisticated capacities digital technologies nowadays have, this analysis adheres to the definition of online manipulation as developed by Susser et al.:

> the use of information technology to covertly influence another person's decision-making, by targeting and exploiting their decision-making vulnerabilities.[25]

Concisely, as Susser et al. contend, manipulation amounts to hidden influence. One can think of the discussed AI systems in stationary retail that keep track of visitors' emotions[26] to customise the in-store experience to maximise visitors' in-store spend.[27] Even if such emotional AI fails to identify visitors, the data processed by the technology reveals information pertaining to individuals, may exhibit certain

---

[20] Dupré (2021); Sacco (2005), p. 596; Rixen (2006), p. 345; Häberle (2005).

[21] Bayefsky (2013), p. 811; Bognetti (2005), p. 89.

[22] Since the adoption of the UDHR in 1948, the legal concept of human dignity has served as (one of) the primary ground(s) for other human rights instruments to prohibit *inter alia* slavery, inhuman or degrading treatment, and commercialisation of the human body. See Dicke (2002), pp. 111–120; Zardiashvilli and Fosch-Villaronga (2020), p. 123; Beyleveld and Brownsword (1998), pp. 661–680.

[23] UNESCO (2019).

[24] McStay (2020), pp. 1–12.

[25] Susser et al. (2019).

[26] Nguyen et al. (2022).

[27] For instance, the company 'eyeQ' has developed an emotional AI system that detects facial emotional reactions as visitors walk through a shop and look at the shelves, to subsequently customise in-store marketing based on this data processing. See McStay (2018).

vulnerabilities, and covertly influence their decision-making, thus amounting to manipulation.

Considered through the lens of human dignity, manipulation is problematic as in short, it undermines people's autonomy.[28] Deploying non-identifying emotional AI to manipulate people, be it in a retail context or elsewhere, is at odds with the prohibition to instrumentalise or objectify people and thus infringes on their dignity.[29] Even if the processing of soft biometric data by emotional AI does not meet the threshold to be considered manipulative, it may still constitute a violation of the right to human dignity cf. Article 1 of the Charter. This is due to the inseparable intertwinement of the right to human dignity and another fundamental right that may be affected by such data processing practices:[30] the right to privacy (Article 7 of the Charter and Article 8 of the ECHR). As emphasised amongst others by the European Data Protection Supervisor (EDPS) in 2015,

> privacy is an integral part of human dignity, and the right to data protection was originally conceived in the 1970s and 80s as a way of compensating the potential for the erosion of privacy and dignity through large scale personal data processing.[31]

Therefore, the processing of soft biometric data by emotional AI that 'merely' constitutes a violation of the right to privacy in Article 8 of the ECHR and Article 7 of the Charter may also amount to an interference with the right to human dignity. This conclusion is endorsed by the EDPS in the following statement:

> turning the human face into another object for measurement and categorisation by automated processes controlled by powerful companies and governments touches the right to human dignity.[32]

3.2 *The Right to Privacy (Article 8 of the ECHR and Article 7 of the Charter) and the Right to Data Protection (Article 8 of the Charter)*

The processing of soft biometric data by emotional AI may jeopardise the right to privacy established in Article 7 of the Charter and Article 8 of the ECHR.[33]

---

[28] Although some definitions of 'manipulation' might allow for manifestations of manipulation that benefit the person exposed to the manipulation, we argue that the definition we adhere to, amounting to 'exploiting decision-making vulnerabilities', leaves no room for positive forms of manipulation.

[29] The principle of non-commercialisation conveys the idea that people lack dignity once they are used by others as mere objects. See, e.g., De Hingh and Lodder (2020), pp. 261–275.

[30] Floridi (2016), pp. 307–312.

[31] EDPS (2015).

[32] Wiewiórowski (2019).

[33] To illustrate the correspondence between Article 7 of the Charter and Article 8 of the ECHR, see, e.g., Case C-400/10 PPU *J McB v LE* (ECJ, 5 October 2010), § 53, in which the ECJ explicitly referred to Article 52 (3) Charter – the linking pin between the Charter and ECHR.

Although Article 8 of the ECHR primarily aims to protect citizens' privacy vis-à-vis governments,[34] in multiple judgments, the European Court of Human Rights (ECtHR) has stipulated that this provision moreover implies the positive obligation for signatory Member States to secure the protection of the right to privacy in relationships between private parties,[35] including horizontal relationships between individuals.[36]

Further, the ECtHR has repeatedly reiterated that the Article 8 ECHR right must be interpreted broadly and covers the right to protection of personal autonomy and self-determination.[37] As argued, these principles are compromised in cases where the processing of soft biometric data by emotional AI amounts to manipulation. Consequently, the deployment of manipulative non-identifying emotional AI surely interferes with the right to privacy. If it is in accordance with the law and necessary in a democratic society in pursuit of one of the legitimate interests set forth in Article 8(2) of the ECHR, an interference with Article 8 of the ECHR by or on behalf of a public authority can be justifiable. However, it seems unlikely that the deployment of manipulative emotional AI to covertly influence citizens' decision-making in pursuit of a legitimate aim would meet the 'necessary in a democratic society' criterion. Therefore, it is fair to conclude that exposing individuals to manipulative non-identifying emotional AI can be considered not only an interference but also a violation of the right to privacy pursuant to Article 8 of the ECHR.

Due to the broad scope of the sphere of private life under Article 8 of the ECHR, the processing of soft biometric data by emotional AI that does *not* meet the threshold of manipulation may interfere with the right to privacy further to Article 8 of the ECHR as well. The ECtHR has ruled that the concept encompasses the bodily and psychological integrity of people and may 'embrace multiple aspects of the person's physical and social identity'.[38] Emotions are pre-eminently a private matter,[39] and while some scholars argue for group conceptions of privacy,[40] it seems that such an extension of the concept is not necessary to conclude that the

[34] ECtHR, *Libert v France,* Fifth Section Judgment of 22 February 2018, Application no. 588/13, § 40–42.

[35] ECtHR, *Bărbulescu v Romania*, Grand Chamber Judgment of 5 September 2017, Application no. 61496/08, §§ 108–111.

[36] ECtHR, *Evans v. The United Kingdom*, Grand Chamber Judgment of 10 April 2007, Application no. 6339/05, § 75; ECtHR, *Marckx v Belgium*, Judgment of 13 June 1979, Series A No. 31.

[37] ECtHR, *Pretty v. the United Kingdom*, Fourth Section Judgment of 29 April 2002, Application no. 2346/02, § 61.

[38] ECtHR, *Denisov v. Ukraine*, Grand Chamber Judgment of 25 September 2018, Application no. 76639/11, § 95; ECtHR, *S. and Marper v. the United Kingdom*, Grand Chamber Judgment of 4 December 2008, Application nos. 30562/04 and 30566/04, § 66.

[39] Research shows that over 50% of UK citizens are 'not OK' with emotion detection by emotional AI, regardless of whether it renders them identifiable or not. Interestingly, people's desire to keep emotions private differs significantly across generations: whereas 66.3% of people aged 65 and older object to emotion detection by emotional AI (regardless of identifiability), this holds for only 31.4% of people aged 18–24. See McStay (2020), p. 10.

[40] Floridi (2014); Van der Sloot (2016).

deployment of non-identifying emotional AI without consent interferes with the individual's right to privacy established in Article 8 of the ECHR.

Non-identifying emotional AI by a public authority can be necessary in a democratic society to pursue a legitimate aim. For instance, the discussed emotional AI in highly autonomous vehicles to enhance road safety may be considered a justifiable interference with passengers' rights to privacy to pursue the legitimate aim of public safety.[41] Assessing this adequately would require an in-depth analysis of the clarity of the law (which is not there yet) and the proportionality of this major interference with privacy, taking into account the contributions of such emotion recognition systems to the public acceptance of autonomous driving, and the impact of autonomous driving on road safety. For now, we conclude that emotional AI processing soft biometric data in highly autonomous vehicles pursuant to forthcoming legislation could entail a justifiable interference with the right in Article 8 of the ECHR. So whether non-manipulative, non-identifying emotional AI violates peoples' right to privacy further to Article 8 of the ECHR is less straightforward. If emotional AI is deployed by a private organisation or in horizontal relationships between citizens, the derogation clause in Article 8(2) of the ECHR bears no relevance, and without consent of the natural person exposed to such emotional AI, a violation of Article 8 of the ECHR seems evident.[42]

Article 8 of the Charter guarantees the protection of personal data, as a separate fundamental right that has no equivalent in the ECHR.[43] By definition, as soft biometric data fails to identify natural persons, the processing of soft biometric data by emotional AI is not covered by Article 8 of the Charter.[44] This provision cannot be viewed in isolation, however, as the ECtHR has asserted that Article 8 of the ECHR includes a right to data protection as well. Interestingly, the concept of data protection to which the scope of Article 8 of the ECHR extends also covers data

[41] The European Commission has expressed its belief in the potential of autonomous driving to compensate for human errors and thereby enhance road safety. See European Commission (2019).

[42] Not all data processing engages Article 8 of the ECHR; if consent for a certain practice is given, that practice does not interfere with the Article 8 rights. See regarding the role of 'consent' in case law on Article 8 of the ECHR, e.g., *Malone v the UK* where the ECtHR held that the release of telephone metering data to the police *without the consent* of the subscriber amounts to an interference with the right guaranteed by Article 8 of the ECHR (emphasis added), ECtHR *Malone v the UK*, Judgment of 2 August 1984, application no. 8691/79, § 84.

[43] See 'Article 8 of the Charter concerns a fundamental right which is distinct from that enshrined in Article 7 of the Charter and which has no equivalent in the ECHR' (Joined Cases C-203/15 and C-698/15, Tele2 Sverige and Watson and Others, EU:C:2016:970, § 129).

[44] The Article 8 Charter right to protection of personal data is based on Article 286 of the Treaty establishing the European Community (now replaced by Article 16 of the Treaty on the Functioning of the European Union (TFEU) and Article 39 TEU) and Directive 95/46/EC (Data Protection Directive). Further to Article 2(a) Data Protection Directive, 'personal data' means 'any information relating to an identified or identifiable natural person'.

"relating to an individual's private life",[45] which might include, e.g., aggregated data and group data.[46] Whether data pertains to one's private life depends amongst others on the nature of the data, the context and results of the data processing.[47] Given its highly intimate nature, it seems plausible to assume that the processing of emotional data falls within the scope of data pertaining to one's private life, protected by Article 8 of the ECHR.[48]

4 EU Regulation on the Processing of Soft Biometric Data by Emotional AI

4.1 Outside the Remit of the General Data Protection Regulation

The GDPR leaves no doubt about its scope: the processing of *personal* data. Article 4(1) GDPR defines 'personal data' as 'any information relating to an identified or identifiable natural person'. Consequently, the processing of data that fail to identify any individual falls outside the scope of the GDPR.[49] With regard to the processing of amongst others biometric data, Article 9(4) of the GDPR offers room for Member States to introduce further conditions, including limitations. In Article 4(14) of the GDPR, 'biometric data' is defined as 'personal data resulting from specific technical processing relating to the physical, physiological or behavioural characteristics of a natural person, *which allow or confirm the unique identification of that natural person*, such as facial images or dactyloscopic data'. Not surprisingly, non-identifying soft biometric data are not included in the definition of biometric

[45] ECtHR, *Amann v Switzerland*, Grand Chamber Judgment of 16 February 2000, application no. 27798/95, § 65; ECtHR *Rotaru v Romania, Grand Chamber Judgment of 4 May 2000,* application no. 28341/95, § 43.

[46] Van der Sloot et al. (2022), p. 76.

[47] ECtHR, *S. and Marper v. the United Kingdom*, Grand Chamber Judgment of 4 December 2008, application no. 30562/04 and 30566/04, § 67; ECtHR, *Uzun v. Germany*, Judgment of 2 September 2010, application no. 35623/05, § 52; ECtHR, *Khelili v. Switzerland*, Judgment of 18 October 2011, application no. 16188/07; ECtHR, *P.G. and J.H. v. the United Kingdom*, Judgment of 25 September 2001, application no. 44787/98; § 57 & 59; Mostert et al. (2017), pp. 1–13.

[48] The ECtHR interpreted the term 'private life' as not being limited to matters of the private sphere of an individual. See ECtHR, *Amann v Switzerland*, Grand Chamber Judgment of 16 February 2000, application no. 27798/95, § 65.

[49] Remarkably, Article 29 Working Party (WP29) already took note of soft biometrics, albeit through a rather undecisive remark: 'Mention should also be made of the use of the so-called soft biometrics defined by the use of very common traits not suitable to clearly distinguish or identify an individual but that allow enhancing the performance of other identification systems', see WP29 (2012).

data. As McStay rightfully argues,[50] if biometric data can single out an individual, they are hard biometric data by definition.[51]

4.2 *The AI Act*

As the first global landmark regulation to govern the development and deployment of artificial intelligence, the AI Act is characterised by a risk-based approach. It defines four levels of risk: (1) AI practices that are prohibited due to unacceptable risk (Article 5), (2) high-risk AI systems (Article 6) subject to strict obligations before they can be marketed, (3) limited risk AI systems, and (4) minimal risk AI systems. The following discussion of the relevant provisions in the AI Act first elaborates upon the provisions of specific relevance to the processing of soft biometric data by emotional AI. Subsequently, the relevant AI Act provisions with a broader scope are analysed.

4.2.1 Biometric Data

Firstly, Article 3(34) of the AI Act defines biometric data, remarkably not adhering to the definition of biometric data laid down in Article 4(14) of the GDPR, but defining 'biometric data' as 'personal data resulting from specific technical processing relating to the physical, physiological or behavioural characteristics of a natural person, such as facial images or dactyloscopic data'. What is noteworthy is that a previous draft of the AI Act sought recourse to the definition of biometric data laid down in the GDPR. In the AI Act, the definition of biometric data is identical to that in the GDPR except for the following phrase only included in the GDPR: 'which allow or confirm the unique identification of that natural person'. Why this phrase is not in the AI Act, and specifically whether this broadens the definition to include soft biometric data, must be considered in a broader context. Firstly, Article 3(33a) of a previous draft of the AI Act presented a definition of so-called 'biometric-based data' as 'data resulting from specific technical processing relating to physical, physiological or behavioural signals of a natural person'. Although the formulation

[50] McStay (2020), pp. 1–12.

[51] Although in earlier scholarship the term 'singling out' has not necessarily been associated with identifiability and the GDPR leaves the term undefined, WP29 defined singling out as 'the possibility to isolate some or all records which identify an individual in the dataset', see WP29 (2014); Wisman and Van der Linden (2008). Interestingly, the European Data Protection Board (EDPB) has not formally endorsed the latter WP29 Opinion, making its status somewhat uncertain, yet Recital 26 GDPR mentions 'singling out' as one of the means one can use to identify a natural person directly or indirectly, thereby associating the term with identifiability as well.

of this definition appeared rather incomplete or at least opaque,[52] the term biometric-based data in this previous draft of the AI Act seemed to address soft biometric data.[53] Nevertheless, the term 'biometric-based data' does not appear in the final version of the AI Act. Omitting the phrase 'which allow or confirm the unique identification of that natural person' from the definition of biometric data in Article 3(34) could reflect an intent to widen the scope of this term.[54] However, to conclude that 'biometric data' under the AI Act also includes soft biometric data would be inadequate: Article 3(34) explicitly limits the scope of biometric data under the AI Act to 'personal data'. As pursuant to Article 3(50), the definition of 'personal data' under the AI Act is equal to that in the GDPR, soft biometric data fall outside the remit of biometric data defined in Article 3(34) of the AI Act.

Consultation of the recitals of the AI Act does not deliver further clarity on what distinguishes the new definition of 'biometric data' from the GDPR. The formulation of Recital 14 merely highlights the opacity that characterises this new definition under the AI Act: 'The notion of 'biometric data' used in this Regulation should be interpreted *in light of* the notion of biometric data as defined in Article 4, point (14) of Regulation (EU) 2016/679 (...) Biometric data *can* allow for the authentication, identification or categorisation of natural persons and for the recognition of emotions of natural persons'. Here, two aspects are particularly unclear. First, what is meant by 'in light of'?[55] Second, 'can allow' is confusing as it seems to suggest that the definition of biometric data in the AI Act has a wider scope than that in the GDPR, which unequivocally states that biometric data 'allow or confirm the unique identification of that natural person'. However, since Article 3(34) of the AI Act limits the scope of 'biometric data' to 'personal data', such expansion of the concept of biometric data as suggested in Recital 14 has not found its way to the provisions of the regulation. Consequently, also under the AI Act, biometric data remains limited to hard biometric data.

---

[52] Strictly speaking, it was not stated that biometric-based data as previously defined in former Article 3(33a) draft AI Act cannot enable the identification of an individual. Moreover, it was unclear how 'signals' in former Article 3(33 a) draft AI Act differed from 'characteristics' in the Article 4(14) GDPR definition of biometric data. This lack of clarity could arguably lead to confusion. Retina scans for example evidently concern the processing of hard biometric data, yet may also meet the definition of 'biometric-based data' under former Article 3(33 a) draft AI Act as the data may relate to physical signals of a natural person.

[53] The addition of the concept of 'biometric-based data' to an earlier draft of the AI Act followed criticism of the original AI Act draft which did not recognise emotion recognition systems not relying on biometric data processing. See Czarnocki (2021).

[54] Another explanation for eliminating these words could be a realisation that the phrase 'which allow or confirm the unique identification of that natural person' in the Article 4(14) GDPR definition of biometric data in fact is redundant, as this is already captured by the term 'personal data' mentioned in this definition.

[55] A previous draft of the AI Act contained a Recital 7, which was unambiguous: 'The notion of biometric data used in this Regulation is in line with and should be interpreted consistently with the notion of biometric data as defined in Article 4(14) of Regulation (EU) 2016/679 of the European Parliament and of the Council'.

4.2.2 Emotion Recognition System

Another concept that needs further discussion is 'emotion recognition system', defined in Article 3(39) of the AI Act as: 'an AI system for the purpose of identifying or inferring emotions or intentions of natural persons on the basis of their biometric data'. This definition does not cover emotion recognition systems that process soft biometric data, since 'biometric data' are personal data. Interestingly, the definition of 'emotion recognition system' in the June 2023 draft of the AI Act included both biometric and biometric-based data, thus covering hard and soft biometric data. In the final AI Act, the definition of 'emotion recognition system' has clearly been narrowed.

Article 5(1)(f) of the AI Act prohibits 'the placing on the market, the putting into service for this specific purpose, or the use of AI systems to infer emotions of a natural person in the areas of workplace and education institutions, except where the use of the AI system is intended to be put in place or into the market for medical or safety reasons'. The AI Act hence categorises the risks associated with these emotional AI systems as unacceptable. It does not address the identifiability of the natural persons exposed to these AI systems, and as such the prohibition's scope extends also to the processing of soft biometric data. The formulation of the prohibition in Article 5(1)(f) raises multiple questions.

Firstly, Article 5(1)(f) only concerns AI systems used to 'infer' emotions. As Article 3(39) defines 'emotion recognition system' as 'an AI system for the purpose of identifying *or* inferring emotions (...)', the legislator clearly distinguishes 'identifying' from 'inferring' emotions. It is however unclear how 'inferring' emotions differs from 'identifying' emotions, and consequently which type of AI-powered emotion recognition technologies fall within the scope of this prohibition. To add to the confusion, Recital 44 contains a third verb, reflected neither in the Article 3(39) definition of 'emotion recognition system' nor in Article 5(1)(f): 'detect': 'Therefore, the placing on the market, the putting into service, or the use of AI systems intended to be used to *detect* the emotional state of individuals in situations related to the workplace and education should be prohibited'. Unfortunately, the AI Act fails to elucidate the differences between 'detect', 'identify' and 'infer'. We hypothesise that 'detect' is the umbrella term that covers both the identification and inference of emotions.[56] However, the AI Act contains no indication that may validate this hypothesis.

Secondly, the restriction to 'areas of workplace and education institutions' raises questions. The rationale behind the prohibition only banning 'AI systems to infer emotions' in the areas of workplace and education institutions is difficult to comprehend. Following considerations on 'serious concerns about the scientific basis of AI systems aiming to identify or infer emotions', highlighting their 'limited

[56] It seems plausible to assume that 'identifying' emotions entails the direct detection or recognition of emotions, and 'inferring' emotions concerns the indirect detection of emotions, whereby data is analysed to derive insights on emotions.

reliability, the lack of specificity, and the limited generalisability', these specific two domains are mentioned in Recital 44 too.[57] Although power imbalance in the context of work or education requires no explanation, power imbalances exist beyond work and education, in horizontal relationships, and notably in vertical relationships between citizens and governments. Why only 'the areas of workplace and education institutions' are included in the Article 5(1)(f) ban remains shrouded in mystery.

Thirdly, it is questionable how the following will play out in practice: 'the placing on the market, the putting into service *for this specific purpose*, or the use of AI systems to infer emotions of a natural person in the areas of (. . .)'. The addition 'for this specific purpose' allows for the putting into service of AI systems that infer emotions of people in the areas mentioned, provided that such is not the specific purpose of the system.

Lastly, a previous version of the AI Act pursued an outright rigid regulatory strategy, pursuant to former Article 5(1)(d c) banning these emotional AI systems entirely from particular areas. The final prohibition in Article 5(1)(f) exhibits more nuance, allowing for the use of these AI systems when they are 'intended to be put in place or into the market for medical or safety reasons'.[58] This added nuance does justice to the value emotional AI may have, e.g., for medical reasons in the field of education. Recalling the AI-powered 'communicative prostheses', for instance, children who experience difficulties in communicating, may greatly benefit from the controlled and consensual usage of such emotional AI systems in schools.[59]

Annex III (1)(c) labels 'AI systems intended to be used for emotion recognition' as high risk. Surprisingly, Annex III (1)(c) does not adhere to any of the definitions in Article 3, so there is reason to assume its scope includes non-identifying emotional AI systems that process soft biometric data. Here, the complicating factor is that pursuant to Annex III (1)(c), those are only classified as high-risk systems if they are '*intended* to be used for emotion recognition'. In practice, this threshold may effectively offer an opportunity for AI system providers to escape the AI Act provisions governing high-risk systems: if the intent criterion is not met, AI systems used for emotion recognition fall outside the scope of Annex III (1)(c) and hence are not considered high-risk under the AI Act. Moreover, remarkably, in a previous version of the AI Act, former Annex III(1)(1)(a a) draft AI Act classified as high risk: 'AI systems intended to be used to make inferences about personal characteristics of natural persons on the basis of biometric or biometrics-based data, including emotion recognition systems, with the exception of those mentioned in Article 5'. This prior draft of the provision hence explicitly excluded from its scope the AI systems

---

[57] Recital 44 contains this sentence: 'Considering the imbalance of power in the context of work or education, combined with the intrusive nature of these systems, such systems could lead to detrimental or unfavourable treatment of certain natural persons or whole groups thereof'.

[58] Recital 44 points out that this includes 'systems intended for therapeutical use'.

[59] Also, allowing the use of these AI systems when they are 'intended to be put in place or into the market for medical or safety reasons' sits well with the potential future installment of emotional AI systems in highly autonomous vehicles, discussed in Sect. 2.

prohibited under Article 5. The lack of that refinement in the final Annex III (1)(c) reduces the clarity of the regulation's risk-based classification system.

The high-risk classification of non-identifying AI systems intended to be used for emotion recognition[60] pursuant to Article 6(2) in conjunction with Annex III(1)(c) leads to the applicability of the strict obligations of Articles 9 to 27. Article 27 is particularly relevant, as this provision mandates a fundamental rights impact assessment for high-risk AI systems to be conducted prior to putting such systems into use. As demonstrated in Sect. 3, the deployment of non-identifying emotional AI may be at odds with several fundamental rights: Article 1 of the Charter, Article 8 of the ECHR and Article 7 of the Charter. Interestingly, a former version of this provision explicitly mandated 'verification that the use of the system is compliant with relevant Union and national law on fundamental rights' (former Article 29 a(d) of the draft AI Act). Such actual fundamental rights compliance assessment is not part of the stripped down final version of Article 27, which is merely limited to amongst others an assessment of 'the categories of natural persons and groups likely to be affected by its use in the specific context' (Article 27(1)(c)) and 'the specific risks of harm likely to have an impact on the categories of natural persons or groups of persons identified pursuant to point (c) of this paragraph (...)' (Article 27(1)(d)). As 'risks of harm likely to have an impact' is utterly generic and detached from relevant Union and national law on fundamental rights, it is questionable whether the significantly diluted Article 27 is still worthy of the name 'Fundamental rights impact assessment for high-risk AI systems'. The fundamental rights impact assessment laid down in Article 27 AI Act appears not sufficiently equipped to safeguard the fundamental rights that may be compromised by the processing of soft biometrics by high-risk emotional AI systems.

4.2.3 Biometric Categorisation System

Article 6(2) of the AI Act in conjunction with Annex III (1)(b) of the AI Act classify as high-risk AI systems: 'AI systems intended to be used for biometric categorisation, according to sensitive or protected attributes or characteristics based on the inference of those attributes or characteristics'. In light of the definition of 'biometric categorisation system' (Article 3(40)),[61] it is not likely that this includes AI systems that process soft biometric data.

---

[60] Yet not prohibited under Article 5.

[61] Pursuant to Article 3(40) of the AI Act, 'biometric categorisation system' means 'an AI system for the purpose of assigning natural persons to specific categories on the basis of their biometric data, unless it is ancillary to another commercial service and strictly necessary for objective technical reasons'.

4.2.4 Generic AI Act Provisions of Relevance

Relevant in the context of manipulative non-identifying emotional AI is the prohibition laid down in Article 5(1)(a) of the AI Act, concerning 'the placing on the market, the putting into service or the use of an AI system that deploys subliminal techniques beyond a person's consciousness or purposefully manipulative or deceptive techniques, with the objective, or the effect of materially distorting the behaviour of a person or a group of persons by appreciably impairing their ability to make an informed decision, thereby causing them to take a decision that they would not have otherwise taken in a manner that causes or is reasonably likely to cause that person, another person or group of persons significant harm'.

In this provision, the thresholds contained have significantly expanded versus its first draft, which prohibited 'the placing on the market, putting into service or use of an AI system that deploys subliminal techniques beyond a person's consciousness in order to materially distort a person's behaviour in a manner that causes or is likely to cause that person or another person physical or psychological harm'. Prima facie, the various thresholds contained in the final Article 5(1)(a) prohibition seem high. In particular, it appears cumbersome to prove that the deployment of subliminal or purposefully manipulative or deceptive techniques has appreciably impaired a person's or group of persons' ability to make an informed decision and has caused them to take a decision that they would not have otherwise taken. If such can be proven, difficulties can be expected with regard to the threshold of a causal relationship between the impairment of decision-making and (the likelihood of) significant harm to that person, another person or a group of persons. Moreover, the lack of clarity on what amounts to 'likely' and 'significant' harm will make it hard to predict what coverage and hence significance this prohibition shall have. Given the range of the thresholds the provision contains, it does not seem unthinkable that the scope of the Article 5(1)(a) shall de facto be marginal.

Secondly, the prohibition codified in Article 5(1)(c) of the AI Act may extend to certain emotional AI systems that process soft biometric data for social scoring purposes. Article 5(1)(c) specifically bans 'the placing on the market, the putting into service or the use of AI systems for the evaluation or classification of natural persons or groups of persons over a certain period of time based on their social behaviour or known, inferred or predicted personal or personality characteristics, with the social score leading to either or both of the following: (i) detrimental or unfavourable treatment of certain natural persons or groups of persons in social contexts that are unrelated to the contexts in which the data was originally generated or collected; (ii) detrimental or unfavourable treatment of certain natural persons or groups of persons that is unjustified or disproportionate to their social behaviour or its gravity'. This provision is of relevance to AI-powered social scoring systems that use emotional AI to infer or predict personal or personality characteristics.

5 Towards Better Protection of Soft Biometric Data

Non-identifying emotional AI may be at odds with several fundamental rights. To reiterate, we distinguish between manipulative non-identifying emotional AI technologies and non-identifying emotional AI technologies that do not manipulate people. Manipulative non-identifying emotional AI technologies violate the right to human dignity established in Article 1 of the Charter as well as the right to privacy pursuant to Article 8 of the ECHR and Article 7 of the Charter. Non-identifying emotional AI technologies that are not manipulative may violate the right to human dignity laid down in Article 1 of the Charter as well and may amount to a violation of Article 8 of the ECHR and Article 7 of the Charter. That is, when non-manipulative non-identifying emotional AI is deployed by a public authority (or by a private organisation to whom a public responsibility has been delegated) in accordance with the law, to pursue a legitimate aim set out in Article 8(2) of the ECHR, it should be assessed on a case-by-case basis whether such interference with privacy can be considered necessary in a democratic society, hence justifiable. In horizontal relationships between citizens or by a private entity (other than in the context of executing a public task), the non-consensual usage of non-identifying emotional AI, also if this does not amount to manipulation, violates the right to privacy in Article 8 of the ECHR and Article 7 of the Charter. Given the intertwinement of the right to privacy and the concept of human dignity, such violation of Article 8 of the ECHR and Article 7 of the Charter arguably constitutes a violation of Article 1 of the Charter as well.

The processing of soft biometric data is not regulated by the GDPR, as these data do not enable identification. Since the AI Act contains several provisions that govern emotional AI systems that process soft biometric data, it provides an interesting basis for the governance of soft biometric data processing by emotional AI systems. However, the AI Act provisions of relevance in the context of soft biometrics and emotional AI mainly give rise to discussions on inconsistencies in formulations and how the various thresholds set out in the provisions ought to be interpreted, rather than to an expectation that the AI Act shall effectively protect the fundamental rights jeopardised by non-identifying emotional AI.

We identify the following opportunities the EU legislator has left unused that would have equipped the AI Act to better protect the fundamental rights that may be compromised by the processing of soft biometric data by emotional AI:

(i) To broaden the scope of biometric data under Article 3(34) to include soft biometric data as well, since in fact not all biometric data are personal data;
(ii) To broaden the scope of the Article 5(1)(f) prohibition to include both AI systems used to infer and identify emotions (or alternatively, abolish the notion of a difference between 'inferring' and 'identifying' emotions in the definition of an emotion recognition system in Article 3(39));
(iii) To lower the thresholds in Article 5(1)(a) concerning the prohibition of in short manipulative AI systems by eliminating the word 'purposefully' (manipulative), the requirement that people's ability to make an informed decision must

be 'appreciably' impaired as well as the significant harm criterion, since manipulation alone is at odds with the right to human dignity established in Article 1 of the Charter;

(iv) To remove the 'intent threshold' in Annex III(1)(c) classifying AI systems 'intended to be used for emotion recognition' as high-risk, in order to prevent potentially easy circumventions of this provision;

(v) To reintroduce the need to verify that the use of the system is compliant with relevant Union and national law on fundamental rights (see former Article 29 a (d) draft AI Act) in Article 27 on the obligation to conduct a fundamental rights impact assessment prior to deploying a high-risk AI system.

6 Conclusion

In this chapter, we have assessed the processing of soft biometric data by emotional AI from a fundamental rights perspective, followed by an analysis of EU legislation governing soft biometrics and emotional AI. We contend that the EU regulatory framework is insufficiently equipped to protect the fundamental rights that may be compromised by the deployment of non-identifying emotional AI: the right to human dignity and the right to privacy. Given the severity of fundamental rights violations associated with the deployment of some non-identifying emotional AI systems, the ubiquitous usage of emotional AI across industries and the consequential at-scale exposure of EU citizens to such technologies would have merited revision of the AI Act. Simultaneously, the EU legislator needs to guard against the overregulation of emotional AI systems that do not harm fundamental rights. We should follow the developments in this area carefully since as we argued also the processing of soft biometric data may violate fundamental rights, and future emotional AI systems are expected to become ever smarter.

References

Albano C (2008) The puzzle of human emotions: some historical considerations from the 17th to the 19th centuries. Dev Med Child Neurol 50(7):494–497

Article 29 Working Party (2012) Opinion 03/2012 on developments in biometric technologies (WP 193)

Article 29 Working Party (2013) Opinion 02/2013 on apps on smart devices (WP202)

Article 29 Working Party (2014) Opinion 05/2014 on Anonymisation Techniques (WP216)

Bayefsky R (2013) Dignity, honour and human rights: Kant's perspective. Polit Theory 41(6):811

Beyleveld D, Brownsword R (1998) Human dignity, human rights, and human genetics. Mod Law Rev 61(5):661–680

Bognetti G (2005) The concept of human dignity in European and US constitutionalism. In: Nolte G (ed) European and US constitutionalism. Cambridge University Press, Cambridge, p 89

Czarnocki J (2021) Will new definitions of emotion recognition and biometric data hamper the objectives of the proposed AI Act? Lecture Notes in Informatics (LNI), Gesellschaft für

Informatik, Bonn. https://dl.gi.de/server/api/core/bitstreams/7b6f9560-ce1b-42bb-89dc-07ac5ffd54bd/content. Accessed 15 Apr 2024

De Conca S (2021) A full house: applying the GDPR to vocal assistants. Unpublished. In BILETA 2021. https://research.vu.nl/ws/portalfiles/portal/151885205/BILETA2021_De_Conca_Smart_Speakers_GDPR.pdf

De Hingh A, Lodder AR (2020) The role of human dignity in processing (health) data building on the organ trade prohibition. In: Synodinou T, Jougleux P, Markou C et al (eds) EU internet law in the digital era: regulation and enforcement. Springer, pp 261–275

De Montjoye Y-A, Hidalgo CA, Verleysen M et al (2013) Unique in the crowd: the privacy bounds of human mobility. Sci Rep 3:1376

Dicke K (2002) The founding function of human dignity in the universal declaration of human rights. In: Kretzmer D, Klein E (eds) Concept of human dignity in human rights discourse. Columbia University Press, New York, pp 111–120

Dupré C (2013) Human dignity in Europe: a foundational constitutional principle. Eur Public Law 19:319

Dupré C (2021) Article 1 – human dignity. In: Peers S, Hervey T, Kenner J et al (eds) The EU charter of fundamental rights, a commentary, 2nd edn. Bloomsbury Publishing, Oxford

European Commission (2019) Road safety: Commission welcomes agreement on new EU rules to help save lives. https://ec.europa.eu/commission/presscorner/detail/en/IP_19_1793. Accessed 22 Apr 2024

European Commission (2023) Success stories: building automated vehicles that are in tune with your emotions. https://projects.research-and-innovation.ec.europa.eu/en/projects/success-stories/all/building-automated-vehicles-are-tune-your-emotions. Accessed 18 Jan 2024

European Data Protection Supervisor (2015) Opinion 4/2015 Towards a New Digital Ethics Data, Dignity and Technology. https://edps.europa.eu/sites/edp/files/publication/15-09-11_data_ethics_en.pdf. Accessed 18 Jan 2024

European Network and Information Security Agency (2018) Privacy and Data Protection in Mobile Applications. https://www.enisa.europa.eu/publications/privacy-and-data-protection-in-mobile-applications. Accessed 25 Jan 2024

Floridi L (2014) Open data, data protection, and group privacy. Philosphy Technol 27:1–3

Floridi L (2016) On human dignity as a foundation for the right to privacy. Philos Technol 29:307–312

Forbes (2018) Rana El Kaliouby CEO Of Affectiva Is Training Robots To Read Feelings. https://www.forbes.com/sites/samarmarwan/2018/11/29/affectiva-emotion-ai-ceo-rana-el-kaliouby/. Accessed 25 Jan 2024

Häberle P (2005) Das Menschenbild im Verfassungsstaat. Duncker und Humblot, Berlin

Hindustan Times Tech (2023) Pizza Hut turns to AI to gauge customers mood, suggest pizzas. https://tech.hindustantimes.com/tech/pizza-hut-turns-to-ai-to-gauge-customers-mood-suggest-pizzas-71684337131772.html. Accessed 18 Jan 2024

Jain AK, Dass SC, Nandakumar K (2004) Soft biometric traits for personal recognition systems. In: Proceedings of the 2004 ICBA International Conference on Biometric Authentication, 15-17 July 2004, Hong Kong, China

Keshav N, Salisbury J, Vahabzadeh A et al (2017) Social communication coaching smartglasses: well tolerated in a diverse sample of children and adults with autism. JMIR Mhealth Uhealth 5(9):e140

McStay A (2018) The rise of empathic media. Sage Publications, London

McStay A (2020) Emotional AI, soft biometrics and the surveillance of emotional life: an unusual consensus on privacy. Big Data Society, pp 1–12

McStay A, Urquhart L (2022) In cars (are we really safest of all?): interior sensing and emotional opacity. Int Rev Law Comput Technol 36(3):472

Mostert M, Bredenoord AL, van der Sloot B et al (2017) From privacy to data protection in the EU: implications for big data health research. Eur J Health Law 24:1–13

Newell S, Marabelli M (2015) Strategic opportunities (and challenges) of algorithmic decision-making: a call for action on the long-term societal effects of 'datification'. J Strategic Inform Syst 24(1):3–14
Nguyen K, Le M, Martin B et al (2022) When AI meets store layout design: a review. Artif Intell Rev 55:5707–5729
Picard RW (1995) Affective computing. MIT Media Laboratory Perceptual Computing Section Technical Report no 321
Rixen S (2006) Würde des Menschen als Fundament der Grundrechte. In: Heselhaus FSM, Nowak C (eds) Handbuch der Europäischen Grundrechte. CH Beck Verlag, Munich, p 345
Roemich K, Schaub F, Andalibi N (2023) Emotion AI at work: implications for workplace surveillance, emotional labor, and emotional privacy. In: Proceedings of the 2023 CHI Conference on Human Factors in Computing Systems, 23–28 April 2023, Hamburg, Germany
Sacco F (2005) Nota sulla dignità umana nel "diritto costituzionale europeo". In: Panunzio SP (ed) I diritti fondamentali e le Corti in Europa. Jovene Editore, Naples, p 596
Somers M (2019) Emotional AI, explained. https://mitsloan.mit.edu/ideas-made-to-matter/emotion-ai-explained. Accessed 31 Jan 2024
Sprokkereef ACJ, Cehajic S (2009) The privacy legal framework for biometrics. FIDIS
Susser D, Roessler B, Nissenbaum H (2019) Technology, autonomy and manipulation. Inter Policy Rev 8(2)
UNESCO (2019) Recommendation on the Ethics of Artificial Intelligence, Paris https://unesdoc.unesco.org/ark:/48223/pf0000381137. Accessed 18 Jan 2024
Van der Sloot B (2016) Do groups have a right to protect their group interest in privacy and should they? Peeling the onion of rights and interests protected under Article 8 of the ECHR. In: Taylor L, Floridi L, van der Sloot B (eds) Group privacy. Philosophical studies series, vol 126. Springer, Cham. https://doi.org/10.1007/978-3-319-46608-8_11
Van der Sloot B, Van Schendel S, Fontanillo López CA (2022) The influence of (technical) developments on the concept of personal data in relation to the GDPR. WODC, The Hague, p 76
Wachter S (2020) Affinity profiling and discrimination by association in online behavioural advertising. Berkeley Technol Law J 35(2). https://doi.org/10.2139/ssrn.3388639
Whittaker M, Crawford K, Dobbe R et al (2018) AI NOW Report. AI Now Institute, New York
Wiewiórowski W (2019) Facial recognition: a solution in search of a problem? European Data Protection Supervisor blog. https://edps.europa.eu/press-publications/press-news/blog/facial-recognition-solution-search-problem_en. Accessed 18 Jan 2024
Wisman T, van der Linden T (2008) My secret life as an average person. Anonieme gegevensverzamelingen en informationele privacy. Tijdschrift voor Internetrecht, pp 86–89
Xiao W, Li M, Chen M et al (2020) Deep interaction: Wearable robot-assisted emotion communication for enhancing perception and expression ability of children with Autism Spectrum Disorders. Fut Generat Comput Syst 108:709–716
Zardiashvilli L, Fosch-Villaronga E (2020) "Oh, Dignity too?" Said the Robot: human dignity as the basis for the governance of Robotics. Minds Mach 30:123

Personal Data Protection in Emotional AI: The Facial Coding Example

Emmanuel Salami

Abstract The processing of emotional data points is fast becoming a critical part of the Artificial Intelligence (AI) data processing component. As these emotional data points can identify natural persons, they thereby fall within the definition of personal data (at least) within the context of EU law. Facial coding involves the observation of a data subject's facial expressions as a means of capturing their emotional reaction in any given time or situation. Ordinarily, processing activities which captured facial images are treated as sensitive personal data for reasons which include the capability of those images to reveal more data than intended. This chapter considers the applicability and impact of EU data protection law on emotional data points. By identifying the compliance gaps and the relationship and intersections between the General Data Protection Regulation (GDPR) and the Artificial Intelligence (AI) Act and proposing possible solution to identified gaps, the chapter attempts to analyse the compatibility of facial coding and data protection law. The chapter achieves this by using facial coding and the (facial) expressions collected from it as a use case. As a result, these considerations will highlight the relationship between emotional AI and data protection law while emphasising areas of divergence and convergence.

1 Introduction

Much research has been carried out on the use of AI systems in various scenarios, and the use of AI within the context of human emotions is no exception.[1] The processing of emotional data points by AI systems and the possibilities that abound therein have the possibility of impacting humanity in a very different way. Traditionally, society always prioritises the freedom of thought and expression of natural

[1] Andrew McStay (2018), p. 1.

E. Salami (✉)
Researcher, Primera Research Institute, Berlin, Germany
e-mail: ME@emmanuelsalami.com

R. Ballardini et al. (eds.), *Emotional Data Applications and Regulation of Artificial Intelligence in Society*, Law, Governance and Technology Series 69,
https://doi.org/10.1007/978-3-031-80111-2_7

persons in a way that ensures independent decision-making.[2] Since society ordinarily promotes the freedom of independent thought, it is hard to conceive of a reason not to extend this to the realm of AI. Therefore, the capability of (emotional) AI to influence the decision-making of natural persons and provoke (emotional) reactions deserves the attention it receives. However, this is not the full story as scholars have also argued that human beings are rational and sovereign beings capable of reaching their own decisions without being swayed in any given direction by external influence.[3] Therefore, while it is believed in some quarters that emotional AI can influence data subjects to act in pre-conditioned ways, some scholars also believe that humans are rational and can act in defiance of such pre-conditioning.

The concepts of AI and emotional data are very critical to this chapter. Article 3 (1) of the AI Act defines AI systems as a machine-based system designed to operate with varying levels of autonomy that may exhibit adaptiveness after deployment and that, for explicit or implicit objectives, infers, from the input it receives, how to generate outputs such as predictions, content, recommendations, or decisions that can influence physical or virtual environments. As will be considered in subsequent parts of this chapter, one of such "outputs" referenced in the above definition is the processing of emotional data points in a manner that influences the emotional reaction of data subjects. As previously referenced in this book,[4] emotional data is defined (inter alia) as biometric and identifiable human based and human directed data, meaning data representing the emotional, psychological or physical status of natural persons by identifying and processing their (facial) expressions, movements, behaviour or other physical or mental characteristics.

Flowing from the above definition, the consideration of the scope and effect of emotional AI lies (among other things), in the fact that the processing of emotional data within the context of AI (facial coding) covers two very critical issues. One of these issues is the fact that emotional AI datasets fall within the classification of special categories of personal data, the processing of which is strictly regulated under the GDPR. The other is that these AI systems process large volumes of data points. When considered together, these two factors highlight the potential severity that arises from the processing of emotional data points within the context of emotional AI systems. The said severity involves the processing of special categories of personal data on a large scale. Where appropriate, this article will exploit the similarities between the facial coding and facial recognition especially because the latter has been subject to regulatory guidance.[5]

This chapter considers the personal data protection of emotional data points as they arise from the processing operations of emotional AI systems. More specifically, by providing a background and description aimed at the proper comprehension

[2] For instance, under the law of contract, 'undue influence' is one of the exceptions, the occurrence of which renders a contract null and void. For further reading, see Nelson Enonchong (2023), p. 1.

[3] Andrew McStay (2018), p. 115.

[4] See in this volume Ballardini, van den Hoven van Genderen and Järvinen.

[5] European Data Protection Board (2023), p. 8.

of the technology, the chapter considers an overview of facial coding. The use cases depicting the (possible) deployment of facial coding are considered thereafter. Subsequently, the intersection between facial coding and data protection law as well as the data protection concerns arising therefrom are also analysed.

2 An Overview of Facial Coding

Facial coding is one of the approaches devised for the measurement and interpretation of the facial expressions and emotions flowing therefrom. It uses biometric data[6] (and by extension sensitive personal data) to gauge emotional reactions deducible from a data subject's face. Partly owing to the similarities between both technologies, including their reliance on computer vision and the processing of biometric data, there is the tendency to conflate facial coding and facial recognition technology.[7] At the risk of over simplifying, facial coding measures human emotions, while facial recognition seeks to identify a human person through their unique facial features. To function effectively, these technologies require some form of template against which the information captured on human faces is measured. In facial coding, the template that is typically used as a benchmark is the Facial Action Coding System (FACS), which is used as the basis for interpreting human emotions. In the case of facial recognition technology, the system compares human faces against a database/template of other faces stored on a smartcard or biometric passport.[8] Furthermore, while facial coding is primarily used for the measurement of human emotion, facial recognition technology can be used for human authentication and identification.[9]

The research of Ekman and Friesen is credited for developing the FACS,[10] the ascription of value to facial movement in humans and the restructuring of the classification of human emotions and facial expressions.[11] As Ekman puts it: facial expressions correspond to changes in the facial configuration due to the movement of facial muscles.[12] These facial expressions help in distilling emotional reactions in any given scenario. In other words, facial coding can be used as a tool for tracking

[6] Art. 4 (14) GDPR.

[7] Max Kalehoff (2024).

[8] European Data Protection Board (2023), p. 9.

[9] European Data Protection Board (2023), p. 9. Human authentication can be used to determine that a person is who they say they are, while human identification can be used to single out a person in a crowd.

[10] FACS is based on Ekman's identification of seven facial expressions of primary emotion which are joy, surprise, sadness, anger, fear, disgust and contempt; three overall sentiments; advanced emotions and 19 action units. See Andrew McStay (2018), p. 58.

[11] Ekman and Friesen (1978).

[12] Paul Ekman et al. (2002).

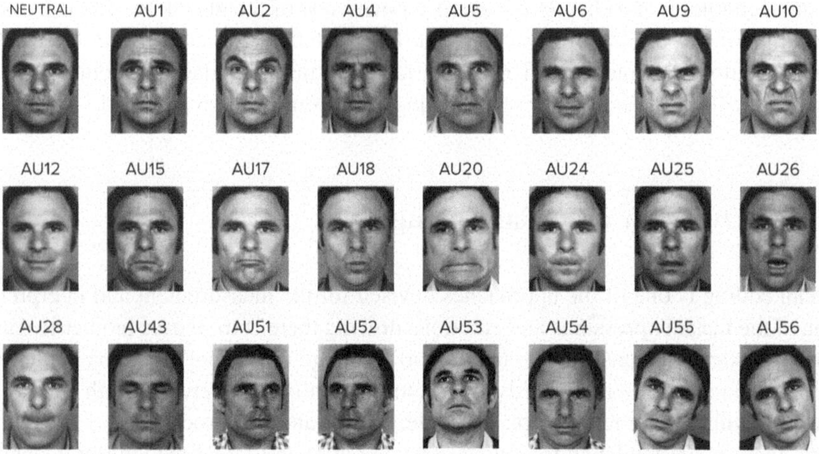

Fig. 1 Categorical approaches to emotions have been used to form the Facial Action Coding System (FACS) depicted below

human emotions. Facial representations of emotions depicted in the FACS are reproduced in Fig. 1.[13]

Facial coding relies on the visual identification of the movement of facial muscles conducted by expert human coders and/or trained software(s).[14] With the aid of computer vision, computers are now able to identify emotional reactions by attributing pixels to facial features and categorizing specific facial movements and expressions into different emotions.[15] However, despite its usefulness in tracking human emotions, facial coding also comes with its shortcomings, as recorded in academic literature, including the absence of context in which a facial expression is displayed.[16] Judging by the fact that more than 25% of Fortune 500 companies use emotional AI,[17] there could be no better time to consider the (privacy and data protection) issues addressed in this chapter. To identify and interpret human emotions, facial coding assesses and interprets several human reactions including the pitch or tone of voice, pace of heart rate, body language/posture, gestures, and facial expressions.

Interestingly, facial coding interacts with human emotions in two possible ways. Firstly, it captures human emotions by recording manifestations of human reactions deducible from the voice, heart rate, body language/gesture analysis, facial analysis, etc. These manifestations of human emotions are then used to provide a glimpse into

[13] Emotiva, Action Units.

[14] Danner and Duerrschmid (2018), pp. 231–252. https://doi.org/10.1016/B978-0-08-101743-2.00010-8.

[15] Andrew McStay (2018), p. 55.

[16] John Prescott (2017), pp. 360–368.

[17] Graham Page and Rana el Kaliouby (2022).

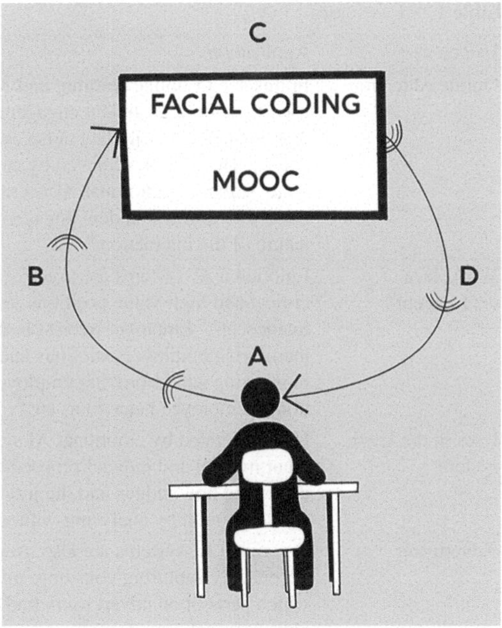

Fig. 2 This hypothetical diagram depicts how facial coding works in the use of a MOOC. In this diagram, "A" represents the data subject who is participating in a MOOC while also being subject to a facial coding processing activity; "B" depicts the emotional data points being collected from A's emotional reaction to the MOOC; "C" is a depiction of the facial coding personal data processing activity; and "D" represents the refined MOOC content being fed back to the data subject ("A") based on the data points collected from their emotional reaction ("B")

how humans might be feeling at a given time or scenario. Secondly, the information deduced from humans through facial coding may also be used to influence human emotions by creating content aimed at triggering a defined emotional reaction in given scenarios. For instance, in the use of Massive Open Online Courses (MOOCs) facial coding can be used to capture moments when students showed less interest in an academic course and this information can be used to rework these sections by learning lessons from the parts of the course that were more captivating for students.[18] The possible interactions between human emotions and facial coding are captured in a MOOC scenario in Fig. 2.

3 Use Cases in the Deployment of Facial Coding

For an enhanced appreciation of the scope and context of this chapter, some of the possible scenarios in which facial coding is (or may be) used are considered in Table 1.[19]

[18] It is acknowledged that Art. 5(1) (f) AI Act prohibits the inferring of emotions from natural persons in the workplace or educational institutions except the AI system is intended for medical or safety reasons. The rationale behind such broad prohibitions is questionable especially because there can be useful use cases for these restrictions. For instance, in the case of MOOCS, facial coding can be used to detect aspects of the course that are more captivating or otherwise to students.

[19] Some of these activities will not be permissible under Art. 5 of the AI Act.

Table 1 AI use cases

Use cases	Application
Online education	In this age of online learning and MOOCs, emotional AI systems can be used to determine student engagement including the measurement of student interest either in the course as a whole or in different aspects of the course. This can be achieved by combining eye movement features and scene features. Emotional AI is critical to MOOCs because it serves as a good way to track student engagement, especially because of the virtual nature of the interaction.[a]
Workplace deployment[b]	Emotional AI systems are used for tracking the emotions of employees in critical and high-value positions, including air traffic control, trading, finance, etc.[c] Employer interest in the deployment of emotional AI includes monitoring employee emotions and moods for various purposes, such as monitoring and improving employee well-being and productivity, prediction of employee behaviour; etc.[d]
Uses in the legal system	Data generated by emotional AI systems are used to replace human judgment in legal and judicial proceedings. Such use cases can be used to determine how judges and the jury perceive a witness, measuring truthfulness/deception by analysing witness behaviour.[e]
Advertising	Emotional AI systems are also used to measure consumer reactions to adverts. By capturing consumer micro-expressions, advertisers can detect which parts of an advert users find more or less captivating thereby optimising ad campaigns.[f]

[a]Xianhao et al. (2022), p. 7321. https://doi.org/10.3390/s22197321 See also McStay (2019), pp. 270–283. https://doi.org/10.1080/17439884.2020.1686016
[b]See footnote 18 above
[c]Andrew McStay (2018), p. 64
[d]Kat Roemmich et al. (2023), pp. 1–20
[e]Andrew McStay (2018), p. 65
[f]Andrew McStay (2018), p. 65

4 The Intersection Between Data Protection and Facial Coding

Facial coding systems are capable of processing personal data because a lot of the data points which they process including voices, heart rates, facial expressions, body postures and gesticulations, to mention just a few, can result in the identification of natural persons. Before going any further, it is pertinent to consider the definition of personal data under EU law.

Under EU law, personal data means any information relating to an identified or identifiable natural person (‘data subject’); an identifiable natural person is one who can be identified, directly or indirectly, in particular by reference to an identifier such as a name, an identification number, location data, an online identifier or to one or more factors specific to the physical, physiological, genetic, mental, economic, cultural or social identity of that natural person.[20]

[20] Article 4(1) GDPR.

Flowing from the definition above, it is clear that the data points processed in the facial coding process relate to natural persons and are such that can result in their identification. In other words, data protection law applies to facial coding as a data processing activity. Within the context of facial coding, the importance of data protection law is further underlined by the fact that a large proportion of the data points processed in those scenarios constitute special categories of data (sensitive personal data). Within the context of EU data protection law, sensitive personal data is defined to include personal data revealing racial or ethnic origin, political opinions, religious or philosophical beliefs, or trade union membership, and the processing of genetic data and biometric data to uniquely identify a natural person, as well as data concerning health or data concerning a natural person's sex life or sexual orientation.[21] In a facial coding context, the personal data being processed by (emotional) AI systems are mostly sensitive in nature because of their ability to reveal some of the data elements listed in the definition of sensitive personal data above.[22] For instance, during the facial coding process, the measurement of facial and emotional reactions (which constitute biometric data) can possibly reveal racial/ ethnic, political and religious affiliations and beliefs through the capturing of hijabs, skull caps, skin colour, etc.

5 Data Protection Compliance in the Use of Facial Coding

As established above, facial coding and data protection share certain intersections which necessitate the issues addressed in this chapter. Therefore, should emotional AI become mainstream, it is necessary to highlight and address the concerns it poses to (data protection) law. Some of these issues are addressed below with the goal of proposing appropriate solutions as deemed necessary.

There is no doubt that the existence of a justifiable legal basis for processing personal data, an encapsulation of the lawfulness principle, is the most fundamental and foundational principle of data protection law. From a facial coding perspective, it is trite law that for it to be lawful, said justifiable legal basis ought to be in existence and defined at the beginning of the processing activity. In a facial coding context, two possibilities abound: the relevant legal basis could apply either to personal data and/or sensitive personal data.[23] For the sake of brevity, this chapter only considers the legal basis in the facial coding scenario as it pertains to the processing of sensitive personal data. The GDPR clearly outlines the legal basis for processing sensitive personal data.[24] As far as facial coding is concerned,

[21] Art. 9(1) GDPR.

[22] Art. 9(1) GDPR.

[23] I am of the view that there are more cases where sensitive personal data will be processed and is likely to be higher in proportion than non-sensitive personal data.

[24] Art. 9(2) GDPR.

(particularly taking the use cases outlined in Table 1 of this chapter into consideration), it would appear that the consent of the data subject is the most applicable legal basis for the processing of the personal data. To be lawful, such consent must have been collected before the commencement of the processing activity, i.e. before the emotional data points are collected from the data subject. Additionally, when consent is to be relied upon as a legal basis, the conditions stipulated in the GDPR must be complied with.[25] Based on the aforesaid points, reliance on consent as a legal basis for processing emotional data can prove difficult in circumstances where there is an imbalance of power between the controller and data subject.[26] This possibility is prevalent in cases where emotional data points are processed during facial coding in an employer-employee or school administration-student context. In such cases, the consent will likely be invalid because of the failure to meet certain prerequisites of the law, including its freely-given element occasioned by said imbalance of power. The same applies when emotional data points collected from the data subjects are used to train or improve the performance of AI systems. For instance, McStay[27] records a scenario where Software Development Kits (SDK) are used to deploy emotional AI.[28] In that scenario, the data collected from data subjects are processed as part of the machine learning process to improve the functionality of the AI systems using the data collected. In such a scenario, the collection of consent for this machine learning activity must have been considered and included in the SDK to ensure the consent request is delivered to data subjects, who can provide or withhold their consent before their emotional data is collected and shared for machine learning-related purposes.

Another interesting (though potentially academic) consideration concerning the deployment of a justifiable legal basis in the use of emotional AI is that the data points to be collected may be largely unknown and unpredictable. As this necessarily lacks the 'explicit' element of consent, doubts are raised about the legality of the consent provided in such context.[29] This is especially relevant because both the data controller/processor and the data subject are not aware at the beginning of the processing activity about the data types to be processed. Traditionally, the data points to be collected during a data processing activity are usually clearly defined and outlined before the commencement of the processing activity.[30] In the case of facial coding, it is arguable that the data points to be collected are unknown and unclear before the commencement of the processing activity and even at the point of data collection. This is because the data controller is unsure of the exact emotion and/or micro-expression that will be gleaned from the face of the data subject.

[25] Art. 4(11) and Art. 7 GDPR.

[26] European Data Protection Board (2020), pp. 7–9.

[27] Andrew McStay (2018), p. 63.

[28] Red hat (2020).

[29] Footnote 31 above.

[30] For instance, Art. 13 GDPR expects data controllers to inform data subjects of the personal data that will be processed throughout the lifecycle of the processing activity.

Therefore, this raises the question of whether the facial coding use case can ever be compliant with the requirement of processing personal data subject to the existence of a justifiable legal basis. By implication, this concern also extends to the transparency and purpose limitation principles the legality of which will ordinarily be impacted upon when the legal basis is not clearly defined. For instance, in the absence of clarity about the data points to be collected, one can argue that the purposes for data processing in such a scenario cannot be clearly defined as anticipated under an applicable law.[31]

Facial coding systems are also capable of automated decision-making, especially when the feedback from these systems is used in reaching decisions which affect the rights and freedoms of natural persons.[32] Hypothetically, facial coding could be used to determine the extent of participation and focus of participants of a MOOC. Assuming the findings from this scenario are used to grade the participants of the MOOC, the automated decision-making process will require privacy compliance. The automated decision-making process can also be influenced by the data that has been used to train the facial coding system. For instance, the use of biased datasets will taint the outcome of the (automated) decision-making flowing out of the use of said tainted data. Consequently, the avoidance of data that has been tainted by bias will ensure that in those cases where facial coding is lawfully used for automated decision-making, such decisions are devoid of bias that traditionally characterises offline data. When facial coding systems are used in making automated decisions, the data subjects ought to be provided with information about the features of the system and how the system arrives at its decision.[33] Furthermore, other requirements of the GDPR including human review of such decisions must be implemented.[34]

Another principle of data protection law which impacts the processing of personal data in a facial coding scenario is the principle of data accuracy.[35] Here, the key consideration is the accuracy of the interpretation that facial coding technologies ascribe to the emotions/emotional reactions derived from data subjects. To appreciate this impact of the data accuracy principle in a facial coding context, one must firstly understand some of the differing approaches relevant to the understanding of emotions. For this purpose, two broad approaches—the categorical and the dimensional approaches—are briefly discussed. The categorical approach posits that there are several universally accepted primary basic emotions which are ingrained in our brains.[36] On the other hand, the dimensional approach rejects the view of the categorical approach and posits that emotions are linguistic and social constructs

---

[31] Art. 5(1) (b) GDPR.

[32] Art. 22 GDPR.

[33] European Data Protection Board (2022), p. 25.

[34] Art. 22 GDPR.

[35] The data accuracy principle requires that personal data should be accurate and up to date. Art. 5 (1) (d) GDPR.

[36] Andrew McStay (2018), p. 56.

attributable to affective states.[37] Therefore, while the categorical approach views emotions as pre-defined and definite across all peoples of the world, the dimensional approach is of the position that our emotions are influenced by our ethnic background, language, and other social factors. As a result of these approaches, it is clear that emotions and the interpretation that might be ascribable to them remains subject to some form of debate amongst experts and industry practitioners alike. This raises the possible question of the accuracy of the interpretations that might be ascribed to these emotions. Although, in the event of divergence in accepted interpretations, this might result in non-compliance with the data accuracy principle, an apparent preference for the categorical school of thought might be the right solution to this concern.[38] For the data accuracy principle to be complied with, there must be a consensus interpretation of emotions among relevant stakeholders.

The major concern with the inaccuracy of emotional measurements in facial coding is the erroneous interpretation of human emotions which places a significant doubt on its reliability. As far as facial coding is concerned, the severity of inaccuracy also depends on the volume of emotional data points being processed. In addressing the data inaccuracy challenge in facial recognition technology, the European Data Protection Board (EDPB) emphasises the importance of data controllers undertaking regular and systematic evaluation of their algorithmic processing to ensure the accuracy, fairness, and reliability of data processing.[39] This recommendation of the EDPB could not be more relevant to facial coding. From a facial coding perspective, beyond a regular and systemic evaluation of algorithms, data controllers must also pay attention to the particular data subjects in question (especially when they constitute minorities) to ensure the interpretation ascribed to their emotions is really that which the particular group intends. This practice will further guarantee the accuracy of emotional data that is processed in those scenarios.[40]

6 Conclusion

There is no doubt that facial coding technologies are an interesting use case for the deployment of emotional AI systems. Moreover, there is no doubt that emotional AI systems are another interesting example of the innovations ascribable to AI systems generally. From a data protection perspective, facial coding (and by extension, emotional AI) undoubtedly impacts the data protection rights of data subjects. The

[37] Ibid.

[38] However, McStay reckons that there is an industry preference for the categorical approach. Ibid.

[39] European Data Protection Board (2023), p. 13.

[40] The issues identified above are not exhaustive but only represent some of the issues relevant from a data protection perspective. Other relevant issues have been addressed, though from the perspective of the law enforcement directive. See European Data Protection Board (2023), pp. 20–28.

criticality of this technology lies not only in the collection of largely sensitive categories of personal data (emotional data points) but also in its ability to influence the emotions of data subjects. Therefore, if data protection compliance is to be achieved, those traditional compliance requirements outlined in the GDPR and enshrined in the EU data protection jurisprudence must be adhered to. Those requirements include the incorporation of privacy by design and default, privacy impact assessments, adherence to the principles of data protection, etc. to the lifecycle of data processing operations. Indeed, to effectively identify and mitigate any possible risks, data controllers/processors must put privacy considerations into perspective before the commencement of data processing.

In conclusion, as deducible from the facial coding use case, emotional AI systems will process sensitive categories of personal data. If not properly managed, these processing activities can result in grave data protection-related consequences for data subjects. The EU is making giant strides in the regulation of AI systems generally, with these giant strides exceeding the scope of data protection law.[41] Beyond the context of legislative language,[42] only time will tell how much of a synergy can be practically achieved among these laws. Time will also tell how the AI Act will impact the data protection aspects of facial coding, and the processing of emotional data points. Though the AI Act has banned certain aspects of emotional data processing, the impact of this ban is yet to be seen on the general development of AI within the EU. What is clear at the time of writing is that some of these prohibitions might be avoidable only if adequate data protection mechanisms are introduced. The adoption of core data protection principles can give emotional AI a greater chance at becoming a mainstream and compliant technology rather than the developmental limitation that might arise as a result of its prohibition. However, one can only hope that a combination of these laws will lead to (data protection) compliance in their use and deployment. Adherence to existing laws and possible consultations with regulators when in doubt might be another good way to achieve compliance well before launch of a product.

References

Danner L, Duerrschmid K (2018) Automatic facial expressions analysis in consumer science. Methods in Consumer Research, Volume 2: Alternative Approaches and Special Applications. pp 231–252. https://doi.org/10.1016/B978-0-08-101743-2.00010-8

Directive of the European Parliament and of the Council on adapting on-contractual civil liability rules to artificial intelligence (AI Liability Directive), COM/2022/496 final" which seeks to regulate the liability of AI systems

[41] See for instance, Directive of the European Parliament and of the Council on adapting on-contractual civil liability rules to artificial intelligence (AI Liability Directive), COM/2022/496—which seeks to regulate the liability of AI systems.

[42] Art. 66 AI Act.

Ekman P, Friesen W (1978) Facial action coding system: a technique for the measurement of facial movement. Consulting Psychologists Press

Ekman P, Friesen WV, Hager JC (2002) Facial action coding system. Manual and Investigator's Guide, Salt Lake City

Emotiva, Action Units. Available at: https://emotiva.it/en/action-units/. Accessed 23 Feb 2024

Enonchong N (2023) Duress, undue influence and unconscionable dealing, 4th edn. Sweet and Maxwell

European Data Protection Board (EDPB): Guidelines 05/2020 on consent under Regulation 2016/679 (2020). https://www.edpb.europa.eu/sites/default/files/files/file1/edpb_guidelines_202005_consent_en.pdf. Accessed 20 Apr 2024

European Data Protection Board (EDPB): Guidelines 05/2022 on the use of facial recognition technology in the area of law enforcement (2023). https://www.edpb.europa.eu/system/files/2023-05/edpb_guidelines_202304_frtlawenforcement_v2_en.pdf. Accessed 20 Apr 2024

Kalehoff M (2024) The clear line between facial coding and facial recognition. Real eyes. Available at: https://blog.realeyesit.com/the-clear-line-between-facial-coding-and-facial-recognition. Accessed 24 Apr 2024

McStay A (2018) Emotional AI. SAGE

McStay A (2019) Emotional AI and EdTech: serving the public good? Learn Media Technol 45(3): 270–283. https://doi.org/10.1080/17439884.2020.168601

Page G, el Kaliouby R (2022) Face value: the power of facial signals in human behavioural research. https://blog.affectiva.com/face-value-the-power-of-facial-signals-in-research. Accessed 16 Jan 2024

Prescott J (2017) Some considerations in the measurement of emotions in sensory and consumer research. Food Quality and Preference. pp 360–368. https://doi.org/10.1016/j.foodqual.2017.04.005

Red hat: What is an SDK? (2020). https://www.redhat.com/en/topics/cloud-native-apps/what-is-SDK. Accessed 26 Dec 2024

Regulation (EU) 2016/679 of the European Parliament and of the Council of 27 April 2016 on the protection of natural persons with regard to the processing of personal data and on the free movement of such data, and repealing Directive 95/46/EC (General Data Protection Regulation) [2016] OJ L 119/1

Roemmich K, Schaub F, Andalibi N (2023) Emotion AI at work: implications for workplace surveillance, emotional labor, and emotional Privacy. In: Proceedings of the 2023 CHI Conference on Human Factors in Computing Systems. Hamburg, Germany. ACM, New York, NY, USA p 20. https://doi.org/10.1145/3544548.3580950

Xianhao S, Bao J, Tao X, Li Z (2022) Research on emotion recognition method based on adaptive window and fine-grained features in MOOC learning. Sensors 22(19):7321. https://doi.org/10.3390/s22197321

Consenting to the Use of Emotional Data by AI-Based Services

Juha Vesala, Juhana Riekkinen, and Viivi Rankka

Abstract In data protection law, consent is a broad and flexible legal basis. While the use of emotion-related personal data in various AI-based services could be based on consent, this involves several practical challenges and unresolved legal questions that extend beyond data protection to other areas of law. In this chapter, we discuss to what extent and under which circumstances consent can be relied upon by providers of emotional AI services and applications. First, we analyse the requirements set by EU data protection law regarding consent as a legal basis for processing emotional data, and the issues raised by the rules concerning automated decision-making in the context of emotional AI. Then, we examine the boundaries and additional requirements imposed by EU competition law and the AI Act regarding the use of emotional AI based on data subjects' consent. Our analysis highlights challenges that arise particularly when emotional AI is used at workplaces or in publicly accessible spaces.

1 Introduction

Emotional AI applications often require the processing of personal data, obtained from sensors (e.g. video, audio, radar) and other sources (e.g. information provided by individuals). For this reason, the use of emotional AI applications requires a legal

J. Vesala (✉)
University of Lapland, Rovaniemi, Finland

University of Turku, Turku, Finland
e-mail: juha.vesala@utu.fi

J. Riekkinen
University of Lapland, Rovaniemi, Finland
e-mail: juhana.riekkinen@ulapland.fi

V. Rankka
University of Helsinki, Helsinki, Finland
e-mail: viivi.rankka@helsinki.fi

R. Ballardini et al. (eds.), *Emotional Data Applications and Regulation of Artificial Intelligence in Society*, Law, Governance and Technology Series 69,
https://doi.org/10.1007/978-3-031-80111-2_8

basis under the General Data Protection Regulation (GDPR)[1] in order to be permitted.

In this Chapter, we examine consent as a legal basis for the processing of personal data and challenges pertaining to it in the context of emotional AI. Specifically, we analyse:

(1) What challenges emotional AI applications raise in terms of meeting requirements for consent?
(2) Which issues does the prohibition on automated decision-making raise in the context of consenting to emotional AI?
(3) Which limitations do EU competition law and the AI Act[2] impose as regards relying on consent from data subjects?

The Chapter highlights challenges raised by the legal requirements relating to consent in selected use cases for emotional AI, particularly when emotional AI is used in physical spaces such as workplaces or publicly accessible spaces.

2 Relevance of Consent for Emotional AI

In the context of emotional AI applications, the consent of data subjects is arguably the broadest and in many cases soundest legal basis for the processing of personal data.[3] This is due to a number of reasons.

First, unlike most other legal bases that are limited to more specific circumstances and uses, consent is capable of covering various use cases, functionalities and implementations of emotional AI.[4] Moreover, consent often provides greater legal

---

[1] Regulation (EU) 2016/679 of the European Parliament and of the Council on the protection of natural persons with regard to the processing of personal data and on the free movement of such data, and repealing Directive 95/46/EC [2016] OJ L119/1.

[2] Regulation (EU) 2024/1689 of the European Parliament and of the Council laying down harmonised rules on artificial intelligence and amending Regulations (EC) No 300/2008, (EU) No 167/2013, (EU) No 168/2013, (EU) 2018/858, (EU) 2018/1139 and (EU) 2019/2144 and Directives 2014/90/EU, (EU) 2016/797 and (EU) 2020/1828 (Artificial Intelligence Act) [2024] OJ L 2024/1689, 12.7.2024.

[3] GDPR Article 6(1)(a) provides the legal basis for data processing based on consent, while further consent related requirements are determined particularly in Article 7, 9 and 22 of the GDPR as regards the topic of this Chapter.

[4] Other legal bases provided in GDPR Article 6(1)(b)–(f) are performance of a contract, compliance with legal obligations, protection of vital interests, performance of public interest tasks and legitimate interest. In the context of emotional AI, for instance, safety considerations could justify processing of personal data without consent under several of these legal bases, depending on the situation. Still, these legal bases do not cover all potential uses of emotional AI as broadly as consent in principle can do. However, it should be noted that also legitimate interest (point (f)) could be a potential legal basis for a relatively broad range of applications, as the interest in question can be of any nature as long as it is lawful, clear, real and present. See, e.g. Article 29 of the Data

certainty than other possibly available legal bases as the assessment is less dependent on ambiguous criteria or balancing of different interests.[5] Second, since personal data belonging to special categories of personal data (e.g. biometric or health data) may be processed as inputs (e.g. sensor data) or inferred when using emotional AI (e.g. health data), explicit consent may be required to process these kinds of data, as limited possibilities exist to process such data without explicit consent.[6] Third, where *prima facie* prohibited automated decision making takes place, explicit consent may also be required in the absence of other legislation permitting the activity.[7] Fourth, consent is an essential element in other legislation, such as the Digital Markets Act (DMA), in that certain practices (e.g. combining personal data) require consent from data subjects pursuant to such legislation.[8]

Throughout the remaining chapter, we highlight consent-related issues relating to certain use cases for emotional AI and technical implementations thereof. Emotional AI applications at workplaces in which sensor data are used to monitor emotional and other wellbeing of employees is one of these use cases examined. It is characterised by the data subjects (employees) being known in advance, alleviating some aspects of acquiring consent, but at the same time the employee-employer relationship giving rise to issues under other elements of consent. Emotional AI applications used in publicly accessible spaces such as shopping centres and public transport facilities used to monitor mood and to detect incidents are examined as the second use case example. Unlike at workplaces, persons in public spaces are not known in advance and methods for informing data subjects and obtaining consent from them are more limited than at workplaces. Data sources for these two use cases can include sensors such as video cameras, radars, audio—potentially biometric data—and the outputs obtained from emotional AI could be used to adjust lighting and room temperature to provide information on screens or otherwise to data subjects, or to alert security or other staff about issues potentially warranting attention.[9]

Protection Working Party (2014). Opinion 06/2014 on the notion of legitimate interests of the data controller. 844/14/EN WP217. Adopted on 9 April 2014, pp. 24–26.

[5] For example, reliance on legitimate interest necessitates a balancing exercise between the legitimate interests in question and the data subject's interests and fundamental rights and freedoms. See, e.g. Kamara and De Hert (2018), pp. 11–17.

[6] GDPR Article 9(2)(a).

[7] GDPR Article 22.

[8] Article 5(2)(c) Regulation (EU) 2022/1925 of the European Parliament and of the Council of 14 September 2022 on contestable and fair markets in the digital sector and amending Directives (EU) 2019/1937 and (EU) 2020/1828 (Digital Markets Act). [2022] OJ L 265/1.

[9] Our use case examples draw on the chapter by Järvinen and Kallio in this volume.

3 Requirements for Consent

In the GDPR, consent is defined as 'any freely given, specific, informed and unambiguous indication of the data subject's wishes by which he or she, by a statement or by a clear affirmative action, signifies agreement to the processing of personal data relating to him or her' (Article 4(11)). If special categories of personal data[10] are being processed, consent must also be explicit (Article 9(2)(a)). Below, these notions of consent—freely given, specific, informed, unambiguous and explicit consent—are discussed in detail in the context of using emotion-aware services in retail, transportation and office environments.

3.1 Freely Given Consent

In order to be regarded as freely given, consent must contain certain elements. Firstly, the data subject[11] must have a *genuine or free choice* as regards to accepting or refusing the terms of the consent. This requires that the data subject is able to decline to consent without any detriment.[12] The European Data Protection Board (EDPB) guidelines mention coercion, intimidation, deception and 'significant negative consequences' as examples of detriment in this regard.[13] Secondly, consent cannot be bundled with other additional terms and conditions (e.g. the performance of a contract[14]).[15]

When using emotion-aware services, a number of challenges arise from the extent of freedom in one's choice. In an example scenario discussed by Järvinen and Kallio,[16] a public transportation environment (trains, buses, trams) contains a

[10] Special categories of personal data refer to data revealing 'racial or ethnic origin, political opinions, religious or philosophical beliefs, or trade union membership, and the processing of genetic data, biometric data for the purpose of uniquely identifying a natural person, data concerning health or data concerning a natural person's sex life or sexual orientation'. GDPR Article 9(1).

[11] i.e. an identified or identifiable natural person, to whom the personal data relates to. GDPR Article 4(1).

[12] GDPR Recital 42.

[13] European Data Protection Board (2020). Guidelines 05/2020 on consent under Regulation 2016/679. Version 1.1. Adopted on 4 May 2020, p. 13. Note that this guideline does not replace the opinions on consent of Article 29 of the Working Party (WP29), which preceded the EDPB. In this chapter, we will refer to both EDPB and WP29 documents.

[14] GDPR Article 7(4). Note that the provision is non-exhaustive: 'any element of inappropriate pressure or influence upon the data subject (which may be manifested in many different ways) which prevents a data subject from exercising their free will, shall render the consent invalid'. European Data Protection Board (2020). Guidelines 05/2020 on consent under Regulation 2016/679. Version 1.1. Adopted on 4 May 2020, pp. 7–8.

[15] Custers et al. (2022), p. 463.

[16] Järvinen and Kallio, in this volume, Sect. 4.3.

monitoring system. If the passenger (the data subject) does not want to consent to data processing, the practical consequences of refusing to consent must be considered. Does the refusal mean that the passenger simply cannot travel? If yes, can such inability to travel be regarded as a *significant* negative consequence? While the inability to travel cannot be regarded as a detriment akin to deception or coercion, however, that does not mean that opting out would be completely free of consequences. If no other options are available, the decision to opt out cannot be regarded as a voluntary one.[17] Furthermore, if the data subject cannot travel because the data subject declines being monitored, then buying the ticket is conditional upon consenting to being monitored.

The third element of a freely given consent is the division of power between the data controller (the body that determines the purposes and means of data processing[18]) and the data subject—consent does not provide a valid legal ground for personal data processing in cases where a clear imbalance of power exists.[19] Vulnerability can be defined as the potentiality of harm, rather than actual occurred harm.[20] The mere existence of a power imbalance does not automatically lead to the impossibility of free choice, rather, the assessment of an imbalance requires case-by-case consideration.[21] A rule of thumb is that the data subject must be able to exercise free will and a real choice.[22]

In an example scenario described by Järvinen and Kallio,[23] an employer wants to monitor the activities of the employees in a workplace. The employee (the data subject) is considered vulnerable because, in terms of hierarchical superiority, the employer (the data controller) is in a position of significant power.[24] What matters in this scenario is whether the relationship between the employees and the employer is the kind where the employees can have a *real choice* in consenting to monitoring. If the employees are dependent on the employer and thereafter hesitant to decline consent, it is unlikely that a real choice can be made. The fact that a power imbalance is considered on a case-by-case basis necessarily means that whether the

[17] '[...] voluntariness is a necessary component for one's token of expressed consent to have a normative force. [...] The expressed consent is insufficient if there was no other viable option otherwise'. Jones and Edenberg (2020), p. 368.

[18] GDPR Article 4(7). Controllership may stem from the factual circumstances of the case ore be defined by law. European Data Protection Board (2020). Guidelines 07/2020 on the concepts of controller and processor in the GDPR. Version 2.1. Adopted on 7 July 2021, p. 11.

[19] GDPR Recital 43.

[20] Malgieri and Niklas (2020), p. 3.

[21] Custers et al. (2022), p. 463.

[22] European Data Protection Board (2020). Guidelines 05/2020 on consent under Regulation 2016/679. Version 1.1. Adopted on 4 May 2020, p. 9.

[23] Järvinen and Kallio, in this volume, Sect. 4.1.

[24] Malgieri (2023), p. 88.

vulnerability of the employee[25] renders the consent not freely given depends on the circumstances of each case.

3.2 Specific Consent

Specific consent requires that the controller specifies the purpose of consent, includes granularity in consent requests, and clearly separates consent-related information from information related to other matters.[26] Though separate consent needs to be given to different data processing operations,[27] if different data processing operations have *the same purpose*, one consent can cover multiple operations.[28] The concept of control is closely linked with the notion of consent because the data subject's control is exercised *through* consent:[29] consent is '[. . .] the most relevant legal basis that can give control of the data back to the data subject'.[30]

In an example scenario from a retail environment, sensors to assess customers' emotional states are being used in a shopping centre.[31] Here, it must be clear for the data controller what the specific purpose of monitoring is. If there are *several* different purposes, the data subjects need to give consent to all such purposes. The GDPR relies heavily on the 'notice and consent' approach.[32] In practice, obtaining several consents in the manner of *first* giving notice and *then* obtaining consent may be challenging, especially in an environment with a high volume of unknown data subjects. If the data subject has no knowledge of the notice, the 'notice and consent' approach becomes meaningless.[33] The manner of informing the data subjects must also be considered: consent must be specific and elaborate while it should be a consolidated and simplified request at the same time.[34] Another challenge is a situation where new purposes emerge while already processing data. This could

---

[25] Interestingly, the vulnerability of the employee as a data subject is recognised in Finland in the Act on the Protection of Privacy in Working Life (759/2004). In the workplace, the employer may not use camera surveillance for the surveillance of a particular employee, unless it is for preventing an apparent threat, investigating crimes, or safeguarding the employee's rights and interests (16 §).

[26] European Data Protection Board (2020). Guidelines 05/2020 on consent under Regulation 2016/679. Version 1.1. Adopted on 4 May 2020, p. 14.

[27] GDPR Recital 43.

[28] GDPR Article 5(1)(b) and Recital 32.

[29] Article 29 of the Data Protection Working Party (2011). Opinion 15/2011 on the definition of consent. 01197/11/EN WP187. Adopted on 13 July 2011, p. 8.

[30] Chen et al. (2022), p. 480.

[31] Järvinen and Kallio, in this volume, Sect. 4.2.

[32] Jones and Edenberg (2020), p. 360.

[33] Milossi et al. (2021), p. 58461.

[34] Steffes et al. (2023), p. 256.

happen if secondary uses of data processing cannot be imagined at the time of the data collection.[35]

3.3 *Informed Consent*

The element of informed consent is connected to the overarching principle of transparency.[36] Transparency of information is one of the fundamental principles of processing personal data (GDPR Article 5(1)(a))—it is 'an essential condition ensuring that consent is valid'.[37] Informed consent requires that the data subject is given all necessary information regarding the data processing.[38] The data subject must be informed of the identity of the controller and the purposes of data processing,[39] as well as of the following: (i) the type of data collected; (ii) the possibility of withdrawing consent; (iii) information on the use of data for automated decision-making; and (iv) the risks of data transfers.[40] Since these concern the minimum requirement of informing, case-by-case consideration is necessary.[41] One rule of thumb is that the data subject understands that personal data are being processed, as well as the purpose of processing.[42] Although the GDPR does not require a certain form for the information,[43] a written form is preferable because the data controller must demonstrate that consent has been given.[44]

One consent-related issue relating to using emotion-aware services is the practical act of informing the data subjects. In an example scenario from a transportation environment, where a bus contains a monitoring system, the question is, how to inform the passengers (the data subjects) in practice in an adequate manner? Though a written form is preferable, it is not feasible in the context of remote sensors, especially with a high number of unknown data subjects. Regardless, all data

---

[35] Politou et al. (2018), p. 5.

[36] Bygrave and Tosoni (2020), p. 184.

[37] Article 29 of the Data Protection Working Party (2011). Opinion 15/2011 on the definition of consent. 01197/11/EN WP187. Adopted on 13 July 2011, p. 9.

[38] Ibid.

[39] GDPR Recital 42.

[40] European Data Protection Board (2020). Guidelines 05/2020 on consent under Regulation 2016/679. Version 1.1. Adopted on 4 May 2020, pp. 15–16.

[41] 'The more complex data processing is, the more can be expected from the data controller'. Article 29 of the Data Protection Working Party (2011). Opinion 15/2011 on the definition of consent. 01197/11/EN WP187. Adopted on 13 July 2011, p. 21.

[42] Korpisaari et al. (2022), p. 150.

[43] European Data Protection Board (2020). Guidelines 05/2020 on consent under Regulation 2016/679. Version 1.1. Adopted on 4 May 2020, p. 16.

[44] GDPR Article 7(1). See also Recital 42: 'where processing is based on the data subject's consent, the controller should be able to demonstrate that the data subject has given consent to the processing operation'; Korpisaari et al. (2022), pp. 153–154.

subjects must *understand* that their personal data is being processed. Perhaps, a layered approach[45] could be an option, where the first layer should convey the most important information. As regards to video surveillance, the EDPB takes a warning sign as an example of the first layer. This warning sign should be positioned in a way that surveillance is clear for the data subjects.[46] Furthermore, when informing the data subjects, it must be clear which party acts as the data controller in a given situation. If passengers are monitored in multiple buses and transportation terminals, it must be clear if every bus company and terminal has their own data controller, or if one single data controller is responsible for all remote sensors in public transportation areas. In addition to the practicalities of informing, the extent of necessary information poses a challenge. The question is, what information should the data subjects receive? Even though the minimum requirements of informing are clear, a case-by-case consideration is necessary when examining whether the data subjects need to know more: 'the more complex data processing is, the more can be expected from the data controller'.[47]

3.4 Unambiguous Indication

Consent must be a clear affirmative action,[48] i.e. the data subject deliberately takes action to consent to a particular data processing.[49] Moreover, consent must be given *prior* to any data processing activity.[50] While consent can be collected via an oral statement or written form (including electronic means), 'silence, pre-ticked boxes or inactivity' do not constitute a valid consent.[51] Indeed, consent request must be presented in an 'intelligible and easily accessible form, using clear and plain language'.[52] Ambiguity must be avoided; the act of consenting must be

[45] A layered approach contains different methods to ensure transparency. The data controller can use different formats in the approach, such as video, leaflet, infographics, QR codes and public signs. Article 29 of the Data Protection Working Party (2017). Guidelines on transparency under Regulation 2016/679. 17/EN WP260 rev.01. Adopted on 29 November 2017, last Revised and Adopted 11 April 2018, p. 20.

[46] European Data Protection Board (2020). Guidelines 3/2019 on processing of personal data through video devices. Version 2.0. Adopted on 29 January 2020, p. 26. See an example of a video surveillance sign on p. 27.

[47] Article 29 of the Data Protection Working Party (2011). Opinion 15/2011 on the definition of consent. 01197/11/EN WP187. Adopted on 13 July 2011, p. 21.

[48] GDPR Article 4(11).

[49] European Data Protection Board (2020). Guidelines 05/2020 on consent under Regulation 2016/679. Version 1.1. Adopted on 4 May 2020, p. 18.

[50] This is evident from the wording of Article 6(1)(a): 'the data subject *has given* consent to the processing [. . .]'. See also Article 29 of the Data Protection Working Party (2011). Opinion 15/2011 on the definition of consent. 01197/11/EN WP187. Adopted on 13 July 2011, p. 9.

[51] GDPR Recital 32.

[52] GDPR Article 7(2).

distinguished from any other actions of the data subject.[53] From a moral viewpoint, consent requests have a practical function: they allow the data subject to express their autonomy by deciding whether or not to accept.[54]

In an example scenario, a shopping centre uses a facial recognition technology (FRT) and needs to obtain consent for it. A customer (the data subject) merely stepping into a shopping centre, and thereafter implicitly consenting to data processing, does not constitute active consent. Customers must be able to make a deliberate act to consent. Consequently, the data controller must consider how to enable the customers to be active in this regard. Another autonomy-related challenge concerns the practicalities of withdrawing consent. The data subject has the right to withdraw consent at any time, and the act of withdrawing must be as easy as it was to give consent.[55] If consent is withdrawn, all data processing based on consent must cease.[56] The question is, how do the customers withdraw their consents to using FRT, and how is the data processing that concerns only some customers ceased?

3.5 *Explicit Consent*

Valid consent requires compliance with all four elements discussed above. If the processing of personal data includes special categories of personal data—such as biometric data[57]—consent must *also* be explicit. Here, the notion of explicit concerns the manner in which the data subject expresses consent.[58] The explicitness of consent requires that the process of providing consent takes place as a 'formally separate process to the other transaction(s) to which the consent attaches'. That process involves the data controller's specific request for permission, followed by the data subject's specific reply.[59]

When emotion-aware services require the processing of biometric data, the main challenge is that consent requirements are stricter in comparison to other data sets that include personal data. With many unknown data subjects, most challenges in,

---

[53] European Data Protection Board (2020). Guidelines 05/2020 on consent under Regulation 2016/679. Version 1.1. Adopted on 4 May 2020, pp. 18–19.

[54] Custers et al. (2022), p. 464.

[55] GDPR Article 7(3).

[56] GDPR Article 17(1)(b).

[57] FRT, for instance, requires the processing of biometric data. European Data Protection Board (2023). Guidelines 05/2022 on the use of facial recognition technology in the area of law enforcement. Version 2.0. Adopted on 26 April 2023, p. 8.

[58] For instance, a written statement would enable the controller to make sure that the consent is explicit. European Data Protection Board (2020). Guidelines 05/2020 on consent under Regulation 2016/679. Version 1.1. Adopted on 4 May 2020, p. 20.

[59] Bygrave and Tosoni (2020), p. 185. Note that the requirement of explicit consent is stricter in comparison to the requirement of non-ambiguity (discussed above in Sect. 3.4.), which merely requires that there is no doubt that the data subject has given consent.

e.g. retail and transportation environments, concern the *act* of requesting consent. The element of explicitness is connected to the manner in which consent is acquired, and hence further complicates the already complex situation.

4 Consenting to Automated Decision-Making

GDPR Article 22(1) lays down a general "prohibition in principle" which applies to certain forms of fully automated individual decision-making and which does not need to be invoked individually by the data subject.[60] In the following, the applicability of this prohibition in relation to emotional AI is analysed. Then, the possibility of making such decisions based on explicit consent, as well as the challenges relating to obtaining such consent and implementing the required safeguards in the context of emotional AI are discussed.

4.1 The Prohibition of Automated Individual Decision-Making

GDPR Article 22(1) applies to (1) decisions (2) based solely on automated processing (3) that produce legal effects or similarly significantly affect data subject(s). If these conditions are fulfilled by an AI system, its use will not be lawful under the GDPR, unless when an exception to the prohibition is applicable. Therefore, before any emotional AI system is taken into use, the data controller must determine whether the system would produce decisions falling under the scope of Article 22.

The automated processing of emotional data can often be understood to create (typically numerous consecutive) decisions that affect individuals. It may be difficult to determine which phases of continuous data processing activities constitute individual decisions in the sense of Article 22.[61] In turn, this ambiguity may complicate determining whether a human being has contributed to this particular decision (as opposed to some earlier or later phase of data processing and/or decision-making), what effects this particular decision causes, and how significant these effects are. In any case, the concept of decision is to be understood broadly.[62]

[60] C-634/12 *SCHUFA Holding*, ECLI:EU:C:2023:957, para 52. The nature of the "right" or "prohibition" in Article 22 had previously been debated in literature. See, e.g. Bygrave (2020), pp. 531–532, Tosoni (2021) and Bygrave (2021), pp. 97–98.

[61] See Binns and Veale (2021), who propose the concept of "multi-stage profiling" to describe decision-making processes that are segmented into difference stages.

[62] GDPR Recital 71; *SCHUFA Holding*, paras 44–46.

Therefore, the first condition (there being a decision) is easily fulfilled in most emotional AI systems that interact with data subjects.

Likewise, the second condition (based solely on automated processing) is typically fulfilled as it may be practically difficult to include meaningful human participation in each individually consequential part of the decision-making procedure, e.g. in the context of the processing of emotional data in robotics or when AI systems interact with a large number of people visiting a physical space such as a shopping centre. This means that if decisions are produced, these often include decisions based on solely automated processing. The fact that human beings may subsequently take further actions or make further decisions does not necessarily disqualify an earlier result of solely automated processing from being a decision in itself in the sense of Article 22(1).[63]

Consequently, the most crucial condition in determining whether Article 22-(1) applies to emotional AI systems seem to be the third one (legal or similar significant effect on data subject). Neither inferring emotions nor using information to affect emotions typically produces direct legal effects, such as the creation of contractual obligations, denial of social benefits, or changes in an individual's legal status.[64] However, in both situations, automated decisions may affect the data subject in various ways. Some effects may be trivial or short-term (such as slight, momentary changes in emotional states) and their significance may thus fall short of the threshold, whereas some effects may be comparable to legal effects in their significance. In particular, a possible outcome of automated decisions that affect the data subject's emotions is that the data subject themselves is encouraged or manipulated to take actions with legal effects, such as buying or selling something.[65] In this case, the automated decision by itself produces no legal effect, but its impact on the data subject may in practice be just as significant. Therefore, a case-by-case analysis of the data processing and decision-making procedures and their effects is needed.

It is important to note that the technical aspects or features of an emotional AI application do not necessarily play the main part in determining how significantly

[63] See Binns and Veale (2021), pp. 325–326, 330. For an example of an automated alert (with the possibility of subsequent investigative actions by humans) as a fully automated decision, see Bygrave (2021), p. 99 (describing the so-called SyRI case). In *SCHUFA Holding*, the automated establishment of a probability value was interpreted to be a decision based on solely automated processing when a third party "draws strongly on that probability value to establish, implement or terminate a contractual relationship with that person" (regardless of whether the third party uses solely automated processing for this purpose). Cf. the concept of semi-automated decision-making in Demková (2023), pp. 34–36, and Palmiotto (2024), who finds that the concept of "solely automated decision" fails to grasp the reality of automated decision-making in practice (p. 235).

[64] Legal effects are not defined in the GDPR. For examples of legal effects in automated decision-making, see Article 29 Working Party (2018). Guidelines on Automated individual decision-making and Profiling for the purposes of Regulation 2016/679. WP251rev.01. Adopted on 3 October 2017, as last Revised and Adopted on 6 February 2018, p. 21.

[65] Emotional AI can be used to exploit emotions for commercial gain. See Valcke et al. (2021), pp. 58–59.

the automated decision-making affects the data subjects. To illustrate this, we can compare two scenarios described in Järvinen and Kallio.[66] One scenario concerns a 5-year-old who drops her popcorn in a cinema. In this example, the "Save the Day" service identifies the event (an upset child) and alerts the staff in order to salvage the customer experience. The alert can be construed as an automated decision under Article 22(1) if it has significant consequences of its own. All further actions, such as cleaning the location and giving the child a new portion of popcorn, are taken by human staff and are not the result of solely automated processing (unless the staff have no authority to use their own judgment on how to best react to the situation). The alert does not produce legal effects, and in this context and as it is directed to customer service staff, it is unlikely to indirectly lead to significant negative consequences for the profiled child. Likewise, erroneously not being flagged by the "Save the Day" system (a *false negative*) would have no severe impact on the data subject. In the absence of an alert, the data subject might be less likely to receive replacement popcorn, but the system does not preclude them from receiving it.[67]

From a technical viewpoint, the emotion-detecting AI application in the "Disturbance Detector" service example might function in a largely similar fashion as the application in the "Save the Day" example. However, there are major, potentially legally significant differences in how and for what purposes these applications are used.

Even in the "Disturbance Detector" scenario, we can again presume that the alert by itself produces no legal effects. In this context, since the alert is directed to security staff (or the police) and may designate an individual as a potential threat, the potential indirect consequences are quite different from the previous example. Although this system is also designed to promote positive effects such as increased safety and comfort, from the perspective of an individual data subject that is flagged as a potential threat by the system, the risk of being subjected to, e.g. removal from the premises or use of force by (human) security staff will clearly increase. As any further decisions and actions after the alert are again taken by human staff, they do not form new automated individual decisions. The automated data processing activity which culminates in the alert does not necessarily lead to the data subject being subjected to violence, removal from the premises or any other negative consequences and if so, there is also human agency involved. Still, alerting the security staff undeniably increases *the risk of such negative consequences*. In addition to merely directing the attention of the security staff towards a specific person, the AI system's assessment of aggressiveness or hostility of the data subject is likely to affect the expectations of the human security staff, the circumstances in which the targeted individual is confronted by the staff, and their behaviour in this

[66] Chapter 2, Sects. 4.2 and 4.3.

[67] However, cf. Bygrave (2020), p. 534, according to whom GDPR Recital 38 intimates that a decision will meet the significant effects threshold if it targets a child. If this was understood as a strict rule, practically all emotional AI systems in public spaces that are not restricted from minors would be likely to fall under GDPR Article 22(1).

interaction.[68] The targeting of security or policing activities with the help of AI systems also carries high risks relating to algorithmic discrimination.[69]

Consequently, the alert by the "Disturbance Detector" would generally have a much more severe impact on the data subject than a similar alert in the context of the cinema example, and arguably it would be at least closer to the threshold of "similarly significantly" affecting the data subject in the sense of Article 22(1).[70] Even in this scenario, not being flagged would not typically produce legal effects (as the data subject would not be excluded from any services or benefits as a result) nor significantly affect *the data subject*. Still, in specific situations, non-interference by the security staff could potentially lead to harm for the data subject, and might well have severe consequences for others. Therefore, the potential significance of the effects of a *false negative* decision by the "Disturbance Detector" would heavily depend on how much the human staff rely on the AI system to detect threats, and the existence of alternative security practices.[71]

Although the processing of emotional data does not always, or necessarily even often, trigger Article 22,[72] some emotional AI applications may meet all three

---

[68] See Selbst (2017), p. 137 (on how officers responding to an erroneous "red" threat level might proceed with an "itchy trigger finger" or be more easily provoked into unnecessary force). Cf. Article 29 Working Party (2018). Guidelines on Automated individual decision-making and Profiling for the purposes of Regulation 2016/679. WP251rev.01. Adopted on 3 October 2017, as last Revised and Adopted on 6 February 2018, p. 21. According to WP29, the threshold may be met when the decision has the potential to "significantly affect the circumstances, behaviour or choices of the individuals concerned".

[69] See, e.g. Selbst (2017), pp. 119–143, Castets-Renard (2021), pp. 99–101 and Galli (2021), pp. 122–123. Cf. also AI Act Recital 18 (highlighting potential discriminatory effects of real-time remote biometric identification systems used in law enforcement). Moreover, data processing related to policing may fall under the scope of the Law Enforcement Directive, i.e. Directive (EU) 2016/680 of the European Parliament and of the Council on on the protection of natural persons with regard to the processing of personal data by competent authorities for the purposes of the prevention, investigation, detection or prosecution of criminal offences or the execution of criminal penalties, and on the free movement of such data, and repealing Council Framework Decision 2008/977/JHA [2016] OJ L 119/89. In the Law Enforcement Directive, automated individual decision-making is regulated in Article 11, and always requires a basis in EU or member state legislation.

[70] Cf. Bygrave (2021), p. 99: In a Dutch judgment concerning the SyRI case, a risk notification indicating that a person is worthy of investigation for possible unlawful behaviour has been considered to have a "significant effect on the private life of the person to whom the notification relates". However, this was a governmental system, and also otherwise not quite comparable with the example here, and the court did not reach a definitive view on the applicability of Article 22.

[71] Beyond the viewpoint of data protection law, it should be noted that safety and security interests may be jeopardised if too much reliance is placed on inaccurate algorithmic systems.

[72] Arguably, regardless of whether Article 22(1) applies, the controller may still need to inform data subjects about any automated decision-making and profiling. In particular, this is needed when the legal basis of processing personal data is consent, which must be informed and specific (see Sects. 3.3 and 3.4). Even when the processing is based on other legal grounds, this kind of information could be interpreted to be required under the general transparency obligations (GDPR Article 5(1) (a) in connection with Article 13 and 14).

conditions. For instance, if we were to replace the human security staff in the "Disturbance Detector" example with AI-controlled robots or barriers, it would be difficult to argue that the automated processing as a whole does not significantly affect the flagged target.

4.2 Automated Individual Decision-Making Based on Explicit Consent

If the prohibition in principle applies, automated individual decision-making may be permissible based on the exceptions defined in GDPR Article 22(2). One of these is explicit consent by the data subject (Article 22(2)(c)).[73] Importantly, for emotional AI applications, under Article 22(4), it is possible to base automated decision-making on data that is classified as health data or biometric data, or any other special category, when the processing is based on the data subject's explicit consent (Article 9(2)(a)). In effect, this makes explicit consent the only widely available basis for automated individual decision-making based on special categories of data in the context of emotional AI.[74]

Whenever automated decision-making is based on explicit consent, all elements of consent must be present. This involves the challenges that have been discussed above in Sect. 3. Notably, the data subject must be appropriately informed of the automated decision-making,[75] and the consent must cover the processing of personal data, and possibly special categories of data, for this particular purpose. Thus, while the applicability of Article 22 may not create completely new kinds of challenges in relation to acquiring and managing the data subjects' consents (beyond the additional requirement of explicitness), fulfilling the requirements of valid consent—in particular those concerning specificity and transparency—will necessitate additional consideration and measures by the data controller.

Furthermore, under Article 22(3), when relying on explicit consent for automated decisions, the data controller must implement suitable measures to safeguard the data subject's rights and freedoms and legitimate interests, including the following:

---

[73] The other two exceptions in GDPR Article 22(2) are necessity for entering into/performance of a contract (point (a)) and specific EU or member state law (point (b)).

[74] Additionally, GDPR Article 22(2)(b) and Article 22(4) give EU and member state legislators the option to allow automated individual decisions based on special categories of data, but only when the processing is necessary for reasons of substantial public interest (GDPR Article 9(2)(g)).

[75] GDPR Articles 13(2)(f) and 14(2)(g) specifically require the controller to provide information regarding "the existence of automated decision-making, including profiling, referred to in Article 22(1) and (4) and, at least in those cases, meaningful information about the logic involved, as well as the significance and the envisaged consequences of such processing for the data subject." Thus, this information must be provided regardless of whether (explicit) consent is the legal basis for processing under Article 6 and/or Article 9 and whether explicit consent is the Article 22 exception on which this automated decision-making is based on.

- the right to obtain human intervention on the part of the controller;
- the right to express his or her point of view; and
- the right to contest the decision.[76]

In the context of emotional AI, this may be problematic. First, it is questionable whether it is practically possible to arrange these minimum safeguards in various contexts where emotional data are processed. Second, even if the controller manages to provide these safeguards, they may be practically useless in safeguarding the data subject's rights, freedoms and interests. For instance, if a robot infers the data subject's emotions and subsequently takes various actions (with consequences significant enough to trigger Article 22) in immediate physical interaction with the data subject, the nature of this interaction may render the right to obtain human intervention or contest the decision meaningless. More concretely, if a robot touches the data subject in a way that generates a negative emotional response or causes physical discomfort, pain or injury, this can hardly be effectively cancelled or reversed by a human being afterwards. Of course, many actions taken by non-physical AI systems—emotional or otherwise—can be similarly irreversible, in which case *ex post* human review and contesting the decision can at most result in the acknowledgement of errors and some form of compensation.[77]

Arguably, the *ex post* minimum measures should be complemented with effective *ex ante* safeguards in most situations.[78] This holds especially true in relation to emotional AI applications with irreversible, immediate consequences for the data subjects (in direct human–robot interaction or otherwise). Similarly, *ex ante* safeguards are crucial for applications such as the "Disturbance Detector", in which the automated output of the AI system does not directly impact the data subject but nevertheless produces an increased risk of severe and possibly irreversible consequences through subsequent human activity, which is pre-conditioned by the output of the AI system. Relevant safeguards include the obligations to use appropriate mathematical or statistical procedures, to implement technical and organisational measures appropriate to ensure that the risk of errors is minimised and inaccuracies are corrected, and to secure personal data in a manner that takes account of the potential risks involved for the interests and rights of the data subject and that prevents discriminatory effects on that person.[79]

When special categories of data are processed based on explicit consent under Articles 9(2)(a) and 22(4), suitable measures to safeguard the data subject's rights and freedoms and legitimate interests must be in place. Unlike Article 22(3), Article

[76] See also *SCHUFA Holding*, paras 65–66, which suggests that the safeguards laid down in national law under GDPR Article 22(2)(b) must likewise include at least these minimum safeguards.

[77] In general, the efficacy of the minimum safeguards has been questioned in literature. See Hawath (2021), pp. 167–168. See also Roig (2017), p. 6.

[78] On the role of *ex post* and *ex ante* safeguards in semi-automated decision-making by European authorities, cf. Demková (2023), pp. 195–200.

[79] GDPR Recital 71; *SCHUFA Holding*, para 66.

22(4) does not specify any mandatory safeguards. Measures similar to those mentioned above could simultaneously contribute to fulfilling this obligation. However, the controller needs to consider what kind of risks are associated specifically with the processing of these special categories of data for the purposes of making automated decisions involving detecting or affecting emotions and how severe these risks are. In turn, the measures should appropriately address these specific risks.

Whether we are talking about safeguards required by Article 22(3) or 22(4), there is a considerable degree of uncertainty as to which safeguards might be legally required in a given situation. The Court of Justice of the European Union (CJEU) has not yet elaborated much on these issues.[80] Without a rigorous case-by-case analysis, it is very difficult to determine which measures by themselves or combined with each other might be efficient in mitigating the specific risks related to the application, use case and scenario at hand.

5 Limitations in Other Legislation on Consent-Based Use of Emotional AI

Even when consent permits the use of emotional AI under data protection legislation, other legislation can limit the acquisition of such a consent or carrying out activities based on the consent. In particular, EU competition law and the AI Act limit the possibility of using emotional AI based on consent from data subjects, as discussed next.

5.1 Required Privacy Terms as Abusively Unfair or Unreasonable Terms

EU competition law prohibits the abuse of a dominant position (Article 102 of the Treaty on the Functioning of the European Union,[81] TFEU). Such abuse of dominance may lie in the imposition of unfair prices and unreasonable terms to trading partners (TFEU Article 102(a)), including privacy terms imposed on consumers.[82] While there have not been cases finding that privacy terms imposed on users constitute this kind of abuse under EU competition law, the German Federal Cartel Office has held that Meta violated a prohibition in German national competition legislation by requiring users of Facebook to consent to the processing of data

[80] See Demková (2023), p. 35.

[81] Consolidated Version of the Treaty on the Functioning of the European Union, [2012] OJ C 326/47 (26.10. 2012).

[82] For an overview of privacy related exploitative abuses, see Botta and Wiedemann (2019).

collected outside of Meta's services.[83] Upon a preliminary reference in the case, the CJEU ruled that a finding under competition law involving a finding of violation of the GDPR is possible under certain conditions.[84]

Although the Meta/Facebook decision cannot be generalised as providing guidance on how EU competition law would treat privacy terms imposed by a dominant undertaking, under the general standards for abuse a requirement that consumers consent to emotional AI use could constitute an unfair price or unreasonable term. This can be the case whether or not the practice is lawful under the GDPR;[85] requiring a consent to accept emotional AI use can be prohibited as abuse of dominance regardless. Abuse associated with seeking consent for emotional AI use could be particularly found in the following circumstances.

5.1.1 Requirement of Dominance in Context of Emotional AI

Dominance on a relevant market is required for the prohibition on abuse of dominance to apply. For this reason, it depends on the market position of the undertaking seeking consent for emotional AI use whether its data protection terms could be abusive. In general, a market share of over 50 percent creates a presumption of dominance on the market,[86] but a lower market share may also suffice. Entry barriers and other such factors also need to be examined when assessing dominance.[87]

In the context of emotional AI, it should be noted that relevant markets for some goods and services can in their geographical dimension be limited (e.g. a town) as consumers are not prepared to switch to producers further away. For example, grocery shopping, public transport and other such services can for this reason in some areas belong to relevant markets in which only a few undertakings operate. Indeed, only one public transport option may exist in some geographic areas for reaching certain destinations, for instance. Dominance is therefore plausible in the context of emotional AI used in physical spaces particularly in such markets (e.g. public transport) even if the undertaking seeking to acquire consent is not dominant nationally, in the EU or worldwide.

---

[83] Decision B6-22/16 of the German Federal Cartel Office dated 6 February 2019 <https://www.bundeskartellamt.de/SharedDocs/Entscheidung/DE/Entscheidungen/Missbrauchsaufsicht/2022/B6-27-21.pdf?__blob=publicationFile&v=3>.

[84] C-252/21 *Meta Platforms Inc and Others v Bundeskartellamt,* ECLI:EU:C:2023: 537.

[85] However, according to the CJEU ruling on Meta/Facebook, ibid, para 63, a competition authority cannot depart from an existing supervisory authority decision and needs to consult the supervisor advisory in case of simultaneous investigation in certain situations where the competition authority suspects that a practice is not consistent with the GDPR.

[86] C-62/86 *AKZO* [1991] ECR I-3359, para 60.

[87] See for assessment of dominance, e.g. Guidance on the Commission's enforcement priorities in applying Article 82 of the EC Treaty to abusive exclusionary conduct by dominant undertakings, [2009] OJ C 45/7, paras 9–18.

5.1.2 Abusively Unfair or Unreasonable Consent to Emotional AI Use

The general legal standards for assessing the imposition of unfair prices or unreasonable terms remain unsettled in EU competition law, and, as noted above, there is no CJEU case law concerning the assessment of data protection conditions under EU competition law. Nonetheless, (1) disproportionality of conditions and (2) unreasonable relationship between the consideration paid by a consumer and the economic value of the product have been applied in other contexts to establish unreasonableness of contractual terms and unfairness of prices.[88]

Following such approaches, privacy terms requiring consent to emotional AI use whose burden on consumers in terms of data protection is in no reasonable relation to the value that consumers receive could constitute an excessively high (non-monetary) price for the service received.[89] This could, for instance, be the case when a consumer is required to consent to the use of personal information for use in emotional AI but does not receive any value in exchange in terms of improved quality of goods or services, or otherwise. Yet, establishing prices as excessively high or low is challenging in itself, and in the context of privacy protection, additional challenges are introduced in the assessment as regards how consumers value privacy as a non-price parameter.[90] Moreover, terms on personal data use for emotional AI purposes that burden the consumer more than necessary for the dominant undertaking to attain its (legitimate) objectives could also amount to abuse.[91] For example, in terms of achieving the objectives of using emotional AI concerned (e.g. safety applications), requiring consent for the use of data for emotional AI that is unnecessary in scope or otherwise could constitute such an unreasonable term.[92]

In sum, EU competition law may prohibit practices whereby a dominant undertaking imposes unfair or unreasonable consents on data subjects to accept emotional AI use. This is not only relevant in the domain of online services but can be a concern also when emotional AI is used in physical spaces (e.g. public transport in some areas). While no finding relating to emotional AI use or other privacy terms has

[88] See for an overview O'Donoghue and Padilla (2013), pp. 742–748 (excessive pricing) and 849–859 (unfair contract terms).

[89] See, e.g. Case C-27/76 *United Brands Company v. Commission*, ECLI:EU:C:1978:22, para 250 (excessive prices can be established by showing the prices are unreasonable in comparison to the economic value of the product).

[90] See on the challenges Botta and Wiedemann (2019).

[91] See, e.g. C-127/73 *Belgische Radio en Televisie and société belge des auteurs, compositeurs et éditeurs v. SV SABAM and NV Fonior*, ECLI:EU:C:1974:25, para 15 (holding the conditions of a collecting society that were not necessary for reaching objectives of the collecting society abusive where they limited the other parties' freedom to exercise copyright unreasonably).

[92] Relatedly, in the case of so-called gatekeepers, combining personal data from different data sources can be prohibited under DMA Article 5(2). For example, this would prevent the combination of personal data from a shopping center with the personal data from a gatekeeper online service. However, such combination of data can be permitted upon specific consent of the end user. DMA Article 5(2).

been made so far under EU competition law, requiring consent to subject one to emotional AI processing could be problematic, particularly if the data subject obtains no value from the use of emotional AI or the scope of consent goes beyond what is necessary for achieving the dominant undertaking's legitimate objectives for using emotional AI. However, as noted above, establishing these forms of abuse is challenging in general and privacy considerations introduce additional challenges in the assessment (e.g. how consumers value their privacy).[93]

5.2 *Prohibitions and Obligations of the AI Act Relevant to Use of Emotional AI Based on Consent*

The AI Act contains prohibitions and other requirements relevant for using emotional AI based on consent. As discussed next, certain uses of emotional AI are entirely precluded, whereas others require the meeting of stringent requirements for high-risk AI systems (e.g. possible third party assessment, human oversight and transparency towards those exposed to certain types of emotional AI).

5.2.1 Emotion Recognition

The AI Act prohibits the use of emotion recognition systems in "the areas of workplace and education institutions".[94] Specifically, the use of emotional AI systems to infer emotions or intentions of natural persons based on biometric data is prohibited.[95] This prohibition thus prevents the use of emotional AI in many environments because many (if not most) are workplaces. Even if emotional AI were aimed at recognising the emotions of customers or other non-employees, the fact that emotion recognition takes place at a workplace could trigger the prohibition. It is not clear from the text of the AI Act whether the ban can be avoided by excluding employees from emotion recognition or by preventing the use of the information concerning employees.[96]

However, not all emotional AI use cases fall under the definition of emotion recognition as defined in the AI Act. For example, fatigue or pain detection does not

[93] Apart from abusively unfair/unreasonable privacy terms examined in this Chapter, requiring consent to emotional AI use could also amount to other kinds of abuse of dominance, such as where emotional AI is used in a discriminatory manner or to exclude competitors of a dominant undertaking. See for an overview Botta and Wiedemann (2019).

[94] AI Act Article 5(1)(f).

[95] Ibid.

[96] AI Act Recital 44 suggests that the imbalance of power at workplaces is a reason for the prohibition. This suggests that the ban is for the benefit of employees and thus possibly not covering the recognition of emotions of others.

constitute the recognition of an emotion but a physical state.[97] Moreover, the ban on emotion recognition at work and education exempts AI systems having medical or safety reasons as their intended use; emotion recognition with such intended purposes is thus not prohibited even at workplaces.[98] Consequently, only some uses cases for emotional AI are subject to the ban on emotion recognition: for instance, in some of the scenarios presented by Järvinen and Kallio,[99] emotions are not inferred (but physiological states or activities) or the intended uses of emotional AI may be safety and medical related. However, non-banned emotion recognition AI systems (e.g. those exempted from the ban on safety/medical use grounds at workplaces) are considered high-risk AI systems subject to stringent requirements relating to their use and development.[100] Moreover, all emotion recognition systems are subject to transparency obligations requiring that those exposed to emotion recognition are informed of that.[101]

5.2.2 Biometric Identification, Categorisation and Facial Recognition

The AI Act bans the categorisation of individuals using biometric data based on certain sensitive factors (e.g. race, religious beliefs) as well as the untargeted collection of facial recognition databases from the internet and CCTV.[102] Other biometric categorisation systems involving sensitive or protected attributes or characteristics, or inferences based on them, as well as remote biometric identification systems are considered as high-risk AI systems.[103] Biometric categorisation systems are also subject to a transparency obligation to inform persons exposed to such categorisation.[104]

Even though these bans and obligations relating to biometric data are not directed at emotional AI, they concern the functionalities and kinds of data often used in emotional AI. Since many emotional AI applications use biometric data (obtained from cameras or other sensors) they may therefore be subject to the above-noted transparency requirements and the stringent criteria for high-risk AI systems if identification or sensitive-parameter based categorisation of individuals is

---

[97] AI Act Recital 18.

[98] AI Act Article 5(1)(f).

[99] Järvinen and Kallio, in this volume, Sects. 4.1–4.3.

[100] AI Act Annex III, paragraph 1(c) classifies biometric AI systems intended to be used for emotion recognition as a high-risk AI system.

[101] AI Act Article 50(3).

[102] AI Act Article 5(1)(g) and (e).

[103] AI Act Annex III, Point 1(a)–(b).

[104] AI Act Article 50(3) provides for transparency relating to biometric categorisation systems. Curiously, remote biometric identification is not mentioned in Article 50 even though is it a high-risk AI system in the AI Act.

involved.[105] Any use of emotional AI to classify individuals based on certain biometrically inferred attributes (e.g. race, sexual orientation) and collection of facial recognition databases from CCTV (arguably any image sensors) is categorically prohibited.

5.2.3 Subliminal Behavioural Manipulation

Another category of prohibited uses of AI systems in the AI Act that can be relevant to emotional AI is the use of subliminal or purposefully manipulative or deceptive techniques with the objective or effect of materially distorting the behaviour of natural persons that materially impairs informed decision-making ability and causes or is reasonably likely to cause the persons significant harm.[106] If, for instance, emotional AI takes actions so as to influence the behaviour of individuals (e.g. employees or consumers), the question arises if this could be of the manipulative kind prohibited in the AI Act.

To avoid this prohibition, emotional AI applications need to refrain from operating in a subliminal, deceptive or manipulative manner or from distorting behaviour in any significantly harmful way. However, it remains unclear what constitutes a subliminal or other manipulative technique under the AI Act—for example whether and which kind of notice is sufficient to avoid that characterisation. For instance, adjusting ambient conditions (e.g. lighting) or "nudging" employees or consumers can be argued to be of manipulative nature.[107] Apart from improving the wellbeing of employees or consumers, emotion-aware environments may also result in harm that triggers the ban (e.g. long-term harm, despite short-term benefits). Harms recognized under the prohibition include not only physiological but also psychological and financial impacts.[108]

To sum up, first, even when the processing of personal data is possible based on consent under the GDPR, the AI Act may ban certain emotional AI uses or impose additional requirements on using emotional AI that go beyond the GDPR. In particular, the AI Act prohibits biometric-based emotion recognition at workplaces, biometric-data-based categorisation of individuals based on certain sensitive parameters, untargeted collection of facial recognition databases, and the use of subliminal

[105] Biometric data is according to recital 14 to be interpreted in light of the corresponding definition in the GDPR Article 4(14). This appears to mean that only data that allows for the identification of a natural person would be deemed as biometric data under the AI Act. If this is the case (which is not clear from the text of the AI Act), emotion recognition or categorisation of individuals based on data not allowing for identification of individuals would not be banned or affected by other requirements. For example, emotion recognition or categorisation of groups of persons could under this reasoning be permitted using sensor and other data that does not enable identification of individuals.

[106] AI Act Article 5(1)(a).

[107] AI Act Recital 29 mentions nudging as potential manipulation and imperceptible audio and video stimuli as examples of deceptive and subliminal techniques.

[108] AI Act Recital 29.

behavioural manipulation techniques. Second, even when not banned, the AI Act imposes obligations on deployers of high-risk AI systems when emotion recognition or biometric categorisation is concerned, such as human oversight and the right to explanation on AI-based automated decisions,[109] as well as that those exposed to certain AI systems are informed about it—in many ways mirroring or complementing similar obligations in the GDPR.[110]

6 Conclusions

Emotional AI applications may have functionalities that require consent from data subjects, as other legal bases for processing personal data are less universal and for many use cases offer less legal certainty. However, ensuring that consent is valid can be challenging in the context of emotional AI. In terms of freely given consent, it may be challenging to enable the data subjects to refuse to consent without any negative consequences and to consent in a way that it is not connected to any other conditional actions. Moreover, the extent of the data subject's vulnerability must be considered, as a clear imbalance of power between the data controller and the data subject may render consent as not being freely given. In terms of specific consent, the issue is the data subjects' ability to exercise control via giving consent to a specific purpose of data processing. Emotion-aware services may require many different purposes of data processing, and new additional purposes may emerge while already processing data. In practice, it may be challenging to make the consent request specific and elaborate, and on the other hand simple and consolidated. As regards to informed consent, challenges concern both the practical act of informing the data subjects and deciphering the extent of information given to the data subjects. Emotion-aware services often target a high number of unknown data subjects, which complicates the matter. In terms of unambiguous indication, it may be challenging to enable the data subjects to express their autonomy actively via consent. The data controller must also consider the practicalities of how to enable the withdrawing of consent and ceasing the processing of personal data. Some emotional AI applications may require the processing of special categories data, such as health data or biometric data. One of the legal bases for processing such special categories of data is explicit consent. Indeed, the notion of explicitness makes the requirements for consent stricter, as explicitness is applied in addition to the other elements of consent.

* * *

Further, some emotional AI applications may entail automated individual decision-making that although is prohibited in principle, is permissible with explicit

[109] AI Act Articles 14 and 86.

[110] See above Sects. 3.3 and 4.2.

consent, as long as certain safeguards are implemented. Acquiring explicit consent for automated decision-making involves similar challenges as discussed above. Explicit consent is also the only widely available basis for automated individual decision-making based on special categories of data in the absence of specific EU or member state laws. Additional challenges and uncertainty are generated by the legal requirements concerning suitable measures to safeguard the data subject's rights and freedoms and legitimate interests, as the measures that are specifically required by law may be difficult to arrange and be ineffective in many data processing scenarios related to emotional AI. Although *ex ante* measures would often seem preferable to *ex post* measures, a thorough case-by-case assessment is vital in determining the exact type and level of measures needed.

Even if consent to emotional AI use were valid under data protection legislation, other legislation can still prevent the use of emotional AI. EU competition law may prohibit the acquisition of consent for emotional AI as an unfair term imposed by a dominant undertaking (e.g. local public transport monopolies). The AI Act prohibits certain uses of emotional AI, including certain biometric categorisation of individuals, emotion recognition at workplaces, and subliminal manipulation. Other biometric categorisation, identification and emotion recognition systems may constitute high-risk AI systems, requiring, for instance, conformity assessments and human oversight, and that those exposed to emotion recognition or biometric categorisation are informed of it. These requirements outside GDPR can prevent the acquisition of consent for data processing, prohibit the use of emotional AI despite consent under data protection legislation, and create additional requirements concerning the development and use of emotional AI beyond data protection law.

References

Binns R, Veale M (2021) Is that your final decision? Multi-stage profiling, selective effects, and Article 22 of the GDPR. Int Data Priv Law 11(4):319–332

Botta M, Wiedemann K (2019) Exploitative conducts in digital markets: time for a discussion after the facebook decision. J Eur Competition Law Pract 10(8):465–478

Bygrave LA (2020) Article 22 automated individual decision-making, including profiling. In: Kuner C, Bygrave LA, Docksey C, Drechsler L (eds) The EU general data protection regulation (GDPR). A commentary. Oxford University Press, Oxford, pp 522–542

Bygrave LA (2021) Article 22 automated individual decision-making, including profiling. In: Kuner C, Bygrave LA, Docksey C, Drechsler, Tosoni L (eds) The EU General Data Protection Regulation (GDPR). A Commentary – 2021 Update. Oxford University Press, pp 96–100. https://fdslive.oup.com/www.oup.com/academic/pdf/law/GDPRCommentary_ArticleUpdates.pdf

Bygrave LA, Tosoni L (2020) Consent in: the EU general data protection regulation (GDPR). In: Kuner C, Bygrave LA, Docksey C, Drechsler L (eds) The EU general data protection regulation (GDPR): a commentary. Oxford University Press, Oxford, pp 174–187

Castets-Renard C (2021) Human rights and algorithmic impact assessment for predictive policing. In: Micklitz H-W, Pollicino O, Reichman A, Simoncini A, Sartor G, De Gregorio G (eds) Constitutional challenges in the algorithmic society. Cambridge University Press, Cambridge, pp. 93–110

Chen J, Dove E, Bhakuni H (2022) Explicit consent and alternative data protection processing grounds for health research. In: Kosta E, Leenes R, Kamara I (eds) Research handbook on EU data protection law. Edward Elgar, Cheltenham, pp 474–502

Custers B, Fosch-Villaronga E, van der Hof S, Schermer B, Sears A, Tamó-Larrieux A (2022) The role of consent in an algorithmic society – its evolution, scope, failings and re-conceptualization. In: Kosta E, Leenes R, Kamara I (eds) Research handbook on EU data protection law. Edward Elgar, Cheltenham, pp 455–473

Demková S (2023) Automated decision-making and effective remedies. The new dynamics in the protection of EU fundamental rights in the area of freedom, security and justice. Edward Elgar, Cheltenham

Galli F (2021) Law enforcement and data-driven predictions at the national and EU level. A challenge to the presumption of innocence and reasonable suspicion? In: Micklitz H-W, Pollicino O, Reichman A, Simoncini A, Sartor G, De Gregorio G (eds) Constitutional challenges in the algorithmic society. Cambridge University Press, Cambridge, pp 111–127

Hawath M (2021) Regulating automated decision-making: an analysis of control of processing and additional safeguards in Article 22 of the GDPR. Eur Data Protect Law Rev 7(2):161–173

Jones ML, Edenberg E (2020) Troubleshooting AI and consent. In: Dubber M, Pasquale F, Das S (eds) Oxford handbook of ethics of AI. Oxford University Press, New York, pp 359–374

Kamara I, De Hert P (2018) Understanding the balancing act behind the legitimate interest of the controller ground: a pragmatic approach. Brussels Privacy Hub Working Paper 4(12)

Korpisaari P, Pitkänen O, Warma-Lehtinen E (2022) Tietosuoja. Alma Talent, Helsinki

Malgieri G (2023) Vulnerability and data protection law. Oxford University Press, Oxford

Malgieri G, Niklas J (2020) Vulnerable data subjects. Comput Law Secur Rev 37(7):3–16

Milossi M, Alexandropoulou-Egyptiadou E, Psannis K (2021) AI Ethics: algorithmic determinism or self-determination? The GDPR approach. IEEE Access 9:58455–58466

O'Donoghue R, Padilla J (2013) The law and economics of Article 102 TFEU. Hart Publishing, Oxford and Portland

Palmiotto F (2024) When is a decision automated? A taxonomy for a fundamental rights analysis. Germ Law J 25:210–236

Politou E, Alepis E, Patsakis C (2018) Forgetting personal data and revoking consent under the GDPR: challenges and proposed solutions. J Cybersecur (Oxford) 4(1):1–20

Roig A (2017) Safeguards for the right not to be subject to a decision based solely on automated processing (Article 22 GDPR). Eur J Law Technol 8:3

Selbst AD (2017) Disparate impact in big data policing. Georgia Law Rev 51(1):109–195

Steffes B, Salemi S, Feth D, Groen E (2023) Generic consents in digital ecosystems: legal, psychological, and technical perspectives. In: Gerber N, Stöver A, Marky K (eds) Human factors in privacy research. Springer International Publishing, Cham, pp 255–282

Tosoni L (2021) The right to object to automated individual decisions: resolving the ambiguity of Article 22(1) of the General Data Protection Regulation. Int Data Priv Law 11(2):145–162

Valcke P, Clifford D, Dessers VK (2021) Constitutional challenges in the emotional AI Era. In: Micklitz H-W, Pollicino O, Reichman A, Simoncini A, Sartor G, De Gregorio G (eds) Constitutional challenges in the algorithmic society. Cambridge University Press, Cambridge, pp 57–77

A Duty of Loyalty for Emotion Data

Woodrow Hartzog and Neil Richards

Abstract Emotion data is dangerous because of how much it reveals about us and how deeply it is coveted by industry and government. This data—purporting to represent the emotional, psychological, or physical status of people by processing their expressions, movements, behaviour or other physical or mental characteristics—is irresistible for companies to use to their advantage. Having failed to recognize this danger, the law has left people open to the exploitative whims of industry and government who process emotion data. This chapter proposes a duty of emotion data loyalty to prohibit recipients of emotion data from acting in ways that conflict with the best interests of the trusting party. The idea behind loyalty is simple: organizations should not process emotion data or design technologies that conflict with the best interests of trusting parties. Our emotions should not be tools with which to manipulate us. Loyalty is the antidote to opportunism: it shifts the legal duty from self-serving to other-serving and has a morality broader than the profit-maximization of neoliberal capitalism. Though loyalty has deep roots in our law, there is more than just abstract ethics and notions of honour to the duty of emotion data loyalty. Loyalty compels firm legal duties and prohibitions that, when breached, give rise to legal liability on the grounds of conflicts of interest or duty.

The authors would like to extend their deep thanks to Kabbas Azhar, Michael Lavine, and Janelle Robins for their extensive research and writing assistance. Portions of this chapter were adapted from the essay "Legislating Data Loyalty," originally published in volume 97 of Notre Dame Law Review Reflection (2022).

W. Hartzog (✉)
Boston University School of Law, Boston, MA, USA
e-mail: whartzog@bu.edu

N. Richards
Cordell Institute, Washington University School of Law in St. Louis, St. Louis, MO, USA
e-mail: nrichards@wustl.edu

R. Ballardini et al. (eds.), *Emotional Data Applications and Regulation of Artificial Intelligence in Society*, Law, Governance and Technology Series 69,
https://doi.org/10.1007/978-3-031-80111-2_9

1 Introduction

Emotion data is eagerly sought governments and industry. It is also dangerous. This data—purporting to represent the emotional, psychological, or physical status of people by processing their expressions, movements, behaviour or other physical or mental characteristics—is irresistible for companies to use to their advantage. Although people are lured (or simply outright compelled) to share emotion data by the seductive claim it might make their lives easier or more enjoyable, these promises reveal little about the true risks of exposure. Emotion data may be inaccurate, biased, invasive, manipulative, and, at a fundamental level, potentially the perfect tool of control. The law has failed to recognize the dangers of emotion data, and thus people are left open to the exploitative whims of industry and government who collect and process it.

A core problem with emotion data is that it encourages self-dealing and opportunism. From an American perspective, current laws in the United States are not enough. Even aspects of the E.U.'s General Data Protection Regulation (GDPR) serve to empower informational self-determination rather than directly preventing opportunism. The procedural aspects of data protection regimes that emphasize informational self-determination do not protect against this kind of self-dealing. In fact, the machinery is built in such a way as to encourage it. "Consent" requests are the starting point for disloyal behaviour online, and serve as little more than window dressing—a "privacy theatre" that gives companies permission to engage in any manner of manipulation to wheedle, extract information, and slice and dice the data of our lives in a million different ways. When companies secure people's "consent" against their own interest for dubious practices, they show how watered-down and ineffective this approach to data privacy has become, particularly in the United States. However, while the law has become a problem, it also offers the possibility of an answer.

This chapter proposes a duty of loyalty for emotion data to prohibit recipients of emotion data from acting in ways that conflict with the best interests of the trusting party whose emotions are being quantified and processed. Loyalty, like much else in the law, is about power. In relationships of trust, the trusting party makes themselves vulnerable to the power of the entity entrusted with the data, which we'll call the "entrustee." In the particular case of an information relationship, power is conferred through the exposure of personal information and submission of agency. When parties deal with each other in technologically mediated environments such as app interfaces, telephone-answering AI decision trees, or social networks, this power is increased. Since the power given to entrustees allows them to make decisions that affect the well-being of the trusting party, inevitably, profit-seeking entrustees will act in their own self-interest in ways that disadvantage trusting parties—another example of what we refer to as opportunism.

Loyalty is the antidote to opportunism. Duties of loyalty are meant to protect against precisely this kind of exploitation. Loyalty shifts the legal duty from self-serving to other-serving. It has a morality broader than the profit-maximization of neoliberal capitalism and engagement business models, and it has deep roots in our law. Yet there is more than just abstract ethics and notions of honour to the duty of loyalty. Loyalty compels firm legal duties and prohibitions that, when breached, give rise to legal liability on the grounds of conflicts of interest or of duty.

The core idea animating a duty of loyalty is that trusted parties must make their own interests subservient to those made vulnerable through the extension of trust. A duty of loyalty for the processing of emotion data would protect people and encourage the interpersonal and institutional trust necessary for humans to thrive.

2 We Need a Duty of Loyalty for Processing Emotion Data

As existing rules do not fully respond to the power disparities and incentives for exploitation of emotion data, we need rules to encourage trust and prohibit self-dealing in these contexts. The processing of emotion data will only be sustainable when people can reliably trust that all such processing will serve their best interests. And a duty of loyalty is best the way to earn and keep that trust for a safe and prosperous future that makes all parties better off.

At bottom, data loyalty is a simple idea: The organizations we trust should not process our data or design their tools in ways that conflict with our best interests. Though it borrows from notions of loyalty in fiduciary law, it is distinct from them. We propose that lawmakers use a two-step process to articulate (1) a primary, general duty of loyalty for processing emotion data, followed by (2) context-specific "subsidiary" duties. In this way, a duty of data loyalty is not just appealing in theory—it can be effectively implemented in practice, just like the other duties of loyalty our law has recognized for hundreds of years. Thus, loyalty is not only flexible but capable of breathing life into America's comparatively weak privacy frameworks.

A duty of loyalty for privacy law is neither perfect nor a tool for all tasks, but loyalty does have one great virtue: it places the focus for information age problems on the relationships that define our social lives rather than on the data which is the by-product of those relationships. Loyalty shifts the law's focus away from the *procedural* rules of privacy law that are too easy to manipulate, and moves it towards the *substantive* question of what practices go too far. It is flexible and adaptable across contexts, cultures, and times. Consequently, loyalty can be a powerful response to what Shoshana Zuboff calls "surveillance capitalism", the claiming of "human experience as free raw material for hidden commercial practices of extraction, prediction, and sales... As significant a threat to human nature in the twenty-first century as industrial capitalism was to the natural world in the nineteenth and twentieth".[1]

[1] Zuboff (2019), p. vii.

Data loyalty has three key features: it is a (1) *relational duty* (2) that *prohibits self-dealing* (3) at the *expense of a trusting party*. Let us now break these three features apart.

2.1 A Relational Duty

Lawmakers regulating the privacy risks of emotion data could begin their task by focusing on one of three different things. First, there is the *data protection approach*: They could focus on the data itself, such as what can be collected and whether datasets are de-identified. This is the approach that most federal and European privacy laws have taken to date with laws such as the GDPR and the California Consumer Privacy Act (CCPA). Second, there is the *structural approach*: for example, by requiring companies to appoint a data privacy officer or focusing on monopoly power, which is the approach familiar to antitrust and corporate law. Third, there is the *relational approach*: Lawmakers could focus on our relationships, such as requiring confidentiality from physicians, lawyers, and other professionals.[2] Each of these approaches have their merits—and they are not mutually exclusive—but we believe that for emotion data, the relational approach should take precedence and focus on the relationships in which emotion data is collected and used.

Relationships are not just one of the oldest contexts in which privacy can flourish; they also have a number of distinct advantages for lawmakers looking to fight the excesses and abuses of data-hungry organizations. Relational duties are acutely sensitive to the *power disparities* within information relationships. Tech companies control what we see, what we can click on, and what sorts of information they want to extract from their customers. In addition, tech companies have incredible resources that help them predict and nudge our behaviour and they also have the financial incentive to keep us ever more exposed. Duties of loyalty protect against self-dealing, which is distinct from protection from the risks of harm that the related duty of care protects against. When it comes to loyalty, the act of betrayal itself is the principal legal wrong rather than any consequential damages. Loyalty duties are more stringent when there is a greater power imbalance greater vulnerability of the trusting party as a result of their exposure.[3]

Relational duties are also a way out of *privacy's consent trap*. For years, lawmakers, regulators, and companies have been debating whether the consent people gave was a truly meaningful, informed, and revocable choice. In reality, people click "I Agree" buttons and slightly wince without reading the terms and conditions because doing so is impossible or unrealistic; consent under such terms is both fictitious and broken. Yet, despite common knowledge that digital consent is rarely meaningful, lawmakers have clung to notice and consent regimes, possibly for

[2] Hartzog and Richards (2020).

[3] E.g. Balkin (2020), pp. 13–14.

lack of a better alternative. We believe that relational duties offer that alternative. These duties decouple choice (picking among alternatives) and consent (a choice with a binding legal consequence), allowing consumers to accept the relationship without accepting the risks of whatever harmful data practices and consequences lurk in the fine print, the business model, or the technology. Moreover, when protected by relational duties (and in particular loyalty's protection from betrayal), people can select from a range of choices without wincing in fear, because they would be protected no matter what they chose.[4]

Last but not least, relationships open the possibility of more *robust enforcement rules* because they are voluntarily entered into and hold a unique place in the law because of it. The concept of contractual privity could also be used to extend relational duties beyond the initial trusting party and entrustee. At the same time, because they regulate relationships rather than information flows, relational duties raise even fewer free expression issues than other forms of data regulation. In relationships, parties assume these duties by soliciting trust and voluntarily entering into these relationships. Moreover, protections for power-imbalanced relationships have a deep tradition in U.S. law in harmony with free expression frameworks. This is, for example, why lawyers do not have a First Amendment right to disclose client confidences, no matter how "newsworthy" those confidences might be.[5] For these reasons, shifting the focus of privacy law from data to relationships offers significant conceptual and practical advantages for effective policy.

2.2 *That Prohibits Self-Dealing*

Many of the problems of surveillance capitalism come down to the problem of self-dealing, where an organization exploits an advantage over a trusting party to its own benefit.[6] The failures of American privacy law have enabled such corporate opportunism and manipulation of consumers using human information. This problem is particularly serious in the context of "personalized" technologies, such as those enabled by emotion data that promise to know us so that they can better satisfy our needs and wants. Insufficiently constrained by privacy law and driven to maximize quarterly profits by corporate law, companies can deploy a potent cocktail of techniques derived from cognitive and behavioural science to "nudge" or otherwise influence the choices we make.[7] Advertised as serving consumers, technologies and

[4]For an extended critique of consent-based models for data processing, see Richards and Hartzog (2019).

[5]See, e.g. Balkin (2016); Volokh (2000), pp. 1057–1058 (explaining that parties who contract to maintain confidentiality have a reasonable expectation of privacy); McClurg (2006); but see Khan and Pozen (2019).

[6]See Cohen (2019); Zuboff (2019).

[7]See Richards (2019), pp. 39–50.

choice architecture have instead become weaponized, serving commodified consumers up to the companies and their commercial and political advertiser clients.[8] The fear of missing out thus becomes one more tool that can be used to drive notification-heavy ad-supported engagement models.[9]

Loyalty rules directly prohibit conflicted self-dealing. In so doing, they can change the incentives and business models of entire industries. Many critics believe that U.S. data privacy law has failed to change the corrosive business models that endanger, manipulate, mislead, and misinform, and polarize people every day. The law, these critics suggest, merely prunes the edges of wrongdoing rather than getting to the core of the problem.[10]

By taking self-dealing off the table as a general matter, a duty of data loyalty would directly address this problem. Indeed, more specific, subsidiary data loyalty rules for practices such as targeted advertising, web scraping, and manipulative interfaces could revolutionize entire industries with clearer rules of the road. Such rules could make certain abusive business models obsolete overnight. This would sharply contrast with the piecemeal and procedural approach of current U.S. data privacy law, which pre-supposes that all possible extraction models can be valid if they follow the right procedures and give people some semblance of control (however fictitious) over their information. Instead, data loyalty rules look directly to corporate profit motives and ask if they conflict with a trusting party's best interests. Rather than exploitation and extraction, they require profit models to be based on the provision of valuable services.

2.3 *At the Expense of a Trusting Party*

Loyalty rules safeguard trusting parties from betrayal, looking to whether a trusting party has been disadvantaged by an organization's self-dealing. When organizations enrich themselves at trusting parties' expense through their data, those trusting people consistently end up paying with their time, attention, mental well-being, reputation, and significant life opportunities.[11] These costs include everything from notifications that advance the platform's interests by interrupting our attention, to manipulative advertising that causes people to buy (or vote) differently in ways that

---

[8] Hartzog (2018)

[9] See Richards and Hartzog (2024), pp. 1168–1172.

[10] See, e.g. Dissenting Statement of Commissioner Rohit Chopra, *In re Facebook, Inc.*, FTC File No. 1823109, July 24, 2019, https://www.ftc.gov/system/files/documents/public_statements/1536911/chopra_dissenting_statement_on_facebook_7-24-19.pdf; Dissenting Statement Of Commissioner Rebecca Kelly Slaughter, *In re Facebook, Inc.*, FTC File No. 1823109, July 24, 2019, https://www.ftc.gov/system/files/documents/public_statements/1536918/182_3109_slaughter_statement_on_facebook_7-24-19.pdf.

[11] See Richards and Hartzog (2024).

serve advertisers, to the well-documented emotional injuries wrought by engagement-driven social media.[12]

Crucially, these costs, impositions, and manipulations, are made substantially more damaging by the "personalization" enabled by self-dealing in personal data. These notifications are not random or serving an individual's interests, such as a reminder to attend a meeting, but are teasing an individual out of the blue that someone they know may have done something interesting. It is not just an ad or a political message, but one calculated to an individual's precisely known psychology and vulnerabilities.[13] Moreover, social media is not just telling an individual what their friends are doing but is doing so in a way that is calibrated to push an individual's buttons to keep them scrolling (or doom-scrolling) with a reckless indifference to their mental health.[14]

The scope of protection that loyalty rules safeguard includes but is broader than recognized privacy harms such as identity theft, emotional harms, breaches of confidence, and dangerous exposure.[15] It also includes more subtle individual and collective costs to our identity, our ability to create relationships, our collectively held truths, and the obscurity that protects our ability to share and move about freely. As such, it protects against the full range of betrayals that powerful parties in an information relationship can perpetrate.

Consequently, loyalty duties are quite straightforward when understood as relational duties that prevent self-dealing at the expense of a trusting party. They accord with basic notions of fairness and decency; if you have power over someone who trusts you, you should not betray them or manipulate them to serve your own interests. It is undoubtedly for these reasons that our law has placed duties of loyalty on relationships with power imbalances for centuries across a wide variety of contexts.

3 A Model for Legislating Data Loyalty

One undeniable virtue of creating a duty of emotion data loyalty is that it would not be necessary to invent it from pure fiction. Loyalty duties have a long and established pedigree in our law, most famously in the law of fiduciaries. A duty of data loyalty

[12] See Hartzog and Richards (2022), pp. 1029–1031 (manipulation); Richards and Hartzog (2024), pp. 1168–1172 (mental health).

[13] This is precisely what happened in the Cambridge Analytica scandal, in which Facebook data was used to try to create finely calibrated psychological profiles of voters identified by their real names, suggesting which kinds of arguments would be most effective at getting them to act in the ways that the paying political advertisers wanted them to. See, e.g. Richards (2019), pp. 25–26.

[14] These are the allegations Facebook whistleblower Frances Haugen presented under oath before lawmakers in the United States and around the world in 2021. See, e.g. Perrigo (2021).

[15] See, e.g. Citron and Solove (2022); Calo (2014).

could draw heavily from this tradition and its proven ability to protect against the power imbalances in relationships in a fair, principled, and meaningful way.

As previously discussed, fiduciary law scholars have identified a two-step process lawmakers use to implement loyalty obligations in a fair and just way: first by articulating the primary duty of loyalty, then by creating and refining context-specific subsidiary duties.[16] A broad and general prohibition on substantial conflicts with the trusting party's best interests would prevent the most egregious forms of disloyalty across the board, generally orienting the company's incentives against betrayal rather than micromanage specific instances. At the same time, specific, substantive subsidiary duties that target particular contexts would ensure accountability and prevent the watering down of these frameworks. Through this "loyalty two-step" approach, a duty of emotion data loyalty could be both general enough to apply across the board, but sensitive enough to individual contexts to act with nuance and precision.

3.1 *First, a General Catchall Duty*

We propose a general rule of data loyalty that would apply to emotion data (and all personal data) as follows:

> Organizations shall not process data or design systems and tools in ways that significantly conflict with trusting parties' best interests that are implicated by their exposure.

Let us explain and define this proposed duty in a little more detail.

3.1.1 A *No-Conflict Rule* for Data and Design

Organizations gain power over trusting parties in two different ways: (1) by collecting and processing data and (2) by controlling our mediated experiences.[17] Loyalty's core mandate is avoiding conflicts. If the duty of loyalty is to accomplish anything, it should prohibit the conflicted design of digital tools and data processing. A general rule against such conflicts is a logical starting point. It could serve as the foundation for a host of regulatory regimes, self-regulatory efforts, and guidance to the public to encourage and nurture their trust.

---

[16] See, e.g. Sitkoff (2019) (explaining that that "[t]he duties of loyalty and care, which we might call the *primary* fiduciary duties, are typically structured as broad, open-ended standards that speak generally… By contrast, the *other* fiduciary duties, which we might call the *subsidiary* or *implementing* fiduciary duties, are typically structured as *rules*, or at least as *more specific standards* that speak with greater specificity".) (emphasis in original).

[17] See, e.g. Richards and Hartzog (2021); Hartzog (2018).

A general no-conflict rule has the remarkable advantage of directing lawmakers, and entrustees themselves, to interrogate not just actions but *motives* and *gains.*[18] Established fiduciary no-conflict rules "do not require the fiduciary to act in any particular way but are instead thought to establish boundaries within which the fiduciary may reasonably be expected to act loyally, at least to the extent that the rules isolate biasing factors that might induce the fiduciary to subjugate the interests of beneficiaries to the interests of others".[19]

Some lawmakers are reluctant to adopt duties of data loyalty because they fear creating a conflict with the exiting duties of loyalty that directors of organizations owe to shareholders.[20] This is an illusory conflict and, at most, can be resolved by lawmakers without substantially remaking corporate law.[21] Fiduciary law scholar Andrew Tuch explains that "imposing user-regarding obligations on corporations will not create untenable frictions between duties to users and duties to shareholders... [T]he primary criticism—that Delaware corporate law undermines the information fiduciary regime—should be dismissed".[22]

If lawmakers were to adopt data loyalty rules, then corporate law would demand that directors adhere to them first and foremost.[23] In fact, if a duty of data loyalty owed by platforms to people is made positive law, a director that acts with the intent to betray customer best interests or fails to act in the face of a known loyalty obligation may be liable for breaching their fiduciary obligation to shareholders as well as their duty to the customers.[24]

If data loyalty is going to work, then trusting parties must be prioritized over other loyalties, particular those firms owe to their shareholders. Such explicit prioritization would resolve any lingering "divided loyalty" concerns. Self-interested actions would be allowed, but only if they do not conflict with trusting parties' best interests, and of course, it is an elementary principle of US constitutional law that a federal duty of loyalty would take precedence over any state duties by operation of the Supremacy Clause.

Furthermore, data loyalty would still allow companies to profit and flourish. The "best interests" polestar of loyalty, by design, accommodates all kinds of self-serving behaviour. It simply limits self-serving behaviour to instances where it aligns

[18] Miller (2011), p. 257 (citing Smith and Getzler (2003), p. 67) ("the motives of the fiduciary are the crucial element in determining whether the fiduciary has acted loyally, and the requirement of motive is quite specific-the fiduciary 'must act (or not act) in what he perceives to be the best interests of the beneficiary.'").

[19] Miller and Gold (2015), p. 557 (2015).

[20] Khan and Pozen (2019), p. 534.

[21] See, e.g. Balkin (2020), p. 23 ("Management's fiduciary obligations to shareholders assume that the corporation will attempt to comply with the legal duties owed to those affected by the corporation's business practices, even if this reduces shareholder value.").

[22] Tuch (2021), p. 1902.

[23] Id.

[24] See id.

with the best interests of the primary trusting party, but such would be the proverbial cases of "win-win" rather than those of extraction or exploitation.[25]

3.1.2 The Collective Best Interests of Trusting Parties

There are a number of different ways to deal with inevitable conflicts among trusting parties as well. The first would be to impose a reasonableness and fairness approach, or a duty of impartiality between people who expose themselves to organizations.[26] Our proposal adopts a collective approach to "best interests", to better avoid conflicts between trusting parties and help free privacy law from its overly individualistic focus. Allowing lawmakers and regulators to focus on the collective best interests of "trusting parties", they can better respond to systemic harms detected sporadically by individuals but strongly at the group level. We recommend that lawmakers specifically prioritize interests that are held collectively by groups of customers, with certain individually held interests holding sway only to the extent they do not conflict with collective customer interests.[27]

A more collective "best interests" approach would be an improvement over the individual self-determination model, which does not compel people to consider the common good or threats to groups they are not members of. When people give consent to data practices, they usually are not motivated to reflect upon how their decision will affect vulnerable groups to which they do not belong.[28] This is similar to some people's indifference to public health when they "choose" not to wear a mask during a pandemic. A reasonableness, context-sensitive approach would require loyalty obligations that are proportional to the risk of abuse. The duty would be the most robust where the volume of data collected is highest and organization's power over people is the greatest.

[25] See Langbein (2005), p. 932 ("[A] transaction prudently undertaken to advance the best interest of the beneficiaries best serves the purpose of the duty of loyalty, even if the trustee also does or might derive some benefit. A transaction in which there has been conflict or overlap of interest should be sustained if the trustee can prove that the transaction was prudently undertaken in the best interest of the beneficiaries.").

[26] Gold (2019), p. 398 ("[C]onflicts among best interests obligations [owed to multiple beneficiaries] are unavoidable. Where such conflicts exist, one answer is to find that loyalty must manifest itself as fairness and reasonableness. Another answer is to impose a duty of impartiality", which would demand "due regard" (though not necessarily equality)).

[27] *Id.* (discussing the hierarchy of obligations approach to how "common shares might ordinarily benefit from fiduciary obligations while preferred shares will only benefit in exceptional circumstances".).

[28] See, e.g. Richards and Hartzog (2019); Hartzog and Selinger (2019).

3.1.3 Limited to Trusting Parties' Exposure

As previously discussed, trust is the willingness to make oneself vulnerable to the actions of others. Our proposed general duty of loyalty would be limited to the extent of a trusting person's vulnerability. Accordingly, "best interests" should not be understood as a general well-being standard but instead be limited to the specific interests affected by the entrustment of data, labour, and attention. This would also direct organizations to ask what interests are implicated by the affordances of their data and human interface designs. For example, systems that allow for microtargeted advertising based on highly detailed profiles make the exploitation of vulnerable parties easier and compound incentives for companies to engineer exposure for financial gains.[29]

In conjunction with a duty of care, a duty of loyalty animates a number of different broad subsidiary duties, such as duties of candour, good faith, non-delegation of key services, and confidentiality.[30] Yet, legislatures and courts often go further and create or delegate authority for the creation of a series of clearer subsidiary obligations that are more like rules rather than vague standards.[31]

3.2 *Second, Rules for Subsidiary Implementing Duties*

More specific subsidiary rules will help resolve the common objection that a duty of data loyalty is just too vague.[32] In this way, the "two step" answers the vagueness objection and reveals that the apparent vice of vagueness is actually a virtue of

[29] See, e.g. Jerome and Johnson (2021).

[30] See Whitt (2019), pp. 94–95.

[31] Robert Sitkoff explains that "[t]he duties of loyalty and care, which we might call the *primary* fiduciary duties, are typically structured as broad, open-ended standards that speak generally. . . .By contrast, the *other* fiduciary duties, which we might call the *subsidiary* or *implementing* fiduciary duties, are typically structured as *rules*, or at least as *more specific standards* that speak with greater specificity". Sitkoff (2019) (emphasis in original). Sitkoff gives the prudent investor rule as an example of a how subsidiary rules develop in trust law. Id. at 421 ("Structurally, the prudent investor rule is an elaborated standard that, by focusing on risk-and-return and diversification, gives specific content to the open-ended, primary duty of care. . . . [R]ather than start from scratch in every fiduciary investment matter, fiduciaries, beneficiaries, and courts may look to the elaboration with the prudent investor rule to discern the application of a duty of care.").

[32] See, e.g. Sitkoff gives the prudent investor rule as an example of a how subsidiary rules develop in trust law. Id. at 421 ("Structurally, the prudent investor rule is an elaborated standard that, by focusing on risk-and-return and diversification, gives specific content to the open-ended, primary duty of care. . . . [R]ather than start from scratch in every fiduciary investment matter, fiduciaries, beneficiaries, and courts may look to the elaboration with the prudent investor rule to discern the application of a duty of care."); Grimmelmann (arguing that when applied to digital platforms, it becomes clear that "the rule against self-dealing is either absurdly under-inclusive, absurdly over-inclusive, or both.").

flexibility.[33] Enacting legislation should also either provide for subsidiary duties or delegate rulemaking authority for future subsidiary rules. These subsidiary data loyalty rules might take a page from non-privacy fiduciary duties such as disclosure, consent, accounting for property (access & portability rights), confidentiality, and the full suite of Fair Information Practice Principles (FIPPS). This would apply some of the most significant obligations compelled by the GDPR. Combined with a duty of care, a duty of loyalty encourages specific rulemaking for concepts such as data minimization and legitimate basis requirements that would be bound together by an anti-betrayal as well as an anti-harm ethos.

However, lawmakers need not stop there. They might also consider rigid prohibitions on specific practices such as the deployment of unreasonably dangerous automated tools or the use of personal data to train those automated systems. They could ban unconstrained surveillance advertising or engagement-first strategies that prey on emotional reactions. Moreover, they could create subsidiary rules for inherently dangerous practices and technologies that, at the systemic level, are in fundamental conflict with the best interests of trusting parties.

One such conflict is emotion recognition systems: a fundamentally misguided and oppressive tool that seeks to collect emotion data by processing facial imagery, speech, and behavioural signals.[34] Such systems are both inherently inaccurate and fundamentally biased against marginalized people and communities.[35] Lawmakers could also craft more rules designed for specific parties, such as explicitly prohibiting social media companies from deploying affect recognition systems on users' photos. Though these rules might be disclosure mandates, process requirements, prohibitions on conduct, or obligated tasks, each should target specific areas where trusted parties have an incentive to engage in self-dealing.[36]

More generally, there are four main areas where the incentives for self-dealing by the powerful party in an information relationship are overwhelming and thus ripe for subsidiary data loyalty rules.[37] These are: (1) *personalization*, i.e. treating people differently based upon personal information; (2) *gatekeeping*, i.e. managing government and third-party access to entrusted data; (3) *influencing*, i.e. levering personal data and digital tools to sway individuals' decision-making; and (4) *mediation*, i.e. creating and administering systems that facilitate interaction between users. These contexts often overlap and involve issues such as discriminatory microtargeting, the harmful amplification of misinformation, failure of process for content moderation, and abusive dark patterns. In each of these areas, we propose

[33] Hartzog and Richards (2022), p. 1015.

[34] For an exploration on the dangers of affect recognition systems see, e.g. Crawford (2021a, b); Stark and Hoey (2021).

[35] *Id.*

[36] See Gold (2019).

[37] See, e.g. Balkin (2020); Scholz (2020), p. 197; Dobkin (2018), p. 17; Barrett, *supra* note ^, 1100 (2019)("[A]n information fiduciary framework should also address manipulation and discrimination in order to ensure that people are protected from the full array of modern digital threats that they face.").

that lawmakers create subsidiary loyalty rules and standards to mitigate disloyal behaviour contextually.

3.2.1 Loyal Personalization

The modern Internet routinely and systemically treats people differently based upon personal information or characteristics. Although targeted and behavioural advertising is the most prominent example of this, first-party product and streaming recommendations, news feeds, default settings, layouts, and more are all designed automatically to look and act differently based on people's personal characteristics. Some of this personalization, such as targeted recommendations for networked connections based upon intentionally revealed data such as where you work or attended high school, would probably be loyal. However, other personalization systems, such as those that wrongfully discriminate or have a disparate impact on protected, marginalized, or vulnerable groups of people, would likely conflict with that trusting collective's best interests. Subsidiary rules built around the concept of loyal personalization could firmly and clearly address a systemic problem in a way that traditional data protection frameworks have been unable to mitigate.

3.2.2 Loyal Gatekeeping

Entrustees have a remarkable ability to facilitate third party access to trusting parties and their data. This access is the source of the power of most major platforms, and everyone wants a piece of the users. Indeed, advertisers clamour for their attention, data brokers and AI developers lust for their data, and governments demand evidence. Entrustees have financial incentives to build portals and facilitate access by third parties. Not all third-party access conflicts with the best interests of trusting parties. For example, contextual advertising usually does not significantly leverage people's own data or limitations against them, nor does it usually expose trusting parties to significant privacy harms. Protocols for interoperability that help people transfer their data from one place may also serve trusting parties' interests.

However, certain lax gatekeeping practices would be disloyal if they endanger trusting parties by obscuring risk while facilitating access to third parties for organizational gains or cost avoidance. The three most resonant privacy scandals in the past decade—the US government surveillance revelations by Edward Snowden, the FBI's request that Apple help them bypass encryption protections, and Cambridge Analytica's massive Facebook data exfiltration—all involved gatekeeping issues. Subsidiary rules built around the concept of loyal gatekeeping would help resolve longstanding debates around what obligations trusted organizations have regarding third-party access through portals, APIs, interfaces, and the automated scraping of websites. In combination with a duty of confidentiality, subsidiary rules could also clarify when directly sharing entrusted emotion data with third parties is disloyal.

3.2.3 Loyal Influencing

Every single design decision made in the creation of a website or app is meant to facilitate or encourage a particular kind of behaviour.[38] The structure of digital technologies will affect people's choices regarding the collection of emotion data even if the effect is not intended by designers. When designers create a drop-down menu, privacy settings, "I agree" buttons, and any other feature that implicates people's privacy, they are influencing them; they cannot avoid it.[39] Given their power, designers should be loyal in exercising their influence.

The most prominent example of disloyal influence involves organizations leveraging "dark patterns" or "malicious interfaces" which are user interface elements meant to influence a person's behaviour against their intentions or best interests.[40] For a variety of reasons, including its highlighting of the nature of the wrong, we prefer the term "disloyal design" to "dark patterns." Companies deploy effort traps, intentionally making account deletion confusing and difficult. They make "cancel" buttons hard to see and press, obscure important details in tiny fonts or walls of boilerplate, and leverage our deeply entrenched and empirically-validated overconfidence regarding risk, deference for conformity, endowment effects, status quo bias, and other biases and mental shortcuts to manipulate us to their ends. Jamie Luguri and Lior Strahilevitz have observed that "dark patterns are strikingly effective in getting consumers to do what they would not do when confronted with more neutral user interfaces".[41]

Even though lawmakers have struggled for years to articulate when attempts at persuasion become harmful,[42] entrustees do need to injure trusting parties to violate a duty of loyalty. As we have already explained, when it comes to loyalty (unlike care), betrayal is harm enough. Subsidiary rules around disloyal attempts to influence would address the most pernicious and dangerous disloyal design strategies head-on.[43] Lawmakers should focus on how the design is meant to take advantage of

[38] See, e.g. Winner (1989), p. 124.

[39] *Id.* ("Human beings...cannot wish [choice architecture] away. Any store has a design; some products are seen first, and others are not. Any menu places options at various locations. Television stations come with different numbers, and strikingly, numbers matter, even when the costs of switching are vanishingly low; people tend to choose the station at the lower number, so that channel 3 will obtain more viewers than channel 53.").

[40] See, e.g. Hartzog (2018); Luguri and Strahilevitz (2021); Calo (2014); Conti and Sobiesk (2009), p. 73; Gunawan et al. (2021); Brignull (2011); Gray et al. (2018), pp. 1–14; Mathur et al. (2019), p. 2; Arunesh Mathur et al. (forthcoming 2021), p. 13; Bosch et al. (2016), p. 248; Waldman (2020), 105, 107–109.

[41] Luguri and Strahilevitz (2021), p. 46.

[42] Id.; see also Daniel Susser et al. (2019).

[43] Luguri and Strahilevitz recommend a multi-factor test to help determine when dark patterns cross the line that looks to considerations such as the defendant's intent, the susceptibility of vulnerable populations, and the magnitude of the dark pattern's costs and benefits.

a person's limitations or vulnerabilities to benefit the designer in a way that is against the trusting party's best interests.[44]

3.2.4 Loyal Mediation

Certain kinds of organizations design their platforms so that their users interact not just with the organization itself, but with each other. Sometimes this can be a good experience for people who use these services. However, things can quickly turn for the worse when companies feel pressured to achieve continual and endless growth. Indeed, companies create systems that reward virality and most outrageous or venomous hot takes instead of the ostensible purpose of meaningful social interaction and social, emotional, and intellectual nourishment. As we have elsewhere written, "[f]ew emotions are more engaging than outrage, which is why engagement creates a toxic forum for the discussion of public issues."[45] Recognizing this fact, companies optimize their algorithms and interfaces to reward our most impulsive and petty reactions. Facebook's "emotion contagion" experiment demonstrated these systems' ability to regulate our emotions but was merely a harbinger of the emotional manipulation we can expect from intermediaries eager to maximize profit.[46] This can lead to acute individual harms such as harassment and emotional health harms as well as systemic harms such as polarization, reduced ability to engage in self-governance, negative public health outcomes, and chilling effects for large groups of vulnerable users.

Though a duty of loyalty cannot solve all of the complex problems of content moderation or harassment, companies do have remarkable power to influence how people using their system interact with each other. When they use this power in a way that conflicts with the best interests of their users in order to optimize growth, they are being disloyal. Naturally, subsidiary rules for loyal mediation are complicated because of the potentially conflicting interests among and between actors and those potentially adversely affected by their actions. However, our proposed "collective best interests" approach would help lawmakers craft clear subsidiary rules to guide organizations in loyal mediation.

[44] Balkin has proposed looking to "techniques of persuasion and influence that (1) prey on another person's emotional vulnerabilities and lack of knowledge, (2) to benefit oneself or one's allies, and (3) reduce the welfare of the other person". Balkin (2018).

[45] Richards and Hartzog (2024), p. 1172.

[46] Selinger and Hartzog (2016).

4 Conclusion

Although emotion data invites harmful self-dealing by data processors that our privacy laws are not able to effectively address, a duty of loyalty for the processing of emotion data and design of technologies that collect and use it can help solve this problem. Nevertheless, duties of emotion data loyalty as part of a broader loyalty duties will take time and effort to meaningfully implement into privacy law. Though data loyalty is a significant and necessary departure from privacy law's ineffective notice and consent approach, lawmakers can confidently embrace loyalty and other relational duties as part of a holistic approach to mitigating the power and abuses of data collectors. If done clearly, carefully, contextually, and with commitment, lawmakers can chart a bold new vision for our privacy rules that is capable of nurturing a sustainable and flourishing future for those who share their personal information as well as those entrusted with it.

References

Balkin J (2016) Information Fiduciaries and the First Amendment. UC Davis Law Rev 49:1183–1234

Balkin J (2018) Fixing social media's grand bargain. Hoover Inst. Aegis Series Paper No. 1814. 14

Balkin J (2020) The fiduciary model of privacy. Harv Law Rev Forum 134:11–33

Barrett L (2019) Confiding in Con Men: U.S. Privacy law, the Gdpr, and information fiduciaries. Seattle Univ Law Rev 42:1057–1113

Bosch C et al (2016) Tales from the dark side: privacy dark strategies and privacy dark patterns. 2016(4) Proceedings on Privacy Enhancing Technologies 237, 248

Brignull H (2011) Dark patterns: deception vs. Honesty in UI design. A List Apart https://alistapart.com/article/dark-patterns-deception-vs-honesty-in-ui-design/. Accessed 12 June 2024

Calo R (2014) Digital market manipulation. Geo Wash Law Rev 82:995–1051

Citron D, Solove D (2022) Privacy harms. Boston Univ Law Rev 102:793–863

Cohen J (2019) Between truth and power. Oxford University Press, Oxford

Conti G, Sobiesk E (2009) Malicious interfaces and personalization's uninviting future. IEEE Security and Privacy (May/June 2009) 73. http://www.rumint.org/gregconti/publications/j3pri.pdf. Accessed 12 June 2024

Crawford K (2021a) Atlas of AI. Yale University Press, New Haven

Crawford K (2021b) Artificial Intelligence Is Misreading Human Emotion. The Atlantic. https://www.theatlantic.com/technology/archive/2021/04/artificial-intelligence-misreading-human-emotion/618696/. Accessed 12 June 2024

Dobkin A (2018) Information fiduciaries in practice: data privacy and user expectations. Berkeley Technol Law J 33:1–50

Gold A (2019) The fiduciary duty of loyalty. In: Criddle E (ed) The Oxford handbook of fiduciary law. Oxford University Press, Oxford

Gray C et al (2018) The Dark (patterns) side of UX design. In: Proceedings of the 2018 CHI Conference on Human Factors in Computing Systems, Montreal, April 2018, pp 1–14 http://dl.acm.org/citation.cfm?doid=3173574.3174108

Gunawan J et al (2021) Towards and Understanding of Dark Patterns Privacy Harms, CHI Workshop, What Can CHI Do About Dark Patterns? https://darkpatternsindesign.com/position-papers/. Accessed 12 June 2024

Hartzog W (2018) Privacy's blueprint: the battle to control the design of new technologies. Harvard University Press, Cambridge

Hartzog W, Richards N (2020) Privacy's constitutional moment and the limits of data protection. Boston College Law Rev 61:1687–1764

Hartzog W, Richards N (2022) The surprising virtues of data loyalty. Emory Law J 71:985–1033

Hartzog W, Selinger E (2019) The inconsentability of facial surveillance. Loyola Law Rev 66:101–123

Jerome J, Johnson AF (2021) AdTech and kids: behavioral ads need a time out. Common Sense Media. https://d2e111jq13me73.cloudfront.net/sites/default/files/uploads/AdTech%20and%20Kids.pdf. Accessed 12 June 2024

Khan LM, Pozen DE (2019) A skeptical view of information fiduciaries. Harv Law Rev 133:497–534

Langbein JH (2005) Questioning the trust law duty of loyalty: sole interest or best interest? Yale Law J 114:932–995

Luguri J, Strahilevitz L (2021) Shining a light on dark patterns. J Legal Anal 13:43–110

Mathur A et al (2019) Dark patterns at scale: findings from a crawl of 11K shopping websites. Proc ACM Hum-Comput Interact 3:2

Mathur A et al (2021) What makes a dark pattern... dark? Design Attributes, Normative Considerations, and Measurement Methods. In: Proceedings of the 2021 CHI Conference on Human Factors in Computing Systems, Yokohama, p 13 http://arxiv.org/abs/2101.04843

McClurg AJ (2006) Kiss and tell: protecting intimate relationship privacy through implied contracts of confidentiality. Univ Cincinnati Law Rev 74:887–941

Miller PB (2011) A theory of fiduciary liability. McGill Law J 6:257

Miller PB, Gold AS (2015) Fiduciary governance. Wm Mary Law Rev 57:557

Perrigo B (2021) Inside Frances Haugen's decision to take on Facebook. Time

Richards N (2019) Why privacy matters. Oxford University Press, Oxford

Richards N, Hartzog W (2019) The pathologies of digital consent. Wash Univ Law Rev 96:1461–1503

Richards N, Hartzog W (2021) A duty of loyalty for privacy law. Wash Univ Law Rev 99:961–1021

Richards N, Hartzog W (2024) Against engagement. Boston Univ Law Rev 104:1151–1179

Scholz LH (2020) Fiduciary boilerplate, locating fiduciary relationships in information age consumer transactions. J Corp Law 46:143–198

Selinger E, Hartzog W (2016) Facebook's emotional contagion study and the ethical problem of co-opted identity in mediated environments where users lack control. Res Ethics 12(1):35–43

Sitkoff RH (2019) Other fiduciary duties: implementing loyalty and care. In: Criddle E (ed) The Oxford handbook of fiduciary law. Oxford University Press, Oxford

Smith L, Getzler J (ed) (2003) The motive, not the deed. In: Rationalizing property, equity and trusts: essays in honour of Edward burn. Oxford University Press, Oxford, pp 53, 67

Stark L, Hoey J (2021) The ethics of emotion in artificial intelligence systems. In: FAccT '21 Proceedings of the 2021 ACM conference on fairness accountability and transparency, New York, Mar 2021, p. 782 https://doi.org/10.1145/3442188.3445939

Susser D, Roessler B, Nissenbaum H (2019) Online manipulation: hidden influences in a digital world. Geo Law Technol Rev 4:1–45

Tuch AF (2021) A general defense of information fiduciaries. Wash Univ Law Rev 98:1897–1937

Volokh E (2000) Freedom of speech and information privacy: the troubling implications of a right to stop people from speaking about you. Stan Law Rev 52:1057–1058

Waldman AE (2020) Cognitive biases, dark patterns, and the "Privacy Paradox". Curr Iss Psych 31: 105, 107–109

Whitt RS (2019) Old school goes online: exploring fiduciary obligations of loyalty and care in the digital platforms era. Santa Clara Comput High Technol Law J 36:75

Winner L (1989) The whale and the reactor. University of Chicago Press, Chicago, p 124

Zuboff S (2019) The age of surveillance capitalism. Public Affairs, New York, p vii

TALKING TO STRANGERS. On the Use of Emotional AI to Prevent and Combat Online Grooming and Sex Chatting with Minors

Anne de Hingh

Abstract At the intersection of emerging AI technologies and the protection of minors against online sexual abuse, fascinating yet worrisome developments unfurl before our eyes. On the one hand, various new forms of online text-based sexual behaviour aimed at minors (online grooming, solicitation of minors, attempted online grooming and online sex chatting) are brought within the scope of criminal law, thus leading to forms of preventive or risk-based criminal law. On the other hand, various (emotional) AI technologies that process and analyse textual/linguistic data are more and more commonly employed as investigative tools to detect or prevent these kinds of (criminal) behaviour or catch online predators in the act. However, not only do these technologies still fall short in many respects and are therefore demonstrably ineffective but their use also poses a potential threat to fundamental rights and online values such as privacy, freedom of expression, confidentiality of communication, online security and safety, especially of the very children they are supposed to protect. This chapter offers a critical review of some of the possible consequences of AI-driven prevention and detection of online text-based sexual offenses, particularly by the use of police bots and large scale, automated scanning of online speech.

1 Introduction and Outline of the Chapter

With the development and the rise of the internet, new forms of criminal offenses arose. Its scalability, transnational nature and its possibilities of operating anonymously, turned the internet into a fertile environment for harmful and illegal behaviour. This certainly also applies to online sexual offences, whether or not

A. de Hingh (✉)
VU Amsterdam, Faculty of Law, Amsterdam, The Netherlands
e-mail: a.e.de.hingh@vu.nl

R. Ballardini et al. (eds.), *Emotional Data Applications and Regulation of Artificial Intelligence in Society*, Law, Governance and Technology Series 69,
https://doi.org/10.1007/978-3-031-80111-2_10

directed against minors, such as online grooming, the solicitation of minors, attempted online grooming and online sex chatting.[1]

Some authors have qualified the regulation of these specific offences as a so-called "kneejerk regulation".[2] In particular, when the online safety of children may seem to be at stake, it appears that legislators are indeed more inclined to immediately impose strict regulation in return. This can lead to new legislation that is motivated by moral considerations or by a certain degree of "techno-panic" about the risks of online technology to minors, rather than by objective numbers and facts.[3]

Another common feature of types of criminal behaviour like online grooming and online sex chatting is that they are by definition communication offenses, as language, i.e. spoken or written text, indeed plays a pivotal role in committing these crimes. Language, written text or speech, is the instrument by which potential groomers approach their potential victims, and by which the victims react to them. Therefore, spoken and written words will automatically also be the evidence on which suspicions of online grooming or sex chatting with minors are based. In itself, this text-based nature of these offences has consequences for the way in which they are enforced. To decide whether actual grooming or sex chatting takes place, naturally (all) online conversations have to be scanned and analysed by law enforcement authorities. And to prevent time-consuming, labour-intensive and ineffective investigative methods, various AI-based tools to detect and investigate illegal speech could solve this problem.

A question related to the theme of this edited volume is to what extent the AI used to detect these text-based online offences could be considered *emotional* AI, as language and emotions naturally relate in various ways.[4] Based on numerous findings in the literature, it can be stated that the specific human language that is used in grooming communication, i.e. the verbal cues in spoken or written form in a conversation between a potential groomer and a potential grooming victim, no doubt represent affections and emotions. Therefore, the AI that is used to detect specific types of communications and is trained to analyse online speech could be qualified as emotional AI.[5] This corresponds to the scholarly literature on emotional or affective AI where emotional AI is often more broadly defined as "any technological application that is used to read and react to emotions and/or make predictions about the emotional states of people using data sources such as facial (micro)-movements,

---

[1] De Hingh (2018), De Hingh (2023a).

[2] Van der Hof and Koops (2011).

[3] Staksrud (2013); Van der Hof (2014).

[4] The various ways in which language and emotion are related can be found in the work of Van Berkum: Van Berkum (2012), Van Berkum (2019).

[5] See also, for example, McStay (2019): "This is a weak form of AI in that these technologies read and react to emotions through text, voice, computer vision and biometric sensing, but they do not have sentience or undergo emotional states themselves. Ultimately based on mathematics, analytics are applied to describe and predict behavioural patterns among people by generating data points from people's words, pictures, intonation, gestures, physiology and facial expressions."

body language, vocal tone or the choice of words".[6] As an addition to the definition used in this edited volume, AI systems that are used for scanning, analysing and responding to grooming language and speech and AI that is capable of communicating with potential groomers itself, evidently are therefore classified as emotional AI.[7]

First of all in this chapter, a concise overview is given of the various forms of online text-based sexual behaviour aimed at minors and how they are regulated and criminalised on a national and international level (Sect. 2). Also, in this section, some observations on the occurrence and prevalence of these crimes are discussed to see whether these justify the emergence of increasingly stringent legislation and intrusive investigative methods based on (emotional) AI in this field. In Sect. 3, existing practices and new legislative proposals on grooming prevention and detection by AI are explained and discussed. These include chatbots and AI-systems that detect, recognize and analyse language. Then, in Sect. 4, it is argued that instead of introducing emotional AI systems into the realm of the prevention, investigation and detection of online grooming and other related types of text-based behaviour directed to minors, other interventions should be given priority for the sake of the online safety of children. In this context, it is concluded that the use of emotional AI detection has major implications on shared European values and fundamental rights such as privacy and the protection of personal data, the freedom of expression and confidentiality of communication, and also especially of the very minors these technologies are supposed to protect. Moreover, AI-based detection and investigation not only pose a threat to values and fundamental rights but also appear to be highly unreliable and ineffective.

2 Text-Based Online Child Sexual Abuse: Regulation and Prevalence

The regulation of text-based online abuse of minors is a relatively new phenomenon. Only in 2007, was online grooming first criminalised when the Council of Europe Convention on Protection of Children against Sexual Exploitation and Sexual Abuse (the Lanzarote Convention) was concluded.[8] Grooming refers to the process during which a potential offender engages with a minor online, builds a friendly relationship with this minor and encapsulates her/him in preparation for a real-world encounter with the purpose of sexually abusing this minor.[9] Grooming is thus a preparatory offense that is committed online with the intention of abusing the child in the offline

[6]Podoletz (2022), p. 1067; McStay (2019), p. 1. Katirai (2023).

[7]See the definition given by Ballardini, van den Hoven van Genderen and Järvinen in this volume.

[8]***Council of Europe Treaty Series - No. 201*** Convention on Protection of Children against Sexual Exploitation and Sexual Abuse, also known as "the Lanzarote Convention", 2007.

[9]De Hingh (2018).

world, in a subsequent phase. Other behaviour, for example, coercing a child to produce "self-generated" sexual imagery or performing sexual acts in front of a webcam, or the actual physical sexual abuse are not part of the criminal act of online grooming.

2.1 Specifics of International and National Grooming Regulation

Article 23 of the Lanzarote Convention sets out the successive elements and phases of online grooming: 1. Online, written or spoken communication between the potential groomer and the minor victim takes place through the use of information and communication technologies, i.e. in chat rooms, on gaming or social media platforms, through texting, emailing etc.; 2. during which the perpetrator makes a proposal to meet in the real world; 3. for the purpose of committing a sexual offence against the minor; 4. and the meeting proposal is followed by material acts leading to such a meeting (e.g. when the potential groomer arrives at the meeting place, buys a train ticket for the victim, or sends an itinerary to the meeting place).

The majority of member states of the Council of Europe (signatories to the Lanzarote Convention) introduced online grooming in one way or another into their domestic law as a criminal offence. On an EU level, the online solicitation of children for sexual purposes or online grooming was regulated in the Child Sexual Abuse Directive.[10] In Article 6 of the Directive, the solicitation of children for sexual purposes was defined as "the intentional conduct of the proposal, by means of information and communication technology, by an adult to meet a child who has not reached the age of sexual consent, for the purpose of committing any of the offences referred to in Article 3(4) and Article 5(6), where that proposal was followed by material acts leading to such a meeting"—fitting in seamlessly with the provision in the Lanzarote Convention.

In the Netherlands, online grooming was introduced in the Dutch Criminal Code (Article 248e of the DCC) in 2010. Here, the scope of the offense has increased considerably as, first of all, in recent years several Dutch courts have more than once convicted suspects of *attempted grooming*—which can be defined as online sexual communication with a minor with a sexual intent *not* resulting in a proposal for a (concrete) meeting and without performing material acts leading to such a meeting.[11]

The terms (online) grooming and solicitation of children for sexual purposes are used alternately and interchangeably in the proposed regulation of the European Commission on child sexual abuse online (the so-called CSAM regulation), which covers among other things the combating and prevention of the online solicitation of minors (see Sect. 3.2 of this chapter). Article 2 of the CSAM regulation offers a

[10] 2011/93/EU.

[11] Van der Hof et al. (2019), pp. 435–436.

definition of online solicitation which refers directly to the above mentioned definition from the Directive on Child Sexual Abuse (2011).

Additionally, again in the Netherlands, a legislative proposal criminalising sex chatting with minors has been adopted by Parliament and has come into effect from July 2024. This new offense criminalizes engaging systematically in sexually communication with minors under the age of 16, without having the intention of meeting and/or sexually abuse the minor (new Article 251 of the Dutch Criminal Code).[12] With this Dutch proposal, an explicit premise of the Council of Europe Convention of Lanzarote was permanently abandoned. Whereas at the time it was emphasized by the negotiators that *"simply sexual chatting with a child, albeit as part of the preparation of the child for sexual abuse, was insufficient in itself to incur criminal responsibility"*, 15 years later the Dutch legislator obviously finds it essential to intervene with criminal law at this early stage.

2.2 Prevalence of Online Grooming and Sex Chatting

When new legislative initiatives are being developed in the fight against the sexual abuse of children, such as the initiative to criminalize online grooming in 2007 and the current Dutch initiative to criminalize sex chatting, one would expect that the necessity for these legislative prohibitions would be firmly substantiated. Indeed, one would expect statistics with regard to the occurrence and increase of these phenomena and the harmful effects on minors underpinning the need for the proposal. However, the data on the prevalence of online grooming are extremely scarce and data on online sex chatting are, as far as I know, not available at all.[13] Any firm statement or position on an assumed increase of these phenomena and their harmful effects on minors are therefore purely speculative.

The very few datasets on the prevalence of online grooming that are available show a mixed picture and do not indicate any substantial increase. In 2020, according to the American National Center for Missing & Exploited Children (NCMEC), a total of 1400 grooming cases were related to the EU, whereas the number of reports *worldwide* was 37,872 (but this number included reported cases of sextortion).[14] In the UK, reporting data show that in 2021/22 there were 6156

[12] De Hingh (2023a). See https://www.eerstekamer.nl/wetsvoorstel/36222_wet_seksuele_misdrijven.

[13] Also, Gorissen et al. (2020), pp. 28–29.

[14] These numbers are based on reports via NCMEC's Cyber Tipline: https://www.missingkids.org/content/ncmec/en/blog/2021/online-enticement-reports-skyrocket-in-2020.html According to NCMEC, compared to 2019, this would mean almost a doubling of the number of reports, which, still according to NCMEC, can be explained by the corona pandemic, as a result of which potential victims and groomers spent more time online. In 2021, 44,155 cases of "online enticement" including sextortion were reported. See also the Impact Assessment Report accompanying the CSAM Proposal, p. 22.

reported offenses related to sexual communication with a child.[15] In the Netherlands, approximately 150 cases of grooming are reported on an annual basis.[16]

Moreover, research shows that only a small percentage of young people are at serious risk on the internet or consider what they experience online as problematic.[17] A large-scale survey by EU Kids Online, a long-term pan-European study by the London School of Economics into the opportunities, risks and safety of the internet for children, showed already in 2010 and again in 2020 that the vast majority of children surveyed had never been confronted with (attempted) grooming.[18] The majority of the children who indicated that they had ever received unsolicited online sexual messages or requests had only rarely experienced this and most of the invitations came from peers and were not perceived as risky or annoying by the minors themselves.[19]

In general, it was found that children who run the risk of falling victim to online grooming make up a very specific, socially more vulnerable group. They appear to be more susceptible to suffer from psychological problems and a lack of self-confidence than other groups, coming from problematic family situations, and are also at greater risk of being victims of *offline* sexual and physical abuse.[20] It seems justified to conclude that the criminalisation of (attempted) grooming and also of online sex chatting does not offer significantly additional protection or provide a solution to the specific problems of this relatively limited group of children.[21]

In line with that criticism, I would argue that also the proposed criminalisation of sex chatting in the Netherlands, despite its unquestionable good intentions, seems disproportionate, poorly worked out and reflects a certain degree of *techno-panic*. A more nuanced approach would help to map out the right intervention measures, which requires more scientific research into the prevention and harmfulness of sex chatting.[22] More attention should also be paid to other, less far-reaching means such

---

[15] National Society for the Prevention of Cruelty to Children (NSPCC) https://www.nspcc.org.uk/about-us/news-opinion/2022/online-grooming-crimes-rise/.

[16] Gorissen et al. (2020), pp. 28–29.

[17] Van der Hof and Koops (2011): 0.11% of the group of children surveyed stated that, after meeting offline with someone they met online, "the other person did something sexual to them". Only 8% of people they saw offline after meeting online were 20 years or older; 92% were peers.

[18] Smahel, D. et al., *EU Kids Online 2020. Survey results from 19 countries*, EU Kids Online, 2020. The percentages are from 73% in Finland to 94% in Croatia and Lithuania. For a comparison with 2010: Livingstone et al. (2011).

[19] Livingstone et al. (2011); van der Hof (2014), pp. 20–21; Smahel et al. (2020), pp. 85–86. Depending on the country, less than 5% (in Switzerland, France and Italy, among others) to 18% (in Germany, Malta and Serbia) of children say they have ever sent a sexual message to someone else.

[20] Staksrud (2013).

[21] Van der Hof and Koops (2011), p. 22.

[22] The EU Kid Online researchers argue that more research is needed to determine the extent to which online sexual approaches to children actually carry the risk of serious harm, see Smahel et al. (2020), p. 88. See also Livingstone (2014).

as intervention programmes, awareness-raising and information campaigns for children, schools, parents and social workers.[23]

3 Prevention and Detection of Grooming and Sex Chatting and the Role of Emotional AI

In various jurisdictions, law enforcement authorities are authorized to use AI to investigate the web and catch groomers in the act. In addition, the aforementioned proposed CSAM-regulation of the European Commission affords provisions regarding the detection, reporting and removal of online grooming (solicitation of children) with the help of AI systems.[24] However, both the automated luring of groomers and the automated detection of "solicitation language" appear to be rather problematic and may yield relatively disappointing results.

3.1 (National) Police Bots: AI Scanning Speech and Communicating to People

In the Netherlands, authorities are allowed to utilize AI as part of covert police work directed at luring potential groomers. These "police chatbots" (also known as virtual adolescent bait or *lokpuber* in Dutch) look and talk like minors and are able to either scan conversations or generate speech themselves.[25]

The introduction of these artificial speakers into Dutch law took place in phases.[26] First of all, not long after the regulation of online grooming in the Dutch Criminal Code, the Dutch police initiated a pilot scheme in which they experimented with policemen simulating to be minors online, the so-called adolescent bait. In 2019, the Dutch grooming provision was revised to accommodate this investigative power. The covert policeman or adolescent bait was added to the criminal offense of online grooming to enable the authorities to catch groomers red-handed. As a result, from that moment onwards, it was also illegal (and punishable) to (attempt to) groom a police officer that uses a fake account/profile online pretending to be a minor, or a

---

[23] For example: https://www.meldknop.nl/, https://slachtofferwijzer.nl/nieuws/grooming-hoe-kun-je-hiervoor-waken/, https://www.helpwanted.nl/, Insafe, Child Helpline International, The Children's Helpline, INHOPE, https://www.vraaghetdepolitie.nl/seks-en-loverboys/misbruik/hoe-voorkom-ik-grooming.

[24] Proposal of the European Parliament and of the Council laying down rules to prevent and combat child sexual abuse, COM(2022)209, 11 May 2022. See Witting and Leiser (2022).

[25] Similar covert techniques including posing as a child online are also used in Australia in child grooming investigations.

[26] The term artificial speaker is from Lamo and Calo (2019).

worried parent or older brother taking over an online grooming conversation from the minor and even so-called paedophile hunters simulating to be minors and having conversations with potential groomers with the intention of dealing with them in the physical world (as a form of private justice).[27]

The provision was soon amended by Dutch MPs who added the so-called virtual creation, a specific artificial intelligent form of adolescent bait, i.e. an AI chatbot provided with a profile of a non-existing victim that is used as an investigative tool (a honeypot) by the police or by other organisations. This virtual minor ("avatar" of a child) would be interacting in conversations with potential groomers while the software used allowed for large numbers of simultaneous conversations with different suspects.

This virtual creation was inspired by the AI adolescent bait known as Sweetie 2.0 that had been developed in 2015 by Terre des Hommes and the Dutch company Tracks Inspector to combat Webcam Child Sex Tourism.[28] This innovative tool enabled the automation of responsive communications with online chat partners using a personified chat robot in various communication channels. The chatbot was a virtualized minor child (aka Sweetie) who would engage in a dialogue using a chatbot engine and 3D imagery ("avatar"). All chat conversations were recorded by the system which assisted analysts in classifying 'online predators' by analysing the data. The chat data were processed per chat and profiles were created for each chat partner to assist with the identification of recurring chat partners.[29] The same AI will be utilized in the prevention and combating of online sex chatting and sexual corruption alike (the proposed Article 251 of the DCC mentioned in the previous paragraph).[30]

Sweetie 2.0 inspired other initiatives too, such as the Norwegian project PrevBOT where a policebot was developed as a preventive tool against online grooming.[31] Based on a machine learning algorithm, this system would be able to generate predictions on possible grooming that it has detected.[32] According to the description of PrevBOT in the literature, the tool could be used to observe people passively (so without interaction capturing ongoing conversations, e.g. by scraping) and as an agent interacting and having chat conversations with potential groomers.[33]

---

[27] De Hingh (2018).

[28] Van der Hof et al. (2019).

[29] For further technological specifications: chapter 3 in Van der Hof et al. (2019).

[30] *Parliamentary Papers II* 2022/23, 36222, no. 3, p. 99 (Explanatory Memorandum to Article 251 of the Dutch proposed Sexual offenses Bill (Wetsvoorstel Seksuele Misdrijven): The virtual decoy adolescent will be used in the detection of sex chatting (sub a), sexual corruption (sub b) and grooming (part c).

[31] Sunde and Sunde (2021), p. 6.

[32] Both indicating and flagging spaces where grooming possibly occurs (chat rooms where children and adults are present), specific persons (that are present in those rooms and are known offenders) and specific risk speech: conversations that can be classified as sexualized speech.

[33] Sunde and Sunde (2021), p. 27.

It should be noted that at the time when these AI applications were conceived and developed, the term *emotional* Artificial Intelligence was not as commonplace as it is today. This means that current insights and also new proposed legislation regarding emotional AI, such as the AI Act, potentially alter perspectives on the detection of grooming by AI technology.[34] Insights about the nature of affectionate relationships, for example, that can arise between humans and machines are increasing—especially in the context of the use of chatbots.[35] Now that AI can already do much more than it could five years ago, it is not inconceivable that governments will need to be much more cautious and restrained in deploying these kinds of technologies and that transparency about such tools requires improvement.[36]

In practice, however, governments tend to be extremely eager to make use of the possibilities of new AI-technologies, often inspired or stimulated to do so by tech industry.[37] These forces may partially explain the fortitude that was demonstrated by the European Commission vis-à-vis the so-called CSAM Regulation, which is discussed in the next section.

3.2 EU detection System: AI Identifying, Analysing, and Storing Speech

In May 2022, the European Commission published a Proposal for a Regulation of the European Parliament and of the Council, laying down rules for preventing and combating child sexual abuse: the much debated, so-called CSAM-regulation.[38] The proposal aimed to tackle two specific forms of online child sexual abuse: the online distribution of child sexual abuse material (CSAM) and the online solicitation or grooming of minors. Obviously, for this chapter, the latter category is of relevance. In the proposed regulation, providers of hosting services (in the broad meaning of the word) and interpersonal communication services (such as WhatsApp and Signal) are to play a pivotal role in preventing and combating the online solicitation of children,

[34] Regulation (EU) 2024/1689 of the European Parliament and of the Council of 13 June 2024 laying down harmonised rules on artificial intelligence and amending Regulations (EC) No 300/2008, (EU) No 167/2013, (EU) No 168/2013, (EU) 2018/858, (EU) 2018/1139 and (EU) 2019/2144 and Directives 2014/90/EU, (EU) 2016/797 and (EU) 2020/1828 (Artificial Intelligence Act).

[35] https://www.rtlnieuws.nl/economie/artikel/5413661/chatbots-ai-liefde-relatie-chatgpt-replika.

[36] The SER, Advisory Board of the Dutch Government, is pointing to the risks of the use of emotional AI like language recognition AI: https://www.ser.nl/nl/actueel/Nieuws/emotion-ai.

[37] On the CSAM Regulation and the commercial interests of, e.g. Thorn, see: https://balkaninsight.com/2023/09/25/who-benefits-inside-the-eus-fight-over-scanning-for-child-sex-content/.

[38] Proposal of the European Parliament and of the Council laying down rules to prevent and combat child sexual abuse, COM(2022)209, 11 May 2022.

as indeed according to the European Commission, grooming communication for the most part takes place on these platforms and through their services.[39]

The proposed regulation includes obligations that are partly new and partly in line with the obligations arising from the Digital Services Act (DSA). For their services offered in the EU, these obligations can be roughly divided in a phase where all relevant providers identify and analyse, and subsequently reduce the risk that the service is used for the solicitation of children. When there is evidence of a significant chance that the service is (still) used for online child sexual abuse and that the measures taken by the provider to reduce the risk of abuse are insufficient, the risk assessment phase is followed by a second phase. In such an event, service providers are obliged to take specific measures in order to detect the solicitation of children on their services (Article 7) and to report and remove all content that is related to these grooming activities: i.e. the evidence of written or spoken "grooming content" exchanged between a groomer and a minor.

For this purpose, according to Article 10 of the proposed regulation, providers should install and operate various detection technologies aimed at detecting online grooming taking place on their services. These detection technologies shall be made available by a newly founded agency: the EU-Centre for Child Protection.[40] The leveraging of AI detection technologies by the providers will undoubtedly be of a semi-permanent nature as the detection order has a duration of up to 12 months. This would—in my view—imply that once providers have installed and operated these detection technologies, there would hardly be any reason to de-install and de-operate the AI applications after that first year.[41] With the help of these (emotional) AI technologies, all suspicious and illegal content found by the providers would then be reported directly to this same EU-Centre for Child Protection.

Most political controversy and debate around the proposed regulation has been focussed on the question to what extent (and against what price) providers should have access to end-to-end encrypted content by applying decryption technologies, for which the proposal very emphatically leaves sufficient room. For this reason, some opponents have qualified the regulation as chat control and mass surveillance.[42] Critics, among others the EDPS, have stressed that such generalised

---

[39] Explanatory note to the proposal, p. 2.

[40] Article 42 of the Proposal for a Regulation of the European Parliament and of the Council laying down rules to prevent and combat child sexual abuse, COM(2022)209, 11 May 2022.

[41] De Hingh (2023b).

[42] https://www.patrick-breyer.de/en/posts/chat-control/. Recent negotations however seem to have mitigated the proposed detection order: "*To avoid mass surveillance or generalised monitoring of the internet, the draft law would allow judicial authorities to authorise [only] time-limited orders, as a last resort, to detect any CSAM and take it down or disable access to it (...). MEPs excluded end-to-end encryption from the scope of the detection orders to guarantee all users' communications are secure and confidential. Providers would be able to choose which technologies to use as long as they comply with the strong safeguards foreseen in the law (...).*" See https://www.europarl.europa.eu/news/en/press-room/20231110IPR10118/child-sexual-abuse-online-effective-measures-no-mass-surveillance.

surveillance that leaves no guarantees for privacy could not be a remedy to the social problems of child abuse and exploitation.[43]

Surprisingly, far less political or societal outrage was heard about the fact that pursuant to this proposal internet service providers would be obliged not only to screen all conversations taking place within their services but also to scan it for suspicious word use and language patterns with the help of AI technologies, select and collect these and send them to the EU-Centre. According to Article 44 of the proposal, the EU-Centre will collect all the detected content in databases. Not only will images, hash values, and indicators of online child abuse material be stored there but also all spoken and written speech (words, dialogues, language patterns, etc.) that are regarded as evidence for the online solicitation of children. In that way, providers will be collaborative to the build-up of a giant thesaurus of *grooming linguistics*.[44]

3.3 Grooming Detection with AI: Unreliable, Ineffective and Privacy-Intrusive

The annex to the European CSAM proposal gives valuable insight into the effectiveness of (emotional) AI technologies that are available for the detection of the speech deployed for the solicitation of children.[45] The technologies would include, for example, a Microsoft anti-grooming technology called Artemis, a tool designed to detect grooming and the solicitation of a child for sexual purposes.[46]

Although the Artemis Project, introduced in 2020, received much media attention, it seems to have faded into the background, most likely because speech recognition technologies such as Microsoft Artemis are not very effective. Microsoft reports that the accuracy of its grooming detection algorithm has an accuracy of 88%, which means that 12% of the messages that are identified as grooming later appear to be false positives, which becomes clear from the examples presented by Microsoft itself. The chance that statements such as "I could be your dad" or questions such as "Is your mum there?" are qualified by emotional AI as grooming material and eventually end up in the EU databases as not imaginary.[47] Since it could

[43]EDPB-EDPS (2022) Joint Opinion 04/2022 on the Proposal for a Regulation of the European Parliament and of the Council laying down rules to prevent and combat child sexual abuse, 28 July 2022.

[44]De Hingh (2023b).

[45]Commission staff working document Impact Assessment Report Accompanying the document Proposal for a Regulation of the European Parliament and of the Council laying down rules to prevent and combat child sexual abuse SWD/2022/209, 11 May 2022 (hereafter: Impact Assessment with the proposed CSAM-Regulation).

[46]Impact Assessment with the proposed CSAM-Regulation, pp. 282–283. Zie https://medium.com/themeetgroup/project-artemisan-overview-9ce4174489db.

[47]EOKM, *Standpunten van het EOKM over de Europese Verordening ter voorkoming en bestrijding van seksueel kindermisbruik*, 22 november 2022, see www.eokm.nl.

ultimately lead to large numbers of internet users being falsely accused of grooming a child, this would make the tool simply useless.[48]

Moreover, contrary to the initiatives the EU-Centre seems to suggest, and to the assumptions that are implicit to tools such as police bots and baits, a general finding across research on the language of online grooming is that the detection of specific language and the creation of databases with "suspicious" keywords is a perilous undertaking—*among others* as there exists only a very limited amount of linguistics research on online grooming.[49]

The scarce research in this field shows that there are no signature words that serve as "a smoking gun" to indicate that grooming or sex chatting is taking place.[50] One interesting outcome which so far has been underexposed is that a substantial part of the conversations, language patterns and word usage will most certainly have an everyday character: '*What you doing after school*'.[51] By definition, parts of grooming conversations do not exclusively consist of sexualized speech per se. After all, by definition, a grooming conversation will (according to the description of the offence) have to include a proposal for a meeting and material acts leading to that meeting—if the conversation conducted or detected by AI is to at least lead to a successful prosecution and conviction of the groomer. Indeed, a conversation about a meeting place, and which train the victim should take to get there, are not blatantly sexualized conversations.

For that matter, the mundanity of conversations does not mean that they are less emotionally charged" or of a less private nature. Every language utterance can be considered as one of the most fundamental private aspects of humankind—touching upon the right of confidentiality of communication and freedom of speech.[52] Sunde & Sunde classify the process of collecting linguistic data and characteristics of a speaker/writer, the qualification of unique characteristics, and the results of technological text analysis of individual internet users with (the taking of) physical fingerprints for a reason.[53] Moreover, even the impact assessment accompanying the proposed CSAM regulation is clear about this: speech detection is the most intrusive form of detection for users.[54] Therefore, the (automated) detection, collection and analysis of language patterns and specific use of words—as well as

---

[48] See Impact Assessment with the proposed CSAM-Regulation, p. 99 and p. 283.

[49] Lorenzo-Dus et al. (2023), p. 72.

[50] Lorenzo-Dus et al. (2023), pp. 70–71: Reasons for this include the fact that groomers often use language in a way that disguises their abusive intentions, such as when building trust (see Section 4.4), and because individual groomers can vary considerably in how they use language to manipulate children.

[51] Lorenzo-Dus et al. (2023), p. 42.

[52] In addition, the connotation of these types of conversations will be partly determined culturally (and therefore differ by country).

[53] Sunde and Sunde (2021), p. 5, so comparable with biometric characteristics.

[54] See Impact Assessment with the proposed CSAM-Regulation, p. 99.

undercover participation in suspicious conversations—undoubtedly constitutes a potential violation of fundamental rights.[55]

4 Some Critical and Concluding Remarks

It is clear that at a national, European and international level, heavy artillery is being deployed in the fight against online text-based offenses directed towards minors (online grooming, attempted grooming, online solicitation and sex chatting). This is striking now that it is not even clear what the prevalence of these offenses is and what actual harm they cause to minors. Arising from an essentially well-intentioned desire to protect children from online dangers, the cure may appear to be more problematic than the disease.

In the previous sections, some practical as well as more fundamental concerns vis-à-vis the use of emotional AI for the detection and prevention of online offences have already been discussed. In this concluding section, some final key objections will be highlighted. One concern is the extent to which commercial interests of tech companies seem to play a decisive role in the development and instalment of new AI driven investigative policies. Companies that themselves have a commercial interest in these kinds of initiatives usually do not seem to be the best advisors. In addition, regulatory bodies at both a national and EU level make themselves depend on commercial actors to develop these AI technologies.[56] As the EDPS noted before (in the context of the automated detection of known CSAM): as the detection techniques are mainly proprietary, this automatically entails that the algorithms are not open for external review. As a result, much of the debate relies on assurances of the companies for the accuracy of the tools.

Moreover, it is not reassuring to think that these different technologies will interfere with each other and that in the near future Dutch virtual creations (the adolescent bait, or police bot) would substantially contribute to the filling of the database of the EU Centre with (more or less suspicious) language identifiers that they have collected in the context of enforcement of online sex chatting and grooming in the Netherlands.

This would have additional negative consequences if it turns out that current AI technology is inadequate and not capable of effectively screening conversations for any harmful content. Indeed, we have already seen how difficult it will be to establish the technological, linguistic standards that should distinguish grooming

[55] See, e.g. Gremsl and Hödl (2022).

[56] Recently, Google, Meta, Discord and other tech companies announced that they would set up a joint platform cum database called *Lantern* through which the tech companies would exchange information and signals of child abuse, such as relevant keywords used to groom minors. On this "first cross-platform signal sharing program", see https://www.technologycoalition.org/newsroom/announcing-lantern. And see https://tweakers.net/nieuws/215386/google-meta-en-anderen-gaan-samenwerken-om-online-kindermisbruik-tegen-te-gaan.html (tweakers.net, 7 November 2023).

communication from other, everyday communication (in the category of "Is your mother at home?"). Similarly, the EDPS have noted that current AI-powered detection technologies (...) having extremely poor statistics would yield unreasonably high false positives which could easily lead to overblocking.

Furthermore, as previously mentioned, AI (speech recognition) technology most certainly does not consider the specific "linguistic" legal criteria in criminalization (such as the meeting proposal and material acts leading to that meeting for behaviour to qualify as the criminal offense of "online grooming). Moreover, by definition, language is culturally and contextually defined, and its meaning is highly dependent on interpretation. Will current AI detection technologies be able to interpret the 24 different languages that are used in the EU? Will the EU Centre's database collect grooming identifiers in all those languages? These are just two of the many questions to which there are currently no answers.

Among some, there is the fear of "repurposing"', the possibility of using existing investigative technologies for other purposes, once they have become established. For example, existing language identification technologies and databases could be transformed and extended quite easily at a later stage to detect other content, such as certain categories of disinformation or political communication deemed undesirable.[57] The same is true for the decryption order, the controversial part of the CSAM proposal: once access to end-to-end encrypted communication is a fact, it easily gives room for all kinds of other investigation and detection possibilities. With regard to the CSAM proposal, especially, it should be emphasised that there are no guarantees that it will only take a targeted approach to the sexual solicitation of children and that it will not form the basis for a general and indiscriminate scanning of the content of almost all types of electronic communications. Within such scenarios, the step from combating online sexual offences to censorship and thought policing is no longer purely imaginary.[58]

Although national authorities (e.g. Dutch and Norwegian) have only taken their first tentative steps in using police chatbots in the context of grooming, and although a final agreement on the exact details of the European CSAM proposal is not yet in sight, the first cautious examples cannot but involuntarily evoke the spectre of a government that will be able to monitor *any* online conversation by means of emotional AI.

---

[57] Similar concerns were expressed by the European privacy watchdogs in their joint opinion EDPB-EDPS (2022), *Joint Opinion 04/2022 on the Proposal for a Regulation of the European Parliament and of the Council laying down rules to prevent and combat child sexual abuse*, 28 July 2022.

[58] Minutes of a meeting of the European Commission have confirmed this concern and showed that Europol requested the European Commission to provide unfiltered access to the data obtained through client-side device scanning (scanning phones for the presence of child abuse material or sexually explicit communications with/about minors). Experts speculate that Europol would like to use that data to develop AI applications for the detection of sexual offences and other types of crimes. The same minutes also show Europol's desire for repurposing and the commercial interests behind the fight against CSAM. See: https://balkaninsight.com/2023/09/29/europol-sought-unlimited-data-access-in-online-child-sexual-abuse-regulation/#:%7E:text=In%20the%20meeting%2C%20the%20minutes,how%20this%20data%20is%20used.

References

de Hingh AE (2018) Grooming in het wetsvoorstel Computercriminaliteit III. Over het verbod op sexchatten met kinderen, robots en politieambtenaren. Computerrecht 2018/162

de Hingh AE (2023a) Het wetsvoorstel seksuele misdrijven. Over online én offline sexchatten en het opsporen van het online seksueel benaderen van kinderen, Computerrecht 2023/3

de Hingh AE (2023b) De preventie en bestrijding van seksueel misbruik van kinderen in de online omgeving: een controversieel Europees voorstel. Tijdschrift voor Internetrecht 2023/2

EDPB-EDPS (2022) Joint Opinion 04/2022 on the Proposal for a Regulation of the European Parliament and of the Council laying down rules to prevent and combat child sexual abuse, 28 July 2022

Gorissen M et al (2020) Het fenomeen online seksueel geweld. Een literatuuronderzoek naar de kennis over omvang, aard en aanpak. NSCR, Amsterdam

Gremsl T, Hödl E (2022) Emotional AI: legal and ethical challenges. Inf Polity 27:163–174

Katirai A (2023) Ethical considerations in emotion recognition technologies: a review of the literature. AI and Ethics 2023

Lamo M, Calo R (2019) Regulating bot speech. UCLA Law Rev 66:988–1028

Livingstone S et al (2011) Risk and safety on the internet: the perspective of European children. Full findings from the EU Kids Online survey of 9–16 year olds and their parents. EU Kids Online. LSE, London

Livingstone S et al (2014) In their own words: what bothers children online? Eur J Commun 29(3): 271–288

Lorenzo-Dus N, Evans C, Mullineux-Morgan R (2023) Online child sexual grooming discourse. Cambridge University Press, Cambridge

McStay A (2019) Emotional AI and EdTech: serving the public good? Learn Media Technol 45(3): 270–283

Podoletz L (2022) We have to talk about emotional AI and crime. AI Soc 38:1067–1082

Smahel D et al (2020) EU Kids Online 2020. Survey results from 19 countries, EU Kids Online. ELS, London

Staksrud E (2013) Online grooming legislation: Knee-jerk regulation? Eur J Commun 28(2): 152–167

Sunde N, Sunde IM (2021) Conceptualizing an AI-based Police Robot for preventing online child sexual exploitation and abuse – Part I The theoretical and technical foundations for PrevBOT. Nordic J Stud Policing 8(2):1–21

van Berkum JA (2012) Zonder gevoel geen taal. (Oratie Universiteit Utrecht 30 September 2011)

van Berkum JA (2019) Language comprehension and emotion: where are the interfaces and who cares? In: de Zubicaray GI, Schiller NO (eds) The Oxford handbook of neurolinguistics. Oxford University Press, Oxford

van der Hof S (2014) Online grooming – a case of technopanic? Strafblad 2014:19–25

van der Hof S, Koops B-J (2011) Adolescents and cybercrime: navigating between freedom and control. Policy Int 3(2)

van der Hof S et al (eds) (2019) Sweetie 2.0 using artificial intelligence to fight webcam child sex tourism. Asser Press, The Hague

Witting SK, Leiser M (2022) Outcome Report on the Expert workshop on EU proposed regulation on preventing and combatting child sexual abuse. 16 December 2022

AI in the Lecture Room: Analysing Two Use Cases in the Context of Higher Education

Anette Alén, Beata Mäihäniemi, and Aušrinė Pasvenskienė

Abstract There is artificial intelligence (AI) in the lecture room, and it cannot be ignored. With unprecedented speed, AI has made its way to the everyday practices of higher education. As such, automation and analytics are nothing new in the academic educational context. However, with more recent AI applications it has truly become impossible to ignore AI in everyday academia and to avoid rethinking pedagogical approaches and solutions. Moreover, following the COVID-19 pandemic, digital tools for higher education are now being systematically developed, with an emphasis on quality and wellbeing of students. At the same time, regulatory instruments for AI are being tailored on various levels.

This chapter discusses AI in higher education from a legal perspective while addressing specific use cases. The chapter briefly touches upon the role of emotions and interaction in learning, linking this to the features of AI in education. Then, the selected use cases are analysed from a regulatory point of view. The focus of this chapter is on EU level legal instruments, alongside various ethical and self-regulatory guidelines that frame the use of AI in education. In particular, the AI Act is analysed in the context of higher education, including the relevant human rights dimensions.

A. Alén (✉)
University of Helsinki, Helsinki, Finland
e-mail: anette.alen@helsinki.fi

B. Mäihäniemi
University of Lapland, Rovaniemi, Finland
e-mail: beata.maihaniemi@ulapland.fi

A. Pasvenskienė
Vytautas Magnus University, Kaunas, Lithuania
e-mail: ausrine.pasvenskiene@vdu.lt

R. Ballardini et al. (eds.), *Emotional Data Applications and Regulation of Artificial Intelligence in Society*, Law, Governance and Technology Series 69,
https://doi.org/10.1007/978-3-031-80111-2_11

1 Making Room for Emotions and AI in Higher Education

During the past few decades, we have observed a boom in the development of various practices and digital tools used in education. This boom has been accompanied by a growing body of literature on educational technologies.[1] For their part, social and psychological dimensions of education have also been of interest to researchers,[2] and increasingly so after the pandemic. Higher education, which has been traditionally associated with knowledge-based approach and rationality, has also been criticized for its sole focus on reason, and overlooking the role of emotions and emotional skills.[3] Indeed, psychological processes, including emotions, are at play in the educational context and have an impact on learning, which has been acknowledged for quite some time.[4] In fact, the overall incorporation of technology, and AI in particular, into the learning process and integration of AI may bring along various emotions, from excitement to even fear of the unknown.[5]

Consequently, there has been a move towards a more comprehensive understanding of the learning process in higher education, including its dimensions beyond cognitive ones, such as those related to emotions. At the same time, digital tools and online teaching are being developed more systematically and with a focus on quality after the emergency remote solutions during the COVID-19 pandemic.[6] Furthermore, a more holistic perspective on quality has also led to increased attention on the wellbeing of students especially since the pandemic.[7] As the latest development, the use of artificial intelligence (AI) has been gaining ground in higher education, together with its legal implications and regulatory frameworks being discussed and developed.

The EU Digital Education Plan (2021–27) aims at high-quality digital education across Europe.[8] Despite its soft law character, European policy on education has a role in framing the landscape of national education systems. However, digitalization of education receives attention not only in EU policies targeting education systems but also in matters of technological innovations. For its part, the EU Artificial

---

[1] See, e.g. Huang et al. (2019); Martin et al. (2019), pp. 34–43.

[2] E.g. Edwards and Harwood (2003).

[3] Hews et al. (2023); Sandomierski and Ben-Ishai (2022).

[4] See, e.g. Pekrun (2014). Research interest on the subject has intensified during the twenty-first century. See, e.g. Pekrun and Linnenbrink-Garcia (2014). Several studies have been conducted on the roles and functions of emotions in diverse educational settings, achievement emotions, recognition of such emotions as confusion though gestures, conversations, and facial movements in intelligent tutoring systems. See Shen and Xiao (2023).

[5] See, e.g. Benites Paradeda and Souza Santos (2022).

[6] Dos Santos (2022).

[7] Douwes et al. (2023), p. 1.

[8] European Education Area (2020).

Intelligence Act (AI Act)[9] entered into force in the summer of 2024. Two years after entering into force, most of the provisions of the AI Act will start being applied.[10] The AI Act is expected to have a largely positive influence of AI on education, including its important role in modernizing education systems, increasing education quality, and accelerating digital education. Nonetheless, the AI Act also includes limitations for educational AI.[11] From a regulatory point of view, there are many open questions which will be addressed when the AI Act with its mechanisms is functioning fully, alongside industry practices. Some self-regulatory and ethical frameworks have been adopted already prior to hard law: these include EU-level ethical guidelines for trustworthy AI (2019)[12] and for AI in teaching and learning (2022).[13]

These educational, technological, and regulatory developments must be discussed in tandem. Therefore, this chapter addresses two specific use cases of educational AI, highlighting the role of emotions and interaction in support of learning. The use cases are analysed from the perspective of regulation, with a focus on the AI Act in particular. To pave the way for the analysis, the general regulatory framework is briefly discussed. Finally, some conclusions are drawn on the opportunities and challenges of emotional AI in an educational setting.

2 AI-Powered Education and the Role of Regulation

AI presents learning opportunities that are increasingly flexible, inclusive, and captivating. AI software is applied to enhance collaborative learning through assisting in the formation of adaptive groups guided by learner models, facilitating online group interactions, and providing summaries of discussions that human tutors can utilize to steer students towards the goals and objectives of a course.[14] In addition, AI software is also available for creating an intelligent virtual reality (IVR) that is used to guide learners in an authentic virtual reality and in game-based learning environments.[15] Some studies also look at the way in which AI can name emotions to address challenges with learning and enhance this.[16] Therefore, in

[9] Regulation (EU) 2024/1689 of the European Parliament and of the Council of 13 June 2024 laying down harmonised rules on artificial intelligence and amending Regulations (EC) No 300/2008, (EU) No 167/2013, (EU) No 168/2013, (EU) 2018/858, (EU) 2018/1139 and (EU) 2019/2144 and Directives 2014/90/EU, (EU) 2016/797 and (EU) 2020/1828 (Artificial Intelligence Act).

[10] European Council (2024); see also European Parliament (2023) and European Parliament (2024).

[11] See AI Act.

[12] High-Level Expert Group on Artificial Intelligence (2019).

[13] European Commission (2022).

[14] Zawacki-Richter et al. (2019).

[15] Zawacki-Richter et al. (2019).

[16] Blanchard et al. (2009).

the educational context, the potential applications of AI are numerous.[17] Surprisingly, however, AI tools have often been discussed as technical concepts separate from the social dimensions of higher education.[18] Moreover, although AI tools increasingly enter the educational sector and gradually make a strong impact on education and administrative activities, it is also important to acknowledge the limits of technology in education. For their part, Popenici and Kerr emphasize the importance of recognizing risks and upholding academic scepticism to navigate this evolving landscape effectively.[19] This includes the ability of educators to distinguish AI tools that are worthwhile and ethical from those that are not.[20]

Together with developing technologies and expanding applicability, the regulation of AI has become increasingly pressing. From a legal point of view, AI has been approached from different angles already for a number of decades.[21] However, with the EU Artificial Intelligence Act, the EU has set out to be the first legislative instrument to regulate AI horizontally, including the educational sector. For their part, the ethical AI guidelines for educators highlight the following classification in connection to specific use cases: using AI to teach students or to support student learning (both student-facing), using AI to support the teacher (teacher-facing), and using AI to support diagnostic or system-wide planning (system-facing).[22] However, the multifaceted classification may also be interpreted in a way which connects the dimensions to each other in a supportive manner.[23] In this regard, one important note is that these dimensions do not expressly include a dimension for educational wellbeing. Nonetheless, AI-powered tools may be utilized in developing higher education from the perspective of student wellbeing, which implies a direct link also to emotional elements of education, even if the concept of wellbeing as such is debated and multifaceted.[24] For their part, Holmes and others have categorized teaching and learning with AI so as to include 'the use of AI to support learners directly, involving tools such as those known as intelligent tutoring systems, dialogue-based tutoring systems, exploratory learning environments, automatic writing evaluation, learning network orchestrators, chatbots and AI to support learners with disabilities; the use of AI to support administrative systems (such as recruitment, timetabling and learning management); the use of AI to support teachers directly (although, with the exception of smart curation of learning materials, there

[17] Bearman et al. (2023), p. 374; Niemi et al. (2023). See, however, Breines and Gallagher (2020), p. 1.

[18] Bearman et al. (2023), pp. 371, 374; Kontiainen et al. (2021). Indeed, technological change is not just about technology but about changes in human interaction and social structures.

[19] Popenici and Kerr (2017), p. 22.

[20] Luckin et al. (2022).

[21] See, e.g. Viljanen and Parviainen (2022); Richards and Smart (2016); WIPO (1991).

[22] European Commission (2022), p. 14.

[23] Council of Europe (2022), p. 22.

[24] Tang et al. (2023).

are few examples)'.[25] Examples of learner-supporting AI include adaptive learning tools; tools that capture and analyse signals, such as those that measure attention; empathy, or emotions; hardware such as headsets; chatbots that support learners; and automatic writing evaluation.[26] Furthermore, when it comes to AI-powered education, UNESCO recommendations emphasize the wide range of skills required, including not only literacy, numeracy, coding but also critical and creative thinking as well as socio-emotional and AI ethics skills.[27]

This chapter focuses on two specific use cases which are linked to the quality of higher education, including its emotional dimensions, learning efficacy, and educational wellbeing. For its part, online teaching may lead to a loss of quality due to lower attention levels affecting learning efficiency.[28] Quality in this regard may arguably be increased by increasing attention levels even if not directly measuring quality as such. However, there is a need for quality assessment tools specifically tailored for online teaching—due to and despite the lack of general level measurement tools for "quality of service in higher education".[29] Moreover, as a complex and holistic phenomenon, student wellbeing may also be challenging to measure for traditional quality assessment and development. In both regards, the usefulness of AI tools is worth considering, as suggested in this article: while the first use case discusses remote lessons and the use of AI tools for measuring attention levels, the second use case addresses the opportunities to increase educational wellbeing while receiving support from AI. Nevertheless, the AI Act includes a complex legal framework for such use cases, as will be discussed in the following section. Via references and taking into account the utilization of data by AI applications, the existing EU regulation on personal data, the General Data Protection Regulation (GDPR),[30] is also integrated into the regulatory framework governing the use of AI. However, this is discussed only so far as its relevance in the context of the selected use cases.

---

[25] Holmes et al. (2022), p. 19.

[26] Holmes et al. (2022), pp. 20–21.

[27] UNESCO (2022), provision 102.

[28] Smallwood et al. (2007).

[29] Ramírez-Hurtado et al. (2021).

[30] Regulation (EU) 2016/679 of the European Parliament and of the Council of 27 April 2016 on the protection of natural persons with regard to the processing of personal data and on the free movement of such data, and repealing Directive 95/46/EC (General Data Protection Regulation).

3 Mapping the Regulatory Background: Towards the Use Cases

Due to the fluidity of its concept, AI has been deemed problematic as a basis for regulation.[31] In addressing various applications, the AI Act, however, also builds on risk levels, whereby four levels of risk are defined in the Act: unacceptable risk, that is prohibited AI practices;[32] high risk;[33] and the rest of applications imposing only limited or minimal risk. Overall, the use of AI in education seems to be encouraged by the AI Act which refers to AI as a tool that can improve "prediction, optimizing operations and resource allocation, and personalizing digital solutions available for individuals and organizations".[34] Similarly, the AI Act stresses how the implementation of AI systems can support high-quality digital education, digital skills and competences, and critical thinking.[35] Despite the opportunities of AI, some additional conditions and limitations concern its use when it comes to emotions and in specific contexts connected to education.

One especially important limitation for the purposes of this chapter is the prohibition in Article 5 on 'the placing on the market, the putting into service for this specific purpose, or the use of AI systems to infer emotions of a natural person in the areas of workplace and education institutions, except where the use of the AI system is intended to be put in place or into the market for medical or safety reasons'.[36] While it seems that this prohibition in Article 5 brings along a total ban on the use of emotional AI in education, this is not the whole picture: The AI Act does not define what the medical or safety reasons would be that would justify putting emotional AI into place. However, some guidelines as to these situations should be provided alongside the implementation of the AI Act which would also ensure protection of students' rights. Nevertheless, a wide array of justifications is possible for the use of emotional AI to ensure safety of students or for 'medical' reasons.[37]

The so-called emotion recognition systems are able to identify and infer emotions or intentions of natural persons from biometric data, that is, data revealing physical

[31] Schuett (2023); Wang (2019). Indeed, the concept of AI was under construction and fiercely debated during the legislative process of the AI Act.

[32] Article 5 of the AI Act.

[33] Classification rules in the Article 6, possible amendments in the Article 7. Requirements for High-risk systems in Section 2 of the AI Act (Articles 8 to 15).

[34] AI Act, recital 4.

[35] AI Act, recital 56.

[36] AI Act, Article 5, para 1 (f).

[37] One scenario would denote situations where students are monitored to ensure that their (mental) health is not deteriorating (e.g. due to switching to remote teaching during another pandemic or individual cases where students have had some health issues). Similarly, there may be some situations where the safety of students needs to be ensured in the class, such as in the case of a school shooting or where some other incident had occurred.

characteristics of a natural person.[38] Furthermore, the AI Act also specifies that anyone exposed to systems which process biometric data for the purposes of identifying or inferring emotions or intensions or grouping them into specific categories (such as according to their sex, ethnic origin, or interests) should be informed of such.[39] Therefore, AI is not to be employed in the recognition of people's facial expressions, movements, pulse frequency, or voice.[40] However, borderline situations can occur where it may be difficult to distinguish between systems that collect only physiological information and ones that infer emotions. Indeed, it may be challenging to define some gesture whether it is the result or manifestation of an emotion or not. For example, a grimace may be both a sign of pain and simply disagreement. Moreover, generalizations are apt to flaws because emotions may be expressed in different ways in different cultures and situations and even in the case of a single individual.[41] Inferring emotions can therefore lead to significant errors in interpretation. Despite AI having emotional intelligence (EI), empathy and context-sensitivity are mastered only by humans.[42] Nonetheless, regarding the potential of these new tools, research demonstrates that emotion recognition can contribute to improving self-learning, learning enjoyment, academic performance, and learning achievement.[43]

In addition to the above limitations, some AI systems in education are viewed as high-risk ones. Such is the case where an AI system is used to determine access or admission or assign persons to educational and vocational training institutions where the AI system affects the decisions on the admission or assigning process.[44] A second case is when the AI system is used to evaluate the learning outcomes of persons in educational and vocational training institutions.[45] The same goes for assessing and influencing the appropriate level of education by means of AI.[46] Finally, high-risk operations include online proctoring, that is, the use of AI for monitoring and detecting prohibited student behaviour during tests.[47] Since these operations may determine the educational and professional course of a person's life and ultimately affect their ability to secure a livelihood, the afore-mentioned uses are classified in the AI Act as high-risk. When improperly designed and used, such

[38] AI Act, recital 18. It is however not the same as the system that could identify the fatigue of drivers to prevent accidents, and the like.

[39] AI Act, recital 132.

[40] See also Farahany (2023).

[41] AI Act, recital 44.

[42] Kumar and Martin (2023); Kontiainen et al. (2021).

[43] Shen and Xiao (2023).

[44] AI Act, use case in Annex III (3a).

[45] Annex III (3b).

[46] Annex III (3c).

[47] Annex III – paragraph 1 – point 3 – point d.

systems can be particularly intrusive and may violate one's right to education and be discriminatory.[48]

Indeed, in a wider sense, the legal framework for the use of AI in education also includes the fundamental rights dimension on a more general level, including the protection of students' fundamental rights, such as the right to education, right to privacy and freedom of speech. In its commentary, the United Nations Committee on Economic, Social and Cultural Rights noted that academics and students are especially vulnerable to political and other pressures and that the right to education can only be ensured if accompanied by the academic freedom of academics and students.[49] In addition, with the increased use of digital technologies in education, academics and students face challenges. For example, surveillance and digitalization of teaching materials and lectures lead to such an environment in the classroom that academics may favour teaching in a conservative way and avoiding controversial topics and discussions.[50] Although a crucial element of academic freedom is the privilege of academics to teach freely, collected classroom data or the digital map of the classroom opens possibilities to extract, interpret, compare or even manipulate.[51] This is an issue from the perspective of freedom of thought and expression and academic freedom, including teaching and the right to education.[52] Digital technologies and monitoring also include privacy concerns, while data protection plays a decisive role in regulating AI. For its part, the AI Act stresses the fact that the development and use of AI-based systems inevitably requires personal data processing, referring, among others to the GDPR.[53] On the use of AI-based applications, the GDPR poses several limitations, which is also evident in the concerns expressed by the European Data Protection Supervisor (EDPS):[54] where high-risk AI systems rely on processing personal data or process personal data to fulfil their task, such a processing might be contrary to data protection rules.[55] Therefore, the EDPS has identified the need to clarify that the use of AI is subject to data protection legislation.[56] Moreover, the EDPS stresses the importance of including the principle of data minimization in the AI Act as well as data protection by design where high-risk AI systems affect privacy and data protection. The concept of 'risk to fundamental rights' must thus be aligned with the principles of GDPR.[57] For its part, the

[48] AI Act, recital 56.

[49] UN Committee on Economic, Social and Cultural Rights (1999).

[50] Carlson (2018), p. 55.

[51] McCluskey and Winter (2014), p. 142. Collected data must have an agreed lifetime and expiration date, as well as criteria to request its deletion. See Renz and Hilbig (2020). See also Avella et al. (2016).

[52] Pasvenskienė (2017).

[53] AI Act, recital 10.

[54] European Data Protection Supervisor (2021).

[55] European Data Protection Supervisor (2021), paras 15 and 75.

[56] European Data Protection Supervisor (2021), para 15.

[57] European Data Protection Supervisor (2021), paras 18 and 76.

principle of purpose limitation allows for data to be gathered for a specific purpose whereby the use of AI to infer emotions is “highly undesirable” and should only be exceptionally allowed for specific use cases and purposes, while including appropriate safeguards.[58]

In the case of emotional AI-based applications, the legal basis for data processing follows those listed in Article 6 of the GDPR, that is, consent or contract with the student, vital interests (to protect someone’s life), as well as legitimate interests (there are however limitations as to how much this legal basis can be used by public institutions such as universities). Even the use of AI tools on a voluntary basis faces the issue of consent, the conditions of which are laid down in Article 7 of the GDPR: Consent not only must be freely given and explicit but also informed and given for the specific purpose. Furthermore, the reasons for processing must be clearly stated. Consent can also be withdrawn. Indeed, the validity of a student’s consent could be questioned in a situation where an educational institution would be directing a student into agreeing to be monitored by AI tools. Moreover, the GDPR points out that the asymmetry of power plays an extremely important role where the other party has more power over terms and conditions under which the whole use of an AI application operates. Consequently, consent would not be valid ‘where there is a clear imbalance between the data subject and the controller, in particular where the controller is a public authority and it is therefore unlikely that consent was freely given in all the circumstances of that specific situation’.[59]

As noted, the EU has AI guidelines on a general level and particularly for education which both focus on a number of basic principles and which can be seen as complimentary in that the latter offers more specific guidance in the context of education.[60] These guidelines build on human agency and oversight which derive from fundamental rights. Moreover, the guidelines also stress transparency as a major element, which consists of traceability, explainability, and communication. Diversity, non-discrimination, and fairness are also represented as crucial elements in AI-powered education. These are ensured by allowing accessibility or universal design. To avoid discrimination, any unfair bias should be identified, and indeed stakeholders of different ages and various genders should also be included. Finally, the use of AI in education needs to focus on societal and environmental wellbeing and privacy combined with data governance.[61] According to the ethical guidelines, these guidelines do not correspond to legal assessments; in this regard, educational institutions, while using high-risk applications, can rely on the use of certificates to ensure the fulfilment of the requirements of the AI Act.[62] On the other hand, it is also

[58] European Data Protection Supervisor (2021), paras 27 and 35.

[59] GDPR, recital 43.

[60] European Commission (2022), pp. 12, 18–19.

[61] European Commission (2022), p. 18.

[62] European Commission (2022), p. 18.

important to note that the ethical guidelines are applicable regardless of the scope of application of the legal framework.[63]

Next, the use cases will be analysed against this regulatory background.

4 Analysis of Selected Use Cases in Higher Education

For this chapter, the use cases selected include measuring students' attention levels in online teaching and supporting student wellbeing, as previously outlined. On the basis of research literature, these use cases are described and elaborated on, while a legal analysis targets the main concerns in light of the AI Act and relevant fundamental rights, while ethical concerns are discussed on the side. This is not to undermine the relevance of ethics, trust, and accountability.[64]

4.1 USE CASE 1: Remote Lessons—Measuring Attention Levels

In higher education, attention levels raise concerns especially in the context of online education, with a focus on quality and learning outcomes. Distraction is one of the main issues that learners face in virtual training due to screen-time fatigue and disturbances (e.g. email notifications, social media), all of which decreases productivity and concentration during learning.[65] For its part, online teaching should also aim at improved interaction as well as increased concentration among students. Overall, the focus should be more on the effectiveness of learning and human interaction rather than the technological systems as such.[66] In this regard, digital tools and AI-powered solutions can serve as support mechanisms. For example, image processing techniques and machine learning enable the measuring of attention. This is possible by looking at the blink rate (reduced if the student is concentrated), as well as facial expression and eye gaze (collected by a tracker during the teaching session), background noise, and body posture.[67] As a result, remote teaching could be accompanied by attention level alarms and notices that are available for students during lectures. While there could be an option to this share data with teachers, teachers could also be provided with group-level information to guide their activity.

---

[63] European Commission (2022), pp. 18–19.

[64] More focus on ethics is needed: what happens, for instance, if the educator does not follow system recommendations. See Holmes (2022), p. 42. See also Smith (2023).

[65] Ramírez-Hurtado et al. (2021), p. 10.

[66] Ramírez-Hurtado et al. (2021), p. 11.

[67] Rahul et al. (2020); see also Shanthakumar et al. (2017).

However, in the educational context, it may be challenging to separate bodily functions from actual emotions, which affects the situation described in the context of Article 5 of the AI Act. This has been also acknowledged in the AI Act where the emotions recognition system with the potential to be used to measure students' attention has received its own specific definition. Even though an AI system identifies or infers emotions or intentions by using a person's biometric data and emotions do not denote physical states nor apparent expressions, expressions are apt for the identification or inference of emotions.[68] Thus, there is a problematic borderline between physiological information and actual emotions, which is also crucial for the intended purpose of the AI tools. Facial expressions and spoken audio data from the students may also indicate their emotional state.[69]

In situations where some devices are used to monitor the emotions and behaviour of students and make predictions or recommendations based on these observations, the issue of cognitive liberty also has an important role.[70] Moreover, surveillance could actually lead to an opposite outcome, that is, an increased level of anxiety among learners and decreased positive framing for social and emotional learning.[71] While such a monitoring can also cause intentional changes of behaviour, students should not be pressured to perform better by constant monitoring as some surveys demonstrate that sometimes the students are keen to trick the system, which can lead to false results.[72] Indeed, students should have the option to opt out of monitoring, that is, the use of attention measuring tools and emotional AI in education would more likely be optional rather than mandatory. At least for now, it would be a supportive tool instead of a crucial application. Any information collected must be used for narrowly defined purposes such as tailoring educational offer for the students and providing support for learning. Moreover, the collection of data through learning analytics should also have an agreed lifetime and expiration date while providing mechanisms that guarantee the deletion of data when requested by the students.[73] While specifying the purpose of gathering data to each student, the use should be based on obtaining valid consent from each student before using such applications to analyse the voice and gaze. However, the role of the student in relation to the teacher and the educational institution is an important factor to consider. This problem is connected to the giving of freely given consent, as previously discussed. Last but not least, any monitoring must also be pedagogically meaningful: Zawacki-Richer argues that educational surveillance and data collection should add value for a good teacher to make pedagogical sense and proactively offer support and guidance where needed.[74]

[68] AI Act, recital 8a.

[69] Luckin et al. (2022).

[70] Farahany (2023), p. 22.

[71] Vuorikari et al. (2020), p. 38.

[72] Chaturapruek et al. (2018).

[73] Renz and Hilbig (2020).

[74] Zawacki-Richter et al. (2019).

4.2 USE CASE 2: Good to Study!—Measuring Emotional Dimensions of Wellbeing

As such, student wellbeing is a complex parameter which must be assessed holistically, while taking into account various fields of life and basic psychological needs.[75] For the purposes of this chapter, the educational context and effect on learning outcomes are especially relevant.[76] Moreover, students' wellbeing is essential to fostering creativity, which is considered a core twenty-first-century skill that remains uniquely human and fundamental for human development.[77] Therefore, information on the wellbeing of a student could be regularly gathered by the use of accessible applications (e.g. via smart phone) including specific study-related questions. Then, upon request, this data could be used to generate automatically a report on the status of the wellbeing of a particular student.[78] Such a process could involve a chat-like feature or an AI tutor providing feedback and support based on the wellbeing status and offering ways to improve an individual student's wellbeing.[79] Indeed, wellbeing reports could be a regular tool for students to use to keep track on their own situation, while the teacher would receive an overall report in order to monitor developments and identify irregularities, for instance, during exam periods.

However, wellbeing measuring and wellbeing enhancing tools cannot be conducted without the digitalization of data collection and situational assessments.[80] This means gathering data on very specific and personal experiences which may include sensitive personal data regulated by the GDPR. Although some objective measures such as physiological data and sleep patterns could be used to measure wellbeing, subjective measures may work better for the assessment where wellbeing is usually relating to a student's own experiences and interpretations.[81] From the perspective of the AI Act, some dimensions of wellbeing might arguably also amount to the justification for the use of emotional AI for 'medical' reasons (Art 5 AI Act), which was discussed above as relatively open category. In any case, the use of sensitive personal data includes the risk of the identification of a student also outside the educational use of that data, and even after anonymization. Therefore, any reports on wellbeing should only be available to students and teachers as specified above, with access to them well protected and the data anonymized if used in any kind of synthesis, while still having to face the issue of inferences. As pointed out by Farahany, new rules need to be put in place to prevent data gathering of neural data and to protect individuals from having their personal information

[75] Vuorikari et al. (2020), p. 26.

[76] European Commission (2022), p. 20.

[77] Markauskaite et al. (2022). See also Alén (2024).

[78] Tang et al. (2023) p. 59.

[79] Tang et al. (2023) p. 59.

[80] Tang et al. (2023) p. 59.

[81] Tang et al. (2023), p. 56.

misused. This implies protecting mental privacy, as people (here students) would be reluctant to share their data unless they are reassured that the data is not used against them.[82]

Since measuring wellbeing may also be challenging as different factors may have a bigger impact on some students, there is a need to separate what is being measured from subjective experiences. Another question to consider is how much information students are willing to reveal about themselves, even when they know that this information may help them in their learning process. There may be cultural differences to how much one wishes to reveal their wellbeing information, alongside other factors, such as one person being more extrovert while another is more introvert. Importantly, transparency is needed to make it evident that the social interaction in the form of wellbeing reporting is simulated and that the AI system itself is unable to feel or be empathic similar to humans.[83] Due to the complexity of wellbeing as a phenomenon, it would however be important to utilize AI in such a way that it enables it to detect factors related to studies and learning activities, which could then support the development of practices at the faculty or university. Moreover, it might be advisable to offer professional emotional support for students in connection with these types of educational transitions.[84]

5 Towards AI-Powered Educational Practices

This chapter has discussed the use of AI in higher education, with a special emphasis on the opportunities for increased quality by focusing on attention levels and wellbeing. As regards the selected use cases, though physiological data could be used in measuring attention levels, this would involve the difficulty of drawing lines to actual emotions. For its part, student wellbeing would mostly rest on subjective experiences and reflection, with the high probability of including sensitive personal data. From a legal perspective, it is advisable to abstain from anthropomorphism and clearly inform on the use of AI in education.[85] Both use cases bring along questions of data protection and the need to stress that the analysis is done by AI applications and not by humans. Indeed, transparency is not only a legal requirement but a core element of AI ethics. Moreover, Khosravi and others suggest that explainable AI in education must be "sensitive to the learning context and consider the different actors in a learning community as potential audiences".[86]

Currently, voluntary tools in the service of students and staff would best suit a higher educational context. Indeed, limiting AI-empowered monitoring to voluntary

[82] Farahany (2023), p. 23.

[83] European Commission (2022), p. 20.

[84] See, e.g. Benites Paradeda and Souza Santos (2022), p. 9.

[85] Mitchell (2023).

[86] Khosravi et al. (2022).

use of the tools and not overriding the rights of students in the name of efficiency or quality should be safeguarded. In some cases, the monitoring of emotions in an educational setting may be beneficial to learners and increase their satisfaction in education. However, this would need to be done with the full consent of students. All in all, it seems that the data protection rules, alongside the ban on the use of emotional AI in education, strongly limit the use of such applications. Moreover, it should be emphasized that the tools must be provided by the educational institutions, and the functionalities and principles must also be understood by the faculty alongside students. In this regard, digital readiness is essential. Academics and students must be prepared to exploit the potential of innovative tools in education. It is also important that educators and learners maintain a critical understanding of innovative tools, their boundaries, limitations, and the extent to which they can be trusted. Higher education curricula must not only accommodate skills required in a working life that includes both humans and machines[87] but education itself should benefit from AI tools in reforming the practices of teaching and learning. However, this needs to be done in a way that satisfies the requirements stemming from ethics and human rights, thus putting machines in the service of humans. Indeed, AI-powered educational tools render the socio-emotional dimensions of teaching even more evident than before.[88] In this way, AI may serve both students and teachers so as to embrace their human capabilities on a scale larger than before.[89]

In terms of further research, legal analysis should be accompanied by socio-political contexts.[90] The way AI systems are designed is largely influenced by a political economy and these choices will also influence AI applications used in education.[91] There might also limitations on the resources different higher education institutions can use in their operations, which is apt to create inequalities between these institutions and consequently between students.

References

Alén A (2024) Designing higher education – lessons for law schools. Eur J Leg Educ 5(1):3–28. https://www.ejle.eu/index.php/EJLE/article/view/88/41

Aoun JE (2017) Robot-proof: higher education in the age of artificial intelligence. MIT Press

Avella JT, Kebritchi M, Nunn SG, Kanai T (2016) Learning analytics methods, benefits, and challenges in higher education: a systematic literature review. Online Learn 20(2):13–29

[87] Aoun (2017).

[88] UNESCO (2019), p. 29.

[89] For a human-centered approach to educational AI, see Romero et al. (2024).

[90] Holmes et al. (2022); See also Council of Europe (2022), p. 51.

[91] See e.g. Creutzig et al. (2022). Most of the developers of AI systems come from the so-called high-income WEIRD countries, meaning western, educated, industrialised, rich, and democratic. See Pinkwart (2016).

Bearman M, Ryan J, Ajjawi R (2023) Discourses of artificial intelligence in higher education: a critical literature review. High Educ 86:369–385. https://doi.org/10.1007/s10734-022-00937-2

Benites Paradeda R, Souza Santos HV (2022) Factors that negatively influence students' transition from the traditional classroom to emergency remote education (ERT). Comput Educ Open 3: 100098. https://doi.org/10.1016/j.caeo.2022.100098

Blanchard EG et al (2009) Affective artificial intelligence in education: from detection to adaptation. AIED 200:81–88

Breines MR, Gallagher M (2020) A return to Teacherbot: rethinking the development of educational technology at the University of Edinburgh. Teach High Educ:1–15. https://doi.org/10.1080/13562517.2020.1825373

Carlson L (2018) Academic freedom in the age of information technology: swimming against the tide. Scand Stud Law 65:39

Chaturapruek S, Dee T, Johari R, Kizilcec R, Stevens M (2018) How a data-driven course planning tool affects college students' GPA: evidence from two field experiments. CEPA Working Paper No.18-10. http://cepa.stanford.edu/wp18-10

Council of Europe (2022) Artificial Intelligence and Education – a critical view through the lens of human rights, democracy and the rule of law. https://rm.coe.int/prems-092922-gbr-2517-ai-andeducation-txt-16x24-web/1680a956e3

Creutzig F, Acemoglu D, Bai X, Edwards PN, Hintz MJ, Kaack LH, Kilkis S, Kunkel S, Luers A, Milojevic-Dupont N, Rejeski D, Renn J, Rolnick D, Rosol C, Russ D, Turnbull T, Verdolini E, Wagner F, Wilson C, Zekar A, Zumwald M (2022) Digitalisation and the Anthropocene. Annu Rev Environ Resour 47:479–509. https://doi.org/10.1146/annurev-environ-120920-100056

Dos Santos LM (2022) Online learning after the COVID-19 pandemic: learners' motivations. Front Educ 7:879091. https://doi.org/10.3389/feduc.2022.879091

Douwes R, Metselaar J, Pijnenborg GHM, Boonstra N (2023) Wellbeing of students in higher education: the importance of a student perspective. Cogent Educ 10:1. https://doi.org/10.1080/2331186X.2023.2190697

Edwards C, Harwood J (2003) Social identity in the classroom: an examination of age identification between students and instructors. Commun Educ 52(1):60–65. https://doi.org/10.1080/03634520302463

European Commission (2020). Digital Education Action Plan 2021–2027. Resetting education and training for the digital age. Communication from the commission to the european parliament, the council, the european economic and social committee and the committee of the regions. COM/2020/624 final. https://eur-lex.europa.eu/legal-content/EN/TXT/PDF/?uri=CELEX:52020DC0624

European Commission (2022) Ethical guidelines on the use of artificial intelligence (AI) and data in teaching and learning for educators. https://data.europa.eu/doi/10.2766/153756

European Council (2024) Artificial intelligence (AI) act: council gives final green light to the first worldwide rules on AI. Press release, 21 May 2024. https://www.consilium.europa.eu/en/press/press-releases/2024/05/21/artificial-intelligence-ai-act-council-gives-final-green-light-to-the-first-worldwide-rules-on-ai/

European Education Area (2021–2027) Digital Education Action Plan. https://education.ec.europa.eu/focus-topics/digital-education/action-plan

European Parliament (2023) Artificial Intelligence Act: deal on comprehensive rules for trustworthy AI. Press release, 9 December 2023. https://www.europarl.europa.eu/news/en/press-room/20231206IPR15699/artificial-intelligence-act-deal-on-comprehensive-rules-for-trustworthy-ai

European Parliament (2024) Artificial Intelligence Act: MEPs adopt landmark. Press release, 13 March 2024. https://www.europarl.europa.eu/news/en/press-room/20240308IPR19015/artificial-intelligence-act-meps-adopt-landmark-law

Farahany NA (2023) The battle for your brain: defending the right to think freely in the age of neurotechnology. St. Martin's Publishing Group

Hews R, Beligatamulla G, McNamara J (2023) Creative confidence and thinking skills for lawyers: making sense of design thinking pedagogy in law education. Think Skills Creat 49:10152. https://doi.org/10.1016/j.tsc.2023.101352

High-Level Expert Group on Artificial Intelligence (2019) Ethics Guidelines for Trustworthy Artificial Intelligence. https://ec.europa.eu/futurium/en/ai-alliance-consultation.1.html

Holmes W, Persson J, Chounta I-A, Wasson B, Dimitrova V (2022) Artificial intelligence and education: a critical view through the lens of human rights, democracy and the rule of law. Council of Europe Publishing. http://book.coe.int. ISBN 978-92-871-9236-3

Huang R, Spector JM, Yang J (2019) Educational technology a primer for the 21st century. Springer

Khosravi H, Buckingham Shum S, Chen G, Conati C, Tsai YS, Kay J, Knight S, Martinez-Maldonado R, Sadiq S, Gašević D (2022) Explainable Artificial Intelligence in education. Comput Educ: Artif Intell 3. https://doi.org/10.1016/j.caeai.2022.100074

Kontiainen L, Koulu R, Mäihäniemi B (2021) Oikeuden digitalisaatio ja juristityön arkipäivä. (Lakimies 2/2021), pp 173–199. https://www.edilex.fi/lakimies/228230002

Kumar H, Martin A (2023) Artificial emotional intelligence: conventional and deep learning approach. Expert Syst Appl 212(13):118651

Luckin R, Cukurova M, Kent C, du Boulay B (2022) Empowering educators to be AI-ready. Comput Educ: Artif Intell 3. https://doi.org/10.1016/j.caeai.2022.100076

Markauskaite L, Marrone R, Poquet O, Knight S, Martinez-Maldonado R, Howard S, Tondeur J, De Laat M, Buckingham Shum S, Gašević D, Siemens G (2022) Rethinking the entwinement between artificial intelligence and human learning: what capabilities do learners need for a world with AI? Comput Educ: Artif Intell 3. https://doi.org/10.1016/j.caeai.2022.100056

Martin F, Ritzhaupt A, Kumar S, Budhrani K (2019) Award-winning faculty online teaching practices: course design, assessment and evaluation, and facilitation. Internet High Educ 42: 34–43. https://doi.org/10.1016/j.iheduc.2019.04.001

McCluskey F, Winter M (2014) Academic freedom in the digital age 22, vol 2. Q Emerald Group Publishing Limited, pp 136–146. https://doi.org/10.1108/OTH-09-2013-0033

Mitchell M (2023) How do we know how smart AI systems are? Science 381(6654). https://doi.org/10.1126/science.adj5957

Niemi H, Pea RD, Lu Y (eds) (2023) AI in learning: designing the future. Springer Cham. https://doi.org/10.1007/978-3-031-09687-7

Pasvenskienė A (2017) A legal justification of academic freedom as a fundamental right: charting vagueness for more clarity. Doctoral Dissertation, Vytauto Didžiojo universitetas

Pekrun R (2014) Emotions and learning. Educ Pract Ser 24(1):1–31

Pekrun R, Linnenbrink-Garcia L (eds) (2014) International handbook on emotions in education. Routledge

Pinkwart N (2016) Another 25 years of AIED? Challenges and opportunities for intelligent educational technologies of the future. Int J Artif Intell Educ 26:771–783. https://link.springer.com/article/10.1007/s40593-016-0099-7

Popenici S, Kerr S (2017) Exploring the impact of artificial intelligence on teaching and learning in higher education. Res Pract Technol Enhanced Learn 12:22. https://doi.org/10.1186/s41039-017-0062-8

Rahul RK, Shanthakumar S, Vykunth P, Sairamnath K (2020) Real-time Attention Span Tracking in Online Education," 2020 IEEE MIT Undergraduate Research Technology Conference (URTC), Cambridge, MA, USA, pp. 1–4. https://doi.org/10.1109/URTC51696.2020.9668900.

Ramírez-Hurtado JM, Hernández-Díaz AG, López-Sánchez AD, Pérez-León VE (2021) Measuring online teaching service quality in higher education in the COVID-19 environment. Int J Environ Res Public Health 18(5):2403. https://doi.org/10.3390/ijerph18052403

Renz A, Hilbig R (2020) Prerequisites for artificial intelligence in further education: identification of drivers, barriers, and business models of educational technology companies. Int J Educ Technol High Educ 17:14. https://doi.org/10.1186/s41239-020-00193-3

Richards NM, Smart VD (2016) How should the law think about robots? In: Calo R, Froomkin AM, Kerr I (eds) Robot law. Edward Elgar Publishing, pp 3–22

Romero M et al (2024) Manifesto in defence of human-centred education in the age of artificial intelligence. In: Urmeneta A, Romero M (eds) Creative applications of artificial intelligence in education. Palgrave studies in creativity and culture. Palgrave Macmillan, Cham. https://doi.org/10.1007/978-3-031-55272-4_12

Sandomierski D, Ben-Ishai S (2022) Modular legal learning: revitalizing the law classroom. Dalhousie Law Journal 45(2):591–614

Schuett J (2023) Defining the scope of AI regulations. Law Innov Technol 15(1):60–82. https://doi.org/10.1080/17579961.2023.2184135

Shanthakumar RRK, Vykunth S, Sairamnath P, Sairamnath K (2017) Real-time attention span tracking in online education. Department of Information Technology, Sri Venkateswara College of Engineering, Sriperumbudur. https://arxiv.org/ftp/arxiv/papers/2111/2111.14707.pdf

Shen B, Xiao H (2023) Measuring emotions in education using wearable devices: a systematic review. Comput Educ 200. https://doi.org/10.1016/j.compedu.2023.104797

Smallwood J, Fishman DJ, Schooler JW (2007) Counting the cost of an absent mind: mind wandering as an underrecognized influence on educational performance. Psychon Bull Rev 14:230–236

Smith B (2023) AI in higher education: an ethical perspective. J Educ Ethics 34:56–74

Tang X, Upadyaya K, Hiroyuki T, Kasanen M, Salmela-Aro K (2023) Assessing and tracking students' wellbeing through an automated scoring system: school day wellbeing model. In: Niemi H, Pea RD, Lu Y (eds) AI in learning: designing the future. Springer, pp 55–71

UN Committee on Economic, Social and Cultural Rights (2019) General Comment No. 13: The Right to Education (Art. 13 of the Covenant), E/C.12/1999/10, 8 December 1999. https://www.refworld.org/legal/general/cescr/1999/en/37937

UNESCO (2019) Artificial intelligence in education: challenges and opportunities for sustainable development. Pedró, Francesc, Subosa, Miguel, Rivas, Axel, Valverde. Working papers on education policy ED-2019/WS/8. https://unesdoc.unesco.org/ark:/48223/pf0000366994

UNESCO (2022) Recommendation on the Ethics of Artificial Intelligence. https://www.unesco.org/en/articles/recommendation-ethics-artificial-intelligence

Viljanen M, Parviainen H (2022) AI applications and regulation: mapping the regulatory strata. Front Comput Sci 3:779957. https://doi.org/10.3389/fcomp.2021.779957

Vuorikari R, Punie Y, Cabrera M (2020) Emerging technologies and the teaching profession: ethical and pedagogical considerations based on near-future scenarios. Publications Office of the European Union, Luxembourg. https://doi.org/10.2760/46933

Wang P (2019) On defining artificial intelligence. J Artif Gen Intell 10(2):1–37. https://doi.org/10.2478/jagi-2019-0002

WIPO (1991) Worldwide Symposium on the Intellectual Property Aspects of Artificial Intelligence, Stanford University 1991 (Geneva 1991)

Zawacki-Richter O, Marín V, Bond M, Gouverneur F (2019) Systematic review of research on artificial intelligence applications in higher education: where are the educators? Int J Educ Technol High Educ 16(39):1–27. https://doi.org/10.1186/s41239-019-0171-0

Fair and Sustainable Data Governance for Responsible Uses of Emotional Data

Rosa Ballardini and Olli Pitkänen

Abstract In the data economy, setting internal standards and data policies for how data is gathered, stored, processed, and disposed has become both crucial and mandatory for companies and organizations. Thus, different models for data governance have been developed to support companies and organizations in their everyday data business. One prominent example is the Finnish Innovation Fund Sitra Rulebook model for a fair data economy, currently used by several data sharing networks across Europe. Although these models generally apply to data governance, *whether and to what extent they are suitable for data governance of more specific contexts, like for emotional data,* is questionable. Through scenario methodology, we address this issue to elaborate on how emotional data through AI will or can be developed and used in the next five years, and assess the suitability of the existing data governance models. We do this by contextualizing the applicability and validity of the Sitra rulebook model in the framework of our developed scenario. Ultimately, we provide new understanding on the benefits, but also possible limitations, of data current governance models in the context of the rapidly upcoming wave of emotional data and AI, while also reflecting on possible needs for further developments.

1 Introduction

The deeper we enter the complexity of global digital ecosystems, the more evident the importance of data becomes evident. Not only is data a core component of the digital economy but it is also an essential resource to secure the green and digital transitions.

R. Ballardini (✉)
Faculty of Law, University of Lapland, Rovaniemi, Finland
e-mail: rosa.ballardini@ulapland.fi

O. Pitkänen
1001 Lakes, Helsinki, Finland
e-mail: olli.pitkanen@1001lakes.com

R. Ballardini et al. (eds.), *Emotional Data Applications and Regulation of Artificial Intelligence in Society*, Law, Governance and Technology Series 69,
https://doi.org/10.1007/978-3-031-80111-2_12

Several studies have identified reasons why so little data is still shared.[1] In particular, these reasons include:

- Technology issues, such as a lack of interoperability in technology and semantics, and insufficient data quality;
- Legal problems, like the lack of frameworks according to data;
- Ethical and social challenges, such as cultural barriers for data sharing and moral concerns about data sharing;
- Security difficulties;
- Business and economical hindrances, especially the digital immaturity of many companies and their inability to see the business benefits of data sharing;
- and—most importantly—a fundamental distrust between the participants, who are often market competitors.

To solve these issues, and to build trust among parties helping governing data sharing networks, the Finnish Innovation Fund Sitra rulebook model for a fair data economy has gained popularity.[2] To note is the pan-European potential outreach of the Sitra rulebook, as an expert group set up by the European Union-funded Data Space Support Centre (DSSC) is currently working on adapting the Sitra Rulebook model into a pan-European DSSC rulebook model. The first version of the DSSC Rulebook model is expected to be published by the end of 2024. Also, as a starting point, it should be pointed out that for the purpose of this chapter, we rely on the definition of the data governance model as provided by the Data Space Support Centre (DSSC) that defines the "Data space governance framework" as: "The structured set of principles, processes, and practices that guide and regulate the governance, management and operations within a data space to ensure effective and responsible leadership, control, and oversight. It defines the functionalities the data space provides and the associated data space roles, including the data space governance authority and participants".[3]

In relation to data sharing, a special group of data is *emotional data,*[4] which has gained considerable importance lately especially due to technological developments and the potentials of artificial intelligence (AI). Since trust is a key factor in digital

---

[1] See, e.g. Jussen et al. (2024); Schlueter Langdon and Schweichhart (2022).

[2] Marko Turpeinen: "Rulebook overcomes the lack of trust in data sharing", 2022, https://mydata.org/2022/08/30/rulebook-overcomes-the-lack-of-trust-in-data-sharing/ "The Sitra rulebook model: Forming trust-based data sharing networks", https://data4food2030.eu/rulebook-feature-the-sitra-rulebook-model-forming-trust-based-data-sharing-networks/; "Traffic Data Ecosystem Rulebook", https://www.fintraffic.fi/en/fintraffic/traffic-data-ecosystem-rulebook.

[3] Data Spaces Blueprint v1.0 at: https://eur02.safelinks.protection.outlook.com/?url=https%3A%2F%2Fdssc.eu%2Fspace%2FBVE%2F357073747%2F2%2BCore%2BConcepts&data=05%7C02%7CRosa.Ballardini%40ulapland.fi%7C3f574ee4ad564fdbc53008dc7fb1a981%7C4c60a66f0a8d446e9ac0836a00d84542%7C0%7C0%7C638525648234262350%7CUnknown%7CTWFpbGZsb3d8eyJWIjoiMC4wLjAwMDAiLCJQIjoiV2luMzIiLCJBTiI6Ik1haWwiLCJXVCI6Mn0%3D%7C0%7C%7C%7C&sdata=bSI2bY3OmaTZ3R0oWTMyXLUIHFq7PZMtmhJlSZ8VTyw%3D&reserved=0.

[4] As defined in the introductory section of this book.

transformation in general and in the development of AI systems that handle emotional data in particular, the question arises as to whether models like the Sitra rulebook can also help to address trust issues related to the sharing of emotional data. Our hypothesis is that regulatory frameworks and currently existing tools for data governance, such as the Sitra rulebook model, should be developed in order to meet the specific needs of emotional AI. Our research question is: how could tools like the Sitra rulebook model be further developed to better embrace the sensitivities of emotional data sharing? To address this question, we rely on scenario methodology and develop a future scenario for how emotional data through AI will or can be developed and used in the next five years. We analyse the applicability of the Sitra rulebook model to shed light over its benefit, but also some possible limitations when applied to data governance in the context of emotional AI.

2 The EU Legal Landscape for Data Sharing

Acknowledging the opportunities but also the high risks and challenges related to the use and processing of data, in 2020, the European Union launched the European data strategy[5] for harnessing existing barriers and creating a single European market for data, while fully respecting EU policies on fundament rights such as privacy, data protection as well as competition law. A driving principle of the data strategy relates to creating an appropriate balance between protection, regulation and innovation 'to allow data to flow freely within the EU and across sectors', in accordance with the 'free movement of data', which is one of the five pillars of the European internal market.

To achieve the ambition of the EU data strategy, various regulatory actions have already been taken, and more legislative initiatives are underway. The Data Governance Act[6] and the Data Act[7] (that are often jointly referred to as the 'Data Acts') are the most recent pieces of law released as part of the European strategy for data. The Data Governance Act, which applies from September 2023, aims to facilitate the voluntary sharing of data by individuals and businesses and harmonises conditions for the use of certain public sector data. On the other hand, the Data Act, which shall apply from 12 September 2025, is a horizontal regulation that covers different regulatory aspects related to personal and non-personal data collected by connected

[5] European Data Strategy. Making the EU a role model for a society empowered by data; at: https://commission.europa.eu/strategy-and-policy/priorities-2019-2024/europe-fit-digital-age/european-data-strategy_en.

[6] Regulation (EU) 2022/868 of the European Parliament and of the Council of 30 May 2022 on European data governance (Data Governance Act), https://eur-lex.europa.eu/legal-content/EN/TXT/?uri=CELEX%3A32022R0868.

[7] Regulation (EU) 2023/2854 of the European Parliament and of the Council of 13 December 2023 on harmonised rules on fair access to and use of data (Data Act), https://eur-lex.europa.eu/legal-content/EN/TXT/?uri=CELEX:32023R2854.

products and related services in the B2B, B2C and B2G contexts. The Data Act will complement the Data Governance Act by better harnessing the potential of data sharing, and providing further opportunities for the reuse of data by tackling the problem that most data remain either unused or that its value is concentrated in the hands of relatively few large companies. In addition to data sharing obligations and access rights, the Data Act contains rules on switching between data processing services and international transfers of non-personal data.

However, the 'Data Acts' do not exist in a vacuum. On the contrary, they strategically complement the already existing EU legal framework for data governance. This comprises *inter alia* the General Data Protection Regulation (GDPR),[8] the Free Flow of Non-Personal Data Regulation,[9] the Open Data Directive,[10] as well as the Database Directive[11] and the Platform to Business Regulation.[12] For instance, the 'Data Acts' link to the GDPR in the sense that they are consistent with existing rules on the processing of personal data and protecting the private life and the confidentiality of communications, as well as any data stored in and accessed from terminal equipment (in accordance with the ePrivacy Directive[13]). Moreover, the 'Data Acts' also complement these privacy-focused provisions, particularly with regards to data generated by a user's product connected to a publicly available electronic communications network.

By ensuring that every organisation should be able to store and process data anywhere in the EU, and ensuring the availability of data for regulatory control, the Free Flow of Non-Personal Data Regulation aims to remove obstacles to the free movement of non-personal data between different EU countries and IT systems in Europe. Moreover, it will introduce codes of conduct to facilitate switching data between cloud services to tackle the problem of 'vendor lock-in'. The Data Act

[8] Regulation (EU) 2016/679 of the European Parliament and of the Council of 27 April 2016 on the protection of natural persons with regard to the processing of personal data and on the free movement of such data, and repealing Directive 95/46/EC (General Data Protection Regulation) (Text with EEA relevance), at: https://eur-lex.europa.eu/eli/reg/2016/679/oj.

[9] Regulation (EU) 2018/1807 of the European Parliament and of the Council of 14 November 2018 on a framework for the free flow of non-personal data in the European Union (Text with EEA relevance.). https://eur-lex.europa.eu/legal-content/EN/TXT/?uri=CELEX%3A32018R1807.

[10] Directive (EU) 2019/1024 of the European Parliament and of the Council of 20 June 2019 on open data and the re-use of public sector information (recast). https://eur-lex.europa.eu/legal-content/EN/TXT/?uri=celex%3A32019L1024.

[11] Directive 96/9/EC of the European Parliament and of the Council of 11 March 1996 on the legal protection of databases. https://eur-lex.europa.eu/legal-content/EN/TXT/?uri=celex%3A31996L0009.

[12] Regulation (EU) 2019/1150 of the European Parliament and of the Council of 20 June 2019 on promoting fairness and transparency for business users of online intermediation services (Text with EEA relevance). https://eur-lex.europa.eu/legal-content/EN/TXT/?uri=celex%3A32019R1150.

[13] Directive 2002/58/EC of the European Parliament and of the Council of 12 July 2002 concerning the processing of personal data and the protection of privacy in the electronic communications sector (Directive on privacy and electronic communications). https://eur-lex.europa.eu/legal-content/EN/ALL/?uri=CELEX%3A32002L0058.

builds on all this, helping even more citizens and businesses to switch between cloud providers and port data.

In addition, the Data Act tackles some of the long-lasting controversies existing in the context of the Database (DB) Directive, the purpose of which is to protect databases that have been created as a result of a 'substantial investment', even when the database itself is not 'original' in the sense of qualifying for copyright protection. Here, a long-standing and highly debated issue relates to whether databases containing data generated or obtained by the use of products or related services, such as machine-generated data, would be entitled to protection under the dictate of the DB Directive.[14] In fact, the Data Act expressly states that, in order not to hinder the exercise of the right of users to access data and share data with third parties under the Data Act "The sui generis right provided for in Article 7 of Directive 96/9/EC shall not apply when data is obtained from or generated by a connected product or related service falling within the scope of this Regulation" (Art. 43 of the Data Act).

Moreover, as a rule, trade secrets must be protected and may only be disclosed if the data holder and the user "take all necessary measures prior to the disclosure" to preserve confidentiality (Art 4(6) of the Data Act). Access and sharing of data may be refused only if the data holder, which is a "trade secret holder", can demonstrate, and duly substantiate, that they are "highly likely to suffer serious economic damage" from the disclosure, on a case-by-case basis (Art. 4(8) and 5(11) of the Data Act).

Last but not least, the 'Data Acts' also complement both the Platform to Business Regulation and the Open Data Directive. The former has imposed transparency obligations, requiring platforms to describe for business users the data generated from the provision of the service, while the latter has defined minimum standards for re-using data held by the public sector and of publicly funded research data made publicly available through repositories.[15]

As previously mentioned, there are also other EU regulations that will impact the current personal and non-personal data governance rules. These regulations include primarily the Digital Markets Act,[16] which requires certain providers of core platform services identified as 'gatekeepers' to provide more effective portability of data generated through business and end users' activities; the Digital Services Act

[14] Pihlajarinne and Ballardini (2019).

[15] For a comprehensive overview on issues related to non-personal data governance see: Olga BATURA, Axel WION, Sofia Noelle GONZALEZ, J. Scott MARCUS, Ilsa GODLOVITCH, Lukas WIEWIORRA, Peter KROON, Serpil TAS and Nico STEFFEN, "The emergence of non-personal data markets", Policy Department for Economic, Scientific and Quality of Life Policies Directorate-General for Internal Policies. Available at: https://www.europarl.europa.eu/RegData/etudes/STUD/2023/740098/IPOL_STU(2023)740098_EN.pdf.

[16] Regulation (EU) 2022/1925 of the European Parliament and of the Council of 14 September 2022 on contestable and fair markets in the digital sector (Digital Markets Act), https://eur-lex.europa.eu/eli/reg/2022/1925/oj.

(DSA);[17] as well as the forthcoming 'Artificial Intelligence Act (AI Act)', an abbreviation of the proposal for a regulation of the European Parliament and of the Council on harmonized rules on Artificial Intelligence,[18] which is particularly relevant in the context of data regulation in relation to AI technologies.

As elaborated in the Introduction of this book, although emotional data is not as such a specific topic to attract its own *ad hoc* legal provision in the EU, sensitive data such as emotions are covered by several of the existing and forthcoming data sharing and data governance EU provisions, particularly the ones related to privacy and data protection like the GDPR as well as the AI Act.

3 Existing Models Built Based on the Legislation to Conduct Data Governance: The Example of Sitra's Rulebook

The Sitra Rulebook model is an example of the aforementioned EU legal framework for data governance, shaping and influencing the development of concrete tools used for data sharing and data governance in practice.

The Finnish Innovation Fund Sitra is a think tank, promoter of experiments and operating models, and a catalyst for co-operation.[19] In 2019, Sitra organized a series of workshops in which experts in the field of emerging data economy developed the idea to promote data sharing with common ground rules manifested in a rulebook. As a result, Sitra initiated a process to develop a model for a rulebook for a fair data economy. Since the publication of the first version of the rulebook model in 2020, there has been a large versatile group of experts from companies, universities, authorities, and industrial associations developing the model. At the time of writing, version 2.0 of the rulebook model is available at Sitra's website in several languages.[20]

The starting point of the rulebook model is that it aims to tackle difficulties in data sharing from both business, ethical, legal, and technical perspectives. It is designed to protect people's privacy and data protection as well as make it easier to initiate data sharing networks and enable growing data ecosystems. The rulebook model is

[17] Regulation (EU) 2022/2065 of the European Parliament and of the Council of 19 October 2022 on a Single Market For Digital Services and amending Directive 2000/31/EC (Digital Services Act) (Text with EEA relevance).

[18] Regulation (EU) 2024/1689 of the European Parliament and of the Council of 13 June 2024 laying down harmonised rules on artificial intelligence and amending Regulations (EC) No 300/2008, (EU) No 167/2013, (EU) No 168/2013, (EU) 2018/858, (EU) 2018/1139 and (EU) 2019/2144 and Directives 2014/90/EU, (EU) 2016/797 and (EU) 2020/1828 (Artificial Intelligence Act), https://eur-lex.europa.eu/eli/reg/2024/1689/oj.

[19] The Finnish Innovation Fund Sitra, https://www.sitra.fi/en/.

[20] Sitra (2022), Rulebook for a Fair Data Economy, version 2.0, https://www.sitra.fi/en/publications/rulebook-for-a-fair-data-economy/.

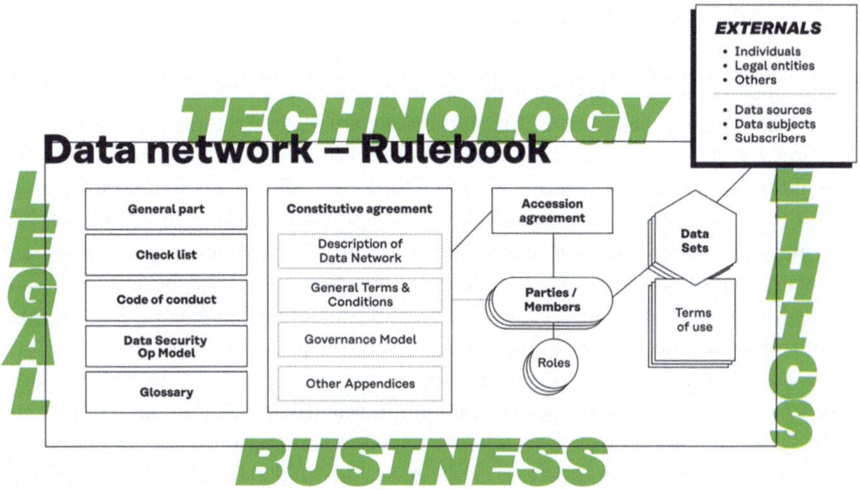

Fig. 1 General structure of a rulebook in accordance with the Sitra model

quite generic as it is not specifically designed for any application area or industry. In particular, it should be noted that emotional AI was not considered when the rulebook model was developed.

The rulebook model consists of two main parts. The first part is an introduction on how to set up a data sharing network, to assess its capabilities and shortcomings, and to create a rulebook for it. It also includes extensive guidelines for data security and ethical principles. The second part of the rulebook model consists of editable templates that enable organisations to create their own rulebooks for their data networks and support when defining the legal relations within networks. The templates are provided in an editable form so that they can easily be made into an actual rulebook to be adopted by a specific data network. They include templates for a description of the data network, for a code of conduct, for a constitutive agreement, for an accession agreement, for a governance model and for a dataset terms of use, as well as the General Terms and Conditions (Fig. 1).

The Sitra rulebook model has already been applied to many data sharing networks (e.g. Fintraffic's Traffic Data Ecosystem[21]) and it is currently attracting growing attention from around Europe. For example, the International Data Spaces Association recognizes and uses the Sitra model in its own rulebook development.[22]

[21] Traffic Data Ecosystem Rulebook, https://www.fintraffic.fi/en/rulebook.

[22] IDSA Rulebook: Legal Dimension, https://docs.internationaldataspaces.org/ids-knowledgebase/v/idsa-rulebook/idsa-rulebook/6_legal_dimension.

4 Method: Scenario Building

In this chapter, we are analysing the applicability of the Sitra rulebook model to emotional AI. Since emotional AI applications are still rare today, we are mostly concerned with future phenomena and therefore our methodology needs to borrow from futures research.[23] Exploring the future of a multi-dimensional topic such as the one in hand here, requires a transdisciplinary approach in order to ensure holistic outcomes and to avoid undesirable tunnel vision. In this regard, scenarios are especially useful when we want to describe how the world will be like and what kinds of legal challenges may occur. In terms of predicting future complex systemic techno-socio developments, scenarios are useful, especially since these developments are often associated with uncertainties and systemic shifts. In fact, scenario development enables uncovering plausible futures and associated impacts of techno-socio systems.[24] In that way, a variety of impacting factors from wide-ranging fields are linked together to generate coherent and understandable 'illustrations' (i.e. scenarios) of the future.[25] These illustrations represent the relationship models between the impacting factors under consideration. These impacting factors (i.e. drivers of change) are the key trends and megatrends that will affect the future occurrence of an event within a defined scope. Change drivers often include uncertainties and assumptions, while trends are events that are happening around any given time. Though trends occur over a shorter period and have local impact, megatrends, on the other hand, are events that have long persisted and that are expected to continue for many years to come with a worldwide impact.

4.1 *Creating Our Future Scenario*

For our purpose, we invited Vesa Kantola, who is an experienced expert in future scenario developing,[26] to co-create with us a future scenario relevant to our context, hypothesis and research question. During the process, Kantola was granted access to scientific material from our conducted literature review. We met with him twice, and communicated with him on multiple occasions through email in order to agree on the details that the scenario should include and to co-create with him the desired settings. The result was the presented scenario below, which is in a form of an imaginary scientific article published in a fictional journal in five years' time, i.e. 2028.

---

[23] Bell (1997); Pitkänen (2006).

[24] Börjeson et al. (2006), pp. 723–739.

[25] Curado and Bontis (2006), pp. 367–381.

[26] Kantola et al. (2013), pp. 589–600. Aalto ARTS Books; Kankainen et al. (2011).

This article was published in the* Scandinavian Journal of Design and Architecture, *September 2028, vol. 3, issue 2
Vesa Kantola:

The Evolution of Public Spaces in the Age of AI

Introduction:

The evolution of public spaces in architecture has been a longstanding discussion. With the integration of sensors and AI, this discourse has taken on a new dimension. This article explores this novel direction using Actor Network Theory (ANT)[1] from Science and Technology Studies[2], which considers even non-living entities as active actors within our networks.[3]

Research Methodology:

The study involved interviews with prominent designers in the United States and China, including Dr. Hio Ho and the artist pseudonym ValtD. Dr. Ho is a key figure in the development of China's social record system, while ValtD's work includes the interaction design of Disney Park Singapore.

Available Technologies:

To identify individuals in public or semi-enclosed spaces, various technologies rely on face recognition, often supported by cameras and wireless sensors. China leads the way in delivering cost-effective solutions, while Clearview AI competes in the US. However, while stringent privacy laws and human rights regulations in the US and Europe have forced Clearview AI to modify its products significantly[4], Chinese AI companies operate with more freedom.

A common cost-effective solution involves a 30x30 metre grid with camera and sensor systems. These systems incorporate various sensors and AI programs, and they can be sourced from different regions to meet specific needs.

The use of loudspeaker systems in public spaces is on the rise, offering immediate feedback to customers through sound, which directly impacts the autonomic nervous system. AI can generate music and sounds based on face recognition, emotions, and personal information, allowing customers to purchase or download music they enjoy.

In security situations, AI-generated sounds can notify security staff discreetly and guide them efficiently. AI-produced sounds can also influence people's emotions, either alerting or calming them.

Staging the Shop Centre:

Taking the *Mall of Rudolph the Red-nosed Reindeer* in Finland as an example, this shopping centre demonstrates how different departments can create unique user experiences. The mall is divided into the Bazar, Classics, and Concierge sections, each catering to different types of products and shopping experiences, where AI plays a role in dynamically pricing items.

(continued)

Each department in the shopping has unique security, logistics, and AI camera-sensor needs, presenting challenges for effective operation and maintenance.

Customers and Their Contracts:

Customer journeys in the Mall of Rudolph the Red-nosed Reindeer vary in complexity. Upon entry to the centre, customers are informed that they are subjects of monitoring. Recognition and data comparison occur, with some customers participating in loyalty programs. Contracts with internet platforms and wearable devices influence the extent to which customers share personal information.

In the Concierge section, valuable items are integrated with RFID tags, and these items are registered under the buyer's digital identification upon purchase.

Questions for Europe:

As ANT theory from the 1990s highlighted the role of non-human agents, Europe faces critical questions in this AI-driven sensory world under the following categories[5]:

Regulation and Geopolitics: Should the EU impose limits on the sale and import of specific software and hardware from the US and China? How should corporations react?

Personnel and Workforce: How should public servants be monitored, and what hybrid roles should they adopt?

Customer Involvement: Can customers make automated contracts through their own AI agents while navigating public spaces?

Business Models: How can databases from various sources be combined to benefit all stakeholders? Can standardized procedures and contracts be established?

Green and Sustainable Policy: The energy consumption of AI-sensory systems is a pressing concern. Europe must consider sustainable solutions in the face of growing energy demands.

Conclusion:

The evolution of public spaces in the age of AI and sensors presents a range of challenges and opportunities for Europe. Addressing these issues will require innovative thinking and the development of new models that consider the role of both humans and non-human actors in our public, business, and private lives.

References:

1. Latour, B. (2005). Reassembling the Social: An Introduction to Actor-Network-Theory. Oxford University Press.
2. Hackett, E. et al. (2007). The Handbook of Science and Technology Studies. MIT Press.

(continued)

3. Kantola, V. (2025). ANT revised – correcting Latour's gravest errors. Doctoral dissertation, Aalto University.
4. E.g. *Clearview AI v Finland,* ECJ C-101/26.
5. Bradford, A. (2023). Digital Empires: The Global Battle to Regulate Technology. Faculty Books.

4.2 Experts' Workshop: Selection of Experts, Preparatory Work and Workshop Setting

To receive feedback regarding the applicability of the Sitra rulebook model in the future scenario created, we organized a workshop for legal experts. We invited a total of four (4) legal experts with proven knowledge on different areas of the EU legal framework relevant to AI and data regulation in general, and to emotional AI regulation in particular. More specifically, legal experts' expertise included both academic and practical experience, with a focus especially on robot law, AI liability, data protection, and competition law. The group was composed by a mix of mid-senior experts with a range between 5 to 30+ years of expertise in these areas.

Before the workshop, the experts had been provided with a link to the Sitra rulebook model and were asked to familiarise themselves with it in advance. While one expert was also already familiar with the details of the Sitra Rulebook model as she had been using it multiple times in conducting data governance analysis in company cases, the others had not used the Sitra model before the workshop.

The workshop was conducted on 14.11.2023 online via Microsoft Teams. Moreover, the experts were asked to use a Miro board (www.miro.com) while providing their answers. At the workshop, the researchers (i.e. the authors of this chapter) asked the experts questions and took notes. The Miro board was also used to capture remarks from the participants. Furthermore, upon permission of the participants, the event was recorded for the researchers' internal verification purposes.

To kick off the workshop, the researchers briefly presented the purpose of the workshop as well as the content of the Sitra model, after which the scenario was shared with the experts, who were given about 10 min to familiarise themselves with it.

The workshop was composed of four (4) parts and a concluding and summing up part. In Part I (7 min), the experts were asked to identify the actors involved in the scenario and their roles as: 1. a customer (i.e. data provider); 2. a shopping centre operator (i.e. service provider, data provider, or end user); 3. a restaurant/shop (i.e. data provider or end user), or 4. an AI-based system provider (i.e. service provider or end user of data). Following this, one role was assigned to each of the experts (i.e. one participant represented the customer, one the shopping centre operator, one the restaurant/shop and one the AI-based system provider).

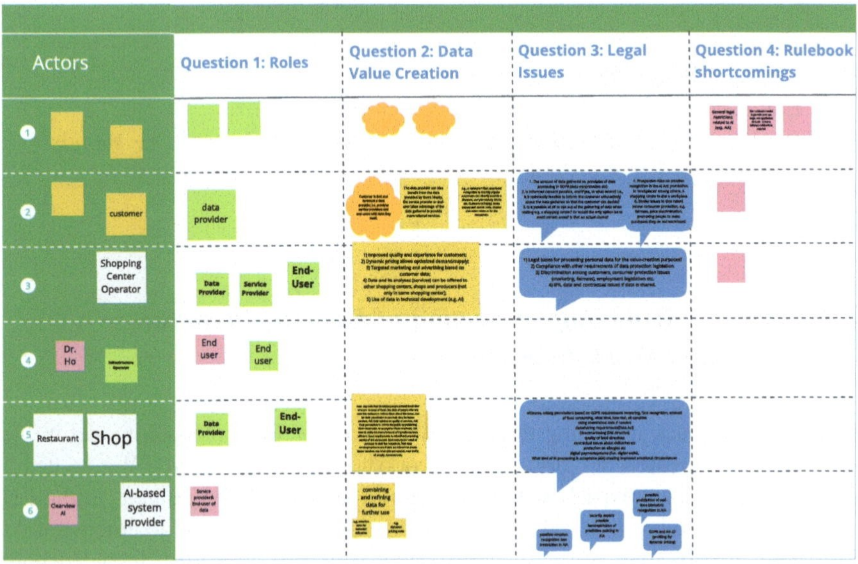

Fig. 2 The resulting Miro board from the workshop

We then continued with Part II, lasting about 25 min, which related to value creation. In this phase, the experts were asked: "Based on the actor and role you have been given, what are the possible ways you can benefit from data and AI in the scenario (e.g. selling data for money, understanding customers to better improve services)?" The experts were first given 10 min to individually consider their answers and report them to the Miro board, and then they were asked to present their views to the group. About 15 min were used for this group discussion.

Part III lasted about 25 min and focused on legal issues. Here, the experts were given the following instructions: "Based on the actor and role you have been given, list legal issues related to the value creation in the previous part (e.g. IPR license to use data is needed, no clear legal basis to process personal data)". Again, the experts were first given time for individual work (about 10 min), followed by group discussions and sharing of views (about 15 min).

Following Part III, Part IV focused on discussing the issues in the context of the Sitra Rulebook model as the experts were asked the following question: "Based on the actor and role you have been given, answer the following question: what, if any, are the current shortcomings of the Sitra rulebook model when applied to emotional data/emotional AI?" The same format was used, starting with individual work using the Miro board (10 min), followed by group discussions (20 min).

Finally, the last 10 min of the workshop were used to collect final remarks on the issues discussed from each of the experts and from summarising the main results of the workshop.

Figure 2 (also provided in readable form as Annex 1) shows the Miro board related results of the workshop.

5 Workshop Results and Reflection on Hypothesis and Research Questions

5.1 Mapping and Understanding Applicable Legislation

We elaborate on the results of the workshop by following an integration method where we present the participants' contribution, combined with our own further analysis and understanding on the matters.

The experts' workshop shed light over several issues relevant to the context of data governance models such as the Sitra rulebook model, both in general and in relation to some specific issues related to applying such models to data governance in the context of sensitive data such as emotional data. Part II and III of the workshop unveiled how different types of EU law could play a role in the scenario, allowing us to map relevant legal provisions and applicable principles. To enable the subsequent stage of understanding the suitability of the Sitra model to the context of the scenario, this mapping of the applicable laws in the context presented was indeed a necessary step.

Notwithstanding the different roles the experts had been assigned, most of the legal issues they pointed out turned out to be applicable to many actors alike. Therefore, it seems more sensible to present the legal areas that were identified as clusters of legal issues, rather than as clusters of legal issues 'per actor' separately. Following this logic, three main categories could be identified:

1. **Privacy and data protection issues** (primarily in relation to the GDPR and relevant parts of the AI Act[27]);
2. **AI and data specific laws** (primarily the AI Act and the various pieces of EU law related to data governance, such as the Data Governance Act and the Data Act, i.e. the 'Data Acts');
3. **Other relevant legal issues** (primarily IPR law and consumer protection legislation).

Indeed, the results from Parts II and III of the workshop confirmed our starting point in terms of which legal frameworks are the most relevant for the context of the scenario.

Generally speaking, issues related to privacy and data protection attracted the majority of the answers and discussions. First, the answers and discussions indicated that a customer who provides data may have concerns about the amount of data gathered and the principles of data processing in the GDPR, such as data minimization. Customers may also wonder if it is technically feasible to inform them exhaustively about the data gathered so that they can decide whether to give informed consent. Additionally, they may question whether it is possible to opt out of data gathering when visiting a shopping centre, or if the only option is to visit

[27] It is to be noted that the actors referred to the version of the AI Act available at that time (i.e. July 2024: https://eur-lex.europa.eu/eli/reg/2024/1689/oj).

certain areas, which may not be an actual choice. In turn, shopping centre operators who provide data and services may have questions about the legal basis for processing personal data for value-creation purposes, as well as compliance with other requirements of data protection legislation. For their part, restaurants and shops that provide data may need to ask permission based on GDPR's requirements for sensory and face recognition, the amount of food consumed (what kind, how fast), and all sensitive information using anonymized data if needed. Finally, AI-based system providers who provide services and use data may need to consider the GDPR and Article 22, which pertains to profiling for dynamic prices.

The second most discussed cluster of legal issues pertained to the domain of 'AI and data-specific legislation', which primarily focused on the Artificial Intelligence Act (AIA) and the 'Data Acts'. First, it was pointed out that, under the AIA, it would be very important to clearly specify whether the type of AI and data processing system that triggers emotional circumstances that is used is acceptable as such or conditional to certain actions required by the type of risks category the system falls into. Secondly, as a shopping centre is *inter alia* also a workplace, the provisions of the AI Act related to emotion-recognition, especially in regard to the prohibition in workplaces, would be relevant. Third, the data sharing requirements included in the Data Act were presented as fundamental issues to be considered. In fact, the Data Act forces companies to provide users (both natural and legal persons) with access to the data generated by their connected Internet of Things (IoT) devices, which also includes cases when trade secrets are involved. In order words, manufacturers and other data holders of connected products will have to make user data accessible for free to users and under fair, reasonable and non-discriminatory (FRAND) terms to third parties in the EU, as well as other third parties outside the EU, albeit not subject to the FRAND terms. Finally, in relation to service providers and end users of data, three main issues all related to the AIA were highlighted: first, issues about the possible emotion-recognition ban or restrictions by the AIA should be carefully monitored; second, a possible ban or restriction of predictive policing in the AIA for security purposes might have repercussions here; third, the possible prohibition of real-time biometric recognition in the AIA is in need to be closely considered in the case at stake. All in all, this part of the workshop not only specified both legal issues to be considered in data governance models for AI in general but also shed light on issues specific to emotional data and emotional AI in particular.

Last but not least, the cluster related to 'other relevant legal issues' was that which attracted the least discussions, and it was focused on highlighting some possible repercussions pertaining to the domain of IPR legislation and consumer law. From the perspective of IPR law, the answers and discussions indicated that IPR, trade secrets and linked contractual issues are indeed crucial to consider, especially in terms of data 'ownership' and data sharing practices. From the point of view of consumer law, it was stressed that discrimination amongst customers as well as consumer protection issues related to fair and transparent marketing and advertising practices, including fairness in price discrimination, or promoting people to make purchases they neither want nor need, are issues of particular importance that the actors of the scenario would mostly likely need to carefully consider. In this regard, relevant marketing laws such as EU Direct marketing (Directive 97/66/EC) would also need to be considered in the assessment.

5.2 *Applicability and Suitability of the Sitra Rulebook Model*

As previously explained, Part IV of the workshop was focused on the actual question related to the applicability and suitability of the Sitra rulebook model in the context of emotional AI and emotional data to address our main research question, based on the results from the previous steps /discussions. Although this discussion mostly highlighted the pros and cons of the Sitra model in general as a tool for data governance management, some issues specific to emotional data governance were also highlighted and could also be derived from the general comments collected. On the positive side, it was indicated that the process of implementing a rulebook for a specific case is often not so much about writing the document but developing a common understanding of the case. Therefore, the Sitra rulebook model, which is quite generic in nature, is very helpful from this point of view. Moreover, the generality of the Sitra rulebook model makes it applicable to many contexts. Nevertheless, having more specific rules could create fragmentation and several versions of the rulebook to choose from, which could add complexity at the general level.

The Sitra rulebook model is extensive, contains a lot of useful information and guidance, and is freely available from Sitra's website. Another advantage of the generic approach followed by the Sitra rulebook model was that there is at least no obvious obstacle to applying it to any AI-based system, including also emotional AI and emotional data governance.

At the same time, however, this level of generality carries counter-sides. In particular, it requires considerable extra work to be able to tailor it to specific situations. It was pointed out that, as such and while it always needs adaptations, the Sitra rulebook model is not directly suitable to anything. Another downside that the experts mentioned was that the Sitra rulebook model is quite difficult to approach as it is quite complicated and takes a considerable amount of time to navigate and learn how to use.

All these issues could be particularly challenging in complex cases, such as those related to data governance of emotional data, or where many entities are involved in data sharing. Indeed, a final point highlighted by the experts was whether the current version of the Sitra rulebook model is usable for emotional data and emotional AI, stressing that any such model should also include procedures for regular monitoring and updating the context to ensure it is current and accurate.

6 Conclusion: Reflection on Data Governance Models for Emotional Data and AI

The experts' workshop discussed several issues related to data governance models, especially the Sitra rulebook model, and how they apply to sensitive data such as emotional data. Three main categories were identified and confirmed as being legal frameworks most relevant for the context of the scenario: privacy and data protection issues, AI and data specific laws, and other relevant legal issues. From their perspective, customers may have concerns about the amount of data gathered, principles of data processing, informed consent, and opt-out options. While shopping centre operators may have questions about the legal basis for processing personal data and compliance with data protection legislation, restaurants and shops may need to request permission based on the GDPR's requirements for sensitive information. Moreover, AI-based system providers may need to consider GDPR and Article 22, which pertains to profiling for dynamic prices.

Secondly, the issues include the need to specify the following: whether the type of AI and data processing system that triggers emotional circumstances is acceptable; the relevance of the provisions of the AI Act related to emotion-recognition; the fundamental issues presented by the data sharing requirements included in the Data Act; and the three main issues related to the AIA, including the restrictions of the emotion-recognition, predictive policing for security purposes, and real-time biometric recognition. Emotion recognition systems that are not prohibited are classified as high-risk systems under the AIA, which also severely restricts the assessment or classification of people over a period of time based on their social behaviour or known, inferred or predicted personal or personality characteristics. The use of real-time remote biometric identification systems in publicly accessible spaces for law enforcement purposes is also prohibited unless strictly necessary for the purposes specified in the AIA.

The discussion highlighted the pros and cons of the Sitra model as a tool for data governance management, and some issues specifically related to emotional data governance were also identified. Although the model is extensive, contains much useful information and guidance, and is freely available from Sitra's website, this level of generality requires considerable extra work to tailor it to specific situations and, as such, the Sitra rulebook model always needs adaptations.

All in all, while it is clear that any data governance model like the Sitra rulebook needs to be regularly updated with legal provisions, whether more specific models should be developed to better accommodate the needs of specific types of data, such as our case emotional data, remains an open question. Indeed, although the Sitra rulebook model is general, this makes it applicable to many contexts—including the context of emotional data and emotional AI. Indeed, having more specific rules could create fragmentation with several versions of the rulebook to choose from, which could add complexity at the general level. In fact, even though we hereby investigated the suitability of the Sitra rulebook model for emotional data, similar studies could be conducted also for other types of data sets or data applications.

Perhaps it could be more advisable to develop a method for adapting the general data governance models, such as Sitra's rulebook, and tailor them to specific cases as needed. That said, we are not in favour of creating multiple ad hoc "Sitra rulebooks" on a case-by-case basis. Instead, we support the development of more methods or tools to make the existing rulebook model more tailored to individual cases. For example, the use of editable templates within the rulebook model allows for customization while maintaining a consistent framework. This approach ensures flexibility and adaptability without the need for entirely new rulebooks. However, we acknowledge that this is a complex and challenging task that requires further investigation in future research. Nevertheless, several products are already available for contract generation and management, examples of which include PandaDoc[28] and Juro.[29] Yet, it will be interesting to see whether such contract automation tools could provide a starting point for reducing the work involved in adapting the rulebook model to different cases and managing parallel versions of rulebooks.

Policy and Laws

Directive (EU) 2019/1024 of the European Parliament and of the Council of 20 June 2019 on open data and the re-use of public sector information (recast). https://eur-lex.europa.eu/legal-content/EN/TXT/?uri=celex%3A32019L1024

Directive 96/9/EC of the European Parliament and of the Council of 11 March 1996 on the legal protection of databases. https://eur-lex.europa.eu/legal-content/EN/TXT/?uri=celex%3A31996L0009

Directive 2002/58/EC of the European Parliament and of the Council of 12 July 2002 concerning the processing of personal data and the protection of privacy in the electronic communications sector (Directive on privacy and electronic communications). https://eur-lex.europa.eu/legal-content/EN/ALL/?uri=CELEX%3A32002L0058

European Data Strategy. Making the EU a role model for a society empowered by data. At: https://commission.europa.eu/strategy-and-policy/priorities-2019-2024/europe-fit-digital-age/european-data-strategy_en.

Proposal for a Regulation of the European Parliament and of the Council laying down harmonised rules on artificial intelligence (artificial intelligence act) and amending certain union legislative acts COM/2021/206 final, https://eur-lex.europa.eu/legal-content/EN/TXT/?uri=celex%3A52021PC0206.

Regulation (EU) 2022/868 of the European Parliament and of the Council of 30 May 2022 on European data governance (Data Governance Act), https://eur-lex.europa.eu/legal-content/EN/TXT/?uri=CELEX%3A32022R0868.

---

[28] See, e.g. Simplified contract management contract: https://www.pandadoc.com/contract-management-software/.

[29] See, e.g. AI-powered contract automation: https://juro.com/.

Regulation (EU) 2023/2854 of the European Parliament and of the Council of 13 December 2023 on harmonised rules on fair access to and use of data (Data Act), https://eur-lex.europa.eu/legal-content/EN/TXT/?uri=CELEX:32023R2854.

Regulation (EU) 2016/679 of the European Parliament and of the Council of 27 April 2016 on the protection of natural persons with regard to the processing of personal data and on the free movement of such data, and repealing Directive 95/46/EC (General Data Protection Regulation) (Text with EEA relevance). At: https://eur-lex.europa.eu/eli/reg/2016/679/oj

Regulation (EU) 2022/1925 of the European Parliament and of the Council of 14 September 2022 on contestable and fair markets in the digital sector (Digital Markets Act), https://eur-lex.europa.eu/eli/reg/2022/1925/oj.

Regulation (EU) 2022/2065 of the European Parliament and of the Council of 19 October 2022 on a Single Market For Digital Services and amending Directive 2000/31/EC (Digital Services Act) (Text with EEA relevance).

Regulation (EU) 2018/1807 of the European Parliament and of the Council of 14 November 2018 on a framework for the free flow of non-personal data in the European Union (Text with EEA relevance.). https://eur-lex.europa.eu/legal-content/EN/TXT/?uri=CELEX%3A32018R1807

Regulation (EU) 2019/1150 of the European Parliament and of the Council of 20 June 2019 on promoting fairness and transparency for business users of online intermediation services (Text with EEA relevance). https://eur-lex.europa.eu/legal-content/EN/TXT/?uri=celex%3A32019R1150.

Online Publications

AI-powered contract automation: https://juro.com/

BATURA O, WION A, Noelle GONZALEZ S, MARCUS JS, GODLOVITCH I, WIEWIORRA L, KROON P, TAS S and STEFFEN N (2023), "The emergence of non-personal data markets", *Policy Department for Economic, Scientific and Quality of Life Policies Directorate-General for Internal Policies*. Available at: https://www.europarl.europa.eu/RegData/etudes/STUD/2023/740098/IPOL_STU(2023)740098_EN.pdf.

Data Spaces Blueprint v1.0: https://eur02.safelinks.protection.outlook.com/?url=https%3A%2F%2Fdssc.eu%2Fspace%2FBVE%2F357073747%2F2%2BCore%2BConcepts&data=05%7C02%7CRosa.Ballardini%40ulapland.fi%7C3f574ee4ad564fdbc53008dc7fb1a981%7C4c60a66f0a8d446e9ac0836a00d84542%7C0%7C0%7C638525648234262350%7CUnknown%7CTWFpbGZsb3d8eyJWIjoiMC4wLjAwMDAiLCJQIjoiV2luMzIiLCJBTiI6Ik1haWwiLCJXVCI6Mn0%3D%7C0%7C%7C%7C&sdata=bSI2bY3OmaTZ3R0oWTMyXLUIHFq7PZMtmhJlSZ8VTyw%3D&reserved=0

IDSA Rulebook: Legal Dimension, https://docs.internationaldataspaces.org/ids-knowledgebase/v/idsa-rulebook/idsa-rulebook/6_legal_dimension

Simplified contract management contract: https://www.pandadoc.com/contract-management-software/

Sitra (2022) Rulebook for a Fair Data Economy, version 2.0, https://www.sitra.fi/en/publications/rulebook-for-a-fair-data-economy/

The Finnish Innovation Fund Sitra, https://www.sitra.fi/en/

Traffic Data Ecosystem Rulebook, https://www.fintraffic.fi/en/rulebook.

Turpeinen M (2022) "Rulebook overcomes the lack of trust in data sharing" https://mydata.org/2022/08/30/rulebook-overcomes-the-lack-of-trust-in-data-sharing/

References

Journal Articles

Börjeson L, Höjer M, Dreborg K-H, Ekvall T, Finnveden G (2006) Scenario types and techniques: towards a user's guide. Futures 38(7):723–739. ISSN 0016-3287. https://doi.org/10.1016/j.futures.2005.12.002

Curado C, Bontis N (2006) The knowledge-based view of the firm and its theoretical precursor. Int J Learn Intellect Cap 3(4):367–381

Jussen I, Möller F, Schweihoff J, Gieß A, Giussani G, Otto B (2024) Issues in inter-organizational data sharing: findings from practice and research challenges. Data Knowl Eng. https://doi.org/10.1016/j.datak.2024.102280

Kankainen A, Vaajakallio K, Kantola V, Mattelmäki T (2011) Storytelling Group – a co-design method for service design. Behav Inf Technol 31(3):221–230. https://doi.org/10.1080/0144929X.2011.563794

Books and Chapters

Bell W (1997) Foundations of futures studies. Transaction Publishers, United States

Kantola V, Simanainen M, Pitkänen O (2013) Designing the future together expanding the paradigm by combining futures studies and design games. In: Riitta S, Olivier I (eds) The Boundary-Crossing Conference on Co-Design in Innovation (Co-Create 2013), Espoo, Finland, pp 589–600

Pihlajarinne T, Ballardini RM (2019) Owning data via intellectual property rights: reality or chimera? In: Ballardini RM, Kuoppamäki P, Pitkänen O (eds) Regulating industrial internet through IPR, data protection and competition law. Kluwer Law International, The Netherlands, pp 115–133

Pitkänen O (2006) Legal challenges to future information businesses. Helsinki University of Technology, Helsinki

Schlueter Langdon C, Schweichhart K (2022) Data spaces: first applications in mobility and industry. In: Otto B, ten Hompel M, Wrobel S (eds) Designing data spaces - the ecosystem approach to competitive advantage. Springer, Switzerland, pp 493–513

Emotional AI and the Consensus-Based Remuneration Regime in Southeast Asia

Artha Dermawan and Péter Mezei

Abstract Some emotional generative AI (GenAI) companies have acquired the power to extract copyright-protected works from anyone in their orbit without prior authorisation. Such monopolistic abuses could potentially disrupt the market for these copyrighted works, thereby forming the basis for numerous lawsuits across multiple jurisdictions. Indeed, the creative industry will be greatly affected by this phenomenon, let alone rights-holders in the Global South including the Association of Southeast Asian Nations (the ASEAN) who have been suffering from ineffective copyright enforcement and restricted freedom of expression for generations. This chapter discusses how to remunerate rights-holders whose work is unlawfully used to train GenAI systems, focusing on the ASEAN and how their non-interference principle (the ASEAN Way) could address this issue. Moreover, a limited Brussels Effect on Text- and Data-Mining (TDM) regulation in the ASEAN is presented. This chapter finds that the ASEAN Way remains relevant to serve as the foundation for remunerating rights-holders in the ASEAN. Furthermore, this chapter proposes that through the Initiation of GenAI Training Remuneration (TDR), stakeholders, following the spirit of 'Gotong Royong' in the Malay Archipelago, could achieve a consensus on a pro-rata model on the amount and method of remuneration for machine learning by emotional GenAI applications.

The authors thank the editors, Silke von Lewinski, Peter K. Yu, Xuan-Thao Nguyen, Doris Long, Jyh-An Lee, Bob Gomulkiewicz, Maggie Chon, Danny Friedmann, Corinne Tan, Tianxiang He, the University of Washington Center for Southeast Asia Studies and Its Diasporas, and participants of the 2023 Inaugural Asian IP Scholars Roundtable at the University of Washington for their suggestions on a previous draft. We also thank the anonymous peer reviewers for their input. Responsibility for the content and any errors remains ours. All internet sources were last accessed on 7 August 2024.

A. Dermawan (✉)
Max Planck Institute for Innovation and Competition, Munich, Germany
e-mail: artha.dermawan@ip.mpg.de

P. Mezei
University of Szeged, Szeged, Hungary
e-mail: mezei.peter@szte.hu

R. Ballardini et al. (eds.), *Emotional Data Applications and Regulation of Artificial Intelligence in Society*, Law, Governance and Technology Series 69,
https://doi.org/10.1007/978-3-031-80111-2_13

1 Introduction

By introducing complex challenges around the creation, use, and distribution of emotionally attached content, the rapid evolution of emotional generative AI (GenAI) is reshaping the copyright landscape.[1] At the forefront of the contemporary copyright debate is the issue of how emotional content generated by AI should be protected and managed. This chapter specifically addresses the unlicensed use of copyright-protected works, replete with emotional expression, for training such emotional GenAI systems. These systems are trained through sophisticated Text- and Data-Mining (TDM) processes to interpret and replicate the complex human emotional expression within literary and artistic works, thereby raising new challenges within copyright law.[2]

The data used during TDM comes from three primary sources: the first comprises data that is not subject to copyright or is in the public domain; the second includes data that is under copyright but is made available under permissive licenses, such as Creative Commons; and the third, and most legally contentious, involves copyright-protected data utilised without permission. This latter category can be further divided into uses that either infringe upon or do not infringe upon the market for the copyright-protected work.[3] This discourse is particularly concerned with uses that could undermine the market value of the original work, rather than its non-commercial aspects. Amid this landscape, the appropriation of copyright-protected emotional expressions for TDM—which could threaten the market value of such expression—has precipitated copyright litigation by rights-holders across numerous jurisdictions.[4] These litigations refute the notion that employing emotionally attached creative works—such as the intricate melodies of musical compositions, the poignant strokes of visual arts, and the rich narratives of literary pieces—for the purpose of training GenAI constitutes a breach of copyright protection.

[1] Works of art created by humans are intrinsically tied to the emotions of their creators and often resonate deeply with their owners. This connection is deeply rooted in various art theories, which posit that art is a fundamental expression of human emotion. Art serves as a medium through which individuals convey their feelings, experiences, and perceptions. Each piece of art is a reflection of the emotional state of its creator at the time of its inception, making it a powerful form of personal and universal communication. Moreover, as previously discussed in the introduction of this book, emotional GenAI is capable of not only generating literary and artistic works, but also emotionally attached content that could entertain its users. See, Shahid et al. (2023), pp. 1–9.

[2] Alpaydın (2004), p. 2.

[3] Sobel (2021), pp. 222–223.

[4] See 'Lawsuits v. AI.' Available at: https://chatgptiseatingtheworld.com/2023/10/19/master-list-of-lawsuits-v-ai-chatgpt-openai-microsoft-meta-midjourney-other-ai-cos/.

In most jurisdictions, including the European Union (EU)[5] and the Association of Southeast Asian Nations (the ASEAN),[6] emotional artistic expressions—products of human intellect—enjoy robust copyright protection. However, the emergence of emotional GenAI highlights the irreplaceable qualities of human authors, such as emotional intelligence and creativity, which AI cannot replicate. The unauthorized use of these works for AI training, particularly when it competes with or substitutes the original market, suggests the need for remuneration. Indeed, recognizing and rewarding the inherent value and profound impact of human-made content on audience engagement is essential, ensuring authors' creativity and individuality are respected within the digital age's copyright framework.

Furthermore, there is a concerted effort to address the implications of emotional GenAI technologies and to safeguard the interests of rights-holders from any potential adverse effects. Within the international arena, jurisdictions including the EU[7] and the ASEAN[8] are at the forefront, enacting regulations and frameworks that ensure the development and use of emotional GenAI is conducted with transparency and accountability. However, to date only the EU, Singapore, and Japan have demonstrably sought to protect rights-holders by introducing TDM exceptions.[9]

This chapter explores how the ASEAN member states, through the proposed ASEAN Guide on AI Governance and Ethics (ASEAN AI Framework) and the principle of non-interference (the ASEAN Way), could protect rights-holders and effectively accommodate TDM within the community. By drawing a comparative analysis with the EU copyright directives, it is suggested that ASEAN could benefit from adopting an author-focused, consensus-based "common approach" for regulating the use of emotionally attached copyright-protected materials in the TDM process. Rooted in the principles of the ASEAN Way, this approach could lead to the establishment of a remuneration scheme that involves Collective Management Organisations (CMOs), emotional GenAI companies, and the rights-holders or

---

[5] See Directive 2001/29/EC of The European Parliament and of the Council of 22 May 2001 on the harmonisation of certain aspects of copyright and related rights in the information society.

[6] See WIPO, 'The Strategic Use of Intellectual Property to Enhance Competitiveness in Select Industries in ASEAN' (WIPO-ASEAN Study). Available at: https://www.wipo.int/edocs/pubdocs/en/intproperty/953/wipo_pub_953.pdf.

[7] Regulation (EU) 2024/1689 of the European Parliament and of the Council of 13 June 2024 laying down harmonised rules on artificial intelligence and amending Regulations (EC) No 300/2008, (EU) No 167/2013, (EU) No 168/2013, (EU) 2018/858, (EU) 2018/1139 and (EU) 2019/2144 and Directives 2014/90/EU, (EU) 2016/797 and (EU) 2020/1828 (Artificial Intelligence Act). Available at: https://eur-lex.europa.eu/eli/reg/2024/1689/oj.

[8] The ASEAN Guide on AI Governance and Ethics highlights the importance of copyright protection within the development and deployment of AI technologies. The guide mandates that AI developers and deployers ensure compliance with existing copyright laws, emphasizing the need for transparency and proper documentation of data used in training AI models. The ASEAN, 'ASEAN Guide on AI Governance and Ethics' (The ASEAN Secretariat, 2024). Available at: https://asean.org/book/asean-guide-on-ai-governance-and-ethics/.

[9] Ueno (2021), p. 213.

their representatives, ensuring fair compensation for the emotional creativity captured and utilised by these advanced AI systems.

2 The ASEAN Way: An Introduction

2.1 Background on the ASEAN and the ASEAN Way

On 8 August 1967, the ASEAN was established under the ASEAN Declaration (Bangkok Declaration) to foster political and economic collaboration and regional stability.[10] Its economic vision is to create a single market and production base, characterised by competitiveness, equitable economic development, and full integration into the global economy.[11] In contrast to the EU's shared values and laws, ASEAN champions the 'ASEAN Way',[12] embodying consensus and non-interference in internal affairs, particularly those concerning politics and security, to bolster community stability.[13] Unlike the EU's fixed institutions such as the Parliament, Commission, and Court of Justice, leadership within ASEAN rotates annually between member states and is coordinated by a secretariat based in Jakarta. Policymaking is primarily conducted during the ASEAN Summit. Comprising the foreign ministers, the ASEAN Coordinating Council (ACC) plays a pivotal role in policymaking, organises the ASEAN Summit, and oversees the execution of its agreements and decisions. The ACC also stipulates the rules for the ASEAN's ad-hoc ministerial meetings, which address pressing issues.[14]

2.2 The ASEAN Intellectual Property Framework

In pursuit of enhanced economic integration and the swift realisation of the ASEAN Free Trade Area, the ASEAN Member States ratified the ASEAN Framework Agreement on Intellectual Property Cooperation in December 1995, aiming to

---

[10] The ASEAN, 'The Founding of ASEAN'. Available at: https://asean.org/the-founding-of-asean/#:~:text=The%20Association%20of%20Southeast%20Asian,%2C%20Philippines%2C%20Singapore%20and%20Thailand.

[11] The ASEAN, 'Economic Community'. Available at: https://asean.org/our-communities/economic-community/#:~:text=Ministerial%20Meetings%20(AEM)-,Highly%20Integrated%20and%20Cohesive%20Economy,as%20the%20global%20supply%20chain.

[12] Art. 2(2)(e) of the ASEAN Charter emphasises that ASEAN and its member states shall act in accordance with the "non-interference in the internal affairs of ASEAN member states. See, the ASEAN Charter. Available at: https://asean.org/asean-charter/. See, Howe and Park (2017), pp. 1–15.

[13] Lengeling (2020). Available at: https://www.ibei.org/ibei-student-paper-57_240434.pdf.

[14] Art. 7 of the ASEAN Charter.

facilitate closer collaboration in IP and related domains as a cornerstone for economic development.[15] This accord contemplates cooperation across all major IP sectors.[16]

Article 3 of the agreement underscores key collaborative efforts: bolstering IP enforcement and protection, fortifying IP administration, enhancing IP legislation, and founding an ASEAN IP Association. The implementation of the agreement is evidenced by various initiatives, notably the ASEAN Intellectual Property Rights Action Plan 2016–2025. However, despite these advancements, IP academics broadly acknowledge that the goals of cooperation remain partially unfulfilled.[17]

3 Analysis of the Text- and Data-Mining Exceptions and Emotional GenAI

3.1 EU Experiences: A Limited Brussels-Effect on the Regulation of AI?

Ever since the creation of the concept of the "digital single market",[18] the number of regulatory sources on online spaces has skyrocketed. Various EU sources of law, especially the General Data Protection Regulation (GDPR),[19] have become reference points on a global level. In other countries, the use of EU norms as a source of domestic legislation has often been coined as "Brussels-effect".[20] With the exponential growth of use of AI technologies, the EU has taken steps to regulate this field as well. For some time, the EU's approach looked like a mosaic of fragmented sections in the Copyright in the Digital Single Market (CDSM) Directive[21] or the

---

[15] ASEAN Framework Agreement on Intellectual Property Cooperation Bangkok, 15 December 1995. Available at: https://asean.org/wp-content/uploads/2021/01/ASEAN-FRAMEWORK-AGREEMENT-ON-INTELLECTUAL-PROPERTY-COOPERATION-BANGKOK-15-DECEMBER-1995..pdf.

[16] Art. 3(1), ibid.

[17] Barizah (2017), pp. 95–112.

[18] Communication from the Commission to the European Parliament, the Council, the European Economic and Social Committee and the Committee of the Regions: A Single Market for Intellectual Property Rights – Boosting creativity and innovation to provide economic growth, high quality jobs and first class products and services in Europe, COM/2011/0287 final, p. 9 et seq.

[19] Regulation (EU) 2016/679 of the European Parliament and of the Council of 27 April 2016 on the protection of natural persons with regard to the processing of personal data and on the free movement of such data, and repealing Directive 95/46/EC (General Data Protection Regulation) (Text with EEA relevance).

[20] Bradford (2020).

[21] Directive 2019/790 of the European Parliament and of the Council of 17 April 2019 on Copyright and Related Rights in the Digital Single Market and amending Directives 96/9/EC and 2001/29/EC, OJ L 130, 17.5.2019 (CDSM Directive). The CDSM Directive has introduced the text- and data-mining exceptions (Articles 3–4); as well as certain other rules, predominantly related to the new

Digital Services Act.[22] Copyright-relevant provisions found their way into the EU's recent horizontal and holistic regulation on the secure but innovative use of AI technologies, namely the AI Act, too.[23]

The CDSM Directive introduced two new exceptions or limitations for TDM in order to deal with the "automated computational analysis of information in digital form, such as text, sounds, images or data".[24] While Article 3 covers a specific, but broad exception allowing research organisations[25] to carry out TDM, Article 4 allows anyone to mine text or data under more limited circumstances. As Article 3 is designed to benefit only non-profit organisations acting in line with their public mission goals, Article 4 remains the primary source of TDM for developers of commercial GenAI algorithms and applications.

Article 4 allows users to reproduce lawfully accessible works and other protected subject matters, including the extraction of parts of a database, and retain such information as long as it is necessary for the purpose of automated analysis of text and/or data in digital form in order to generate information which includes but is not limited to patterns, trends and correlations.[26] To counterbalance the use of information for commercial purposes, rights-holders are allowed to reserve their rights for TDM. Such reservation shall be expressed in an "appropriate manner, such as machine-readable means",[27] including "metadata and terms and conditions of a website or a service".[28]

A number of uncertainties surround the new rules in general and its relevance for GenAI specifically. These concerns stem, first, from the fact that while EU Member States are obliged to introduce their domestic version of Article 4, the directive itself allows for flexible transplantation (e.g. the introduction of an exception or a limitation). Nonetheless, one of the first comprehensive and comparative analyses of the implementation of the new TDM rules evidenced that EU Member States followed a rather "defensive" approach by implementing these provisions almost verbatim.[29]

Therefore, we might need to look at those numerous open terms of Article 4 and the accompanying recitals, which include "lawfully accessible" works and other

platform liability under Article 17, that necessitate the reliance on automated technologies for, e.g. content recognition or complaint-and-redress mechanisms.

[22] Regulation (EU) 2022/2065 of the European Parliament and of the Council of 19 October 2022 on a Single Market For Digital Services and amending Directive 2000/31/EC (Digital Services Act) (Text with EEA relevance).

[23] The EU AI Act, n.8. There are two provisions relevant to the copyright, see Article 53(1)(c) and (d).

[24] Recital 8 CDSM Directive.

[25] Article 2(1) CDSM Directive.

[26] For the definition of (commercial) TDM, see altogether Article 2(2), Article 4(1)-(2) and recital 18 CDSM Directive.

[27] Article 4(3) CDSM Directive.

[28] Recital 18 CDSM Directive.

[29] Sganga et al. (January 16, 2023). Available at https://ssrn.com/abstract=4325376, p. 523.

subject matter;[30] retaining copies "as long as necessary" for the purposes of TDM;[31] and the reservation of rights via "computer-readable means".

From these uncertainties, the rights reservation (or simply "opt-out") rules under Article 4(3) require a closer look as they clearly reflect that even if the TDM exceptions were designed in light of the developments of AI,[32] they were not drafted in light of GenAI. Both the substance and the functioning of such an opt-out is a mystery. How shall the "computer readable form" of reservations be deployed? What is the proper scope (general v. specific) and the timing (ex ante v. ex post) of opting out? Who is entitled and obliged to deploy such reservations (namely, shall reservations be expressed by the rights-holders or can GenAI developers control opting out by their own procedures?)? Moreover, it remains open how the lawful access and the rights reservation prongs of Article 4 interplay. Can an expressed term of an end-user license agreement to exclude the lawfulness of TDM practically outrule the necessity of any computer readable reservation of rights at the same time? Last but not least, can (and should) a rights reservation slow down the massive use of training data for machine learning purposes?

Needless to say, while we are struggling with these open questions, the number of different opt-out models has grown exponentially. These include, e.g. the ex-ante "TDM Reservation Protocol" that creators might deploy on their websites,[33] or the ex-ante masking of copyright protected images by creators via Glaze.[34] There are numerous solutions for the ex-post reservation of rights (that is following the reproduction or extraction of text or data), e.g. Spawning API's service[35] or Stability AI's own opt-out system.[36] Quite recently, OpenAI has launched both an ex-ante disallowment of scraping solution and an ex-post opt-out mechanism;[37] and Google also published a new ex-ante "scalable control" mechanism through robots.txt, called Google Extended.[38] Whether (any or all of) these solutions fit into the statutory concept of rights reservation is far from being clear.[39]

In light of this, it is questionable whether the CDSM Directive has reached a *de facto* full harmonization on this field. Indeed, we are rather convinced that the CDSM Directive needs some (re)calibration to effectively apply for GenAI.

In the EU, the regulation of GenAI is far from being final. Although the AI Act has passed the so-called trilogue phase of the negotiations, it is not yet formally accepted and published. This regulation is aimed to provide for a compact, holistic

[30] Compare to Rosati (2021), pp. 76–77.

[31] Ibid., p. 89.

[32] Compare to the text of recital 8 CDSM Directive, cited in the accompanying text to footnote 25.

[33] See https://www.w3.org/2022/tdmrep/.

[34] See https://glaze.cs.uchicago.edu/.

[35] See https://spawning.ai/.

[36] See https://stability.ai/faq.

[37] See https://share.hsforms.com/1_OuT5tfFSpic89PqN6r1CQ4sk30.

[38] See https://blog.google/technology/ai/an-update-on-web-publisher-controls/.

[39] In greater detail see Mezei (2024), pp. 461–469.

set of rules on AI, including GenAI. Among other provisions, on the *input* side of machine learning, GenAI requires that general purpose AI providers shall, on the one hand, "put in place a policy to respect Union copyright law in particular to identify and respect, including through state of the art technologies, the reservations of rights expressed pursuant to Article 4(3) of Directive (EU) 2019/790";[40] and, on the other hand "draw up and make publicly available a sufficiently detailed summary about the content used for training of the general-purpose AI model, according to a template provided by the AI Office".[41] These new requirements would necessitate GenAI providers to seriously log and report publicly and in a detailed form their practices so that rights-holders can judge whether their contents were used for machine learning purposes. On the *output* side, the draft AI Act intends to oblige users of deep fake applications to disclose the deep fake nature of the content as well as the name of the creator of such outputs.[42] This transparency obligation is limited in case such use is necessary to exercise the right to freedom of expression and the right to freedom of the arts and sciences.[43] However, the same paragraph recommends a special rule for "evidently artistic, creative, satirical, fictional analogous work or programme", where the transparency obligations are "limited to disclosure of the existence of such generated or manipulated content in an appropriate manner that does not hamper the display or enjoyment of the work".[44]

Although these transparency requirements look straightforward, it is hard to foresee their practical functioning, and they are not completely unique at all. Although "transparency" is one of the magic keywords for the regulation of AI, policy-makers are prompted to design such requirements in line with their own legal system's standards. Such transparency standards might differ heavily from these draft ideas of the European Parliament.

We believe that the EU approach towards regulating TDM might only have a limited "Brussels-effect" on extra-EU jurisdictions.[45] This belief is partially supported by the concerns and open questions surrounding the existing TDM exceptions as well as the new, but not truly unique transparency requirements under the AI Act. Equally importantly, the pace of the legislative process is simply slow in the EU. By the time the AI Act is applicable in the EU, other jurisdictions shall have their own rules in place—otherwise they will fall behind in the global AI race.

---

[40] Article 53(1)(c) of the EU AI Act, see, n.8.

[41] Article 53(1)(d) of the EU AI Act.

[42] Ibid., Article 50(4). Although deep fake contents form only a fragment of GenAI outputs, but they pose serious concerns related to the ethical nature of GenAI. See, Willman (April 17, 2023) (https://variety.com/2023/music/news/fake-ai-generated-drake-weeknd-collaboration-heart-on-my-sleeve-1235585451/).

[43] Ibid., recital 134.

[44] Ibid., Article 52(3).

[45] Compare to Siegmann and Anderljung (August 2022) (https://arxiv.org/ftp/arxiv/papers/2208/2208.12645.pdf); Almada and Radu (2024), pp. 1–18, doi: 10.1017/glj.2023.108.

It is therefore advisable for nations of, e.g. the ASEAN, to consider whether they can approach GenAI and TDM in line with their own traditions. Hence, we shall cast our eyes on these countries' traditional understanding of copyright and their possibilities as regards regulating AI.

3.2 *Copyright Law in the ASEAN: Status Quo*

Within the ASEAN, a notable diversity in copyright laws exists among its members, largely shaped by three distinct legal traditions.[46] While Malaysia, Singapore, and Myanmar have aligned with common law principles,[47] nations such as Laos, Vietnam, Thailand, Cambodia, and Timor-Leste have integrated civil law into their copyright statutes.[48] Blending both common and civil law elements into its copyright regime, the Philippines stands out.[49] Traditionally adhering to civil law, Indonesia has moved with its copyright law amendments from 1982 to 2014 towards a distinctive system that reflects its own socio-political conditions and the demands of its burgeoning creative sectors.[50]

A critical examination reveals that the effectiveness of copyright enforcement in the ASEAN is compromised by several factors, including the absence of dedicated IP courts and the varying adherence to international copyright treaties. Notably, Cambodia, Myanmar, and Timor-Leste have not ratified pivotal agreements such as the Berne Convention and the WIPO Copyright Treaty. This disparity in copyright protection and enforcement underscores a broader issue within the ASEAN, placing rights-holders at a disadvantage and weakening their bargaining power. This situation is exacerbated by regulations that may not fully support rights-holders, such as restrictions on freedom of expression prevalent across the member states.[51] Moreover, the unauthorized use of copyright-protected works in emotional GenAI training not only challenges existing copyright laws but potentially places further strains on copyright holders.

[46] Harding (2015), pp. 813–818.

[47] Relating to the legal traditions in Malaysia, see, Neoh (2010). For the legal tradition in Singapore, see, Tan and Chan (2015). On the legal tradition in Myanmar, see, Southalan (2006), pp. 4–24.

[48] Relating to the legal traditions in Laos, *see,* Ministry of Justice Law of Lao People's Democratic Republic, 'Customary Law and Practice in Lao PDR.' (2011). Available at: https://www.undp.org/sites/g/files/zskgke326/files/migration/la/Customary_Law_Laos2011_english_master1.pdf. For the legal tradition in Vietnam, see, Nguyen (1989), p. 141. On the civil law tradition in Thailand, see, Harding and Pongsapan (2021). For the legal tradition in Cambodia, see, Peng et al. (2012). On Timor Leste, see, Stanford Law School, 'Legal History and the Rule of Law in Timor-Leste.'

[49] Mahy and Sale (2015).

[50] Antons (2018), pp. 73–88.

[51] Artist at Risk Connection, 'Arresting Art: Repression, Censorship, and Artistic Freedom in Asia.' (2023), pp. 10–18. Available at: https://culture360.asef.org/resources/arresting-art-repression-censorship-and-artistic-freedom-asia/.

3.3 The ASEAN AI Framework: The ASEAN Way and Author-Centric Approach

3.3.1 The ASEAN AI Framework

Given the state of rights-holders in the ASEAN, and taking into account the political instability which plays a significant role in ensuring effective copyright protection within the community, the question arises whether the ASEAN Way is still fit for this purpose. Is it the time for full copyright harmonization where each member state could intervene? A full economic integration and IP harmonization might be possible in the future since the ASEAN is already heading in that direction through the establishment of the ASEAN Free Trade AREA (AFTA) in 1992[52] and the ASEAN Economic Community Blue Print 2025.[53] However, prior to setting such an important direction, the ASEAN Member states shall, e.g. end or at least reduce the development gap as agreed upon in the Phnom Penh Declaration,[54] disparities in IP creation, utilization and exploitation.[55]

In light of the rapid development of emotional GenAI, taking into account the political instability, the potential of market-encroaching uses of copyright-protected training data[56] and socio-cultural conditions in the ASEAN, a possible solution could be to include recommendations on the protection of copyright in the ASEAN AI Framework, and such protection could be developed based on the ASEAN Way. As such, the ASEAN approach in regulating AI could be different from the EU AI Act. Indeed, rather than something that is legally binding, the ASEAN-wide formalisation of AI policy could be based on 'best practice by consensus'.[57]

The ASEAN Way of regulating AI could be combined with the author-centric approach, which aims to prioritize the rights and interests of individual creators in the ASEAN and should recognize the unique challenges posed by GenAI while seeking to ensure that rights-holders are fairly compensated for the use of their work.

---

52 ASEAN Secretariat, 'Southeast Asia A Free Trade Area.' (2002). Available at: https://asean.org/wp-content/uploads/images/archive/pdf/AFTA.pdf.

53 ASEAN Secretariat, 'ASEAN Economic Community Blue Print 2025.' (2015). Available at: https://asean.org/wp-content/uploads/2021/08/AECBP_2025r_FINAL.pdf.

54 ASEAN, Phnom Penh Declaration on ASEAN: One Community, One Destiny, 1 (2012). Available at http://www.asean.org/archive/documents/pp_declaration_3%20April_FINAL.pdf.

55 Ng (2013), p. 32. Available at: https://digitalcommons.pace.edu/cgi/viewcontent.cgi?article=1330&context=pilr.

56 See, Jérôme De Cooman, 'The Economic Consequences of Generative AI on the Art Market.' (RAILS, 2023). Available at: https://blog.ai-laws.org/the-economic-consequences-of-generative-ai-on-the-art-market/?cn-reloaded=1&cn-reloaded=1.

57 Kristina F. S. Leng, 'ASEAN's New Dilemma: Managing the Artificial Intelligence Space.' (*ISEAS*, 2023). Available at: https://www.iseas.edu.sg/articles-commentaries/iseas-perspective/2023-65-aseans-new-dilemma-managing-the-artificial-intelligence-by-kristina-fong-siew-leng/.

It also includes the development of mechanisms that allow rights-holders to retain control over their works, allowing them to determine how their work is used and distributed during GenAI training processes. Therefore, the ASEAN AI framework could be construed on the basis of consensus and trust from all stakeholders, i.e. GenAI companies, rights-holders and the public. This consensus-based deliberation may have been inspired by the concept of *Gotong Royong* adopted by several of the ASEAN Member States such as Indonesia, Malaysia, Singapore and Brunei Darussalam. In general, *Gotong Royong* could be defined as "helping each other,"[58] "sharing burdens"[59] or "mutual assistance".[60] *Gotong Royong* is a local wisdom which served as the foundation for political discourse on the nature of power and the features of life in the Malay Archipelago.[61]

3.3.2 On the ASEAN Way: The Initiation of GenAI Training Data Remuneration

Drawing on an author-centric approach, the spirit of *Gotong Royong* and reflection on the EU's approach to TDM, the ASEAN AI Framework could recommend several copyright protection measures as follows: First, Member States should be encouraged to introduce a TDM exception which provides an opt-out mechanism in an appropriate manner, i.e. through machine-readable means for rights-holders as well as a remuneration option, should the opt-out not be desirable.[62] So far, Singapore is the only ASEAN Member State that has provided TDM exceptions.[63] Such initiatives are greatly appreciated and yet unable to balance the various interest of market-encroaching uses implicate, given the absence of opt-out provisions.[64] Unlike the EU, the establishment of an effective opt-out mechanism with a remuneration option should be possible in the ASEAN considering that all Member States except Singapore have their own centralised copyright registration regimes and the ASEAN itself is moving towards a centralised IP database and registration, as envisaged in art. 3(1) of the ASEAN Framework Agreement on Intellectual Property Cooperation and the ASEAN Intellectual Property Rights Action Plan 2016–2025.

---

[58] Simarmata et al. (2020), pp. 15–20.

[59] Rahmi et al. (2001), pp. 119–134.

[60] Bowen (1986), pp. 545–561.

[61] See, Leong (2000), pp. 436–455; Abdullah and Rahman (2015), pp. 221–229.

[62] Sobel, ibid., pp. 236–241.

[63] See, Singapore Copyright Act 2021, Art. 243. Available at: https://sso.agc.gov.sg/Act/CA2021?ProvIds=P15-P28-#P15-P28-.

[64] However, in general, the Singapore TDM exceptions should be appreciated because it offers lawful access requirements and TDM provision that cannot be overridden by contract. See, art. 244 of the Copyright Act 2021.

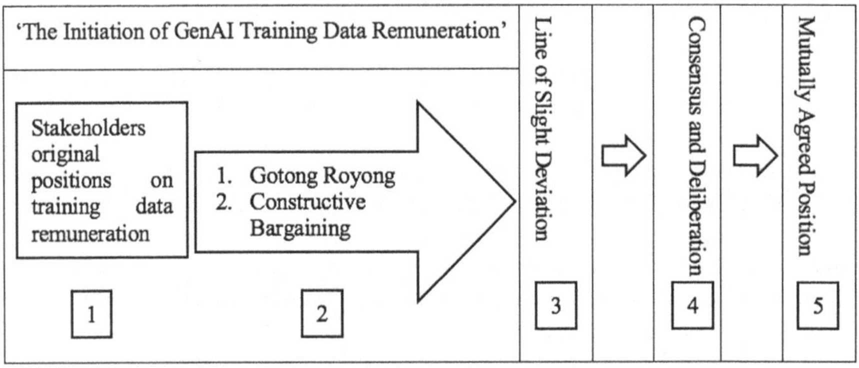

Fig. 1 The process of constructing the TDR in accordance with the ASEAN Way

Second, to ensure the protection of the training data, through their national collective management organization (CMO),[65] Member States could initiate the establishment of GenAI TDR, where the CMO could facilitate consensus, in accordance with the ASEAN Way, between GenAI companies and rights-holders or their representatives to mutually agree on a proportional model of remuneration,[66] and would do so with minimal transaction cost. The TDR could be in the form of a revenue sharing program or remuneration payments for the use of their works during the TDM process.[67]

As illustrated in Fig. 1 below, through the initiation of GenAI TDR, transparent and mutually agreed-upon remuneration arrangements, which include the amount and distribution method of the remuneration, could be reached. Additionally, such an author-centric consensus-based framework seems to conform well with Melamed and Calabresi's distinction of property and liability rules.[68]

Third, to facilitate the implementation of the first and second recommendations, ASEAN Member States should be encouraged to develop the identification or labelling mechanism of the training data, the introduction of an evidence disclosure mechanism as well as the copyright clearance infrastructure. On labelling, one attractive solution could be the establishment of decentralised content identification

[65] CMO plays a critical role in protecting and managing the rights of creators by licensing their works, collecting royalties, and ensuring fair distribution of revenues to rights holders.

[66] Several legal scholars have proposed the remuneration options, such as among others: Sobel (2021), pp. 236–237; Lucchi (2023), pp. 17–21; Senftleben (2023); Geiger and Iaia (2023), pp. 1–15.

[67] Lucchi, ibid., p. 19.

[68] Melamed and Calabresi's distinction between property and liability rules lies in the allocation of control over the use of resources: property rules grant absolute control to the owner who can exclude others unless they agree to a voluntary transaction, while liability rules allow others to use the resource without the owner's consent, provided they compensate the owner as determined by law. See, Calabresi and Melamed (1972), pp. 1089–1092. Available at: https://cyber.harvard.edu/openlaw/DVD/articles/calabresi.html.

that could be used as the protocol for the remuneration scheme, i.e. using ISCC codes (ISO/CD 24138)[69] and Verifiable Credentials (VCs)[70] to create trust in claims and attribution of the training data. This allows one to inseparably connect terms and a license to the digital media asset with no need for embedding, watermarking or centralised registry. This is because the robots.txt may work for content that is published online or embedded in html but not on the content that is not publicly accessible.[71] Furthermore, the identification of copyright protected works in the training data could potentially serve as signalling to the users/consumers and may prevent market-encroaching uses.[72]

3.3.3 Remuneration Calculation Methods: Flat Rates and Pro-Rata Model

Taking Melamed and Calabresi's distinction of property and liability rules as a benchmark for the remuneration, the initiation of GenAI TDR should be straightforward to implement. Using the music industry as an example, the establishment of GenAI TDR should not require additional transaction costs, as in the music industry, for example, information on artist remuneration should already exist in the CMO; and (ii) GenAI TDR will lead to a new licensing regime, where the parties involved may negotiate which licensing arrangement is suitable.[73] Through the initiation of the GenAI TDR, all parties should be encouraged to develop a menu of different agreements so all parties have options to best accommodate their needs. This approach would allow for flexibility and customization, ensuring that each ASEAN country can tailor the training data licensing to their specific requirements and priorities. During the initiation process, all parties involved may discuss the remuneration, could it be a lump-sum payment or an on-going remuneration. If the latter option is preferred, all parties could discuss the amount of flat rates, and the remuneration distribution method to be used. On the distribution regime, a difficult

[69] These codes are a standardized system used to classify and identify different types of products and services. See, 'ISO/CD 24138, Information and Documentation – International Standard Content Code (ISCC).' Available at: https://www.asist.org/2022/11/10/iso-cd-24138-information-and-documentation-international-standard-content-code-iscc/.

[70] VCs could be used in AI training data to protect rights-holders from unauthorized use or manipulation of their data to ensure that AI models are trained on reliable and trustworthy information, ultimately leading to more ethical and responsible AI systems. See, 'Verifiable Credentials Data Model v1.1.' Available at: https://www.w3.org/TR/vc-data-model/.

[71] Santanu Kolay, et al., 'A Larger Scale Study of Robots.txt.' (2018) Available at: https://dl.acm.org/doi/10.1145/1367497.1367711.

[72] Jérôme De Cooman, n.56.

[73] Google and Universal Music are currently negotiating the licensing regime for the voice and melody being used in the GenAI training data. *See,* The Guardian, 'Google and Universal Music Working on Licensing Voices for AI-generated Songs.' (2023) Available at: https://www.theguardian.com/technology/2023/aug/09/google-and-universal-music-working-on-licensing-voices-for-ai-generated-songs.

question arises: which copyright-protected works in the training datasets would be given credit for the newly generated outputs produced by GenAI users? It seems that one possible allocation could be through the quantity of content that rights-holders have contributed to the datasets.

Determination of Flat Rates

To determine the flat rates and to achieve economic success, GenAI providers may consider the number of subscriptions, advertising and procurement costs before establishing their average flat rates.[74] By taking the music industry as an example, in determining flat rates, GenAI providers could take around 30% of the entire subscriptions revenue to cover their overhead costs with the following formula: total subscriptions revenue × 30%.[75]

Determination of Remuneration: The Pro-Rata Model

Having established the amount of the flat rate, it is important to determine on how the money collected by the AI Gen providers through the flat rate is allocated to the rights-holders. By nature, a remuneration based on allocating the amount of content contributed by the rights-holders to the dataset would be pro-rata. If GenAI algorithms consider large amount of works from 'Author X' to be the right fit to generate an output based on the prompt provided by the users, then 'Author X' should be entitled to a higher amount of remuneration. Therefore, in the GenAI business model, the problem lies in consumption behaviour, not in the way the remuneration gets distributed.

Going further, the pro-rata model would perform better than the user-centric approach considering that the user's activity in enjoying a task becomes the benchmark for determining remuneration. However, with the GenAI system, users are unable to decide which copyright-protected works to be used in the training data to generate an output based on a particular prompt. In the pro-rata model, GenAI companies could take all the money generated from users, whether through advertisements or subscriptions, and put it in a big pot. They then could divide that pot by the total number of the copyright-protected work of rights-holder being used during the training process.[76] As can be seen in Fig. 2 below, with a subscription of €10 as an example, GenAI providers could take around 30% of the entire subscriptions

[74] Meyn et al. (2023), pp. 114–131.

[75] Calculation as follows: Total subscriptions revenue × 30% = On-demand music platforms revenue. For example the total revenue is €40 (4 users × €10) × 30% = €12. GenAI providers then will take €12 as their training data revenue to cover overhead costs. Taking the music industry as an example, *see,* Pedersen (2020), p. 4. Available at: https://www.koda.dk/media/224782/meta-study-of-user-centric-distribution-model-for-music-streaming.pdf.

[76] Taking the pro-rata model in music industry as an example. See, Pedersen, ibid., p. 4.

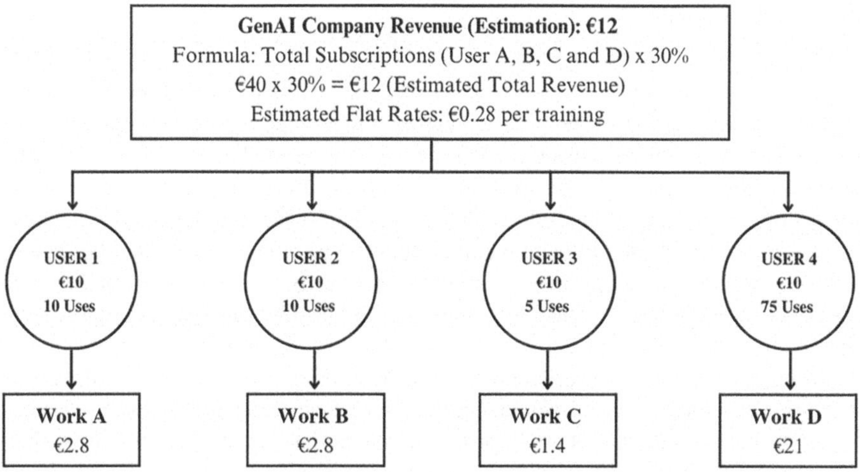

Calculation method for each copyright-protected works being used to train GenAI model:

$$Ra = \frac{Sa}{T} x\ Rt$$

Fig. 2 Overview of GenAI Training Data Remuneration Calculation with the Pro Rata Model (Where: Ra = revenue for Track A; Sa = streams of Track A; T = total number of streams; Rt = Net total licensing revenue. The Illustration is based on a similar calculation at Pedersen, ibid, p. 5)

revenue to cover their overhead costs.[77] In the pro-rata model, all revenues per month are put together according to the number of total number of the copyright protected work being used during TDM and shared between individual generations of AI outputs.[78]

Going further, the pro-rata model could potentially establish a human-centric approach that significantly benefits rights-holders. Its core principle, which advocates for remuneration proportional to the volume of content each rights-holder contributes to emotional AI's training datasets, underscores a dedication to fairness and the acknowledgment of individual efforts. This approach inherently values the creative labour of rights-holders by proposing a system where the total revenue from emotional AI companies—whether via advertisements or subscriptions—is distributed based on the usage extent of their work in training data. This method could potentially ensure a more equitable financial benefit distribution while respecting the intrinsic human creativity and effort that underlie copyright-protected works.

[77] Calculation as follows: Total subscriptions revenue × 30% = On-demand music platforms revenue. €40 (4 users × €10) × 30% = €12. On-demand music platforms then will take €12 as their streaming revenue to cover overhead costs. See, Pedersen, ibid, p. 5.

[78] Muikku (2017) at 5(14). Available at: http://www.digitalmedia.fi/wp-content/uploads/2018/02/UC_report_final_171213.pdf.

4 Conclusion

In the previous section, we systematically analysed the approach of the EU and the ASEAN as regards TDM. As indicated earlier, the EU approach was among the first to regulate this certain aspect of automated/AI-supported use of text and data. However, the ultimate EU rules cannot honestly be treated to be the best example for nations of Asia. Both the fundamentals of ASEAN nations' legal systems differ significantly from those of the civil or common law traditions of EU Member States, and the author-centric approach, elaborated above, is a much better fit for such countries' copyright law. This paper therefore argues that external examples, most notably that of the EU, can serve as a reasonable starting point for the regulation of TDM for emotional GenAI applications, but ASEAN nations shall follow their own traditions in setting the requirements for the use of such AI technologies. As a part of the TDR, the pro-rata model might provide a human-centric solution that recognizes individual contributions, potentially leading to a fairer distribution of remuneration by allocating revenue from emotional AI companies according to the use of copyright-protected works in training data.

References

Abdullah NN, Rahman MA (2015) The use of deliberative democracy in public policy making process. Public Policy Adm Res 5(3):221–229

Almada M, Radu A (2024) The Brussels side-effect: how the AI act can reduce the global reach of EU policy. German Law J 32:1–18

Alpaydın E (2004) Introduction to machine learning. MIT Press, Cambridge

Antons C (2018) Copyright law in Indonesia: from a hybrid to an endogenous system? The reconceptualisation of copyright. In: Gilchrist J, Fitzgerald B (eds) Copyright, property and the social contract: the reconceptualisation of copyright. Springer, Switzerland, pp 73–88

Barizah N (2017) Harmonisation of ASEAN's intellectual property rights law: is it possible? Ind Law Rev 1(3):95–112

Bowen JR (1986) On the political construction of tradition: gotong royong in Indonesia. Asian Stud 45(3):545–561

Bradford A (2020) The Brussels Effect: how the European Union rules the world. Oxford University Press, UK

Calabresi G, Melamed D (1972) Property rules, liability rules, and inalienability: one view of the cathedral. Harv Law Rev 85(6):1089–1092

ChatGPT is eating the world (2024) Lawsuits compilation. https://chatgptiseatingtheworld.com/2023/12/27/master-list-of-lawsuits-v-ai-chatgpt-openai-microsoft-meta-midjourney-other-ai-cos/. Accessed 5 Aug 2024

Geiger C, Iaia V (2023) The forgotten creator: towards a statutory remuneration right for machine learning of generative AI. Comput Law Secur Rev 52:1–15

Harding A (2015) Legal traditions of Southeast Asia. In: Wright JD (ed) International encyclopedia of the social & behavioral sciences, pp 813–818

Harding A, Pongsapan M (eds) (2021) Thai legal history from traditional to modern law. Cambridge University Press

Howe BM, Park MJ (2017) The evolution of the "ASEAN Way": embracing human security perspectives. Asia-Pac Soc Sci Rev 16(3):1–15

Information and Documentation – International Standard Content Code (2024). https://www.asist.org/2022/11/10/iso-cd-24138-information-and-documentation-international-standard-content-code-iscc/. Accessed 5 Aug 2024

Lengeling I (2020) (Non-)Intervention is always for someone and for some purpose. A critical theory analysis on the principle of non-interference within ASEAN. Institut Barcelona Estudis Internacionals Student Paper Series No. 57

Leong HK (2000) Citizen participation and policy making in Singapore: conditions and predicaments. Asian Surv 40(3):436–455

Lucchi N (2023) ChatGPT: a case study on copyright challenges for generative artificial intelligence systems. Eur J Risk Regul:17–21

Mahy P, Sale JP (2015) Classifying the legal system of the Philippines: a preliminary analysis with reference to labor law. Labor Ind Relat:19–30

Meyn J et al (2023) Consequences of platforms' remuneration models for digital content: initial evidence and a research agenda for streaming services. J Acad Mark Sci 51:114–131

Mezei P (2024) A saviour or a dead end? reservation of rights in the age of generative AI. EU Int Rev 46(7):461–469

Muikku J (2017) Pro rata and user centric distribution model: a comparative study. Available via Digital Media Finland. http://www.digitalmedia.fi/wp-content/uploads/2018/02/UC_report_final_171213.pdf. Accessed 7 Aug 2024

Neoh J (2010) Legitimacy of the common law in post-colonial Malaysia. Law Assc Asia Pac 59(1): 1–15

Ng ESK (2013) ASEAN IP harmonization: striking the delicate balance. Pace Int Law Rev 25:129–145

Nguyen LQ (1989) Traditional Vietnamese Law – The Le Code – and Modern United States Law: a comparative analysis. Hastings Int Comp Law Rev 14:141–151

Pedersen RR (2020) A meta study of user-centric distribution for music streaming. Available via Koda. https://www.koda.dk/media/224782/meta-study-of-user-centric-distribution-model-for-music-streaming.pdf. Accessed 25 July 2024

Peng H, Phallack K, Menzel J (eds) (2012) Introduction to Cambodian law. Konrad Adenauer Stiftung

Rahmi DH et al (2001) Rukun and gotong royong: managing public places in an Indonesian kampung. Public Places Asia Pac Cities 53:119–134

Rosati E (2021) Copyright in the Digital Single Market - Article-by-Article Commentary to the Provisions of Directive 2019/790. Oxford University Press, UK

Senftleben M (2023) Generative AI and author remuneration. Int Rev Intellect Prop Compet Law 54:15–30

Sganga C et al (2023) Copyright flexibilities: mapping and comparative assessment of EU and national sources. Available via SSRN. https://ssrn.com/abstract=4325376. Accessed 25 July 2024

Shahid A, Latif S, Qadir J (2023) Generative emotional AI for speech emotion recognition: the case for synthetic emotional speech augmentation. ArXiv

Siegmann C, Anderljung M (2022) The Brussels Effect and Artificial Intelligence: how EU regulation will impact the global AI market. Available via Arxiv. https://arxiv.org/ftp/arxiv/papers/2208/2208.12645.pdf. Accessed 5 Aug 2024

Simarmata N et al (2020) Gotong Royong in the millennial era. Digit Press Soc Sci Humanit 5:30–45

Sobel B (2021) A taxonomy of training data disentangling the mismatched rights, remedies, and rationales for restricting machine learning. In: Lee JA, Hilty R, Liu KC (eds) Artificial intelligence & intellectual property. Oxford University Press, pp 222–223

Southalan J (2006) Burma and the Common law? an uncommon question. Leg Issues Burma J 1(10):4–24

Tan E, Chan GKY (2015) The Singapore Legal System. Laws of Singapore, Research Collection School of Law

The ASEAN Secretariat (2012) Economic community. https://asean.org/our-communities/economic-community/#:~:text=Ministerial%20Meetings%20(AEM)-,Highly%20Integrated%20and%20Cohesive%20Economy,as%20the%20global%20supply%20chain. Accessed 25 June 2024

The ASEAN Secretariat (2023) The ASEAN Charter. https://asean.org/asean-charter/. Accessed 25 June 2024

The ASEAN Secretariat (2024) ASEAN guide on AI governance and ethics. https://asean.org/book/asean-guide-on-ai-governance-and-ethics/. Accessed 5 Aug 2024

The ASEAN Secretariat (2024) The founding of the ASEAN. https://asean.org/the-founding-ofasean/#:~:text=The%20Association%20of%20Southeast%20Asian,%2C%20Philippines%2C%20Singapore%20and%20Thailand. Accessed 25 July 2024

The Guardian (2023) Google and Universal Music Working on Licensing Voices for AI-generated Songs. https://www.theguardian.com/technology/2023/aug/09/google-and-universal-music-working-on-licensing-voices-for-ai-generated-songs. Accessed 25 June 2024

Ueno T (2021) A general clause on copyright limitations in civil law countries: recent discussion on Japanese-style fair use clause. In: Balganesh S, Loon W, Sun H (eds) The Cambridge handbook of copyright limitations and exceptions, pp 213–210

Willman C (2023) AI-Generated Fake 'Drake'/'Weeknd' Collaboration, 'Heart on My Sleeve,' Delights Fans and Sets Off Industry Alarm Bells. Variety. https://variety.com/2023/music/news/fake-ai-generated-drake-weeknd-collaboration-heart-on-my-sleeve-1235585451/. Accessed 25 July 2024

WIPO-ASEAN study on the strategic use of intellectual property to enhance competitiveness in select industries in ASEAN (2010). https://www.wipo.int/edocs/pubdocs/en/intproperty/953/wipo_pub_953.pdf. Accessed 25 June 2024

Damage Caused by Emotional AI: Do Existing and Prospective Liability Rules Provide Sufficient Protection?

Béatrice Schütte

Abstract Emotionally intelligent AI can process the most personal and intimate of information. When this is not handled with the utmost care, it can cause discrimination and stigmatization, violate a person's privacy and it can cause other infringements of fundamental rights. This is particularly relevant in relationships with significant power asymmetry, such as that between an employer and an employee or a public authority and a citizen. In such cases, damage inflicted upon individuals is not tangible, meaning that it does not result in actual physical injury or damage to items of property, and often there is no consequential economic loss either. Still, the damage can cause serious distress to the affected person.

This chapter examines whether existing and prospective liability rules provide affected parties with sufficient protection. Relevant frameworks referenced will be the General Data Protection Regulation (GDPR), the AI Act, the proposed Directive on AI Liability and national civil liability laws of EU Member States. Special focus will be placed on the recoverability of immaterial harm. To date, many national laws—and courts—are reluctant to provide compensation for non-material harm. Therefore, the question is whether this reluctance is still appropriate considering the significant risks AI poses for fundamental rights and other immaterial interests.

1 Introduction

AI systems are becoming ever more sophisticated and are able to harvest and process an increasingly wide range of information from humans. This includes very intimate information, namely our emotions. Depending on the situation, we might not be

B. Schütte (✉)
University of Lapland, Faculty of Law, Rovaniemi, Finland

Fellow 2023–2025 at the Information Society Law Center (ISLC) at the University of Milan, Milano, MI, Italy

University of Helsinki, Faculty of Law, Legal Tech Lab, Helsinki, Finland
e-mail: Beatrice.Schutte@ulapland.fi

R. Ballardini et al. (eds.), *Emotional Data Applications and Regulation of Artificial Intelligence in Society*, Law, Governance and Technology Series 69,
https://doi.org/10.1007/978-3-031-80111-2_14

willing to disclose these emotions even to our closest friends and family members. Given that in professional surroundings, showing certain emotions such as sadness or anger may be seen as a weakness, a sign of incompetence, what if we are surrounded by devices that are able to extract this information from us, whether we want it or not? Will it change our behaviour? Will it cause harm?

Depending on the situation, we do not even have complete control over certain features such as facial expressions or the tone of our voice as these might come as a reflex.[1] In particular, when information about our emotional state is gathered against our will, this amounts to a significant infringement of our privacy. While many people are able to hide their emotions from others at least to a certain extent, AI systems can be trained to recognize micro-expressions that are not noticeable to the human eye. When such information ends up 'in the wrong hands', the consequences can be discrimination or stigmatization.[2] Moreover, it may lead to repercussions in the workplace or in education.

As well as this, one must bear in mind that such applications are not flawless, especially against the background that emotions are difficult to categorize, and the ways of expression vary across cultures and even among individuals.[3] An algorithm connected to a CCTV camera may register aggression between two people and dispatch law enforcement, when in fact it is just a loud and lively conversation.

From an employee's facial expression, a camera system installed in someone's workstation might conclude that the employee is mocking a colleague's statement when the person is actually just making an effort not to cry because their spouse has passed away. Consequently, emotional AI, or affective computing,[4] has been called a threat to human opacity.[5]

In this regard, a central question is who is liable when the use of emotional AI causes damage to a person. Related aspects to examine are the types of damage these AI systems can cause and whether and to what extent they are actually recoverable.

While the AI Act as the core framework on the regulation of this technology entered into force in August 2024,[6] any harmonised rules on liability for damage caused by AI are not yet in sight.[7]

---

[1] Kumar et al. (2024), p. 4.

[2] Mantello and Ho (2022), p. 1.

[3] Recital 44 to the AI Act, Regulation (EU) 2024/1689 of the European Parliament and of the Council of 13 June 2024 laying down harmonised rules on artificial intelligence and amending Regulations (EC) No 300/2008, (EU) No 167/2013, (EU) No 168/2013, (EU) 2018/858, (EU) 2018/1139 and (EU) 2019/2144 and Directives 2014/90/EU, (EU) 2016/797 and (EU) 2020/1828 (Artificial Intelligence Act) (Text with EEA relevance), *OJ L, 2024/1689, 12.7.2024,* ELI: http://data.europa.eu/eli/reg/2024/1689/oj.

[4] The terms 'affective computing' and 'emotional (or: emotion) AI' are often used interchangeably. See, e.g. Weber-Guskar (2021), p. 602.

[5] Kumar et al. (2024), p. 4.

[6] European Commission, 'European Artificial Intelligence Act comes into force', Press release 1 August 2024, https://ec.europa.eu/commission/presscorner/detail/en/ip_24_4123.

[7] The proposed AI Liability Directive (AILD) focuses on procedural aspects. See below, Sect. 4.

The purpose of this contribution is to shed light on the applicable rules in the EU and its Member States in cases where emotional AI inflicts harm on a person and to examine whether existing and planned rules are actually providing adequate protection and remedies in such cases. Where applicable, I will also suggest improvements to current legislation by means of a *de lege ferenda* analysis.

Section 2 of this contribution will give an overview of how emotional AI is regulated at the EU level, while in Sect. 3, I will provide examples of the types of damage that can be caused by emotional AI. Section 4 examines selected liability rules in regard to their applicability to damage caused by emotional AI. Then, the findings of the first four sections will be discussed in Sect. 5, before the chapter ends with brief concluding remarks.

2 The Regulation of Emotional AI Under EU Law

This section will introduce how emotional AI will be regulated at the EU level. In this regard what is most relevant are the AI Act and the General Data Protection Regulation (GDPR).[8]

2.1 Emotional AI Under the AI Act

Emotion recognition systems are addressed in the recently adopted AI Act.[9] They are defined in Article 3 (1) (39) of the AI Act as AI systems 'for the purpose of identifying or inferring emotions or intentions of natural persons on the basis of their biometric data'. Pursuant to Article 5 (1) (f), emotion recognition AI cannot be used at educational institutions and in workplaces, except for medical and safety reasons. The emotion recognition AI systems that are not covered by these provisions are classified as high-risk.[10] In the earlier versions of the proposal, these systems were classified as limited risk, which meant that there would only be a duty to inform individuals that they are interacting with an AI system that can recognise their emotions.[11]

[8]Regulation (EU) 2016/679 of the European Parliament and of the Council of 27 April 2016 on the protection of natural persons with regard to the processing of personal data and on the free movement of such data, and repealing Directive 95/46/EC (General Data Protection Regulation), *OJ L 119, 4.5.2016, pp. 1–88.*

[9]Proposal for a Regulation of the European Parliament and of the Council laying down harmonised Rules on Artificial Intelligence (Artificial Intelligence Act) and amending certain Union Legislative Acts, COM(2021) 206 final.

[10]See Annex III 1 (c) of the AI Act.

[11]See Article 52 (2) of the AI Act Proposal of 21 April 2021 (n 9).

Under certain conditions, the scope of the ban on emotion recognition AI is not completely clear since the AI Act fails to provide a definition of the core terms 'workplace', 'education institutions', and 'medical or safety reasons'. For instance, in the context of workplace environments, it is not obvious if the legislator meant to refer to offices, or to any space where humans work. Indeed, many publicly accessible spaces, such as train stations or shopping centres are also workplaces. The same applies to a construction site in the street. Thus, this could lead to a very wide scope of the ban. In terms of educational institutions, it should be clarified if this covers only institutions for minors or all of them. Additional clarification is also required in regard to the exception of 'medical or safety reasons'. In this context, Recital 44 only mentions that the 'prohibition should not cover AI systems placed on the market strictly for medical or safety reasons, such as systems intended for therapeutical use', which is only one example. Although the standards on health and safety at work differ across sectors and across EU Member States, even a mere reference to such standards would already provide some clarification. Otherwise, guidelines would be desirable.

Under the AI Act, other emotion recognition AI systems shall be classified as high-risk AI systems, as per Annex III, paragraph 1 (c). In addition, Article 50 (3) sets out that deployers of an emotion recognition system or a biometric categorisation system not prohibited under Article 5 shall inform people exposed to such a system. Moreover, personal data must be processed in accordance with the GDPR, the Regulation on the Protection of Personal Data processed by Union Institutions, Bodies, Offices and Agencies[12] and the Data Protection Law Enforcement Directive,[13] as applicable.

During the legislative process, a complete ban on emotion recognition systems has been discussed and also requested by several initiatives.[14] Considering other prohibitions of AI systems enshrined in the AI Act, these discussions are not completely unheard of. As an example, Article 5 (1) (a) prohibits:

> the placing on the market, the putting into service or the use of an AI system that deploys subliminal techniques beyond a person's consciousness or purposefully manipulative or deceptive techniques, with the objective, or the effect of materially distorting the behaviour of a person or a group of persons by appreciably impairing their ability to make an informed decision, thereby causing them to take a decision that they would not have otherwise taken in

[12] Regulation (EU) 2018/1725 of the European Parliament and of the Council of 23 October 2018 on the protection of natural persons with regard to the processing of personal data by the Union institutions, bodies, offices and agencies and on the free movement of such data, and repealing Regulation (EC) No 45/2001 and Decision No 1247/2002/EC (Text with EEA relevance), *OJ L 295, 21.11.2018, pp. 39–98.*

[13] Directive (EU) 2016/680 of the European Parliament and of the Council of 27 April 2016 on the protection of natural persons with regard to the processing of personal data by competent authorities for the purposes of the prevention, investigation, detection or prosecution of criminal offences or the execution of criminal penalties, and on the free movement of such data, and repealing Council Framework Decision 2008/977/JHA, *OJ L 119, 4.5.2016, pp. 89–131.*

[14] See, e.g. Woollacott (2023); European Digital Rights (EDRi) (2021).

a manner that causes or is reasonably likely to cause that person, another person or group of persons significant harm.

Further, Article 5 (1) (b) prohibits 'the placing on the market, the putting into service or the use of an AI system that exploits any of the vulnerabilities of a natural person or a specific group of persons due to their age, disability or a specific social or economic situation, with the objective, or the effect, of materially distorting the behaviour of that person or a person belonging to that group in a manner that causes or is reasonably likely to cause that person or another person significant harm'.

Depending on the concrete use case, an emotional AI system can be manipulative and distort a person's behaviour. For some individuals, the mere knowledge of being exposed to such a system can have a chilling effect on their behaviour, and it may make them deviate from their normal behaviour and decision-making. Against this background, and taking into consideration that the technology will evolve further in the future, it is likely that also a complete ban of such systems will be discussed (again). Therefore, the revised risk-classification, i.e. from limited risk to high-risk, is appropriate. This is also supported by Recital 44 to the AI Act, which sets out that emotion recognition systems give rise to serious concerns because emotions and expression of emotions vary strongly across cultures and situations, and they can even differ between individuals. Naturally, there is difficulty in specifying and generalising emotions.

In any event, further clarification as to the regulation of emotion recognition, and particularly the prohibitions and exceptions therefrom, remains necessary. This also concerns the question if certain ways of using emotional AI fell under the scope of the prohibitions in Article 5 (1) (a) and (b) of the AI Act. A noteworthy example of manipulative technology was an experiment conducted by Facebook in 2012 showing selected users either more positive or more negative posts in their timeline. In this example, those users with the positive timelines were themselves more likely to post positive content compared to those being shown negative content.[15]

2.2 *Emotional AI Under the GDPR*

In addition, the GDPR also regulates emotional AI, even though it does not explicitly mention emotional AI or emotional data. As this regulation is meant to be technology-neutral, it does not refer to any specific technology.[16] Naturally, at the time the GDPR was drafted and entered into force, the field of emotion recognition technologies was far less developed than it is today.[17]

[15] Steindl (2022), p. 318.

[16] See Recital 15 to the GDPR; see also https://commission.europa.eu/law/law-topic/data-protection/reform/what-personal-data_en.

[17] Steindl (2022), p. 312.

However, the GDPR defines biometric data, to which the AI Act refers for the purpose of defining emotion recognition systems. According to Article 4 (14), these are 'personal data resulting from specific technical processing relating to the physical, physiological or behavioural characteristics of a natural person, which allow or confirm the unique identification of that natural person, such as facial images or dactyloscopic data'. There is consensus that physiological responses can provide information on a person's emotional state.[18] In addition, the relevant data can also fall under the scope of health data as per Article 4 (15) of the GDPR.[19] Biometric data, and health data, belong to the special categories of data enjoying a particular level of protection under Article 9 of the GDPR. The processing of such data is in principle forbidden if these data allow one to identify or somehow single out an individual. If this is not the case, the data fall outside the scope of the GDPR.[20] However, the European Data Protection Supervisor stated already in an opinion of 2015 that under certain circumstances Big Data should be considered personal data even where anonymisation techniques have been applied as it is constantly becoming easier to identify people by means of combining allegedly anonymous data with other datasets, including, for instance, public information on social media.[21] In this context, Big Data are collected data sets that are so large and complex that they require new technologies such as AI to process.[22] Article 9 (2) sets out a number of exceptions where the processing of special categories of data is permitted. Among these exceptions are consent, the protection of the data subjects' vital interests, substantial public interest, or public health. In practice, the most relevant exception will be the data subject's consent. In this regard, recital 32 to the GDPR clarifies that

> consent should be given by a clear affirmative act establishing a freely given, specific, informed and unambiguous indication of the data subject's agreement to the processing of personal data relating to him or her, such as by a written statement, including by electronic means, or an oral statement. This could include ticking a box when visiting an internet website, choosing technical settings for information society services or another statement or conduct which clearly indicates in this context the data subject's acceptance of the proposed processing of his or her personal data. Silence, pre-ticked boxes or inactivity should not therefore constitute consent. Consent should cover all processing activities carried out for the same purpose or purposes.

Whether consent is indeed given freely, it is often problematic in relationships of power imbalance, which may be one of the reasons why emotion recognition is prohibited in workplaces and education. An additional problem in this regard is so-called 'consent fatigue' which has been observed in relation to ticking boxes

[18] Healey (2014), p. 213.

[19] See also Steindl (2022), p. 312.

[20] McStay (2020), p. 3, 4.

[21] European Data Protection Supervisor, Opinion 4/2015, 'Towards a new digital ethics: Data, dignity and technology', 6.

[22] https://www.europarl.europa.eu/topics/en/article/20210211STO97614/big-data-definition-benefits-challenges-infographics.

when visiting a web page: people just tick the box without reading further as they wish to access the respective content.[23]

3 Potential Damage Caused by Emotional AI

From a general perspective, critical properties of AI, such as opacity, complexity, data dependency and autonomy, may lead to the violation of some of the fundamental rights enshrined in the EU Charter of Fundamental Rights.[24]

Depending on the context in which they are used, emotional AI systems can have severe consequences for those people affected by these systems. Currently, major tech companies such as Apple, Meta, Google or Microsoft are working on tools for emotional AI to develop "empathic products" for different applications and settings.[25] As emotions are highly subjective, a major risk in emotional AI is bias. Apparently, certain ethnicities are more prone to being assigned negative emotions than others.[26]

When used in e-commerce, information gained about consumers can be (ab)used to nudge them into purchase decisions they would not take under normal circumstances.[27] Indeed, in the workplace, the employer might—consciously or unconsciously—take decisions relating to the fate of an employee based on the gathered emotional data.

The fact that the AI Act prohibits the use of such systems in the workplace does not mean that they will never be used. Decisions taken based on emotional data can lead to discrimination or stigmatisation of the employee, for instance, when it results in the denial of a promotion, firing an employee or the omission of hiring a person. From a fundamental rights perspective, this affects, for instance, the right to a private life and data protection. Moreover, it may infringe the right to mental health.[28] Surveillance, even the mere perception of it, may have a chilling effect on human behaviour. As a consequence, it can have a significant impact on the extent to which we use our rights to, e.g. freedom of expression or to assembly and association.[29]

What the above-mentioned examples of infringements that may result from the use of emotional AI have in common is that they will all lead to non-material harm. Its recoverability depends on the applicable legal framework, as the following sections will show.

---

[23] See, e.g. Nouwens et al. (2020), p. 9.

[24] See, e.g. AI Act proposal April 2021 (n 9), Explanatory Memorandum, 11.

[25] Gremsl and Hödl (2022), p. 164.

[26] Purdy et al. (2019).

[27] Pusztahelyi (2020), p. 14.

[28] Ibid.

[29] Valcke et al. (2021), p. 65.

4 Applicable Liability Regimes

This section will examine the potential bases of liability for damage caused by emotional AI. The selected frameworks are those on data protection, e-privacy, product liability, AI liability and, as an example of national law, the relevant provision in German law.

4.1 Article 82 of the GDPR

Article 82 (1) of the GDPR establishes that 'any person who has suffered material or non-material damage as a result of an infringement of this regulation shall have the right to receive compensation from the controller or processor for the damage suffered'. The provision sets out the liability of the data controller when the damage is caused by processing, which infringes the GDPR. By contrast, the data processor is liable for damage caused by processing only when they have not complied with the obligations enshrined in the regulation, or where they have acted outside the scope of or contrary to the lawful instructions of the controller.

Depending on the context, the processing of emotional data might infringe the rules set out in the GDPR. Emotional data are biometric and identifiable human based and human directed data, meaning data representing the emotional, psychological or physical status of natural persons by identifying and processing their (facial) expressions, movements, behaviour or other physical or mental characteristics. However, as mentioned above, the GDPR does not explicitly address emotions or emotional data, but some of these data might fall under the scope of biometric data. This is further supported by the AI Act, which explicitly refers to biometric data in the definition of emotion recognition systems.[30]

Particularly relevant infringements of the GDPR in relation to emotional AI can be the processing of a category of personal data that must not be processed, the infringement of the principles of transparency or accuracy, the infringement of the principle that persons have the right not to be subject to profiling or the infringement of the right not to be subject to automated decision-making.[31] With regard to the processing of personal data, data subjects should be made aware of the risks, rules, safeguards and rights in relation and how to exercise their rights in relation to such processing.[32]

As regards the recoverable damage under Article 82 of the GDPR, 'the concept of damage should be broadly interpreted in the light of the case-law of the Court of Justice in a manner which fully reflects the objectives of this regulation'.[33] Relevant

[30] See Article 3 (39) of the AI Act; see above Sect. 2.1.

[31] See also, e.g. Häuselmann (2021), p. 250, 252, 255.

[32] See recital 39 GDPR.

[33] Recital 146 GDPR; see also Menezes Cordeiro (2019), p. 492, 494.

harm or causation are not defined in the GDPR, nor are there rules on the burden of proof. Consequently, national rules and traditions regarding compensation for non-material harm, for instance, or requirements in terms of showing causation, can have a significant impact on whether and what kind of compensation is ultimately awarded.

A compensation claim under Article 82 of the GDPR requires material or non-material damage, unlawfulness, causality and culpability. 'Unlawfulness' relates to an infringement of the GDPR, meaning any infringement and not restricted to certain cases. This also includes the violation of rights, obligations or legal prohibitions that are only indirectly related to data processing or of a complementary nature.[34] While material damage refers to any financial impairment, including a loss of profits, non-material damage must be interpreted autonomously. It can be awarded in case of, for example, discrimination, damage to reputation, identity theft, loss of confidentiality of personal data protected by professional secrecy, significant social disadvantages for the concerned data subject, the unlawful processing of sensitive data or data with criminal relevance, or if personal data of vulnerable natural persons is processed unlawfully. Furthermore, it includes unwelcome public exposure or restraints on personal development.[35]

Relevant to the recoverability of non-material harm under Article 82 (1) of the GDPR is also the judgment in the *Österreichische Post* case[36] handed down by the Court of Justice of the European Union (CJEU). In this case, the questions for the preliminary ruling focused on several issues, including non-material damage resulting from the unlawful processing of data: compensation for such data processing and assessing the seriousness of such a non-material harm.[37]

In his Opinion, the Advocate General Campos Sánchez-Bordona stated that the mere breach of the rules enshrined in the GDPR is insufficient for awarding damages as the damage must be connected to harm suffered as a result of the breach. Moreover, the non-material harm must consist of something more than only 'annoyance or upset', 'a mere feeling of displeasure due to another person's failure to comply with the law'. Unfortunately, the Advocate General has left the difficult task of assessing the 'fine line between mere upset (which is not eligible for compensation) and genuine non-material damage (which is eligible for compensation)' for the national courts to deal with.[38] After all, the long-awaited clarification in this context has unfortunately not been provided by the judgment, and it is expected that fragmentation across EU Member States remains.

In this context, it is worth mentioning that German courts, for example, have stressed the need for damages for non-monetary losses that arise from infringement of the GDPR to be high enough to ensure the deterrent effect of the law and the

[34] Menezes Cordeiro (2019), p. 493.

[35] See, e.g. recital 75 GDPR.

[36] Case C-300/21 *UI v Österreichische Post AG* [2021] OJ C 320/25.

[37] Ibid.; see also Opinion of AG Campos Sánchez-Bordona delivered on 6 October 2022, para 14.

[38] Opinion of AG Campos Sánchez-Bordona delivered on 6 October 2022, para 116.

effectiveness principles.[39] When it comes to non-material harm, the challenge is that it is hard to quantify such in monetary terms, since it not only comprises pain or suffering but also extends to emotional harm.[40] Its definition may be particularly difficult where 'the line between physical inconvenience and discomfort and mental distress and disappointment is narrow'.[41]

In view of the above, Article 82 (1) of the GDPR can serve as a basis of liability for damage caused by emotional AI when the damage is the consequence of an infringement of the GDPR.

4.2 E-privacy Framework

In addition to the GDPR, the ePrivacy framework, which is meant to complement the regulations on data protection, might also give rise to liability for damage caused by emotional AI.[42] The ePrivacy Directive[43] shall ensure that all communications over public networks maintain respect for fundamental rights. Moreover, regardless of the technology used, data protection and privacy shall be granted. Under the scope of the ePrivacy Directive, EU Member States shall warrant that users grant their consent before cookies are stored and accessed in computers, smartphones or other devices connected to the Internet.[44] In order to adapt the framework to the current state of digitalisation, the European Commission issued in 2017 a proposal for an e-privacy Regulation.[45] This proposal was also a consequence of the Cambridge Analytica scandal.[46] The proposal contains rules regarding the protection of fundamental rights and freedoms of natural and legal persons in the provision and use of electronic communications services, and in particular the rights to respect for private life and

---

[39] See, e.g. Amtsgericht Frankfurt am Main, Urteil v. 10.07.2020 - Az.: 385 C 155/19 (70), available at https://www.datenschutz.eu/urteile/DSGVO-Schadensersatzanspruch-bedarf-es-einer-ernsthaften-Beeintraechtigung-Amtsgericht-Frankfurt_aM-20200710/.

[40] Havu (2019), p. 492.

[41] Yates (1973), p. 535, 536.

[42] Voss (2017), p. 3.

[43] Directive 2002/58/EC of the European Parliament and of the Council of 12 July 2002 concerning the processing of personal data and the protection of privacy in the electronic communications sector (Directive on privacy and electronic communications), OJ L 201, 31.7.2002, pp. 37–47.

[44] European Commission (2023), Digital Privacy, see https://digital-strategy.ec.europa.eu/en/policies/digital-privacy.

[45] Proposal for a Regulation of the European Parliament and of the Council concerning the respect for private life and the protection of personal data in electronic communications and repealing Directive 2002/58/EC (Regulation on Privacy and Electronic Communications), COM(2017) 10 final.

[46] Buruiana (2021), p. 47, 53.

communications and the protection of natural persons with regard to the processing of personal data.[47]

4.2.1 The ePrivacy Directive

The ePrivacy Directive, dating from 2002, is currently applicable. Pursuant to its Article 1, it provides for the 'harmonisation of the national provisions required to ensure an equivalent level of protection of fundamental rights and freedoms, and in particular the right to privacy and confidentiality, with respect to the processing of personal data in the electronic communication sector and to ensure the free movement of such data and of electronic communication equipment and services in the Community'. The directive was enacted to complement the Data Protection Directive (DPD),[48] which was later replaced by the GDPR, and it is *lex specialis* in relation to it.[49] The directive does not contain any reference to emotions, emotional AI or affective computing, which is not surprising given that it entered into force more than 20 years ago. Article 15 (2) of the ePrivacy Directive refers to the DPD for questions on liability, sanctions and judicial remedies, which means that the relevant provision nowadays would also be Article 82 of the (1) GDPR.[50]

4.2.2 The ePrivacy Regulation

As opposed to the ePrivacy Directive, the proposed ePrivacy Regulation refers to emotions in Recitals 2 and 20. Pursuant to Recital 2, emotions are considered highly sensitive information, and Recital 20 sets out that terminal equipment containing information about an individual's emotional, political and social complexities requires enhanced protection. If the ePrivacy Regulation enters into force, it might lead to different levels of protection for emotions or emotional data, depending on whether the GDPR or the ePrivacy Regulation is applicable.[51] Rightful criticism has been brought forward against the limitation of emotions to the recitals and not addressing them in the actual text of the proposed Regulation, given the increasing

[47] Proposal for a Regulation of the European Parliament and of the Council concerning the respect for private life and the protection of personal data in electronic communications and repealing Directive 2002/58/EC (Regulation on Privacy and Electronic Communications), COM(2017) 10 final, Explanatory Memorandum, 1.1., Recitals 1–3.

[48] Directive 95/46/EC of the European Parliament and of the Council of 24 October 1995 on the protection of individuals with regard to the processing of personal data and on the free movement of such data, OJ L 281, 23.11.1995, pp. 31–50.

[49] European Commission (2017), p. 15.

[50] Etteldorf (2019), p. 228.

[51] Häuselmann (2021), p. 250.

significance in data analytics, by means of, for instance, social media sentiment analysis or Big Data inferencing.[52]

In terms of liability, Article 22 of the proposed ePrivacy Regulation sets out that 'any end-user of electronic communications services who has suffered material or non-material damage as a result of an infringement of this Regulation shall have the right to receive compensation from the infringer for the damage suffered, unless the infringer proves that it is not in any way responsible for the event giving rise to the damage in accordance with Article 82 of Regulation (EU) 2016/679'. Compared to the ePrivacy Directive, the formulation in the proposed regulation is clearer and more explicit, and it establishes liability with a reversed burden of proof. Indeed, the proposed ePrivacy Regulation is better aligned with the GDPR and adapted to the current state of digitalization.

4.3 The AI Liability Directive and Emotional AI

In September 2022, the European Commission published a proposal for a directive on civil liability for damage caused by AI (AILD).[53] This section will examine if the proposed directive will impact liability for damage caused by emotional AI.

The AILD does not establish any rules on the substance of liability.[54] According to Article 1 of the AILD, it 'lays down common rules on the disclosure of evidence on high-risk artificial intelligence (AI) systems to enable a claimant to substantiate a non-contractual fault-based civil law claim for damages, and on the burden of proof in the case of non-contractual fault-based civil law claims brought before national courts for damages caused by an AI system'. These aspects are particularly important considering the common information asymmetry between the provider of an AI system and the person who has suffered harm. If the latter does not have specialised knowledge on the functioning of an algorithmic system, it will be difficult or even impossible to prove essential elements like causation or fault.[55]

To this end, Article 3 of the proposed directive introduces the possibility for the EU Member State courts to order—upon request by the claimant or the potential claimant (before filing a lawsuit)—providers of AI systems and persons subject to the obligations of a provider pursuant to Article 24 or Article 28(1) of the AI Act, or users to disclose relevant evidence at their disposal of a specific high-risk AI system suspected of having caused damage. However, courts may not order the disclosure at

[52] McStay (2020), p. 3.

[53] Proposal for a Directive of the European Parliament and of the Council on adapting non-contractual civil liability rules to artificial intelligence (AI Liability Directive), COM(2022) 496 final.

[54] As opposed to the European Parliament resolution of 20 October 2020 with recommendations to the Commission on a civil liability regime for artificial intelligence (2020/2014(INL)).

[55] See also, e.g. European Commission (2020b).

their own initiative. If the defendant fails to comply with such an order, there is a rebuttable presumption of non-compliance by the defendant.

This newly introduced obligation has the potential to supplement the transparency obligations as enshrined, for instance, in the AI Act. In this context, what is relevant are Articles 12 and 13 of the AI Act. Article 12 of the AI Act sets out the obligation to design and develop a high-risk AI system in a way that it automatically records events so as to enable the tracing of its functioning. In turn, Article 13 of the AI Act shall enable the deployer[56] to use the system's output in an appropriate manner. This relates, among others, to information about the high-risk AI systems purpose, metrics or capabilities. The transparency requirement in Article 13 shall also facilitate the provider's and deployer's compliance with obligations set out in Chapter III, Section 3 of the AI Act, such as the provider's duty of information in case of the high-risk AI system's suspected non-conformity with the AI Act or the deployer's duty to monitor the operation of the high-risk system based on the instructions of use as per Article 26 (5) of the AI Act. If it can help them to prove their claim, Article 3 of the AI Liability Directive obliges the user[57] to share this information with the claimant or the potential claimant.

Interestingly, the AILD seems to ignore prohibited AI systems completely. While it implements a lower threshold in relation to the burden of proof for high-risk AI systems, and briefly mentions AI systems not classified as high risk, no reference whatsoever is made to what should apply in cases where someone provides or deploys a prohibited AI system which then causes damage. In this context, one may well raise the question whether it would not be appropriate to lower the threshold even further if, for instance, an employer uses emotion recognition to gain insights on their employees' work ethics.

The AILD regime will have to be applied in combination with the relevant civil liability rules of the EU Member States. In itself, it is—at this stage—not a basis for liability, but a liability framework in name only.

4.4 *Product Liability*

The Product Liability Directive (PLD)[58] establishes a regime of no-fault liability for certain economic operators.[59] In March 2024, the European Parliament adopted a

[56] The deployer is defined in Article 3 (4) of the AI Act as a 'natural or legal person, public authority, agency or other body using an AI system under its authority except where the AI system is used in the course of a personal non-professional activity'.

[57] In earlier versions of the AI Act, the 'deployer' was called the 'user'. So far, no changes have been made to the AILD, which refers to the definition included in the AI Act.

[58] Council Directive 85/374/EEC of 25 July 1985 on the approximation of the laws, regulations and administrative provisions of the Member States concerning liability for defective products, OJ L 210, 7.8.1985, pp. 29–33.

[59] De Luca (2023), p. 2.

revised version pf the PLD, fit for the digital age, which entered into force in November 2024.[60] Among other updates, it includes a broader scope of the notion of a product, which makes it now applicable to software, even when supplied as standalone software.[61] Services will remain outside the scope, unless they are interconnected with the product in such a way that the product would be unusable without the service.[62] In addition, it refers to online platforms in Recital 38 and Article 8 of the PLD as potentially liable economic operators. This can be relevant when an online platform sells consumer products with emotional AI features. The Directive is applicable to AI-enabled computer programs, other software applications such as mobile phone apps, as well as AI-enabled tangible products, which can gather data (excessively). In this context, common examples include smart-home devices such as robot vacuum cleaners, smart thermostats or fridges, or virtual assistants like Alexa. In particular, smart-home devices need to gather certain data in order to function properly, and especially smart home assistants are likely to be able to recognise a consumer's emotions based on, for instance, the tone of their voice.

For an injured party to have a claim under the PLD, the product must also be defective. According to Article 7 (1) of the revised PLD, a product is defective if it does not provide the safety that a person is entitled to expect or that is required under Union or national law. Article 7 (2) continues to state that all circumstances must be taken into account. Among others, this includes the presentation and the characteristics of the product, including its labelling, design, technical features, composition and packaging and the instructions for its assembly, installation, use and maintenance; the reasonably foreseeable use; the effect on the product of its ability to continue to learn or acquire new features after it is placed on the market or put into service; the reasonably foreseeable effect on the product of other products that can be expected to be used together with the product, including by means of interconnection or relevant product safety requirements, including safety-relevant cybersecurity requirements.

This can be understood in the sense that if the description of an AI-enabled product or software states that only certain types of data are collected and processed, while in fact the data collection reaches further, the product or software is to be considered defective. The same would apply if faulty programming during the production process leads to excessive data gathering. Failure to comply with safety-relevant cybersecurity requirements could also possibly lead to excessive data gathering through the AI-enabled product.

Under the scope of the PLD, the injured party can recover material losses resulting from death, and personal injury including medically recognised harm to psychological health and property damage, apart from damage to the defective

[60] European Parliament legislative resolution of 12 March 2024 on the proposal for a directive of the European Parliament and of the Council on liability for defective products (COM(2022)0495 – C9-0322/2022 – 2022/0302(COD)).

[61] See Article 4 (1) revised PLD; see also, e.g. Li and Schütte (2023), p. 576.

[62] See Recital 17 to the revised PLD.

product itself and to property that is exclusively used for professional purposes.[63] Property damage includes damage to data, which, pursuant to Recital 20, means the loss or corruption of data, for instance, when data is stored on a hard drive. As to the harm to psychological health, Recital 21 clarifies that the definition of harm must be that which affects the victim's general state of health and could require therapy or medical treatment, taking into account, inter alia, the International Classification of Diseases by the World Health Organization.

The unreasonable gathering of emotional data by a defective product is not likely to cause actual physical harm to a person. However, depending on how far the excessive data gathering goes, there is a risk that the invasion of privacy will cause psychological distress to an extent that treatment is required. In that case, it would count as recognised harm to psychological health. Violations of privacy as such that do not cause psychological distress to an extent that it needs to be treated will count as immaterial harm that cannot be recovered based on the PLD.

Therefore, only in very rare cases, the PLD will likely serve as a basis of a claim for damage caused by emotional AI.

4.5 German Law as an Example

As the proposed AILD does not establish any rules on the substance of liability for damage caused by AI, but instead delegates this part to the national laws of the EU Member States, it is worth exploring what liability under such national law might look like. This section will analyse what potential liability under German law, in combination with the AILD, would look like.[64]

Pursuant to § 823 I BGB,[65] 'a person who, intentionally or negligently, unlawfully injures the life, body, health, freedom, property or another right of another person is liable to make compensation to the other party for the damage arising from this'. Liability under § 823 I BGB requires the violation of one or more of the legally protected interests, liability-founding causation, unlawfulness, fault, and liability-specifying causation.[66] As is the general rule in the law of civil procedure, the burden of proof regarding all the requirements of liability usually lies with the claimant.[67]

---

[63] See Article 6 of the revised PLD.

[64] One question that keeps arising is whether the AI system itself can be liable. In German national law, to date, you can only be responsible if you are able to hold rights and obligations. In addition, also an AI would have to be able to display faulty behaviour, that is, to act intentionally or negligently. In Germany, the prevailing approach is that AI systems are deterministic and do not have the cognitive abilities to act faultily. See, e.g. Konertz and Schönhof (2020), pp. 117, 118.

[65] Bürgerliches Gesetzbuch – the German Civil Code.

[66] Stürner (2021) § 823.

[67] Beibringungsgrundsatz – the principle of the production of evidence. See, e.g. Bard and Morell (2023).

As regards the protected interests, the wording 'or another right' relates to rights of the same character as property, life or health, meaning that they must be rights of exclusive character that can be invoked *erga omnes*.[68] Those who have suffered harm can claim compensation when the wrongdoer's act or omission was the cause for the suffered harm, when no defences are applicable, and when the behaviour was intentional or negligent. The provision of § 823 I BGB can be applied alongside Article 82 of the GDPR.[69]

The use of emotional AI could lead to the infringement of personality rights, which falls under the scope of 'another right' within § 823 BGB.[70] This includes, for instance, the unauthorised power of disposition over sensitive personal data, the unauthorised investigation into personal data going beyond what is publicly accessible, or transferring personal data beyond what is permitted under the scope of the Federal Data Protection Act. Individuals have the right to informational self-determination, which means that they are the ones to decide what kind of personal information may be transferred to the public and/or to third parties.[71]

For a long time, it was disputed whether immaterial harm is recoverable under the scope of § 823 I BGB. However, over time, the Federal Constitutional Court and the Federal High Court of Justice have handed down ground-breaking judgments answering the question affirmatively.

Based on the analysis above, § 823 I BGB, individually or in combination with the AILD regime, is a suitable basis of a claim for damage caused by emotional AI. As opposed to a claim based on Article 82 (I) of the GDPR, there is no restriction to data protection infringements. However, before the AILD is in force, the injured party will have to prove all the requirements of § 823 I BGB.

5 Discussion

The preceding sections have shown that the use of emotional AI can lead particularly to non-material harm in persons exposed to different systems. However, at this stage it can be difficult to obtain compensation if harm occurs. Indeed, injured parties can only rely on Article 82 of the GDPR or on national laws.

[68] Palandt (2020) § 823, marginal no. 11.

[69] See, e.g. OLG Düsseldorf, Beschl. v. 16.03.2021 (16 U 269/20), available at Wybitul T, Jacquemain T, 'DATA AGENDA UND LATHAM & WATKINS LLP DS-GVO-Schadensersatztabelle', as of January 2022, 16; FG Berlin-Brandenburg, Beschluss vom 27.10.2021 - 16 K 16155/21, available at https://openjur.de/u/2379890.html.

[70] Palandt (2020) § 823, marginal no. 19.

[71] The right to informational self-determination was first formulated by the German Federal Constitutional Court (Bundesverfassungsgericht) in 1983, with the 'Volkszählungsurteil' (Census Judgment). See BVerfG, Urteil des Ersten Senats vom 15. Dezember 1983 - 1 BvR 209/83 -, Rn. 1-215, available at https://www.bverfg.de/e/rs19831215_1bvr020983.html.

In terms of the GDPR, one must keep in mind that biometric data or health data do not cover the whole of what can be understood as emotional data. In the absence of an official definition, Ballardini et al. have suggested to define emotional data as 'data representing the emotional, psychological or physical status of natural persons by identifying and processing their (facial) expressions, movements, behaviour, or other physical, physiological or mental characteristics'.[72] Further, the term 'emotion recognition system' does not equal the broader term of emotional AI or affective computing. An emotional AI system may well include components to detect pain or fatigue, which is excluded from the scope of 'emotion recognition systems as per the AI Act'.

As regards Article 82 of the GDPR, hopes were high that the *Österreichische Post* judgment would provide actual clarification as to the threshold for non-material harm, but it was re-delegated to EU Member States. This seems to reflect the general reluctance of EU Member States concerning any harmonisation or approximation of liability rules, or private law in general.[73] The same can be said for the current version of the AILD, which seems a 180 degree turn compared to the proposal for a regulation issued by the European Parliament in October 2020, which enshrined actual liability rules, setting out the liability of the 'operator'. The operator was a person having a degree of control over an AI system, and they would have been strictly liable for damage caused by high-risk AI, while liability for harm inflicted by AI systems not classified as high-risk would be based on fault.[74] However, the provision on the recoverability of immaterial harm had room for improvement. The fact that it required 'significant immaterial harm that results in a verifiable economic loss'[75] made it even contradictory to existing EU law, which entails that compensation for immaterial or non-material harm is not understood as compensation for economic losses but for non-material harm 'itself'.[76]

As national laws can differ significantly across Member States, so do the courts' approaches to awarding compensation for non-material harm. While, for instance, Germany already in the late 1950s acknowledged that infringements of personality rights give rise to compensation,[77] and has repeatedly confirmed this, and courts have awarded reasonable sums to injured parties, other countries are more reluctant in that regard.[78] This is also relevant with a view to the question of which courts will have jurisdiction in such liability cases. In terms of online infringements of

[72] Ballardini et al. (2024), p. 2.

[73] See, e.g. Terryn (2010), p. 8.

[74] European Parliament resolution of 20 October 2020 with recommendations to the Commission on a civil liability regime for artificial intelligence (2020/2014(INL)).

[75] Ibid., Annex B, Article 3 (i).

[76] See, e.g. Opinion of Advocate General Wahl, Case C-150/17 P Kendrion, ECLI:EU:C:2018:612, paras 107–110, 124–128; Case C-337/15 P Staelen, ECLI:EU:C:2017:256; Havu (2019).

[77] See, e.g. Herrenreiter Judgment, Federal Supreme Court of Justice in 1958, BGHZ 26, 349, available at https://openjur.de/u/190815.html.

[78] For instance, the 2020 Finnish Guidelines of the Personal Injury Commission Regarding the Amounts of Compensation Payable under Chapter 5 of the Finnish Tort Liability Act for Pain,

personality rights, in 2011, the CJEU clarified that the injured party can bring claims to the Courts in their Member State of residence.[79] It remains to be seen whether this will be translated to the use of AI systems. While the country of residence is of advantage for the injured party insofar as they are likely to be more familiar with any procedures, it may well be a disadvantage if the injured party resides in a Member State where the courts are reluctant to award compensation for non-material harm.

As an EU framework, although the GDPR provides for the recovery of non-material harm, as it is sector specific legislation, it has a limited scope. Emotional data are only relevant insofar as they fall under the scope of biometric data. While emotions are explicitly protected under the ePrivacy framework, its scope is even more limited as it applies only to electronic communications. In addition, neither the GDPR nor the ePrivacy framework provide for any harmonised amounts of compensation. Against this background, legislation in terms of liability in this context is fragmented and still very far away from the level playing field that the EU legislator envisions with regard to AI.[80]

Thus, there is no framework or provision in force that provides for a comprehensive recoverability of harm caused by emotional AI. Persons suffering damage resulting from the use of emotional AI systems are at a significant risk of not receiving any compensation. This can also provide the wrong incentives to providers and users of such systems: being at a relatively low risk of facing damages claim could prompt them not to observe the required standard of care.

In general, the regulatory piecemeal across EU Member States creates considerable legal uncertainty for all parties involved. In addition to potentially injured parties at risk of not receiving compensation, the providers and deployers of emotional AI systems are also fishing in troubled waters, not knowing what claims to expect or how courts might decide. This might lead to risks becoming uninsurable due to the unpredictable situation, and have a chilling effect on innovation and the uptake of these technologies.

However, the EU legislator is also facing the difficult task of finding the balance in protecting legally relevant interests and fundamental rights while at the same time enabling innovation and ensuring that the EU is not falling behind in what has been called the race to AI.[81] Nevertheless, in this context, it does not help to leave essential terms undefined or incompletely defined.

Other Temporary Harm, Permanent Harm, and Suffering award rather moderate sums even for pain and suffering related to severe injuries, e.g. up to 8000 Euros for severe heart injuries.

[79] Judgment of the Court (Grand Chamber), Joined Cases C-509/09 and C-161/10 eDate Advertising GmbH v X and Olivier Martinez, Robert Martinez v MGN Limited.

[80] European Commission (2020a), p. 8.

[81] See, e.g. Smuha (2021), p. 57.

6 Conclusion

This chapter analysed which rules could be applicable in cases where the use of emotional AI causes harm. As this harm will mostly be non-material, quantification is difficult—as in most cases of non-pecuniary loss. However, the prospective regulatory framework in this regard does not make it easier for injured parties to obtain compensation, nor does it give a positive outlook in terms of predictable and just case outcomes. It already starts with strong fragmentation of the general regulatory framework relating to the technology: the gaps outlined in the previous sections make it even difficult for providers, deployers and data processors to map out their obligations properly.

Generally, while overregulation is seen as an obstacle to the development and use of new technologies, the legal uncertainty created by fragmented regulations that fails to clarify stakeholders' obligations and potential users' rights will have the same negative effect. Therefore, the EU legislator should consider introducing another special category of data, namely emotional data, to the GDPR and correspondingly define emotional AI or affective computing in the AI Act. Additional clarification is necessary for terms such as 'subliminal techniques' or 'medical reasons and safety reasons'. This does not require an amendment of the regulation as such, but could be done by means of guidelines, as in the case of the Machinery Directive.[82]

References

Ballardini RM, van den Hoven van Genderen R, Nokelainen T (2024) Legal incentives for innovations in the emotional AI domain: a carrot and stick approach? J Intell Prop Law Pract 19(8):658–667. https://doi.org/10.1093/jiplp/jpae041

Bard V, Morell A (2023) Der Beibringungsgrundsatz: Eine Rechtfertigung unter besonderer Berücksichtigung der Passivität der nicht beweisbelasteten Partei. Anwaltsblatt ZPO Blog, 5 October 2023. Available via https://anwaltsblatt.anwaltverein.de/de/zpoblog/der-beibringungsgrundsatz-eine-rechtfertigung-unter-besonderer-beruecksichtigung-der-passivitaet-der-nicht-beweisbelasteten-partei. Accessed 19 Aug 2024

Buruiana A (2021) The legal consequences of the Facebook-Cambridge Analytica scandal on the EU information society; the proposal of E-Privacy regulation. Law Annals Titu Maiorescu University, pp 47–58

De Luca S (2023) European Parliamentary Research Service, Briefing, New Product Liability Directive. Available via https://www.europarl.europa.eu/RegData/etudes/BRIE/2023/739341/EPRS_BRI(2023)739341_EN.pdf. Accessed 19 Aug 2024

Etteldorf C (2019) EDPB on the interplay between the ePrivacy Directive and the GDPR. Eur Data Protect Law Rev 5(2):224–231. https://doi.org/10.21552/edpl/2019/2/12

European Commission (2017) Evaluation and review of Directive 2002/58 on privacy and the electronic communication sector. Available via https://digital-strategy.ec.europa.eu/en/library/

[82]European Commission (2023), 'Guide to application of the Machinery Directive 2006/42/EC - Edition 2.2'.

evaluation-and-review-directive-200258-privacy-and-electronic-communication-sector. Accessed 19 Aug 2024
European Commission (2020a) 'White Paper on Artificial Intelligence' COM(2020) 65 final
European Commission (2020b) 'Report on the Safety and Liability Implications of Artificial Intelligence, the Internet of Things and Robotics', COM(2020) 64 final
European Commission (2023) Guide to application of the Machinery Directive 2006/42/EC - Edition 2.2
European Commission (2024) European Artificial Intelligence Act comes into force. Press release 1 August 2024. Available via https://ec.europa.eu/commission/presscorner/detail/en/ip_24_4123. Accessed 19 Aug 2024
European Data Protection Supervisor (2015) Opinion 4/2015: Towards a new digital ethics: Data, dignity and technology. Available via https://www.edps.europa.eu/sites/default/files/publication/15-09-11_data_ethics_en.pdf. Accessed 19 Aug 2024
European Digital Rights (EDRi) (2021) Civil Society Statement: An EU Artificial Intelligence Act for Fundamental Rights. Available via https://edri.org/wp-content/uploads/2021/12/Political-statement-on-AI-Act.pdf. Accessed 19 Aug 2024
Gremsl T, Hödl E (2022) Emotional AI: legal and ethical challenges. Inf Polity 27:163–174. https://doi.org/10.3233/IP-211529
Häuselmann A (2021) Fit for purpose? Affective computing meets EU data protection law. Int Data Priv Law 11(3):245–256. https://doi.org/10.1093/idpl/ipab008
Havu K (2019) Damages liability for nonmaterial harm in eu case law. Eur Law Rev 44(4):24–46
Healey J (2014) Physiological sensing of emotion. In: Calvo RA, D'Mello S, Gratch J et al (eds) The Oxford handbook of affective computing. Oxford University Press, Oxford, pp 204–216. https://doi.org/10.1093/oxfordhb/9780199942237.013.023
Konertz R, Schönhof R (2020) Das technische Phänomen "Künstliche Intelligenz" im allgemeinen Zivilrecht. Nomos, Baden-Baden. https://doi.org/10.5771/9783748910503
Kumar M, Aijaz A, Chattar O et al (2024) Opacity, transparency, and the ethics of affective computing. IEEE Transact Affective Comput 15(1):4–17. https://doi.org/10.1109/TAFFC.2023.3278230
Li S, Schütte B (2023) The proposal for a revised product liability directive: the emperor's new clothes? Maastricht J Eur Comp Law 30(5):573–596. https://doi.org/10.1177/1023263X231216941
Mantello P, Ho MT (2022) Why we need to be weary of emotional AI. AI Soc 39:1447–1449. https://doi.org/10.1007/s00146-022-01576-y
McStay A (2020) Emotional AI, soft biometrics and the surveillance of emotional life: An unusual consensus on privacy. Big Data & Society 7(1). https://doi.org/10.1177/2053951720904386
Menezes Cordeiro AB (2019) Civil liability for processing of personal data in the GDPR. Eur Data Protect Law Rev 5(4):492–499. https://doi.org/10.21552/edpl/2019/4/7
Nouwens M, Liccardi I, Veale M et al (2020) Dark Patterns after the GDPR: scraping consent pop-ups and demonstrating their influence. In: Proceedings of the 2020 CHI Conference on Human Factors in Computing Systems, Honolulu, USA, April 25–30, 2020. https://doi.org/10.1145/3313831.3376321
Palandt O (ed) (2020) Bürgerliches Gesetzbuch, 79th edn. C.H. Beck, Munich
Purdy M, Zealley J, Maseli O (2019) The risks of using AI to interpret human emotions. Harvard Business Review. Available via https://hbr.org/2019/11/the-risks-of-using-ai-to-interpret-human-emotions. Accessed 19 Aug 2024
Pusztahelyi R (2020) Emotional AI and its challenges in the viewpoint of online marketing. Curentul Juridic 23(2):13–31
Smuha N (2021) From a 'race to AI' to a 'race to AI regulation': regulatory competition for artificial intelligence. Law Innov Technol 13(1):57–84. https://doi.org/10.1080/17579961.2021.1898300
Steindl E (2022) Does the European data protection framework adequately protect our emotions? emotion tech in light of the draft AI act and its interplay with the GDPR. European Data Protection Law Review 8(2):311–319. https://doi.org/10.21552/edpl/2022/2/20

Stürner R (ed) (2021) Jauernig, Bürgerliches Gesetzbuch, 21st edn. C.H. Beck, Munich

Terryn E (2010) The Common Frame of Reference: an optional instrument? Note for the European Parliament, Directorate General for Internal Affairs. Available via https://www.europarl.europa.eu/document/activities/cont/201004/20100430ATT73925/20100430ATT73925EN.pdf. Accessed 19 Aug 2024

Valcke P, Clifford D, Dessers VK (2021) Constitutional challenges in the emotional AI era. In: Micklitz HW, Pollicino O, Reichman A et al (eds) Constitutional challenges in the algorithmic society. Cambridge University Press, Cambridge, pp 57–77. https://doi.org/10.1017/9781108914857.005

Voss WG (2017) First the GDPR, now the proposed eprivacy regulation. J Intern Law 21(1):3–11. https://papers.ssrn.com/sol3/papers.cfm?abstract_id=3008765

Weber-Guskar E (2021) How to feel about emotionalized artifcial intelligence? When robot pets, holograms, and chatbots become afective partners. Ethics Inform Technol 23:601–610. https://doi.org/10.1007/s10676-021-09598-8

Woollacott E (2023) Europe's AI Act moves forward with increased privacy protections. Forbes, online, 11 May 2023. Available via https://www.forbes.com/sites/emmawoollacott/2023/05/11/europes-ai-act-moves-forward-with-increased-privacy-protections/. Accessed 19 Aug 2024

Yates D (1973) Damages for non-pecuniary loss. Mod Law Rev 36(5):535–541. https://www.jstor.org/stable/1094803

Commercializing Emotions in a Lawful and Responsible Manner: The Limitations, Possibilities and Dilemmas in an Emotional AI Service Business Concept in the Workplace

Amanda Drake

Abstract While commercial possibilities of emotional AI for businesses are manifold, so are the risks this technology brings. Currently, debate on legal and ethical aspects in the area of commercial emotional AI is ongoing and even a ban is being considered, potentially endangering innovation and the commercial uptake of emotional AI in the EU. It is safe to say that the provision of this technology takes place in a grey area at the moment, causing particular attention to legal and ethical dilemmas. This chapter is an explorative study about collision, dependency and compatibility of law, ethics and practice in the area of commercialization of certain type of emotional AI—emotion-aware systems at workplaces. If the processing of emotions—one's own and others'—by people is already complex and at times risky, how can a company utilize emotional AI commercially in both a legally and ethically responsible manner? Firstly, this chapter explores how the relevant legislation in terms of AI balances the risks and possibilities of emotional AI. Following this, the chapter explores how a company can navigate in practice through the current obstacles in its way to the provision of lawful and responsible emotional AI services.

1 Introduction

Humans' ability to innovate in the field of technology no longer sufficiently fits the framework of current law and ethics. AI has revolutionized the limits of human capability and consequently challenged the old concepts of regulating technology.[1] Regulating technology is regulating business, and from smart cars to diagnostic medical devices and from movie recommendation systems to chatbots, AI has been

[1] See more on the challenges at Scherer (2016), p. 359.

A. Drake (✉)
University of Lapland, Faculty of Law, Rovaniemi, Finland
e-mail: amanda.drake@ulapland.fi

R. Ballardini et al. (eds.), *Emotional Data Applications and Regulation of Artificial Intelligence in Society*, Law, Governance and Technology Series 69,
https://doi.org/10.1007/978-3-031-80111-2_15

introduced to business operations and innovations at an increasing pace in various fields. However, some fields are more ethically multidimensional and thus more likely to give rise to scrutiny, public disagreement and legal and ethical discussion than others. To identify the emotions of humans, emotional AI involves the utilization of biometric data, and as complex as emotions are, so is the potential operational field in commerce. While commercial opportunities for emotional AI services could thrive, the potential risks include intrusiveness to rights and freedoms of natural persons, loss of privacy, bias, discrimination and disregard for cultural differences.[2] It is safe to say that emotional AI is considered as having been debated, and its providers and deployers must plan its utilization diligently. Yet, what are the legal and ethical aspects of the utilization of emotional data commercially?[3]

This chapter focuses on a particularly interesting and debated potential use case of emotional AI: emotion-aware services in a work context, as illustrated in the chapter by Järvinen and Kallio. From this service area, this chapter reviews a specific service concept, performance booster service in terms of its purpose to assess (I) the emotions of **individuals** and (II) **overall** atmosphere and feeling in the workplace[4] (hereinafter referred to as **"emotional AI services"**).

Focusing on relevant provisions of the Regulation (EU) 2016/679 of the European Parliament and of the Council of 27 April 2016 on the protection of natural persons with regard to the processing of personal data and on the free movement of such data, and repealing Directive 95/46/EC (General Data Protection Regulation), hereinafter referred to as "GDPR", and the Regulation (EU) 2024/1689 of the European Parliament and of the Council of 13 June 2024 laying down harmonised rules on artificial intelligence and amending Regulations (EC) No 300/2008, (EU) No 167/2013, (EU) No 168/2013, (EU) 2018/858, (EU) 2018/1139 and (EU) 2019/2144 and Directives 2014/90/EU, (EU) 2016/797 and (EU) 2020/1828 (Artificial Intelligence Act), hereinafter referred to as "the AI Act", this chapter sheds light on the legal field in which a service provider and system deployer both must currently navigate. The chapter will then review how a company can contribute to the promotion of ethical and responsible emotional AI business by means of corporate social responsibility. This chapter reviews the current situation of law and ethics, pointing out possibilities and dilemmas in the field of emotional AI, which arguably has commercial potential but is simultaneously being protected against by legal prohibitions and has made calls for even considerations of "neuro rights".[5] Is this technology actually a gross violation of privacy which should be banned or a developing technology, the exploitation possibilities of which can be benevolent and useful, or is it something in between? From the viewpoint of

---

[2] Purdy et al. (2019) and the AI Act, Recital 44.

[3] Emotional AI's ability to perform has been widely contested, for example, on the basis of emotions being "complex human phenomena that cannot be clearly assigned to a set of nonverbal and verbal indicators". Policy Department for Citizens' Rights and Constitutional Affairs (2021), p. 17.

[4] See Järvinen's and Kallio's chapter in this book, Sect. 4.1.

[5] Policy Department for Citizens' Rights and Constitutional Affairs (2021), p. 10.

emotional AI services, this chapter reviews such questions and aims to shed light on the practical side of the legal and ethical issues indicated as well as concretizing the legal uncertainty a company in the field of emotional AI must currently navigate in.

2 Commercializing Emotional AI: Business Case

A company conceptualizing a new business model must have a map of the relevant legal field the requirements of which its service must meet. Regulatory compliance is an essential part of service development, but the emotional AI service provider must navigate in an uncertain legal and ethical situation at the moment. However, no complete ban on the commercial use of emotional AI is foreseeable and a rapidly developing variety of different emotional data-based business models shows that this is an area of increasing commercial interest. Nevertheless, use of emotional data as raw materials of a service and as the core of the business emphasizes the importance of adherence to both law and ethics.

2.1 Emotional AI Service Business Concept

In their chapter, Järvinen and Kallio illustrated various service concepts regarding commercial use cases of emotional AI. This chapter's legal review will focus on emotional AI services in the workplace, which services aim to create more efficient, comfortable and productive workplace with the help of emotional AI.[6]

In addition to remote measurements, the emotional AI service would use wearable sensors to capture physiological data, movement patterns, and environmental factors directly from natural persons. In addition, over a long period, the service would monitor the activities, experiences, work patterns, productivity and well-being of a known user or group of users. The emotional AI service intends to assess two elements which will be illustrated as scenarios in this chapter. Firstly, it will assess **individuals'** emotions, comfort levels and employee experience; monitor individuals' presence, movement, and activity within meeting rooms; observe behaviours at desks; identify anomalies in behaviour and environmental conditions **(hereinafter "scenario I")**. Secondly, it will assess the **overall** atmosphere and feeling in the office space, including, e.g. energy levels, boredom, drowsiness and enthusiasm **(hereinafter "scenario II").**[7] In the following sections, we

[6] See emotional AI service i.e. performance booster service in Table 1 in Järvinen's and Kallio's chapter in this book, Sect. 4.

[7] See Järvinen's and Kallio's chapter in this book, Sect. 4.1. Concepts are slightly adjusted and categorized herein to fit the scope of this chapter.

systematically go through the endurance of this business concept in relation to relevant legislation.[8]

3 Legal Emotional AI Business: Insights on Relevant Legislation

With respect to the interface between technical solutions and data protection, the GDPR[9] has shed light on difficulties faced by the practitioners in the implementation field, caused by vagueness in the legislation. From a company's point of view, a combination of multi-million euro sanctions and ambiguous legal requirements does not offer a very manageable foundation for functioning compliance. This section reviews the relevant provisions of two major AI related items of legislation—the GDPR and the AI Act—in terms of their applicability and potential dilemmas to emotional AI services.

3.1 The GDPR

3.1.1 Emotions as Personal Data?

As part of its compliance work, the deployer company, a controller company in this case, must assess whether the GDPR applies to the provision of the service. This assessment begins with determining whether personal data is processed as part of the emotional AI service or not. Although this sounds straightforward, the fact that emotions are not explicitly mentioned in the GDPR gives an indication of the possible interpretation challenges to be faced.

While 'emotions' as such are not included in verbatim in the scope of the GDPR, an analysis of provisions applicable to emotional AI services derives from the actual source data of such solutions, usually biometric data.[10] When biometric data as defined in Article 4 (14) of the GDPR is used to derive emotions, such processing

[8] It should be noted that outside the scope of this chapter there are other applicable laws to the service, such as more specific rules for the processing of employees' personal data in the employment context which member states, as per Article 88 of the GDPR, may have in place. For example, the Finnish Act on the Protection of Privacy in Working Life (759/2004) includes a cooperation procedure requirement for organizing technical monitoring of employees (Section 21) and service provider should adhere to such or similar legislation if applicable to its service.

[9] The GDPR has applied from 25th of May 2018.

[10] According to Article 4 (14) of the GDPR, "biometric data means personal data resulting from specific technical processing relating to the physical, physiological or behavioural characteristics of a natural person, which allow or confirm the unique identification of that natural person, such as facial images or dactyloscopic data".

leads to application of the GDPR. However, this only applies if such data allow or confirm the unique identification of the data subject. Therefore, a system based on "pulse frequency, body temperature and non-unique facial expressions (such as smiling, raising of the brow or yawning) or non-unique voice signals (such as volume or trembling)"[11] would fall outside the scope, provided that such data cannot be used to identify a person.

Since an essential part of our business concept is the systematic and extensive collection and processing of person-specific data, anonymous processing does not come into question for scenario I (assessing individual data as defined in Sect. 2.1). Indeed, the collection of remote measurements, physiological data, movement patterns and data derived from the wearables would consist of such a multidimensional and comprehensive set of information that would very likely allow or confirm the unique identification of the person in question.

However, with regard to scenario II (assessing the overall data as defined in Sect. 2.1), in case only remote measurements were used to assess the overall atmosphere, such processing could in theory be conducted without the unique identification of a specific person in the space, provided that no natural person could be identified or identifiable from the data detected from the environment. Compared to a billboard screen in a busy street broadcasting targeted advertisements to passing pedestrians based on their age, gender and mood without identifying them,[12] in an office environment, however, the fulfilment of such a requirement would be challenging. First at all, the number of possible identities of people are already limited and controlled in the working environment.[13] Secondly, if the service is being used in a meeting room, for example, and a person enters the controlled environment, the adjusted attributes in the environment thereafter (change in environment, for example, addition of refreshing bright lights or calming music if such feature is part of the service) could reveal emotions (anger, for example) of a person to others. Therefore, it is likely that the data collected in scenario II would be considered personal data.

3.1.2 Emotions as Special Categories of Personal Data?

Further to the determination of whether emotional data is considered personal data is to understand if Article 9 of the GDPR applies, i.e. does the data collected via a service belong to a special category of personal data? A recent study has concluded

[11] Policy Department for Citizens' Rights and Constitutional Affairs (2021), p. 67. Note also the GDPR, Recital 51 according to which "the processing of photographs should not systematically be considered to be processing of special categories of personal data as they are covered by the definition of biometric data only when processed through a specific technical means allowing the unique identification or authentication of a natural person".

[12] Häuselmann et al. (2023), p. 3.

[13] For instance, if the service was used in a meeting room, the employer would know the attendees who have booked the room. If only one person would attend the meeting, the data would be very identifiable.

that the answer to such a dilemma depends on the data collecting approach of the system used to detect emotions.[14] As such, emotional data seems to not constitute special category data.[15] However, systems which use physiological data-based emotion recognition systems, i.e. systems that derive emotions based on the heart rate or blood pressure of the data subject, do process special category data. This is due to such data falling into the health data category, another type of special category data listed in Article 9.[16]

On the other hand, alternative system approaches such as systems using non-health data, e.g. audio emotion- or visual recognition based on facial expressions and body movements, would not fall under Article 9, provided that the purpose of the processing did not uniquely identify a natural person.[17] In terms of biometric data, this is because a prerequisite for application of Article 9 is that the processing takes place "for the purpose of uniquely identifying a natural person".[18] This would not be case in emotional AI services since when an identification purpose answers the question "Who is this person?",[19] the purpose of the service in question is to determine "what is this person feeling?". In such an event, instead of biometric identification, it is biometric detection which takes place.[20]

In terms of scenario I, since the service would use wearable sensors to capture physiological data such as heart rate and body temperature, the controller company would have to comply with Article 9, leading to more strict requirements for establishing a legal basis for the processing of data concerning health. In terms of scenario II, the rule above applies to any physiological data collected which can be linked to a person as well. In both scenarios, Article 9 would not apply in terms of any non-physiological data collected.[21]

To sum up, if it is not possible to collect data anonymously, then the GDPR applies, and depending on the nature of the data that is used to detect the emotions (Is it physiological data or not, and what is the purpose of processing?), either the GDPR will be applied generally or on the basis of Article 9.

[14] Häuselmann et al. (2023), p. 3.

[15] Steindl (2022), p. 313.

[16] Häuselmann et al. (2023), pp. 3–4.

[17] Häuselmann et al. (2023), p. 4.

[18] See more: Policy Department for Citizens' Rights and Constitutional Affairs (2021), p. 81.

[19] Policy Department for Citizens' Rights and Constitutional Affairs, (2021), p. 20.

[20] See more about the distinction of biometric identification, categorisation, and detection at: Policy Department for Citizens' Rights and Constitutional Affairs (2021), pp. 20–21.

[21] Another matter is whether emotions could in some scenarios be directly considered data related to health—for instance—as it could be argued that emotions such as sadness and anger would be attributes to a mental health diagnosis, for example, and thus make such data health related, potentially.

3.1.3 Brief Analysis of Other Relevant Provisions: Legal Basis, Data Protection Principles and Risk-Based Implementation

This section briefly reviews other relevant articles of the GDPR to which the controller company should give particular attention. Firstly, the controller company should establish a legal basis for processing data, either on the basis of Article 6 or Article 9 of the GDPR, depending on the nature of the data collected, as discussed in the previous section. In terms of processing falling under Article 9 (especially scenario I, assessing individual data), consent as the legal basis would most likely be applied. Interestingly Article 9 (2)(e) also includes the possibility to process personal data which are manifestly made public by the data subject. It is interesting to consider the relation of this option to emotions that can sometimes manifest strongly outwards as outbursts. In addition, putting additional focus on the intended purpose of the system, Article 9 (2)(h) also includes a legal basis on the foundation of the assessment of the employee's working capacity, which could be argued to be emotion-related in certain working environments.[22]

In terms of processing falling under Article 6, although the controller company could seek to establish the legal basis on other alternatives, arguably consent as a legal basis could be the most appropriate option.[23] Indeed, it is unlikely that the controller company could justify the processing on the basis of employee contract performance, adherence to law or other interests set out in Article 6.

The aforementioned consent has been proposed as a legal basis for the processing of personal data in emotional AI service. However, due to the asymmetrical relationship between employer and employee, it should be carefully assessed whether the employee can in fact give voluntary consent to data processing. In terms of using facial recognition software, an imbalance has been found in a school environment with regard to students and the controller.[24] The question is, does the employee have an actual opportunity to refuse processing without adverse effects?[25]

---

[22] This legal basis could come into question if there was a medical or safety reason for the system as later discussed in Sect. 3.2.3. It should be also noted that if the purpose of the system would be to automatedly analyse or predict aspects concerning that employee's performance at work (see definition of 'profiling' in the GDPR Article 4 (4)), the provisions regarding profiling would become applicable. This could also make the processing fall under Article 22 if the processing could lead to the denying of employment opportunities or other significant effects (Data Protection Working Party (2018), p. 22).

[23] In addition to challenges regarding the validity of the consent, there are also practical challenges, especially in scenario II. If consent was the legal basis of the service, how could overall atmosphere be assessed, e.g. in a meeting room, if only certain employees had given their consent and employees who have not consented would enter the same controlled space?

[24] A school in Sweden received GDPR fines for using facial recognition technology for monitoring student's attendance. Among other deficiencies, the consent given by the students was not valid due to an imbalance between the data subject and controller. See more: European Data Protection Board (2019) and Policy Department for Citizens' Rights and Constitutional Affairs (2021), pp. 40–41.

[25] It should be noted that a ban on emotional AI systems in the workplace (as is seen later in this chapter) has been justified on the basis of "the imbalance of power in the context of work or education" in the AI Act, Recital 44.

According to the GDPR, consent must be "freely given, specific and unambiguous".[26] Moreover, it shall be based on a real choice and control of the data subject, and its validity depends on whether the data subject can actually refuse giving consent without any negative consequences.[27] The problematics of the validity of consent in the work context has been analysed in Guidelines 05/2020 by the European Data Protection Board. These Guidelines conclude that due to the imbalance of power in the employment context, while consent should not be the legal basis for the majority of processing activities, in exceptional cases where refusal of consent would not lead to adverse consequences, consent could be relied upon.[28]

Demonstrating the validity and voluntariness of the consent is a challenge. However, the controller company can support the validity with its choices regarding the intended purpose of the system. For example, if the service was a "personal recommendation system" type of service for the employee, where the use of the service and detected emotions and recommendations proposed based on them were only for the benefit of the employee (and for their sole decision to consent to the service and adjust or not to adjust their working behaviour accordingly), the setting would be more balanced. In the same way as with the use or non-use of other work tools such as a calculator, an employee could refuse using the service with no negative consequences.[29] Nevertheless, the collected emotions would not be directly processed by the employer, other than in terms of its role as the controller company; and a service rendering and processing data would be the responsibility of the data processor (third party emotional AI service provider). Therefore, since the employer could not act on the basis of the emotions, a freely given consent would be better justified in this business model.

In addition to diligent consideration of the legal basis, adherence to the data protection principles of Article 5 may be challenged by the processing of emotional data and should therefore be given particular attention in both design and compliance work. For example, principles of fairness, transparency and accuracy have been raised in a study as particularly relevant in terms of issues of emotional data processing.[30] In terms of the emotional AI service discussed in this chapter, it should be especially advisable to carefully assess whether all data and data collection methods are necessary in relation to the purposes for processing (data minimization), especially in scenario I where both remote measurements and wearable sensors are

[26] See definition of 'consent' at Article 4 (11) of the GDPR. See also Recitals 32 and 43 of the GDPR.

[27] The European Data Protection Board (2020), p. 7.

[28] The European Data Protection Board (2020), pp. 8–9.

[29] Could the consent procedure even be designed in such a way that the employer would not get information about which employees specifically use, thus have consented to the use of the service? Depending on the hardware equipment required by the service to function, this could be difficult to implement in practice.

[30] See more about challenges in said data protection principles: Häuselmann et al. (2023), p. 4.

used to collect an extremely considerable data set, covering fundamentally all events happening to the data subjects at work.[31]

Due to the narrow definition of the term 'biometric data', the protection of data subjects under the GDPR has been considered insufficient.[32] However, it should be pointed out that although the GDPR at first glance is surprisingly lenient towards the processing of emotional data, its risk-based approach means that the controller company must diligently put forth its processing activities taking into consideration the objectively assessed risks of the processing.[33] Since the use of emotional data is under ethical debate and a potential partial legal ban, it would be advisable for an emotional AI service controller company to pay particular attention to such provisions of the GDPR where the nature, scope, context and purposes of the processing should determine the probability and severity of the risk to the rights and freedoms of the data subjects, and assess the potential risks of the services carefully. Consequently, this should correlate with the extent of measures implemented thereafter, including but not limited to a data protection impact assessment. Ultimately, the controller company should foster especially high-quality compliance work in terms of data protection (Table 1).[34]

3.2 *The AI Act*

On a mission to balance technological development and rights of natural persons, legislators are exposed to the challenge of building a new type of legal framework for an ensemble, even referred to as 'the new electricity",[35] i.e. AI. In the form of an AI regulation, the EU has taken the first steps in regulating AI, thus revolutionizing the way AI is assessed legally.

At the core of the regulation is the application of a risk-based approach. Instead of a 'one-size-fits-all' type of approach, where the legislation would apply equally to all AI solutions, the applicability of the requirements is subject to the gravity of the risk such a solution bears.[36] Consequently, the AI Act defines the limits for permissible

---

[31] See the complete list of data planned to be collected in Järvinen's and Kallio's chapter in this book, Sect. 4.1.

[32] Häuselmann et al. (2023), p. 4, and Policy Department for Citizens' Rights and Constitutional Affairs (2021), p. 67.

[33] See also the GDPR, Recital 76.

[34] Additionally, it should be noted that especially legislations with a risk-based approach—such as the GDPR—enable a wide-ranging application regarding the interpretation of the requirements. For instance, in terms of principles relating to the processing of personal data, the principle of data minimization requires that "Personal data shall be...(c) adequate, relevant and limited to what is necessary in relation to the purposes for which they are processed". (GDPR Article 5 (1)(c)) What actually is "necessary" is subject to the controller's determination.

[35] WIPO Magazine (2019).

[36] See an illustration of a risk pyramid at: European Parliamentary Research Service (2024), p. 7.

Table 1 Summary of the key findings

Emotional AI service scenario	Type of data processed	Intended purpose	Is it personal data?	Is it special category of personal data under Article 9?	Legal basis
I (assessing individual data as defined in Sect. 2.1)	Emotions of an individual derived from **physiological data** (such as heart rate, skin conductance or blood pressure[a]). Emotions of an individual derived from **non-physiological data** (such as audio, facial expressions, body gestures[b]).	Identifying or inferring **emotions** of a natural person on the basis of their data in the workplace.	Yes	Yes, in terms of physiological data (data concerning health). No, in terms of non-physiological data.	In terms of the processing of physiological data (data concerning health), legal basis under Article 9. In terms of the processing of non-physiological data, legal basis under Article 6.
II (assessing overall data as defined in Sect. 2.1)	Overall emotions of many individuals derived from **physiological data**. Overall emotions of many individuals derived from **non-physiological data**.	Identifying or inferring **overall emotions** of natural persons **in the same space** on the basis of their **combined data** in the workplace.	Likely, yes, since the extensive amount of data is collected from controlled, limited and known set of individuals, enabling identification. No, if the data is of such a generic nature that it is not linked to a specific employee (anonymous data).	Yes, in terms of physiological data (data concerning health) if such data falls under the definition of personal data. No, in terms of non-physiological data. N/A if the data is anonymous.	In terms of the processing of physiological data (data concerning health), legal basis under Article 9. In terms of the processing of non-physiological data, legal basis under Article 6. N/A if the data is anonymous.

[a]Häuselmann et al. (2023), p. 4
[b]Häuselmann et al. (2023), p. 4

and non-permissible technological innovation in the field of AI, also emotional AI, as is to be seen in this chapter.

Creating a legal framework for rapidly developing technology innovation brings challenges. A review of the phases of the legislative process of the AI Act already shows how emotional AI has challenged the regulating of AI. The ethical multidimensionality of emotional AI is well illustrated by the different stages of the regulatory process. Emotional AI systems—or emotion recognition systems, as defined in the AI Act[37]—have sailed through different levels of the risk pyramid of the AI Act during various phases of the legislative process and have attributed heated discussion.[38] Currently, emotional AI will be regulated as a prohibited practice, as a high-risk system, and also be subject to certain specific transparency obligations. Next, we will review what this means in practice for our business case.

3.2.1 Emotional AI as a Prohibited Practice

According to the Article 5(1)(f) of the AI Act, "the placing on the market, the putting into service for this specific purpose, or the use of AI systems to infer[39] emotions of a natural person in the areas of workplace and education institutions, except where the use of the AI system is intended to be put in place or into the market for medical or safety reasons" is prohibited.[40] Serious concerns regarding the scientific basis of emotion recognition systems, limited reliability,[41] deficiency of specificity and

[37] According to Article 3 (39) of the AI Act "'emotion recognition system' means an AI system for the purpose of identifying or inferring emotions or intentions of natural persons on the basis of their biometric data".

[38] In an earlier version of the AI Act (version: Brussels, 21.4.202, COM(2021) 206 final, 2021/0106 (COD)), emotional AI was regulated directly only as a limited risk system. More about criticism regarding this overturned approach, see: Steindl (2022), pp. 315–316.

[39] Interestingly, even though the definition of emotion recognition system in Article 3 (39) includes "...purpose of *identifying* or inferring emotions...", the prohibition at Article 5 (1)(f) omits "identify" and includes only "infer" in the scope of the prohibition. In fact, Article 5 does not explicitly refer to the definition of "emotion recognition system" set out in Article 3 (39) at all in verbatim, while it refers to the systems as "AI systems to infer emotions of a natural person" and not to the defined term "emotion recognition system". This may lead to uncertainty and challenges in the classification of emotional AI systems, as, for example, only the definition in Article 3 (39) includes the requirement of *biometric data* to be used to identify or infer emotions. Then again, the definition of "biometric data" in Article 3 (34) includes the requirement of it being considered a personal data. What would the risk classification be if a company used non-biometric data to identity or infer emotions? Also, Annex III (1)(c) fails to refer to emotion recognition systems in verbatim (... "AI systems intended to be used for emotion recognition"). This all causes unclarity as to whether the definition of 'emotion recognition system' applies equally to these provisions and confuses classifying emotional AI generally.

[40] The AI Act, Article 5(1)(f).

[41] For a study regarding challenges to inferring emotion from human facial movements see: Barrett et al. (2019).

generalizability, imbalance of power between the actioners, intrusive nature, and risks of discrimination have been mentioned in Recital 44 of the AI Act as justifications for the prohibition in question.

For an emotional AI service intended to be used in a work context, this does not look encouraging. Indeed, such a large-scale ban in this particular field would arguably have implications for the innovation and commercialization of emotional AI in the context of the workplace. In this section, we will discuss this prohibition in more detail in terms of our business case.

3.2.2 Prohibition Based on a Place Instead of Consequences

First at all, what makes the prohibition deviant is the contextualization of the prohibition on the basis of solely an undefined place—the workplace[42]—instead of actual acts of harm or other more specific prerequisite related to the system itself. As a comparison, Article 5 (1)(a) on manipulative systems includes various prerequisites for application of the ban in question based on the actual harm caused or likely to be caused by the system in question. The contrast between the subsections is significant, since Article 5 (1)(f) focuses merely on the physical place of the system, ignoring disproportionally the wide-ranginess of risks different emotional AI solutions bear, and thus not applying the risk-based approach.

These aspects emphasize and question the purpose of the regulation to balance technological innovation and the safety of natural persons. The prohibition in Article 5(1)(f) does not distinguish applications based on what the intended use is of the inferred emotions. Instead, as long as the solution is used in the workplace, the ban applies. However, as the emotional AI business service concept shows, the risks of this technology vary depending on the intended purpose of the system.[43] For example, in scenario I, a personified performance booster system solely aiming to help the employee to regulate the cognitive load with personal recommendations (regarding, e.g. rest, lighting or noise cancellation), without the employer receiving any of the input or output data, would minimize potential risks regarding the use of the data by the employer to impact employment and the rights of the user. Moreover,

[42]The AI Act fails to define "workplace" which may challenge implementing parties. For example, it is uncertain, whether using the solution while working remotely would fall under the ban. Article 5(1)(f) of the AI Act uses the phrase "in the areas of workplace". However, Recital 44 uses the phrase "systems intended to be used to detect the emotional state of individuals *in situations related to the workplace*...". The latter form could indicate remote working as well. Also, if a service identifies emotions of customers instead of employees, but is used upon customers at the company's employee's workplace, does the ban apply? Moreover, since the majority of spaces outside one's own home can be considered someone's workplace, the ban while lacking the definition of "workplace" leaves ambiguity upon where in fact this technology could actually be used, with all this potentially leading to the risk of fragmentation of the interpretation of law and a decrease in legal certainty.

[43]Or as AI HLEG (2019), p. 3 states "different situations raise different challenges".

the employee could always ignore the recommendations or stop using the service.[44] With such limitations regarding the use and recipients of the emotional data, risks related to the service could be moderated reasonably.[45] In this light, the ban seems disproportionate in terms of this kind of user-driven use of emotional AI. Therefore, it should be considered whether instead of focusing on the physical place of the solution, the limit of this technology's acceptability should be drawn to its consequences, similarly, for instance, as in regard to the prohibition on social scoring in Article 5 (1)(c).

3.2.3 Medical or Safety Reasons?

Considering Article 5(1)(f), the crushing commercial effects on the continuation of the emotional AI service business concept would be undeniable. This is unless the system's medical or safety necessity can be established. The prohibition in Article 5(1)(f) includes exceptions for cases of medical or safety reasons, the applicability of which should be analysed here. The emotional AI service aims "to create more efficient, *comfortable*, and productive workspace for employees[46]". Depending on the nature of the workplace, could increasing comfort be considered to increase safety in the space as well, if, for instance the solution would identify anger and aggression and seek to bring calmness and, by that token, safety to the workplace? Could a solution which seeks to prevent escalations and conflicts in fact improve safety in the workplace?

As to the exception on medical reasons, at least theoretically, it could be possible that the business model would have health benefits in an effort to reduce stress. However, it is unclear whether application of the exception would require the solution to be a medical device, in accordance with the medical device legislation. After all, Recital 44 of the AI Act states "*strictly* for medical or safety reasons". Nevertheless, while it fails to define "medical and safety reasons", the current wording in the exception in Article 5 (1)(f) leaves ambiguity and legal uncertainty as to the scope of the exceptions since many uses of emotional AI services could be considered to attribute to safety or health, at least indirectly.[47] However, if the purpose of the system was to solely increase efficiency and performance in the workplace, the exception would not apply.

---

[44] An employee could be considered to have a similar freedom of decision, for example, with a blood pressure monitor that the employer has made available for the employees in the lounge area of the workplace.

[45] Interestingly, 'recommender systems' have been listed as an example of minimal-risk AI systems in an illustration of a risk pyramid at: European Parliamentary Research Service (2024), p. 7.

[46] Järvinen and Kallio, in this book, Sect. 4.1.

[47] Therapeutical use has been given as an example in the AI Act, Recital 44.

3.2.4 Emotional or Physical State?

According to Recital 18 of the AI Act, "The notion (of emotion recognition system) refers to emotions or intentions such as happiness, sadness, anger, surprise, disgust, embarrassment, excitement, shame, contempt, satisfaction and amusement. It does *not include physical states*, such as pain or fatigue...".[48]

Interestingly then, if the emotional AI service solely detected physical states such as fatigue of the employee, which in a work context is a very beneficial trait to detect and mend, the service would not be considered an emotion recognition system in terms of the AI Act and would therefore not fall under the prohibition.[49]

Consequently, it becomes very essential to consider the differences between emotional and physical states. In addition to other measurements, the emotional AI service intends to detect employee stress. Work stress is one of the most significant causes of work-related illnesses and can lead to various health problems—annually causing a financially significant loss in work input.[50] However, is stress a physical state referred to in the Recital 18 of the AI Act or an emotion falling under prohibition in Article 5(1)(f)? From the viewpoint of an emotional AI service provider, this is a very relevant distinction business-wise, and examination of this question reveals a possible ambiguity, even a paradox in the regulation.

According to the definition by the American Psychological Association, "emotion" is "a complex reaction pattern, involving experiential, behavioural, and physiological elements, by which an individual attempts to deal with a personally significant matter or event".[51] On the other hand, "stress" is defined as "the physiological or psychological response to internal or external stressors"[52] and also as "the effects of anything that seriously threatens homeostasis".[53] In these terms, there seems to be an overlap as emotions incur and can be measured in physical form (e.g. excitement as an increased heart rate) as well and could therefore be referred to as "physical states" as well.[54] Therefore, the exception set out in Recital 18 is inconclusive and rather paradoxical and thus should be specified. Otherwise, there is a risk that by categorizing emotions only into physical states, this would enable circumvention of the Article 5 (1)(f) prohibition.[55] The question is, if emotional and

---

[48] According to the AI Act, Recital 18 the definition does not refer to systems used in detecting the state of fatigue of professional pilots or drivers for the purpose of preventing accidents.

[49] Naturally, as physiological data would still be collected, GDPR Article 9 would apply, as earlier discussed in Sect. 3.1.2.

[50] Juvani (2019), p. 2057.

[51] Definition of "Emotion" at American Psychological Association (2018).

[52] Definition of "Stress" at American Psychological Association (2018).

[53] Schneiderman et al. (2005), p. 1.

[54] See Sect. 3.1.2 on how physiological data is used for detecting emotions.

[55] To illustrate the ambiguity of the matter, let us consider a scenario where a company would like to detect the emotion of sadness experienced by its employees, but cannot conduct this within the framework of Article 5 of the AI Act. Instead, the company decides to collect the physical display of sadness, the appearance of liquid from glands in eyes of the people (i.e. tears). Would this fall under Article 5?

physical states are not completely distinguishable in a medical or psychological sense, how can the legislator clarify the issue? One option could be to define 'emotion' in the AI Act, but although basic emotions, such as joy and sadness can generally be listed, an exhaustive list of emotions (or physical states) in the definition could raise several challenges. For service providers, it can however be concluded that identifying or inferring physical states, such as fatigue (and possibly stress) of natural persons in the workplace, is not prohibited under the AI Act Article 5 (1)(f).

3.2.5 Emotional AI as a High-Risk Solution

According to Annex III 1 (c), high-risk AI systems pursuant to Article 6(2) include AI systems intended to be used for emotion recognition.[56] What this means in practice for emotional AI service providers is that, for instance, extensive regulative requirements in chapter III of the AI Act become applicable.[57] Due to the prohibition in Article 5, this would however be the case only if the service provider in our service model established a medical or safety reason for the system, or alternately detected physical states instead of emotions.

Depending on the intended purpose of the system, in the latter case above, instead of being an emotion recognition system, the solution could potentially be considered high-risk on the basis of it being (i) an AI system "intended to be used for biometric categorization,[58] according to sensitive or protected attributes or characteristics based on the inference of those attributes or characteristics" (Annex III 1 (b)), or (ii) an AI system intended "to allocate tasks based on individual behaviour or personal traits or characteristics or to monitor and evaluate the performance and behaviour of persons in such relationships" under Annex III 4 (b).[59]

In terms of concerns regarding emotional AI generally, some corresponding provisions for high-risk solutions mitigating the said risks include Article 10 (2) (f), (examination in view of possible biases), Article 9 (establishing risk management system), Article 13 (transparency) and Article 15 (accuracy). In addition, according to Article 26 (7) "before putting into service or using a high-risk AI system in the workplace, deployers who are employers shall inform workers' representatives and the affected workers that they will be subject to the use of the high-risk AI system".

---

[56] See also Recital 54 of the AI Act: "...emotion recognition systems that are not prohibited under this Regulation, should be classified as high-risk".

[57] This is of course provided that the service is considered an emotion recognition system as defined in the AI Act Article 3 (39). See more on this matter in footnote 39.

[58] Potentially, a physical state could form a category, as categorization means assigning natural persons to specific categories relating to, e.g. behaviour or personality traits on the basis of their biometric data. See more on defining 'categorization': The AI Act, Recital 16.

[59] Depending on the intended purpose of the system, Annex III (4)(b) regarding employment could apply as it determines as a high-risk solution "AI systems intended to be used to make decisions affecting terms of work-related relationships, the promotion or termination of work-related contractual relationships, to allocate tasks based on individual behaviour or personal traits or characteristics or to monitor and evaluate the performance and behaviour of persons in such relationships".

Table 2 Summary of the key findings

Intended purpose of the emotional AI service	Types of data collected	Prohibited under Article 5(1) (f)?	Risk category?
Identifying or inferring **emotions** of natural persons on the basis of their biometric data in the workplace.	Emotions on the basis of biometric data.	Yes	Unacceptable risk
Identifying or inferring **emotions** of natural persons on the basis of their biometric data **for safety or medical reasons** in the workplace.	Emotions on the basis of biometric data.	No	High-risk under Annex III 1 (c)
Identifying or inferring **physical states** (such as fatigue, potentially stress) of natural persons on the basis of their biometric data in the workplace.	Physical states on the basis of biometric data.	No	High-risk under Annex III 1 (b)/ Annex III 4 (b), if applicable

Perhaps overlappingly, emotional AI has also been subjected to specific transparency obligation of Article 50 (3) (Table 2).[60]

4 Responsible Emotional AI Business: Insights on Ethical Implications

4.1 Ethical Implications of Emotional AI Services and Corporate Social Responsibility

Earlier, we conceptualized the framework and foundations of achieving a legal emotional AI service. However, an integral part of the evaluation of commercialization is also the ethics of the business concept.[61] Emotional AI has raised ethical concerns, especially in terms of its relation to human dignity, integrity and mental privacy,[62] even raising discussion on the need for "neuro-rights".[63] It is therefore

[60] According to Article 50 (3) of the AI Act, "Deployers of an emotion recognition system or a biometric categorisation system shall inform the natural persons exposed thereto of the operation of the system, and shall process the personal data in accordance with Regulations (EU) 2016/679 and (EU) 2018/1725 and Directive (EU) 2016/680, as applicable".

[61] The AI HLEG's Ethics Guidelines for Trustworthy AI identify lawfulness and ethics as components of trustworthy AI, in addition to robustness. HLEG (2019), p. 5.

[62] Emotional AI could identify aspects of people's mental state that the person him or herself would not be aware of. On the other hand, the system could inaccurately claim such a mental state to be present. The setting is challenging from many perspectives and to add an element of commercialization to the picture, the matter gets more complex. See also grounds for planned partial prohibition of emotional AI at the AI Act, Recital 44.

[63] Policy Department for Citizens' Rights and Constitutional Affairs (2021), p. 57.

particularly important that a company operating in emotional AI service business understands its ethical implications, naturally implementing corporate social responsibility simultaneously.

While risk-bearing AI solutions are developed at the increasing phase, corporate responsibility is required, scrutinized and proclaimed increasingly. Corporate social responsibility, "the responsibility of enterprises for their impacts on society",[64] demands companies to identify the harmful effects related to their operations and try to prevent and reduce them.[65] Earlier in this chapter, we addressed the effects of legislation on the commercial use of emotional AI. However, although corporate responsibility is currently a subject to judicialization,[66] the basis of corporate responsibility has been that a company not only commits to comply with the applicable law but also exceeds the minimum requirements set forth therein.[67] Ideally, since this 'exceeding' would originate from the ethics of the company, it is important for companies to comprehend not only the legal dimensions of corporate responsibility but also the essential and foundational element beyond it, i.e. ethics.[68]

Similarly, as in the determination of what is legal and illegal, the determination of right and wrong is influenced by the operational field of a company.[69] Certain services are ethically more multidimensional than others and thus more likely to give rise to public disagreement and scrutiny. Emotional AI, in fact, is such an example. Consequently, the sensitive, primitive and fundamental role of emotions highlights the due diligence expected in the commercialization of emotional AI. Yet, what does that mean in practice for our emotional AI service?

4.2 *Certain Elements of Responsible Emotional AI Service Concept*

In order to evaluate the emotional AI service's impact on society and simultaneously its ethical endurance, it is essential to identify the risks emotional AI operations may entail. In terms of the emotional AI service discussed in this chapter, adverse effects

---

[64] European Commission (2011), p. 6.

[65] Vanhala et al. (2022), p. 24.

[66] Directive (EU) 2022/2464 as regards corporate sustainability reporting entered into force on January 5th, 2023. See also recently adopted Corporate Sustainability Due Diligence Directive.

[67] Vanhala et al. (2022), p. 242. See also AI HLEG (2019) p. 12 according to which also "adherence to ethical principles goes beyond formal compliance with existing laws".

[68] See Vanhala et al. (2022), p. 35.

[69] Policy Department for Citizens' Rights and Constitutional Affairs (2021), p. 57: "However, it is difficult to make any general statements about different degrees of ethical sensitivity, as context and purposes of both biometric categorisation and biometric detection may vary to a great extent".

on society associated with the service could include human rights violations, especially in terms of right to privacy;[70] the risk of discrimination and cultural bias; and adverse effects attributable to the imbalance of power between the actioners and limited reliability of the system.[71] Although deeper understanding and thorough identification of applicable risks and measures would require an extensive in-depth assessment, few insights follow.

The use of emotional data as raw materials of a service and as the core of the business emphasizes the importance of having a strong ethical foundation on which the service is built. Therefore, accountable measures to operationalize ethical values should be adopted. A code of conduct, a set of company norms also encouraged by the AI Act,[72] should be in place to embody the principles. Especially if rules of a code of conduct are made legally binding towards the value chain contractually,[73] particularly in terms of any processors of emotional data, it may help to build trust and reduce fears regarding emotional AI. Naturally, this is only the case if the code is implemented in practise through measurable actions and processes which are strictly complied with and that the compliance is monitored in reality.

In addition, particular attention should be given to the potential adverse effects attributable to the imbalance of power.[74] Measures to mitigate any risks regarding the service's underlying asymmetrical roles between employee and employer should be reflected at least as follows: (i) in the company's code of conduct; (ii) in the design and development choices regarding the service (whether to choose scenario I and/or II, what kind of data is collected, for what purpose and how); and (iii) in the communication policies and risk management processes. Having a continuous and transparent dialogue[75] with the end-users, i.e. the employees, is especially important when developing and using the emotional AI service. Questions to consider include: on what basis exactly should employees trust the company to process their emotions? How can the company sustain trust? Is either, neither or both of the service scenarios safe from the employee's and employer's points of view?

It is important that fears regarding AI are not underestimated, and that the concerns of stakeholders are taken into account in corporate responsibility work. Consequently, as part of its sustainability strategy, a company should proactively see beyond the mandatory legal framework and define, document, implement, monitor and communicate their own ethical standpoints and principles.

---

[70] On risks of AI generally, see especially UN. Human Rights Council (2019), p. 3.

[71] See the AI Act, Recital 44.

[72] See Article 95 of the AI Act regarding codes of conduct for voluntary application of specific requirements. See also the AI Act, Recital 165.

[73] See also Vanhala et al. (2022), pp. 165–168, where the authors present methods on establishing legally binding obligations related to corporate responsibility.

[74] See AI HLEG (2019), p. 12.

[75] For reference, see Article 35 (9) of the GDPR, according to which in terms of data protection impact assessment "where appropriate, the controller shall seek the views of data subjects or their representatives on the intended processing, without prejudice to the protection of commercial or public interests or the security of processing operations".

5 Conclusions

Today, an emotional AI service provider and deployer must navigate and make business strategic decisions in an uncertain situation. Currently, the shifting position of emotional AI in the legislative process, regulative dilemmas and complex ethical challenges epitomize the difficulty in dealing with this technology commercially.

In terms of the GDPR, neither business scenario I nor II is subject to a direct ban. However, in the absence of clear emotional data related provisions, a company operating in emotional AI service business must identify the applicable legal provisions on the basis of the nature of the information used to detect emotions. There are still issues, since (i) the use of system approaches collecting physiological data leads to the processing of special data; (ii) establishing consent as a valid legal basis is challenged by the imbalance of power; and (iii) managing the massive amount of data planned to be collected may not comply with data protection principles.

However, the controller company can attribute to the resolution of these issues by (i) if possible, favouring emotional AI approaches which do not collect data that falls under Article 9; (ii) adjusting the intended purpose of the system to a personal recommendation tool for the use (or non-use) and access of the employee only; (iii) fostering especially high-quality compliance work in terms of data protection principles and provisions which require assessing the risk the processing entails.

In terms of the AI Act, a review of the phases of the legislative process already shows how emotional AI has challenged the regulating of AI, especially the recent decision to prohibit the use of emotional AI in the workplace in Article 5 (1)(f) of the AI Act. Consequently, business scenarios I and II would likely both be subject to the prohibition.

However, this chapter argues that instead of legal bans tied simply to a physical area—the workplace—it would be more practical, innovation-friendly and proportionate to focus any bans of emotional AI to an actual harmful intended purpose or harm caused or likely to be caused by the solution. After all, this has been the logic of bans in some of the Article 5 subsections otherwise. It is undeniable that certain uses of emotional AI in the workplace should be restricted and the asymmetry of power should not be underestimated in any case. However, the ban in its current form is not in proportion to the objectives of the regulation. In particular, in terms of scenario I, it is unlikely that the service in a "personal recommendation system" form would cause significant harm or have any legal effects towards the employee.

Nonetheless, by adjusting their business idea quite drastically, there are ways in which the service provider could be able to offer a comparative emotional AI solution in the workplace on the EU market. These include establishing a safety or medical reason for the solution, or by using the system to only detect a physical state, such as fatigue of the employees. However, since emotions can be considered physical as well, the true meaning and effect of this exception is unclear. Similarly and simultaneously, the clarity and practicality of Article 5 (1)(f) is also undermined by the lack of definitions for the "workplace" and "medical and safety reasons". All these unclarities challenge the companies as interpreters and implementers of the law and may potentially lead to fragmentation of interpretations regarding the law and ultimately decrease in legal certainty. Therefore, it is important that these matters are specified by the legislator.

In addition to efforts to provide and deploy a legal emotional AI service, the emotional AI service provider and deployer must foster ethical business conduct and corporate social responsibility particularly diligently. The use of emotional data as the heart of a business emphasizes the importance of having a strong ethical backbone and accountable measures such as binding codes of conduct to operationalize the ethical values adopted. Since the role of emotions contributes to the due diligence by which any commercialization of emotional AI should be subjected, a company building its business around emotional AI should proactively see beyond the mandatory legal framework and have their own ethical standpoints and principles fostered and monitored.

References

Legislation

Directive (EU) 2022/2464 of the European Parliament and of the Council of 14 December 2022 amending Regulation (EU) No 537/2014, Directive 2004/109/EC, Directive 2006/43/EC and Directive 2013/34/EU, as regards corporate sustainability reporting. Available at: https://eur-lex.europa.eu/legal-content/EN/TXT/?uri=CELEX:32022L2464

Finnish Act on the Protection of Privacy in Working Life (759/2004, amendments up to 347/2019 included). Available in English: https://www.finlex.fi/en/laki/kaannokset/2004/en20040759.pdf

Directive (EU) 2024/1760 of the European Parliament and of the Council of 13 June 2024 on Corporate Sustainability Due Diligence and amending Directive (EU) 2019/1937 and Regulation (EU) 2023/2859. Available at: https://eur-lex.europa.eu/eli/dir/2024/1760/oj

Regulation (EU) 2024/1689 of the European Parliament and of the Council of 13 June 2024 laying down harmonised rules on artificial intelligence and amending Regulations (EC) No 300/2008, (EU) No 167/2013, (EU) No 168/2013, (EU) 2018/858, (EU) 2018/1139 and (EU) 2019/2144 and Directives 2014/90/EU, (EU) 2016/797 and (EU) 2020/1828 (Artificial Intelligence Act). Available at: https://eur-lex.europa.eu/eli/reg/2024/1689/oj

Regulation (EU) 2016/679 of the European Parliament and of the Council of 27 April 2016 on the protection of natural persons with regard to the processing of personal data and on the free movement of such data, and repealing Directive 95/46/EC (General Data Protection Regulation). Available at: https://eur-lex.europa.eu/legal-content/EN/TXT/PDF/?uri=CELEX:32016R0679

Literature and Other Sources

American Psychological Association (2018) APA Dictionary of Psychology. Available at: https://dictionary.apa.org/

Barrett LF, Adolphs R, Marsella S, Martinez AM, Pollak SD (2019) Emotional expressions reconsidered: challenges to inferring emotion from human facial movements. Psychol Sci Public

Interest 20(1):1–68. https://doi.org/10.1177/1529100619832930. Erratum in: Psychol Sci Public Interest. 2019 Dec; 20(3) pp. 165-166. PMID: 31313636; PMCID: PMC6640856. Available at: https://pubmed.ncbi.nlm.nih.gov/31313636/

Data Protection Working Party (2018) Guidelines on Automated individual decision-making and Profiling for the purposes of Regulation 2016/679. Available at: https://ec.europa.eu/newsroom/article29/items/612053/en

European Commission, Communication from the Commission to the European Parliament, The Council, The European Economic and Social Committee and the Committee of the Regions, A renewed EU strategy 2011-14 for Corporate Social Responsibility (2011). Available at: https://op.europa.eu/en/publication-detail/-/publication/ae5ada03-0dc3-48f8-9a32-0460e65ba7ed/language-en

European Data Protection Board (2019) Facial recognition in school renders Sweden's first GDPR fine. Available at: https://www.edpb.europa.eu/news/national-news/2019/facial-recognition-school-renders-swedens-first-gdpr-fine_sv

European Data Protection Board (2020) Guidelines 05/2020 on consent under Regulation 2016/679. Available at: https://www.edpb.europa.eu/our-work-tools/our-documents/guidelines/guidelines-052020-consent-under-regulation-2016679_en

European Parliamentary Research Service (2024) Artificial intelligence act. March 2024. Available at: https://www.europarl.europa.eu/RegData/etudes/BRIE/2021/698792/EPRS_BRI(2021)698792_EN.pdf

Häuselmann A, Sears A, Zard L, Fosch-Villaronga E (2023) EU Law and Emotion Data. 11th International Conference on Affective Computing and Intelligent Interaction (ACII). Available at: https://doi.org/10.48550/arXiv.2309.10776

High-Level Expert Group on Artificial Intelligence (HLEG) (2019) Ethics Guidelines for Trustworthy AI. Available at: https://digital-strategy.ec.europa.eu/en/library/ethics-guidelines-trustworthy-ai

Juvani A (2019) Työstressin vaikutus työuriin. Lääketieteellinen aikakauskirja Duodecim, 2019; 135(21):2057–2064. Available at: https://www.duodecimlehti.fi/duo15224

Policy Department for Citizens' Rights and Constitutional Affairs (2021) Biometric Recognition and Behavioural Detection. Available at: https://www.europarl.europa.eu/RegData/etudes/STUD/2021/696968/IPOL_STU(2021)696968_EN.pdf

Purdy M, Zealley J, Maseli O (2019) The risks of using AI to interpret human emotions. Harv Bus Rev. Available at: https://hbr.org/2019/11/the-risks-of-using-ai-to-interpret-human-emotions

Scherer U (2016) Regulating artificial intelligence systems: risks, challenges, competencies, and strategies. Harv J Law Technol 29(2) Available at: http://euro.ecom.cmu.edu/program/law/08-732/AI/Scherer.pdf

Schneiderman N, Ironson G, Siegel SD (2005) Stress and health: psychological, behavioral, and biological determinants. Annu Rev Clin Psychol 2005:607–628. Available at: https://www.ncbi.nlm.nih.gov/pmc/articles/PMC2568977/

Steindl E (2022) Does the European data protection framework adequately protect our emotions? Emotion tech in light of the draft AI act and its interplay with the GDPR. Eur Data Protect Law Rev (EDPL) 8(2):311–319. HeinOnline

UN. Human Rights Council (2019) The right to privacy in the digital age. Available at: https://digitallibrary.un.org/record/3837297?v=pdf

Vanhala A, Ristaniemi M, Dahlqvist M, Heasman L, Lautjärvi K, Kumpula A, Lehtonen A, Malminen T, Mähönen J, Rajavuori M, Salminen J, Turunen T, Viljanen M, Wasastjerna M, Wuolijoki S (2022) Yritysvastuu & Oikeus. Kauppakamari, Helsinki, p 459

WIPO Magazine (2019) Artificial intelligence: the new electricity. 3/2019. Available at: https://www.wipo.int/wipo_magazine/en/2019/03/article_0001.html

Design Science Methodology for AI-Based Contract Design Research

Jouko Nuottila, Anna Hurmerinta-Haanpää, and Hilja Autto

Abstract Contract design matters. The literature confirms that different contract designs can induce varying emotions, feelings, behaviour, and views of the contractual relationship. Specifically, prevention- and promotion-framed contracts and contract clauses seem to induce different emotions, which have been shown to impact the development of trust and even relationship performance. In addition, as many traditional contracts lack a design perspective, they may induce many negative emotions, such as confusion and frustration, among contract users. On the other hand, well-designed contracts can empower and engage contract users.

Although (emotional) AI enables new venues for contract design and legal technology related research, it requires the adoption of new research methodologies. This chapter presents a novel methodology for legal research—design science methodology—that originates from computer science and serves a dual purpose: creating new scientific knowledge while developing and evaluating an information systems artefact. To illustrate how the methodology can be applied in practice, the chapter presents a research setting in which design science methodology can be used for developing and evaluating an AI-based contract design tool that is based on the guiding principles of proactive contract theory and that takes into account the social and psycho-cognitive effects of contracts.

J. Nuottila · H. Autto
University of Lapland, Rovaniemi, Finland
e-mail: Jouko.Nuottila@ulapland.fi; Hilja.Autto@ulapland.fi

A. Hurmerinta-Haanpää (✉)
Aalto University, Espoo, Finland
e-mail: anna.hurmerinta-haanpaa@aalto.fi

R. Ballardini et al. (eds.), *Emotional Data Applications and Regulation of Artificial Intelligence in Society*, Law, Governance and Technology Series 69,
https://doi.org/10.1007/978-3-031-80111-2_16

1 Introduction

Legal contract research has been mostly interested in the theoretical or doctrinal studies of contracts and contract law.[1] However, more recently, legal researchers have started to study empirical realities of contracts leading to the use of both qualitative and quantitative research methods.[2] Also, with the rise of AI, scholars have started to study possibilities and challenges related to the use of AI in contract design and contract interpretation.[3] To develop this field of research further, this chapter presents a novel methodology for legal research[4]—*design science methodology*[5]—that originates from computer science and serves a dual purpose: creating new scientific knowledge while developing and evaluating an information systems artefact.[6] To illustrate how the methodology can be applied in practice, we present a research setting for developing and evaluating an AI-based contract design tool that is based on the guiding principles of proactive contract theory and that takes into account the social and psycho-cognitive effects of contracts.

The chapter proceeds as follows. Following the introduction, we present the guiding principles of proactive contract theory and contract design research that the developed contract design tool will be based on. Thereafter, we present the design science methodology and describe how it can be applied in a research setting developing and evaluating an AI-based contract design tool. Finally, a short summary concludes the chapter.

2 Our Theoretical Approach to Contract Design: Proactive Contract Theory

2.1 Guiding Principles of Proactive Contract Theory

Proactive contract theory focuses on the operational side of contracts to ensure that the parties reach the desired outcomes of their agreement. Thus, contracts need to focus on (1) facilitating what is desirable and (2) preventing undesired outcomes. These points are called the promotive and preventive dimensions of proactive contract theory, and they are grounded in the psychological theory of regulatory

[1] Silverstein (2021), p. 224; Hurmerinta-Haanpää and Berger-Walliser (2024).

[2] For Finnish empirical research by contract law scholars, see e.g., Nuottila et al. (2016); Viljanen et al. (2018a, b); Hurmerinta-Haanpää (2021); Laurikainen-Klami (2022a, b); Kaave (2022).

[3] See e.g., Arbel and Becher (2022); Kolt (2022); Autto et al. (2024).

[4] Dickhaut et al. (2024) have earlier applied Design science research approach to develop design patterns for lawful AI-based assistants (such as Amazon's Alexa).

[5] Kuechler and Vaishnavi (2008); Peffers et al. (2012); Dresch et al. (2015). For more about the design science methodology, see Sub-chapter 3.

[6] Hevner et al. (2004); Kuechler and Vaishnavi (2008).

focus (RFT).[7] While the preventive dimension aims to prevent problems before they occur, the promotive dimension is aimed at detecting and realizing opportunities to enable business success.[8]

In addition, the promotive and preventive dimensions can be applied to contract *framing*, which refers to heuristics that guide decision making by directing a reader's attention to certain messages or events while dismissing other elements.[9] Research on contract framing suggests that the optimal framing of a contract depends on transactional attributes[10] and the desired type of interorganizational relationship. While preventive contract clauses that frame goals as obligations and describe safeguards in terms of penalties are better suited for relationships that require precision, promotively framed contracts facilitate experimental, flexible business relationships and give rise to greater trust.[11]

Moreover, proactive contract theory adopts a process view on contracts,[12] seeing them as dynamic and adaptable business tools that have multiple functions. For example, while contracts need to safeguard party interests and rights, they also need to coordinate responsibilities, build frames for collaboration, be tools for intra- and interfirm communication, and, to an ever-growing extent, build frameworks for sustainable business relationships.[13]

Proactive contract theory gives much emphasis to contract design and user-centricity.[14] Contract design can cover the design of the contract, including content, language and presentation, and the design of the contracting process. Content design designs the substance content of the contract, which varies according to the purpose and nature of the contract, the objectives of the parties, their roles, rights and

---

[7]Regulatory focus refers to the different strategic means that people and organizations use to obtain desirable outcomes and avoid negative outcomes. According to RFT, introduced by professor of psychology and business Tory Higgins, two regulatory focuses affect people's emotions and drive behavior: preventive and promotive. Preventively focused people see goals as minimal targets that must be met. If the goal is not met, a person with preventive regulatory focus experiences high-intensity negative emotions. Conversely, if the person attains the goal, they experience low-intensity positive emotions. Promotive regulatory focus, in turn, leads to the interpretation of a goal as maximal. Thus, people with promotive regulatory focus experience low-intensity negative emotions if the goal is not met and high-intensity positive emotions if it is (see e.g., Higgins (1997)). For more about RFT in the context of proactive contracting, see Siedel and Haapio (2010), pp. 660–661.

[8]See e.g., Haapio (2013), pp. 38–39.

[9]Tversky and Kahneman (1981), p. 453; Weber (2017), p. 747.

[10]Transactional attributes refer to transaction's distinct characteristics that determine the best way to govern the transaction. According to transaction cost economics, the main transactional attributes are asset specificity, frequency, uncertainty, complexity, and interdependence. See e.g., Williamson (1979), pp. 233–261; Schepker et al. (2014), pp. 195–198.

[11]See e.g., Weber et al. (2011), pp. 196–198; Weber and Mayer (2011), pp. 58–61; Weber and Bauman (2019); Rich et al. (2022).

[12]For more about the process view of proactive contracting, see Kujala et al. (2015), p. 96.

[13]Hurmerinta-Haanpää (2021), p. 77.

[14]Passera and Haapio (2013), pp. 40–43.

obligations, and the legal framework. In turn, language design is the designing of contract language to make it more understandable, using tools such as plain language, while designing presentation refers to the structure, layout and visual appearance of the contract.[15] For user-centricity, it is decisive that insights from information design research, such as knowledge on the literacy proficiencies of people, memory, information processing and overload, and understanding, are taken into account, and information design methods, such as experimentation, user-testing and prototyping, are used in the contract design process.[16]

Finally, proactive contract theory sees contract design as a multiprofessional endeavour, requiring input from not only legal but also commercial, technical, and other professionals. The reason for this is that different professionals hold different kinds of contracting capabilities: while lawyers are well-suited to plan and draft legal clauses, such as clauses on dispute resolution and intellectual property rights (IPRs), engineers have been shown to be more apt to design more flexible and experimental contract clauses.[17] Moreover, as the end users can represent different professions, a multiprofessional contract design team ensures that the various user groups and their varying information needs are taken into account in the process.[18]

2.2 *Proactive Contract Design and Emotions*

In addition to the guiding principles of proactive contract theory, the developed contract design tool is guided by contract design research that relates to the social and psycho-cognitive effects of contracts. Essentially, this research shows that contract design can induce varying emotions, feelings, behaviour, and views of the contractual relationship.

First, different contract frames seem to induce different emotions, which have been shown to impact the development of trust and even relationship performance. As described earlier, research on contract framing suggests that a contractual frame must be selected on the basis of transactional attributes, task characteristics and the type of relationship desired.[19] Essentially, preventive contract-framing that highlights obligations and penalties for non-compliance is a better fit for mission-critical exchanges where the continuation of the relationship is of lesser importance, while promotive contract-framing supports more exploratory, collaborative, and

[15] See e.g., Hurmerinta-Haanpää (2022), pp. 164–165; Haapio (2013), pp. 57–58; Passera (2017), p. 62.

[16] Hurmerinta-Haanpää and Nuottila (forthcoming).

[17] Mayer and Weber (2009), pp. 14–16.

[18] See e.g., Haapio (2006); Nystén-Haarala et al. (2010); Siedel and Haapio (2010); Haapio (2013); Kujala et al. (2015); Nuottila et al. (2016).

[19] See e.g., Weber et al. (2011), pp. 196–198; Weber and Mayer (2011), pp. 58–61; Weber and Bauman (2019); Rich et al. (2022).

long- term relationships.[20] In addition, framing seems to influence the creation and development of interorganizational trust.[21] Specifically, there is evidence that promotively framed contracts give rise to greater trust than preventively framed contracts.[22]

Second, traditional contracts that lack a design perspective seem to induce many negative emotions among contract users, such as confusion and frustration, while contracts that are designed according to the guiding principles of proactive contract theory induce positive emotions. For example, in a contract design project reported in Passera et al. (2016), researchers conducted a single case study with a sales team to create visualizations and improve understandability of a company's operations and maintenance (O&M) outsourcing agreement. In the study, the researchers found that visualizations developed during the project, such as service concept maps and pricing model diagrams, helped to bridge three knowledge gaps in the contracting process: interfirm; cross-professional; and between contracting phases. Also, the researchers suggested visualizations to allow for more effective communication and coordination by increasing clarity and helping the parties to frame the contract and their burgeoning relationship positively.[23]

Similarly, in studies by Passera (2015, 2018), a better structured and visualized contract or a user guide to contracts were found to support both user comprehension and user experience.[24] In the research reported in Passera (2015), the contract used in the experiment was a tenancy agreement for student apartments, with the participants being master's students from different European universities. The experiment compared the performance of three groups, one using the original, text-only version of the tenancy agreement; a second in which the text was re-ordered more logically, divided into bullet lists, and given more informative headings; and a third where the better structured document was also complemented with thematic companion icons, each positioned next to a section of the agreement. Relating to emotions, the visual/restructured contract was evaluated as much more pleasant to use as well as more useful and functional. In turn, research reported in Passera (2018) compared the terms of public procurement of services (the JYSE 2009 SERVICES)[25] to a visual guide of the terms developed in the research. The comparison was made via an experimental evaluation, and it was complemented with pre-test and post-test questionnaires and qualitative focus group discussions for civil servants. Compared to using the original JYSE document, the results from the research indicated that the

[20] Mayer and Weber (2009), pp. 12–13; Weber and Mayer (2011), pp. 58–61; Weber et al. (2011), pp. 196–198.

[21] Mayer and Weber (2009); Bertrandias et al. (2010); Weber and Mayer (2011); Weber and Bauman (2019).

[22] Weber and Bauman (2019).

[23] Passera et al. (2016).

[24] Passera (2015, 2018).

[25] Ministry of Finance, Finland (2009).

civil servants experienced a higher level of positive affect and a lower level of negative affect when using the visual guide.[26]

3 Design Science Methodology

Design science methodology[27] originates from information systems and software engineering research[28] and is widely used in multidisciplinary human-computer interaction studies.[29]

Following the epistemological foundations of information systems research,[30] design science methodology is based on pragmatism,[31] which views truth as provisional[32] and situational[33] rather than absolute and fixed.[34] In scientific inquiry, pragmatism provides a tool for continuous reflection, in which theories are instruments for scientific work rather than the ultimate goal of research.[35] Pragmatism closely links theory and practice[36] and provides a good foundation for methodologies used in social sciences,[37] business and management research,[38] and information systems research.[39]

Design science methodology creates new scientific knowledge in the process of developing and evaluating an information systems artefact[40] that will address an identified problem.[41] The artefact can include social innovations and it can develop new properties of technical, social, or informational resources to create solutions to an identified problem.[42]

Design science methodology has already been used in a wide variety of research settings. In the field of software engineering and computer science, research focuses on studying technology systems and the technical implementation problems of the

---

[26] Passera (2018).

[27] Kuechler and Vaishnavi (2008); Peffers et al. (2012); Dresch et al. (2015).

[28] Peffers et al. (2007).

[29] Adikari et al. (2006).

[30] See e.g., Goldkuhl (2004, 2012).

[31] Not to be confused with legal pragmatism (see e.g., Posner (1989)).

[32] Jacobs (2010).

[33] McCaslin (2008).

[34] Jacobs (2010).

[35] Peirce (1905); James (1907).

[36] Greenwood and Levin (2005).

[37] Joas (1993); Morgan (2014).

[38] Pfeffer (2008); Simpson (2018).

[39] Goldkuhl (2004); Hevner et al. (2004).

[40] Hevner et al. (2004); Kuechler and Vaishnavi (2008).

[41] Peffers et al. (2007); Wieringa (2014).

[42] Peffers et al. (2007); Dresch et al. (2015).

systems.[43] Also, the methodology is applied for application and user experience studies of information systems,[44] for example, in the context of management information systems,[45] e-learning solutions,[46] smart grids[47] and augmented reality applications.[48] Moreover, design science methodology is used for the development of autonomous robot systems.[49] Finally, design science methodology has been used in social research context, as in developing electric mobility services in smart cities.[50]

The research process of the design science methodology includes several stages. Though there are many descriptions of the research process in the literature that vary in their details, the overall process is always similar. Here, we present a process that is based on Peffers et al. (2006)[51] and Venable et al. (2017).[52] The research process is illustrated in Fig. 1.

As shown in Fig. 1, *Problem identification and motivation* refers to the research interest in question. It is a current state problem definition added with a desire to change the current state towards something better with an effective artefactual solution.[53] At this stage, the goal is also to achieve an aligned understanding of the problem between researchers and a possible audience or users of the solution.

Objectives of a solution is a stage in which researchers infer the objectives for the planned solution rationally from the problem specification.[54] At this stage, researchers should describe how the artefact is going to solve the problem.

At the *Design and development* stage, the needed software components are designed, developed, acquired and integrated to build the solution,[55] while at the *Demonstration and evaluation* stage, the artefact is taken into use with intended users,[56] where researchers observe and measure how well the artefact supports the solution to the problem. The evaluation can include both quantitative and qualitative performance measures. Based on the evaluation, researchers decide whether to iterate back to the Design and development stage to improve the solution or continue to Communication stage.

---

[43] Ozdenizci et al. (2010); Schinle et al. (2020); Halonen et al. (2015).

[44] Adikari et al. (2011).

[45] Rajamäki et al. (2022).

[46] Schmitt (2019).

[47] Vereno et al. (2022).

[48] Haugstvedt and Krogstie (2012).

[49] Garcıa et al. (2018).

[50] Bokolo et al. (2020).

[51] Peffers et al. (2006).

[52] Venable et al. (2017).

[53] Peffers et al. (2006).

[54] Peffers et al. (2006).

[55] Peffers et al. (2006); Venable et al. (2017).

[56] Venable et al. (2017).

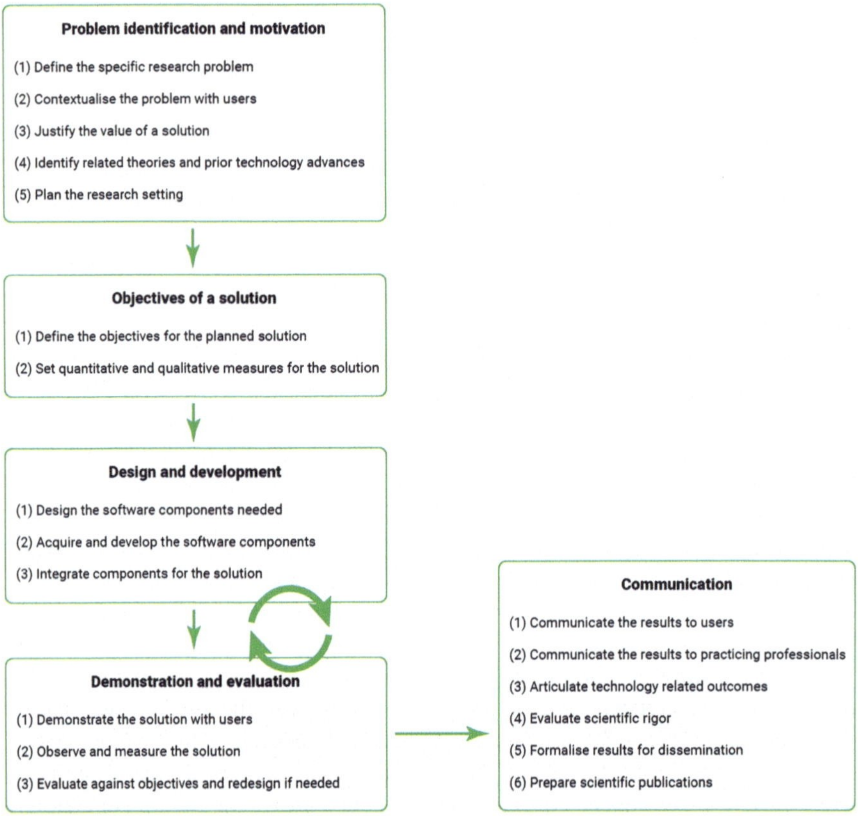

Fig. 1 Research process of design science methodology.

Finally, at the *Communication* stage, the results of the research are communicated to practicing professionals, the research community and other relevant audiences.[57] In scientific publications, the research is reported following the common structure for empirical papers, including problem definition, literature review, data collection, analysis, discussion and conclusion.

The systematic and structured research process qualify design science methodology as a rigorous scientific research approach that serves a dual purpose: solving a practical problem and creating new scientific knowledge. To illustrate how design science methodology can be applied in practice, we next present a research setting for developing and evaluating an AI-based contract design tool.

[57] Peffers et al. (2006).

Table 1 Artefact composition, research team composition, user, and artefact development environment in different research phases

	Phase 1	Phase 2	Phase 3
Artefact composition	ChatGPT + Plugins	OpenAI API to ChatGPT + Custom developed software including document upload	Open AI Studio integrated in Azure development environment + custom developed software
Research team composition	Contract Design Research Team	Contract Design Research Team + Computer Science Team	Contract Design Research Team + Computer Science Team
User	Contract Designer (Researcher)	Contract Designer (Researcher)	Contract Designer (Researcher)
Artefact development environment	Commercial version of ChatGPT	Commercial version of Open AI API + Software development environment	Commercial version of Azure development environment + OpenAI Studio + OpenAI Services + Software development environment

4 Applying Design Science Methodology for AI-Based Contract Design Research

Our research setting includes four phases that we will describe in detail below. The first three phases focus on developing an AI-based contract design tool and the fourth phase on demonstrating and evaluating the tool. While the first two phases have already been conducted and reported in detail in Autto et al. (2024),[58] the final phases are still in progress. The development of the contract design tool is based on the guiding principles of proactive contract theory and research on the psycho-cognitive effects of contracts.

4.1 *Phases 1–3: Designing and Developing the Tool*

In our research setting, the design and development of the artefact is done in three phases, which are illustrated in Table 1. The table describes artefact composition, research team composition, user, and artefact development environment of each phase. Phase one was conducted solely by contract design researchers, while the other phases were conducted in collaboration with computer scientists. In all three phases, the user for the artefact was a contract design researcher.

[58] Autto et al. (2024).

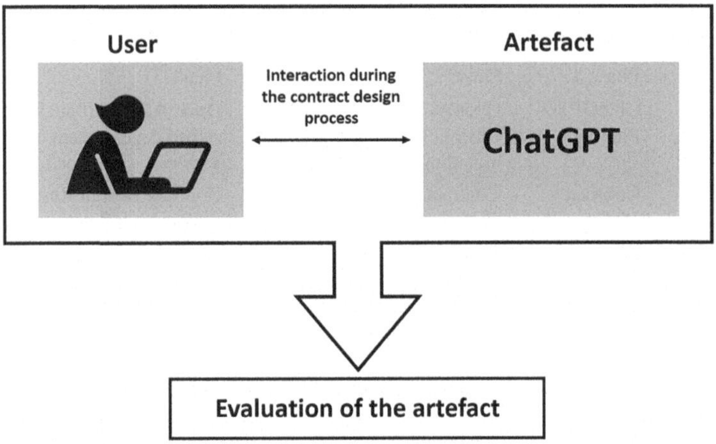

Fig. 2 Phase 1 research setting

4.1.1 Phase 1

The first phase focused on studying how a publicly available AI system specialized in natural language processing with a pre-trained large language model can help shape the content, language and presentation of contracts, according to the guiding principles of proactive contract theory. After evaluating the options, we selected ChatGPT[59] to be used as the publicly available AI system. Moreover, we chose the European Union's Ecodesign for Sustainable Products Regulation (ESPR)[60] as our regulatory framework. The phase one research setting is illustrated in Fig. 2.

In this phase, we first requested ChatGPT to suggest issues that contracting parties should consider in light of the ESPR. ChatGPT provided a good starting point for planning the content of the contract, including references to relevant legal and other sources. Second, we continued our research by requesting ChatGPT to draft contract clauses. Language wise, the first output was rather legal jargon and not very user-friendly. Next, we requested ChatGPT to explain these clauses in ordinary language to an engineer responsible for developing new products and product information. As it translated legalese into ordinary language, ChatGPT successfully provided clearer explanations and improved sentence structure. Third, we requested ChatGPT to produce a layered layout and arrange it in a specific way: the main clause on the right, an explanation in the middle, and FAQ headings on the left. ChatGPT not only wrote the content but organised it the way we wanted, for example, in columns.

[59] ChatGPT is developed and owned by a company called OpenAI.

[60] Regulation (EU) 2024/1781 of the European Parliament and of the Council of 13 June 2024 establishing a framework for the setting of ecodesign requirements for sustainable products, amending Directive (EU) 2020/1828 and Regulation (EU) 2023/1542 and repealing Directive 2009/125/EC.

While ChatGPT had several features that supported contract designer's work in improving contract content, language and presentation, according to the guiding principles of proactive contract theory, it lacked some important features to make contract design more efficient. In particular, we missed an opportunity to train the system to behave exactly as we desired. Also, the system was not capable of adding visual information and graphical instructions into the contracts. Furthermore, uploading training or fine-tuning data was not possible; the only option was to copy and paste instructions as prompts for the ChatGPT. Based on this phase, we concluded that there is a need to modify the AI system so that it would be more helpful for contract designers.

4.1.2 Phase 2

The findings of the first phase helped us to understand the capabilities and restrictions of a publicly available AI system for contract design purposes. For the second phase, we selected the Open AI's API which is an application programming interface to be used for interaction with the functions of ChatGPT. In this phase, the contract design research team defined the features to be developed while the computer science team was responsible for developing the features. The most important features defined and developed in this phase were:

- The possibility to upload documents that presented examples of good contract design in order to train the AI system to perform better and consistently;
- The possibility to provide visual design patterns[61] and graphical elements for contracts.

The phase two research setting is illustrated in Fig. 3.

The development of the features was done in two iterations. During the first iteration, the functionality of the Open AI API was analysed and programming was done to verify the correct functionality of the provided API. The second iteration focused on feature development. Unfortunately, the API provided by the OpenAI did not make it possible for one to upload complete documents to fine-tune the behaviour of ChatGPT. Instead, sending restricted amount of data in text format was allowed, which meant that we could not use example contract documents in the way we thought we could. Moreover, as the API introduced a maximum memory allocation per session, there was a limit on the amount of data one could upload at once, and a limit on the cumulative amount of data.

The functionality of ChatGPT through the API was similar to the system in phase one. For example, ChatGPT could produce simplification of contract documents. However, as in phase one, the system was not capable of producing graphical

[61] For contract design patterns, see e.g., The Contract Design Pattern Library by WorldCC Foundation, Stefania Passera, and Helena Haapio, available at https://contract-design.worldcc.com/ (accessed 2 April, 2024).

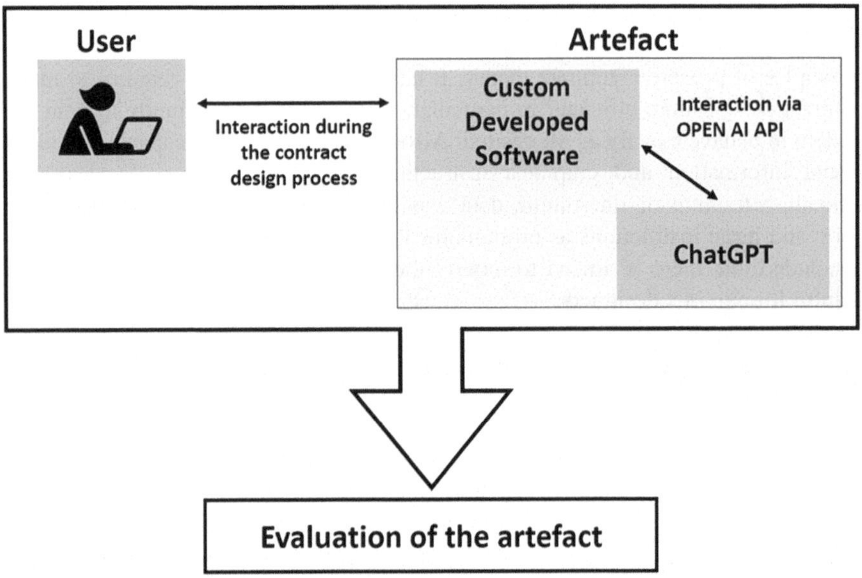

Fig. 3 Phase 2 research setting

contract design elements such as visual patterns or simplifying icons and other graphical presentations. Thus, there was a need for a more capable technological environment to be developed in phase three.

4.1.3 Phase 3

Based on the evaluation of the market, we decided to conduct phase three with Azure OpenAI Studio by Microsoft, which offers OpenAI Studio and OpenAI Services to their current Azure customers. Though Azure OpenAI Studio provides access to similar features as ChatGPT, it has additional customization features. Furthermore, as it is integrated in the Azure development environment, it also provides a lot of functionalities to develop features and user interface. In addition, the environment enables one to operate with one's own documents as training and fine-tuning data. The phase three research setting is illustrated in Fig. 4.

4.2 *Phase 4: Demonstrating and Evaluating the Tool in Redesigning Project Contracts*

In phase four, which is yet to be conducted, we will demonstrate the artefact and evaluate the developed contract design tool in the context of complex industrial

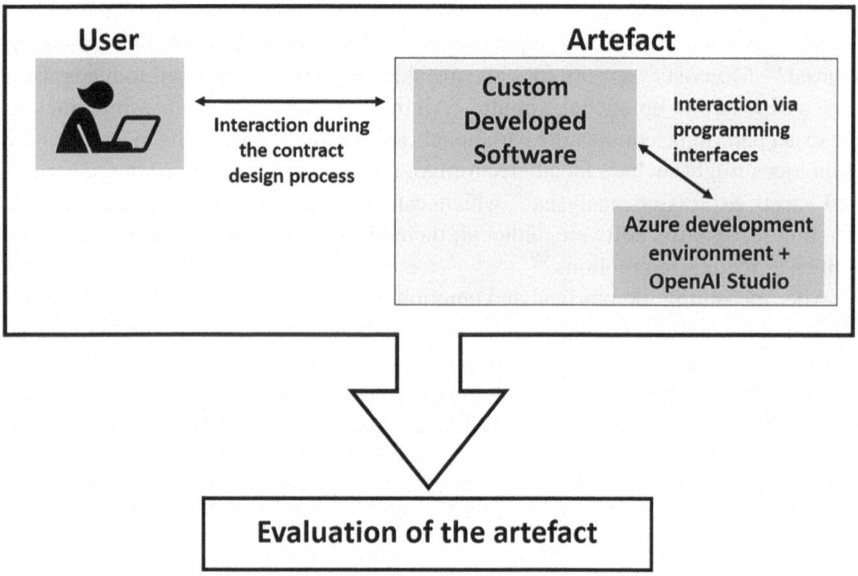

Fig. 4 Phase 3 research setting

project contracts by observing selected contract users in a laboratory environment. We will work with selected companies that operate in complex industrial project settings, which require deep collaboration between project participants.

In this phase, we will first request the developed tool to use contract design patterns that are based on the guiding principles of proactive contract theory, including organization of the contract document, framing, layering, and visuals, amongst others, to improve existing project contracts to facilitate collaboration without compromising the legal rigor of the contract.

Second, once the tool had been used to redesign the contracts, we will study the emotional responses of selected contract users, such as project managers, to the redesigned contract. The selected contract users will be invited to a laboratory to analyse the emotions induced by the redesigned contracts and to evaluate their influence on collaboration characteristics, for example, trust. Research participants will be seated in front of a specifically equipped computer, and they will be connected to sensors measuring markers for their emotional reactions. There are several techniques for this kind of measurement. For example, eye movement tracking is one of the most used measurement techniques and it includes many variables and applications for controlled user observation.[62] With digital tools, eye movement tracking enables the recording of heatmaps,[63] which show the parts in which the user spends the most time when reading the contract. This might indicate

[62] Reyneke (2019).

[63] Georges et al. (2016); Courtemanche et al. (2018).

some of the problematic or complex clauses in the contract. As another example, it is possible to track changes in pupil size, which can be used to identify emotional arousal.[64] Moreover, sensors for galvanic skin response can be used to recognize a user's exposure to emotional stimuli.[65] All these methods are useful while tracking the exact part of the contract the participants are reading. Some of the more advanced techniques might include facial electromyography,[66] facial action coding system,[67] and facial expression analysis,[68] which can be integrated with an advanced AI emotion recognition software, although there are some controversies on their capabilities to recognize emotions.[69]

After measuring the physical and emotional reactions to the redesigned contract, we will also interview the participants to evaluate their views on the original and the redesigned contracts and to see if the views are aligned with the measured physical and emotional reactions. As is often the case with research applying design science methodology, the tool will be likely further developed based on the results of the observations and interviews. Finally, the results of the research will be communicated to practicing professionals, such as project managers, lawyers, and contract designers, research community and other relevant audiences.

The phase four research setting is illustrated in Fig. 5.

5 Conclusions

In this chapter, we introduced the reader to a novel methodology in legal research—design science methodology—and described how it can be applied in AI-based contract design research. The example research concerns the development and evaluation of an AI-based contract design tool that is based on the guiding principles of proactive contract theory and that takes into account the social and psycho-cognitive effects of contracts.

We argue that design science methodology could be used more widely in legal research, especially in relation to contract design research or legal technology related research which use (emotional) AI to develop different information systems artefacts. The methodology is well suited for these kinds of pragmatic research projects

[64] Reyneke (2019).

[65] Shi et al.(2007).

[66] Munim et al. (2017).

[67] Ekman and Friesen (1976); Yurkin and Saradgishvili (2023).

[68] Lopez-Aguilar et al. (2021).

[69] Emotional AI still faces significant challenges compared to human capabilities as it does not understand human emotions in the same nuanced, contextual and culturally diverse way. For example, current emotional AI systems lack cultural and racial sensitivity, and the interpretation of gestures or tone of voice can vary significantly between cultures. See e.g., Somers (2019). Thus, in our research, the analysis by emotional AI would be complemented by human-made analysis.

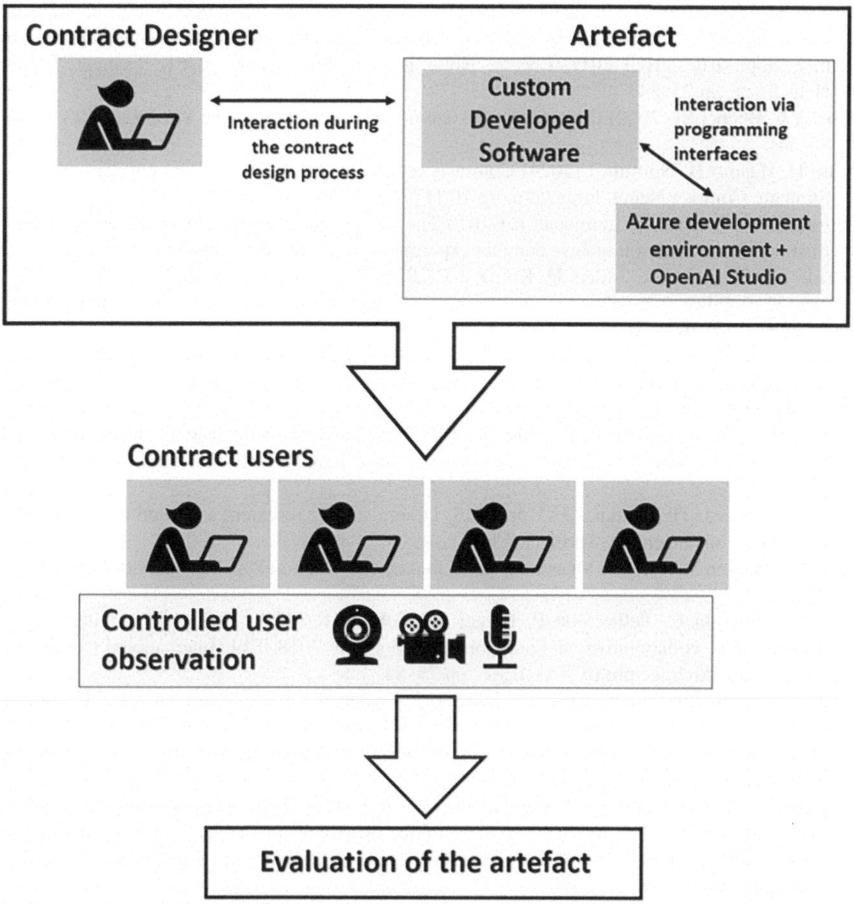

Fig. 5 Phase 4 research setting

by offering a structured and systematic process to develop an information systems artefact and create new scientific knowledge.

By introducing a new methodology for legal technology related research, we hope to widen the methodological narratives and encourage the use of different interdisciplinary research approaches in legal research.

References

Adikari S, McDonald C, Collings P (2006) A design science approach to an HCI research project. In: Kjeldskov J, Paay J (eds) Proceedings of the 18th Australia conference on computer-human interaction: design: activities, artefacts and environments. Association for Computing Machinery, New York, pp 429–432

Adikari S, McDonald C, Campbell J (2011) A design science framework for designing and assessing user experience. In: Jacko JA (ed) Human-computer interaction. design and development approaches. HCI 2011. Lecture Notes in Computer Science 6761. Springer, Berlin, Heidelberg, pp 25–34

Arbel YA, Becher SI (2022) Contracts in the age of smart readers. George Wash Law Rev 90(1): 83–146

Autto H, Haapio H, Nuottila J (2024) Contracts rethought and redesigned: a new era with AI. J Strategic Contract Negot. https://doi.org/10.1177/20555636241261278

Bertrandias L, Fréchet M, Lumineau L (2010) The role of contract framing in the emergence of trust: evidence from a franchise contract experiment. Acad Manage Ann Meet Proc 1:1–6

Bokolo AJ, Petersen SA, Ahlers D, Krogstie J (2020) Big data driven multi-tier architecture for electric mobility as a service in smart cities: a design science approach. Int J Energy Sector Manage 14(5):1023–1047

Courtemanche F, Léger P-M, Dufresne A, Fredette L-LMÉ, Sénécal S (2018) Physiological heatmaps: a tool for visualizing user's emotional reactions. Multimedia Tools Appl 77: 11547–11574

Dickhaut E, Janson A, Söllner M, Leimeister JM (2024) Lawfulness by design – development and evaluation of lawful design patterns to consider legal requirements. Eur J Inform Syst 33(4): 441–468

Dresch A, Lacerda DP, Antunes JAV Jr (2015) Design science research: a method for science and technology advancement. Springer, Cham

Ekman P, Friesen WV (1976) Measuring facial movement. Environ Psychol Nonverb Behav 1:56–75

Garcıa S, Menghi C, Pelliccione P, Berger T, Wohlrab R (2018, April) An architecture for decentralized, collaborative, and autonomous robots. In: 2018 IEEE International Conference on Software Architecture (ICSA). IEEE, pp 75–84

Georges V, Courtemanche F, Sénécal S, Baccino T, Fredette M, Léger P-M (2016) UX Heatmaps: mapping user experience on visual interfaces. In: Proceedings of the 2016 CHI Conference on Human Factors in Computing Systems. Association for Computing Machinery, New York, pp 4850–4860.

Goldkuhl, G (2004) Meanings of pragmatism: ways to conduct information systems research. In: Proceedings of the 2nd International Conference on Action in Language, Organisations and Information Systems (ALOIS). Institutionen för datavetenskap, Linköping University, Linköping, pp 13–16.

Goldkuhl G (2012) Pragmatism vs interpretivism in qualitative information systems research. Eur J Inform Syst 21(2):135–146

Greenwood DJ, Levin M (2005) Reform of the social sciences and of universities through action research. In: Denzin NK, Lincoln YS (eds) The sage handbook of qualitative research, 3rd edn. Sage Publications Incorporated, Thousand Oaks, pp 43–64

Haapio H (2006) Business success and problem prevention through Proactive Contracting. In: Wahlgreen P (ed) A proactive approach. Scandinavian studies in law 49. Stockholm Institute for Scandinavian Law, Stockholm, pp 149–194

Haapio H (2013) Next generation contracts: a paradigm shift. Lexpert, Helsinki

Halonen R, Martikainen O, Naumov V, Zhang Y (2015, December) Algorithm for time-constrained paths to deliver services. In: 2015 15th International Conference on Intelligent Systems Design and Applications (ISDA). IEEE, pp 569–574

Haugstvedt AC, Krogstie J (2012, November) Mobile augmented reality for cultural heritage: A technology acceptance study. In: 2012 IEEE international symposium on mixed and augmented reality (ISMAR). IEEE, pp 247–255

Hevner AR, March ST, Park J, Ram S (2004) Design science in information systems research. MIS Quart 28(1):75–105

Higgins ET (1997) Beyond pleasure and pain. Am Psychol 52(12):1280–1300

Hurmerinta-Haanpää A (2021) The many functions of contracts – how companies use contracts in interorganizational exchange relations. University of Turku, Turku
Hurmerinta-Haanpää A (2022) The functional contracting framework: assessing the impacts of contract functions, framing, and regulatory focus. In: Corrales Compagnucci M, Haapio H, Fenwick M (eds) Research handbook on contract design. Edward Elgar Publishing, Cheltenham, pp 158–179
Hurmerinta-Haanpää A, Berger-Walliser G (2024) Joint value creation: a functional, proactive approach to contract governance. Am Bus Law J 61(4):261–283
Hurmerinta-Haanpää A, Nuottila J (forthcoming) The proactive contracting approach: the first 25 years and beyond. In: Masson A, Bouthinon-Dumas H, Voss WG, Do Carmo Silva JM (eds) Handbook on law & management. Oxford University Press, Oxford
Jacobs DC (2010) Pragmatism. In: Mills AJ, Durepos G, Wiebe E (eds) Encyclopedia of case study research. Sage Publications Incorporated, Thousand Oaks, pp 724–725
James W (1907) Pragmatism: a new name for some old ways of thinking. Longmans, Green & Co, New York
Joas H (1993) Pragmatism and social theory. The University of Chicago Press, Chicago
Kaave P (2022) Irti vakiosopimustoiminnan polkuriippuvuudesta ennakoivalla sopimisella: Empiirinen tutkimus pankkien yritysluottosopimuksista. Lakimiesliiton Kustannus, Helsinki
Kolt N (2022) predicting consumer contracts. Berkeley Technol Law J 37(1):71–138
Kuechler B, Vaishnavi V (2008) On theory development in design science research: anatomy of a research project. Eur J Inform Syst 17:489–504
Kujala J, Nystén-Haarala S, Nuottila J (2015) Flexible contracting in project business. Int J Managing Projects Bus 8(1):92–106
Laurikainen-Klami R (2022a) Urakkasopimussuhteiden ongelmakohdat ja funktionaalinen sopimusteoria niiden ymmärtämisessä. Lakimies 1:33–58
Laurikainen-Klami R (2022b) Insentiivirakenteen toiminta ja vaikutus urakka-allianssissa. Liikejuridiikka 1:36–65
Lopez-Aguilar AA, Bustamante-Bello R, Navarro-Tuch SA (2021) Advanced system to measure UX in online learning environments. In: Proceedings of the 2021 IEEE Global Engineering Education Conference (EDUCON). IEEE, pp 779–782
Mayer KJ, Weber L (2009) Unpacking contract capabilities: shaping behavior by implementing appropriate contract framing. Atlanta Competitive Advantage Conference Paper. https://doi.org/10.2139/ssrn.1349247. Accessed 2 April 2024
McCaslin ML (2008) Pragmatism. In: Given LM (ed) The sage encyclopedia of qualitative research methods. Sage Publications Incorporated, Thousand Oaks, pp 672–675
Ministry of Finance, Finland (2009) General terms of public procurement in service contracts JYSE 2009 SERVICES. http://vm.fi/documents/10623/1169934/JYSE_2009_services.pdf/5e7c7960-9e15-4bc3-8157-f5062b297d17. Accessed 2 Apr 2024
Morgan DL (2014) Pragmatism as a paradigm for social research. Qualitative Inq 20(8):1045–1053
Munim KM, Islam I, Khatun M, Karim MM, Islam MN (2017) Towards developing a tool for UX evaluation using facial expressions. In: Proceedings of the 3rd International Conference on Electrical Information and Communication Technology. IEEE, pp 1–6
Nuottila J, Kauppila O, Nystén-Haarala S (2016) Proactive contracting: emerging changes in attitudes toward project contracts and lawyers' contribution. J Strategic Contract Negot 2(1-2):150–165
Nystén-Haarala S, Lee N, Lehto J (2010) Flexibility in contract terms and contracting processes. Int J Managing Projects Bus 3(3):462–478
Ozdenizci B, Aydin MN, Coskun V, Kerem O (2010, November) Design science in NFC research. In: 2010 International Conference for Internet Technology and Secured Transactions. IEEE, pp 1–6
Passera S (2015) Beyond the wall of text: How information design can make contracts user-friendly. In: Marcus A (ed) Design, user experience, and usability: users and interactions.

Lecture Notes in Computer Science. Springer International Publishing, Cham, Switzerland, pp 341–352
Passera S (2017) Beyond the wall of contract text: visualizing contracts to foster understanding and collaboration within and across organizations. Aalto University, Helsinki
Passera S (2018) Flowcharts, swimlanes, and timelines: alternatives to prose in communicating legal–bureaucratic instructions to civil servants. J Bus Technical Commun, 32(2): pp. 229–272.
Passera S, Haapio H (2013) Transforming contracts from legal rules to user-centered communication tools: a human-information interaction challenge. Commun Design Quart Rev 1(3):38–45
Passera S, Smedlund A, Liinasuo M (2016) Exploring contract visualization: clarification and framing strategies to shape collaborative business relationships. J Strategic Contract Negot 2(1–2):69–100
Peffers K, Tuunanen T, Gengler CE, Rossi M, Hui W, Virtanen V, Bragge J (2006) The design science research process: a model for producing and presenting information systems research. In: Proceedings of the first international conference on design science research in information systems and technology. Claremont Graduate University, Claremont, pp 83–106
Peffers K, Tuunanen T, Rothenberger MA, Chatterjee C (2007) A design science research methodology for information systems research. J Manage Inform Syst 24(3):45–77
Peffers K, Rothenberger M, Tuunanen T, Vaezi R (2012) Design science research evaluation. In: Peffers K, Rothernberger M, Kuechler B (eds) Design science research in information systems: advances in theory and practice. Springer, Berlin, pp 398–410
Peirce CS (1905) What pragmatism is. The Monist 15(2):161–181.
Pfeffer J (2008) What ever happened to pragmatism? J Manage Inq 17(1):57–60
Posner RA (1989) What has pragmatism to offer law? Southern Calif Law Rev 62:1653–1670
Rajamäki J, Lahdenperä J, Shalamanov V (2022, December) Design science research towards ECHO governance and management information system. In: 2022 12th International Conference on Dependable Systems, Services and Technologies (DESSERT). IEEE, pp 1–7
Reyneke R (2019) Improving interactive user experience with microinteractions: an application of biometric and affect detection systems on landing pages. Master's thesis, Harvard Extension School
Rich B, Weber L, Bauman CW (2022) Prevention and promotion approaches to contracting: implications for negotiator focus and contract frames on exchange performance and relationships in the digital age. In: Corrales Compagnucci M, Haapio H, Fenwick M (eds) Research handbook on contract design. Edward Elgar Publishing, Cheltenham, pp 239–257
Schepker DJ, Oh W-Y, Martynov A, Poppo L (2014) The many futures of contracts: moving beyond structure and safeguarding to coordination and adaptation. J Manage 40(1):193–225
Schinle M, Erler C, Vetter AR, Stork W (2020, August) How to disclose selective Information from permissioned DLT-based Traceability Systems? In: 2020 IEEE International Conference on Decentralized Applications and Infrastructures (DAPPS). IEEE, pp 153–158
Schmitt U (2019, September) Interoperability of managing knowledge and learning processes for sustainable e-Education. In: 2019 Conference on Next Generation Computing Applications (NextComp). IEEE, pp 1–6
Shi Y, Choi EHC, Ruiz N, Chen F, Taib R (2007) galvanic skin response (GSR) as an index of cognitive load. In: CHI '07 Extended Abstracts on Human Factors in Computing Systems. Association for Computing Machinery, New York, pp 2651–2656
Siedel GJ, Haapio H (2010) Using proactive law for competitive advantage. Am Bus Law J 47(4): 641–686
Silverstein JM (2021) The contract interpretation policy debate: a primer. Stanf J Law Bus Finance 26(1):222–293
Simpson B (2018) Pragmatism: a philosophy of practice. In: Cassell C, Cunliffe AL, Grandy G (eds) The Sage handbook of qualitative business and management research methods: history and traditions. Sage Publications Incorporated, Thousand Oaks, pp 54–68
Somers M (2019, Mar 8) Emotion AI, explained. MIT Sloan School of management. https://mitsloan.mit.edu/ideas-made-to-matter/emotion-ai-explained. Accessed 2 Apr 2024

Tversky A, Kahneman D (1981) The framing of decisions and the psychology of choice. Science 211(4481):453–458
Venable JR, Pries-Heje, J, Baskerville R (2017) Choosing a design science methodology. In: Proceedings of the Australasian Conference on Information Systems 2017. Australasian Association for Information Systems, Hobart
Vereno D, Polanec K, Neureiter C (2022, April) Evaluating and improving model-based assessment of contextual data quality in smart grids. In: 2022 IEEE Power & Energy Society Innovative Smart Grid Technologies Conference (ISGT). IEEE, pp 1–5
Viljanen M, Salminen J, Hurmerinta-Haanpää A (2018a) Funktionaalinen sopiminen, osa 1: kohti uudenlaista sopimusajattelua. Oikeus 47(1):65–80. (Viljanen et al., 2018a)
Viljanen M, Salminen J, Hurmerinta-Haanpää A (2018b) Funktionaalinen sopiminen, osa 2: sopimisen muutokset käytännössä. Oikeus 47(2):155–167. (Viljanen et al., 2018b)
Weber L (2017) A sociocognitive view of repeated interfirm exchanges: how the coevolution of trust and learning impacts subsequent contracts. Organ Sci 28(4):744–759
Weber L, Bauman CW (2019) The cognitive and behavioral impact of promotion and prevention contracts on trust in repeated exchanges. Acad Manage J 62(2):361–382
Weber L, Mayer KJ (2011) Designing effective contracts: exploring the influence of framing and expectations. Acad Manage Rev 36(1):53–75
Weber L, Mayer KJ, Macher JT (2011) An analysis of extendibility and early termination provisions: the importance of framing duration safeguards. Acad Manage J 54(1):182–202
Wieringa RJ (2014) Design science methodology for information systems and software engineering. Springer-Verlag, Berlin
Williamson OE (1979) Transaction-cost economics: the governance of contractual relations. J Law Econ 22(2):233–261
Yurkin VA, Saradgishvili SE (2023) Digital product UX research with facial expression recognition. In: Arseniev DG, Aouf N (eds) Cyber-physical systems and control II. CPS&C 2021. Lecture Notes in Networks and Systems, vol. 460. Springer, Cham, pp 282–292.

Index

R. Ballardini et al. (eds.), *Emotional Data Applications and Regulation of Artificial Intelligence in Society*, Law, Governance and Technology Series 69,
https://doi.org/10.1007/978-3-031-80111-2

W

The manufacturer's authorised representative in the EU is Springer Nature Customer Service Centre GmbH, Europaplatz 3, 69115 Heidelberg, Germany. If you have any concerns regarding our products, please contact ProductSafety@springernature.com

Printed and bound by CPI Group (UK) Ltd, Croydon, CR0 4YY
30/09/2026
02225600-0008